LELAND STANFORD: MAN OF MANY CAREERS

LELAND STANFORD

LELAND STANFORD:
MAN OF MANY CAREERS

NORMAN E. TUTOROW

Pacific Coast Publishers • Menlo Park, California 94025

12-13-73

To My Wife and Son
and
Don E. Fehrenbacher

PREFACE

To Thomas Carlyle we owe the observation that "biography is the only true history;" his younger contemporary, Ralph Waldo Emerson, phrased the same idea only slightly differently when he wrote that "there is properly no history, only biography." Anyone who has ever undertaken the task of writing the story of a man's life soon discovers as well that there is no biography without history. It is the inevitable historical dimension of biographies that has prompted so many "life and times of" in their titles. The life of a significant man is part of the history of his times and cannot be told entirely divorced from that history; in fact, the biographer struggles constantly with the temptation to make his narrative more a history of the times than the story of a single life.

This temptation is especially alluring when one treats the life of a man like Leland Stanford, a man involved in some of the greatest movements of his age, a man prominent in a myriad of enterprises. The biographer of Stanford has a fascinating story to tell of a career—indeed a series of careers—but he must write about Leland Stanford, Governor of California and United States Senator, without writing a political history of California. He was Governor of the Golden State during the Civil War, but one must not retell the story of that war, not even as it related to California. Perhaps the most difficult aspect of writing a life of Stanford is doing so without rechronicling the oft-told account of the building of the Central Pacific Railroad.

This man had many careers—law, politics, horsebreeding and horseracing, viticulture, and education—and he had as many avocations. His achievements in a number of fields were greater than all but a few recognize, yet very little has been done to preserve his memory. Stanford University students have been quoted as not knowing that he had anything to do with the construction of the first transcontinental railroad. Students of California history come away from textbooks and college classes knowing nothing about him except that he was one of the "Big Four," itself a loaded term that prejudges him unfairly as little more than a greedy railroad swindler.

Almost nothing has been done on Stanford's many specialized interests or activities, each of which would warrant a scholarly monograph. The bibliography attached to this volume testifies to how little the life and career of the man have captured the imagination of specialists in California history. There are no studies on his relationship to Theodore D. Judah, Aaron Sargent, or even Collis P. Huntington. Even so titillating a subject as Stanford and spiritualism has failed to attract attention. It is hoped that this biography will rescue him from his near-oblivion, and that it will bring him enough to life to prompt further study of some of his many careers.

The growing distinction of Stanford University, the recent centennial of the transcontinental railroad and the bicentennial of California, and the prominence California has achieved among the states of the Union point up a need for a biography of one of the Golden State's foremost sons—Leland Stanford, truly a man of many careers.

This book would not have been possible without the assistance of a number of people. In the research for and the writing of every part I have received much help. I would like to take this means of thanking those who have given so generously of their time and talents to improve the manuscript.

Members of the staff of the Stanford University Library have assisted me immeasurably, particularly Mr. Ralph Hansen, University Archivist; Mrs. Alexis Rubin, Assistant Archivist; Miss Patricia Palmer, Manuscripts Librarian; and Mrs. Florence Chu, Interlibrary Loan Service. Thanks also to the staffs of the New York City Library, the Huntington Library, and the Bancroft Library.

I am indebted to Professors Thomas A. Bailey and Don E. Fehrenbacher for proofreading the manuscript and pointing out a number of factual errors, infelicitous expressions, and awkward syntactical constructions. It goes without saying, of course, that I am responsible for the shortcomings which remain.

I am especially grateful to my wife, Mrs. Sue Carol Tutorow, for laboriously typing the manuscript through several preliminary editions, and to my son, James, for doing much of the routine card catalog work and helping me with the tedious task of proofreading the footnotes for each succeeding revision.

N. T.

CONTENTS

ILLUSTRATIONS

Illustrations (Cont)

LELAND STANFORD CHRONOLOGY

1824   Born on March 9.
1836   Moved to Elm Grove Farm on Albany-Schenectady Turnpike.
1841   Enrolled at Clinton Liberal Institute.
1844   Enrolled at Cazenovia Seminary.
1845   Left Cazenovia.
        Began reading law in Albany.
1848   Admitted to New York Bar.
        Moved to Port Washington, Wisconsin.
        Began law practice with Wesley Pierce.
1849   Brothers Charles and DeWitt went to California.
1850   Admitted to Wisconsin Bar on January 8.
        Nominated as a Whig for District Attorney of Washington County.
        Brother Charles and DeWitt went to California.
        Married Jane Lathrop in Albany on September 30.
1851   Elected Port Washington village trustee on May 31.
1852   Brothers Thomas and Philip went to California in February.
        Much of Port Washington destroyed by fire on March 16.
        Sailed alone from New York for California in June.
        Opened a store with Nick Smith in Cold Springs, Eldorado County, California.
1853   Opened a store in Michigan City, Placer County.
1855   Father-in-law Dyer Lathrop died in May.
        Sailed for Albany in June.
        Returned to California with Jane in the fall.
        Bought Sacramento store from Josiah and Philip.
1856   Helped organize Republican party in Sacramento.
        California's first Republican state convention held in Sacramento on April 30.
        Moved into new Sacramento store at Front and L Streets.

1856	On August 27, chosen delegate to party convention which selected presidential electors.
1857	Nominated for Alderman of Sacramento's First Ward in April. Michigan City burned, including Leland's former store, on June 22. In July, elected as a delegate to Republican County Convention and state convention. Nominated for state treasurer in July. Defeated in race for treasurer on September 3.
1858	Vice-president of state convention on August 4 and 5.
1859	Became majority stockholder of Amador Quartz Mine. Nominated for governor on June 8. Defeated in race for governorship on September 7.
1860	Delegate at Republican convention in Sacramento, on February 22, where he was chosen as presidential elector. Not aboard ship when electors sailed east on April 5. Presided over Republican convention in Sacramento, which ratified nomination of Abraham Lincoln, on June 20.
1861	In January, sailed east to participate in distribution of federal patronage. Endorsed for governor by Sacramento County Republican Convention, on June 8. Nominated for governor in June. Elected president of Central Pacific Railroad on June 28. Purchased Fogus house on San Francisco Peninsula in July. Elected governor on September 4.
1862	Inaugurated governor on January 10.
1863	Central Pacific Railroad began laying track in October. Became a private citizen on December 10.
1867	Contract and Finance Company organized.
1868	Leland Jr. born in Sacramento on May 14. Central Pacific gained control of Southern Pacific.
1869	Purchased Warm Springs Ranch near San Jose. Pacific Express Company organized. Central Pacific and Union Pacific joined near Ogden, Utah, on May 10.
1870	Southern Pacific consolidated into Central Pacific system. Purchased Occident, his first race horse, in July.
1871	Began experimenting with winemaking. Charles Crocker withdrew from Central Pacific Railroad.
1872	Hired photographer Eadweard Muybridge to get a picture of Occident with all four feet off the ground.
1873	Crocker returned to Central Pacific Railroad in September.
1874	Stanfords moved to San Francisco. Occidental and Oriental Steamship Company organized, with Stanford as first president.

1876	San Francisco house completed.
	Purchased Gordon estate and other property on San Francisco Peninsula.
1877	Muybridge got photograph of Occident with all four feet off the ground.
1878	Stanford's first serious illness.
	Mark Hopkins died.
	Elected president of Occidental and Oriental, a position held until his death.
	Muybridge copyrighted in his name a series of photographs of a horse in motion.
	Charles Marvin hired as trainer and driver.
1879	Motion picture projected at Palo Alto home.
1880	Mussel Slough tragedy on March 11.
	First European tour.
	Stanford's horses set their first world's records.
	President Hayes visited the Stanfords in Sacramento.
1881	Purchased first tract of land near Vina.
1882	Southern transcontinental completed.
	Planted first vines at Vina.
	Published *Horse in Motion*.
	Appointed to Board of Regents of University of California, on September 14.
1883	Withdrew his name for consideration for University of California regency, in January.
	Second European tour.
1884	Leland Jr. died in Florence, Italy, on March 13.
	Conferred with Harvard president Charles W. Eliot about plans to endow a school.
	Southern Pacific of Kentucky organized.
1885	On January 20, Republican caucus in California legislature selected Stanford as nominee for United States Senator.
	Elected to United States Senate on January 28.
	Central Pacific leased to Southern Pacific of Kentucky.
	Became president of Southern Pacific of Kentucky.
	Became a United States Senator on March 4.
	Read deed of grant to trustees of Stanford University on November 14.
1886	First Senate speech on February 9.
1887	Made first wine at Vina.
	Laid cornerstone of Stanford University on May 14.
1888	First presidential boom.
	Third European tour.
1890	On February 28, agreed to step down from presidency of Southern Pacific.

1890	Resigned presidency of Southern Pacific on April 9.
	Presented money bill to Senate on May 23.
	Fourth European tour.
1891	Reelected to Senate on January 14.
	President and Mrs. Harrison visited California.
	Opening exercises of Stanford University on October 1.
1892	Fifth European tour.
	Second presidential boom.
1893	Died at Palo Alto home on June 20.

LELAND STANFORD: MAN OF MANY CAREERS
1824–1893

CHAPTER I

ATTORNEY-AT-LAW

The township of Watervliet, New York, in which Amasa Leland Stanford was born on March 9, 1824, was part of rural America and shared in the robust drama of the never-ceasing westward movement.[1] Leland and his five brothers, sons of a farmer who regularly engaged in sundry small business ventures, including innkeeping and civil construction projects, shared the hardy physical labor of farm life and early became acquainted with the rough and tumble crowds stopping over on the westward trek.[2] They listened eagerly to the endless chatter of adventurous folk bubbling with the enthusiasm characteristic of hearty pioneers moving on into unfamiliar territories in search of new homes and jobs.

The Stanfords traced their family origins to England, from where they had emigrated to Massachusetts in the early seventeeth century, before finally finding their way west to New York.[3] Elizabeth Phillips, the mother, was related to two famous New Englanders, Wendell Phillips and Phillips Brooks.[4] Abner Stanford, Leland's great grandfather, was a veteran of the Revolutionary War, having served in the Continental Army from 1775 to 1783.[5] His son Lyman, Leland's grandfather, moved westward from the family home site in Massachusetts and settled in 1799 in Lisha's Kill, New York, a small hamlet located between Albany and Schenectady. He later helped build the turnpike which connected these two towns.[6] Lyman earned his livelihood as an innkeeper and was recognized as an enterprising and respected citizen. In 1811 he was made a justice of the peace.[7]

Josiah Stanford, the father of Leland, followed his own father's occupation as an innkeeper, and was proprietor of the Bull's Head Inn on the Troy Road when Leland was born.[8] The location of the family home, across the Hudson from Troy and north of the bustling town of Albany, was ideal for rearing a family of boys. It was rural enough for farming and near enough to through traffic to make business steady and reasonably profitable. At that time Albany was located on one of the busiest thoroughfares westward and was near the head of sloop navigation and of tidewater.[9] It was estimated that on some days 2,000 wagons passed up and down the main street of the town; many of these conveyances belonged to transients just passing through.

In 1836 the Stanfords moved to Elm Grove farm, on the Albany-Schenectady turnpike, where they passed many long and happy years. But they were much more than farmers, and the father was considerably more than an innkeeper. Josiah Stanford had contracted to build a number of roads and bridges and was keenly interested in the building of the Erie Canal. As one of its first advocates, he watched its progress from inception to completion. The father of the boy who would later have an important part in building the first transcontinental railroad also held contracts for grading the roadbed between Albany and Schenectady.[10] The influence of this enterprise upon the young Leland is incalculable. The railroad passed so near Elm Grove that Leland's Saturdays were often spent watching the construction in which even then he was greatly interested.[11]

Young Stanford's later business sense was already in evidence at the age of six, when he made his first money selling horseradish; it was dug with his father's permission from the family garden, cleaned carefully, and carted into town.[12] The following year he and one of his brothers collected and sold five bushels of chestnuts for five dollars each, a tidy sum of cash for two young boys to have at any time. From age fifteen to seventeen Leland worked on contracts with his father, delivering large quantities of wood from the nearby forests to various towns in the vicinity. In this limited but profitable enterprise he got his first taste of business management.

When he was eighteen he earned almost $2,600 selling wood. Wood sold at the time for slightly more than one dollar per cord, but rather than contenting himself with the results of his own labor, he hired a number of men to cut and cord wood for him. By the time his project was completed he had ready for market 2,600 cords.[13]

In 1840 the elder Stanford bought the 323-acre farm at Elm Grove, which to that time had been leased. He kept it until 1858, when he sold it and moved to the Locust Grove farm near Schenectady.[14]

The younger Stanford boys spent many of their most impressionable years at Elm Grove, surrounded by an atmosphere of domestic felicity and parental affection which they long remembered. Farm life gave them character, and Leland learned to work. He also learned the value of time and money and the necessity of keeping up with his father and brothers and the hired hands. Long afterward Leland wrote lovingly to his aging and widowed mother of his many fond memories of her goodness and affection and of the sacrifices she had made for him and his brothers.[15]

Until 1836, when he was twelve years old, Leland attended public schools near his home, but after moving to Elm Grove, which was not within riding distance of school, the father hired teachers to come regularly to the farm and teach the boys at home.[16] Leland was known as one of the more studious of the Stanford boys, although no one would go so far as to call him brilliant. Those who later recalled his youth remembered him as an outdoors and outgoing type, large, healthy, good-natured, always a favorite because of his good sense and cheerfulness, but decidedly impatient of scholarship.[17] Like most boys, he preferred the active outdoor life to the indoor life of school. A later, over-adulatory writer reported that as a lad on the farm every leisure moment found him with a book in his hand.[18] Another, however, recorded that so far as formal schooling was concerned, the boy was rather dull.[19] Leland's favorite childhood reading included Mason Weems' "biographies" of George Washington, Benjamin Franklin, and General Francis Marion.[20] One of his grandfathers, impressed with what appeared a scholarly bent, predicted that one day Leland would become a judge.[21]

After leaving school, Leland continued to read in a variety of subjects. It was later recalled that he was greatly interested in theoretical as well as practical matters, with the philosophy of history, social studies, and political economy among his favorite subjects. His favorite authors included Alexis de Tocqueville, John Stuart Mill, Henry Buckle, and Herbert Spencer, and in the way of lighter reading he was said to have preferred the writings of Oliver Goldsmith, Walter Scott, and Washington Irving.[22]

Perhaps owing to the seriousness with which they approached their studies and the promise of success they showed as young scholars, the parents decided that Leland and his younger brother Thomas Welton were to be trained for professional careers — Leland in law and Thomas in medicine. Accordingly, in 1841, at the age of seventeen, Leland was sent for his preparatory studies to the Oneida Institute of Science and Industry, a small school in the town of Whitesborough, New York, about one hundred miles west of Albany. Oneida sought to create a balanced student, one who knew something besides what he learned from books, and to this end arranged a daily routine combining three hours of manual labor with the academic work.[23] Leland, who had worked hard all of his life at various kinds of jobs, immediately took a dislike to Oneida; possibly he felt that he had had enough manual labor for awhile and now wanted to concentrate on mental achievement. At any rate, after only one night there, hardly long enough to give the school a fair trial, and after talking the matter over with one of the teachers, he left. Traveling to the town of Clinton, about ten miles away, he enrolled at the Clinton Liberal Institute. By way of explaining this unexpected move, he complained to his father about the three hours of daily labor required, which he considered excessive, and called Oneida a small, broken-down place having only twenty-five students. Also, it was a thoroughly abolitionist school where "whites and blacks all ate at one table," and besides, it was not as good as Clinton, where his brother Charles had studied a few years before.[24]

Clinton Liberal Institute was opened in 1831 by Universalists as a protest against the narrowness and intolerance of the sects dominating the other schools.[25] Yet it was itself religiously oriented. School opened and closed each day with Scripture reading, and students were required to attend religious exercises at least once every Sunday. Any student indulging in "profane language" or guilty of "immoral conduct" was subject to immediate expulsion.[26]

Clinton was relatively diversified in its offerings for a school of its kind and boasted that it afforded unusual facilities for the attainment of a thorough preparation for business, entrance to college, or the study of a profession. For the more advanced and ambitious students who wanted to avail themselves of additional educational opportunities, Clinton students could attend at no expense lectures at Hamilton College, which was within walking distance of the Institute.[27]

Almost nothing is known now of Leland's career at Clinton, for the next knowledge we have of him as a student was a letter written two years later notifying his father that he had arrived safely in Clinton.[28] It is not clear from this letter whether Leland was in his third year or whether he was then returning following an interruption of his studies, but it does shed some light on the curriculum taught, as well as on his social life. He was studying English grammar, arithmetic, geometry, and algebra, and, in addition to his academic studies, he participated in two student organizations, serving for a time as president of one. In both these groups he engaged in formal debates, an experience which would no doubt prove of considerable value in his later political career.[29] All Clinton students were required to take part in exercises in speaking and composition. In addition, opportunities were offered by the Literary Society for improvement in extemporaneous debate and general literature.[30] There is also some evidence that Leland was a boxer of sorts.[31]

While still attending Clinton, young Stanford was looking ahead to his educational future, inquiring about Cazenovia Seminary, a Methodist school in a small town near Syracuse. More advanced than Clinton, it was much larger, having 160 students as compared to Clinton's thirty-five.[32] In 1843 it was the third largest academy in the state in enrollment and budget.[33] Cazenovia was a three year school, each year of which had three fifteen-week terms, and granted diplomas upon completion of a course of studies. In 1844 he made the change.

Leland appears to have enjoyed his single year at Cazenovia, where he lived alone in a small, modestly furnished room.[34] He wrote home often, sending exceptionally well-written and respectful letters to his parents, and communicated with his brothers on a variety of matters, especially girls. The girls and boys lived in separate buildings, but they ate together, studied the same subjects, and recited in the same classes.[35] Riding with girls was permitted once or twice each term, but none of the fifty females at Cazenovia interested Leland. In letters to his brothers he was constantly poking fun at marriage, revealing by this kind of levity what was on his mind a great deal of the time.[36]

Cazenovia was a combination academy, preprofessional school, and college preparatory institution. Several of young Stanford's classmates were planning to go from there to college. In addition to his normal academic load, Leland maintained the interest in debating which he had developed at Clinton. The debating society at Cazenovia counted among its numbers fifteen of the "elite of the school," and even possessed its own library. On the whole, Leland was well satisfied with Cazenovia, regarding it as a good school, though probably a bit too strict in its religious observances.[37]

While at school, Leland expressed continuing interest in some unidentified railroad project going forward at home. In some way this involved either his father or the Elm Grove property. On several occasions he requested more information about a contract with the railroad.[38] He expressed satisfaction with some unexplained settlement with a railroad company, which he called as equitable as he had expected and one that would probably lead to the building of a store on the home premises.[39] Perhaps part of the farm had been sold as a right-of-way, or maybe his father was contracting to build or supply materials to builders; in any case, there was a continuation throughout his school days of the interest he had early shown in railroads and which he would have the rest of his life.

Writing home to his father, Leland apologized for not being able to assist him in his labors, since he was to direct his attention toward a profession.[40] Evidently his education at this point was on a part-time basis; he said that at the present rate he would not graduate until he was twenty-six. This meant six years for three years' study. To make things worse, he experienced considerable mental anguish at having to ask constantly for more money.[41]

Leland approached most of his academic subjects with enthusiasm, but there were some exceptions. He reported making average progress in Latin, but to like the class, he said, would have been tantamount to loving a chastening rod.[42] His lack of interest in or love for Latin was due in part to the fact that he was in a class too advanced for him; while he was studying assiduously just to keep up, the other students were merely reviewing. The ensuing frustrations, he wrote, prompted him on occasion to "commit sin sometimes in the shape of oaths."[43]

Philosophy seems to have been more to his liking; at any rate, he received his highest marks in this subject. And though Pierce's Algebra, which was taught at the college level, was his hardest subject, a later writer, whether drawing on first-hand information or pure hearsay, reported that mathematics and the sciences were the life blood of his studies while at school.[44] In overall classwork, he received in one term a ninety-one percent, compared to a class average of between seventy and eighty percent; this he attributed to a near-perfect score in philosophy.[45] Apparently Leland did consistently well in most studies and was reported to be in the favor of his teachers. He boasted that they were all friendly and that they spoke well of him; in fact, he was told that he enjoyed an enviable reputation with his teachers.[46]

In letters to his brothers, the subject of girls continued to intrude, but he recognized that if he were to complete his studies and become a lawyer he would have to avoid marriage for eight or ten years.[47] No matter what the sacrifice necessary to fulfill his ambitions and those of his family, Leland was firmly persuaded that it was worth it; and he was determined to prosecute his chosen profession to the utmost, without settling for mediocrity.[48]

Leland's letters from the Cazenovia Seminary provide valuable insight into his thinking on a wide variety of subjects. In politics, for example, he expressed great satisfaction on one occasion that the Whigs were doing so well.[49] During the 1844 presidential campaign Cassius M. Clay, the fiery Kentuckian, spoke at the school or in the nearby town and Leland was favorably impressed by the famous abolitionist's speech on behalf of the Henry Clay candidacy. He especially praised the speaker for his willingness to sacrifice all possibility of political preferment to his antislavery principles. He believed Clay's advocacy of the cause of the slave and the extension of human liberty was a "glorious example for all to imitate."[50]

There were frequent and periodic evangelistic revivals at Cazenovia during Leland's student days, but all attempts at converting him failed. Many had tried, but all had given it up as a bad job. Not only did he personally resist the promptings of the spirit, but he was accused of having stood in the way of the conversion of some of his fellows. Though he was not favorably disposed toward the brand of Christianity preached by the itinerant evangelists, he was not in any sense irreligious, but generally avoided the subject of religion whenever he could.[51]

Leland did not graduate from Cazenovia; he hinted in early 1845 that he might quit school.[52] The twenty-one-year-old youth left Cazenovia at the end of the winter term of 1845, declining an invitation to teach in a district school he had earlier attended, and entered a legal apprenticeship in the Albany law firm of Wheaton, Doolittle, and Hadley.[53] This in-service training by reading law with licensed attorneys until competent enough for recommendation for admission to the bar was then the customary procedure. In 1848 he was admitted to practice and was offered a position with the firm where he had taken his training. He must have shown unusual promise, for he was offered Doolittle's place in the law firm when the latter retired.[54]

II

The young attorney turned down all job offers and directed his gaze westward. In 1848 he joined the never-ending stream of pioneers and emigrants moving to the Great Lakes area. He chose the young, exciting town of Chicago. Tradition has it that mosquitoes drove him from Chicago; whether this or something else, the young New Yorker passed quickly through the Windy City and pushed northward to the small village of Port Washington in Wisconsin, the nation's newest state, and hung up up his shingle. Leland

Stanford, attorney-at-law.[55] The big and strong young man of twenty-four was aptly suited to the rough and challenging atmosphere of his adopted home; life in this rural, almost frontier village would not be too dissimilar to that in his home state.

In this rapidly growing community, Stanford formed a partnership with another lawyer, Wesley Pierce.[56] His practice appears to have been financially rewarding, for he saved $1,200 his first year.[57] Thanks to his father, who had presented him with a sizeable collection of books when he left home, Stanford began his practice with probably the best law library north of Milwaukee. It was said that judges often borrowed from his library when writing their decisions.[58]

Some confusion surrounds Stanford's position before the Wisconsin bar. He began his law practice in 1848 — the same year Wisconsin became a state — when the first of eight cases signed by him and Pierce was recorded on July 29, but he was not admitted to the bar until January 8, 1850.[59] A possible explanation is that only one partner in a firm had to be a member of the bar. If so, it explains why Stanford joined the bar in 1850, for at that time the partnership was dissolved and Pierce moved away.[60]

Stanford participated actively in Port Washington politics, and on occasion wrote articles for a Milwaukee newspaper. At one point he showed some interest in a journalistic career and joined with others in negotiating the purchase of a used printing press. But before they could act, it was sold, and, without sufficient funds to buy a new press and have it shipped from New York, they abandoned the project.[61]

Stanford got his first taste of political involvement in 1850, when he was nominated as a Whig for district attorney of Washington County, and was pitted against a popular Democrat, Eugene Turner. The Democrats in 1848 had polled three times as many votes as had the Whigs and Free Soilers combined, in round numbers about 1,500 to 500, and, unfortunately for Stanford, the county was still overwhelmingly Democratic.[62] With this handicap

EARLY LITHOGRAPH OF THE VILLAGE OF PORT WASHINGTON.

Author's Collection

Stanford should have been neither surprised nor unduly disappointed when he lost by only 600 votes, but it was reported that the canvass was very heated and destroyed much of the friendship that had existed between himself and Turner.[63] Though far from home for the first time in his life, Stanford stayed in close contact with his family in New York. He wrote often to his younger brother, Thomas Welton, who was in school in West Poultney, Vermont, studying to become a physician. Leland offered him advice on a variety of matters, such as how to write more clearly, on the necessity of daily but discriminating reading, and on how to conduct himself in school. The younger Stanford apparently never resented this fatherly advice, coming from a slightly older brother.[64]

One of the few things known with certainty about Stanford's social life while still a bachelor in Port Washington was that he joined the Masons, and on November 19, 1849, applied for membership in the Ozaukee Lodge.[65] He was initiated on December 17 and was passed the following March. On March 17, 1850, he became a Master Mason, and later was one of the organizers of the Masonic Lodge in nearby Cedarburg.[66]

Early Port Washington settlers, his older contemporaries, remembered Stanford as a stout, dark-complexioned young man with thick lips and a slight impediment in his speech that made him appear at bad advantage in social gatherings and tended to make him bashful and retiring.[67] Despite this, he continued an old school interest: he joined a debating and literary society in Port Washington. He was also listed as one of the "managers" of the Washington Birthday Ball on February 22, 1850.[68]

Stanford earned the respect and gratitude of Port Washington by his sacrificial efforts in an 1849 cholera epidemic.[69] It was reported many years later that he and a Mr. S. A. White abandoned their businesses entirely to care for the victims of the scourge. Day and night, according to the recollections of one witness, these two men went about among the people, nursing and administering to their wants, succoring the living and burying the dead.[70]

Reminiscences by contemporaries throw some light on this period when the young pioneering attorney was enjoying Wisconsin's frontier village life to the fullest, but some of them do not agree with what is generally believed today. For example, one story claims that this "clumsy young fellow," who was "decidedly phlegmatic and dull," could take "all the tricks in that day of the hardy pioneers" when it came to consuming alcohol. Years later it was alleged that during his Port Washington days he could "stand up at the village bar, put all the other fellows to sleep and walk away with a clear head."[71]

Nothing is known of Stanford's loves, if he had any, and little is known about how he and Jane Lathrop, his wife, ever became romantically linked. They were acquainted as children and were close neighbors during his legal apprenticeship in Albany, but there is not a hint of any romantic involvement. Much of this obscurity is due to Mrs. Stanford's desire to keep her personal life private. All intimate letters from Leland were destroyed after his death, but there is no evidence that these included any from the Port Washington period. The first clue that Leland was aware of Jane is a story that when working his way through school on a woodhauling contract, he would use the back streets of Albany to avoid passing her house for fear that she would see him in his red flannel shirt and heavy woolen muffler.[72]

While studying law, Leland lived on the same street in Albany as did the Lathrops; he became acquainted with Jane's brother Daniel, and soon was a regular guest at the Lathrop home. Mrs. Stanford's biographer said that Leland and Jane became engaged during this time, prior to his going west.[73] After the engagement became known, Jane was invited to spend a week at the Stanford home so that she and Mrs. Stanford might become better acquainted.

If, indeed, they were engaged during his first two years in Port Washington, it is not disclosed in the surviving correspondence. Jane is not mentioned in any of Stanford's letters home. The only serious comment concerning any young lady is of a Miss Hannah Clark, to whom he wrote what is as close to a love letter — and not very close at that — as has been found. Hannah had returned to her home in the East after visiting friends in Port Washington. In a letter to her, Stanford reminisced about the many happy hours they had shared in the parlor from which he was writing. He told her that they missed her because she was "very dear" to them. He teased about her rumored engagement to a Dr. Bryant, and begged her to clarify the matter. "Are we never again," he asked, "to have one of those pleasant walks?"[74]

This was in June, 1850, and it is useless to speculate on how much Leland cared for the young lady on the basis of one sketchy letter. Certainly it cannot be said that Jane got Leland on the bounce when they married only three months later. The fact that Leland returned to Albany in the summer of 1850 lends credence, although not certainty, to a previous romance with Jane. They were married on September 30 by the pastor of the North Pearl Baptist Church and left shortly thereafter for Port Washington, where they took up housekeeping for two years, a time Jane later referred to as the happiest of her life.[75]

Their first modest apartment was a one-room unit in the Powers House, just over the barroom. Mrs. Stanford was dissatisfied with not being able to entertain friends in this apartment, and soon they rented a story-and-a-half brick cottage on the edge of a small stream. Gifts of furniture from her father made life comfortable in their new home.[76]

Little is known of the Stanfords' social life. Social functions in the village were exceedingly simple. Mrs. Stanford engaged actively in "promoting social relations," but these were generally limited to dances at the Powers House or to picnicking in one of the many groves near the village. Even in these simple affairs, Mrs. Stanford generally confined her activities to making sandwiches and punch.[77]

Stanford Library

LELAND AND JANE STANFORD, wedding picture, 1850.

Undaunted by defeat in his earlier bid for county-wide office, Stanford, after settling down with his bride, participated actively in small-town politics. The first minutes of the village of Port Washington show that on March 31, 1851, he was elected a village trustee, and in June, 1851, the board held its regular meeting in his law office. From September, 1851, to July, 1852, he was president pro tem of the town council.[78]

Catastrophe struck Port Washington on the morning of March 16, 1852, when a disastrous fire destroyed an entire block of buildings, including Stanford's office and law library, located over a grocery store in a frame building on Franklin Street.[79] The present-day "Stanford Building," at 117 East Main Street, is undoubtedly not the building which housed Stanford's office and library.[80] Even before the fire, the Wisconsin community no longer held out the rewards or presented the challenge that it once had. Heavy immigration to the region had ceased with the exhaustion of timber and as a consequence Stanford's law business began to decline. Before this he had secured an appointment as a notary public, probably to supplement his income; today there remain many deeds and mortgages on file bearing his signature.[81] Another difficulty was that by 1850 the county had become predominantly German, and the German population was increasing so rapidly in Port Washington that it was almost necessary for the success of an attorney to understand the German language.[82]

Somehow the story has grown in Wisconsin that Stanford left because of profound disappointment over his loss to Eugene Turner in the 1850 race for county office. But the story is based upon ignorance of chronology, and upon the human tendency to repeat baseless stories. Even more current accounts in some Wisconsin papers assert without hesitation that Stanford left Port Washington because he lost the election, simply repeating one story that said: "Stanford left Port Washington in disgust in 1852 after he had been defeated for a $300-a-year post as district attorney" — as though his departure followed hard on the heels of his defeat.[83]

This same journal later repeated an even more erroneous version of this story, asserting that Stanford practiced law in Port Washington with Pierce from 1848 to 1852, when he was defeated by Eugene Turner, then, "In disgust, Stanford headed west."[84]

Stanford, of course, did not practice law with Pierce for four years. He was not defeated by Turner in 1852, he did not head west from Port Washington, but returned first to Albany. This error of conjoining events which occurred two years apart has been made repeatedly, and not always by journalists. The compiler of the correspondence of Theodore Hartwig, a friend and associate of Stanford, asserted that when Stanford was defeated in the race for district attorney and decided to go to California, he asked Dr. Hartwig to go with him, giving no hint of the two intervening years.[85]

If Stanford left in a huff over his loss, it must have been a two-year huff. The election was held in 1850, but he did not leave until 1852. Why did the newlyweds return to Wisconsin after their marriage if Stanford was so dissatisfied with the place? Moreover, he really had no hope of winning this election, so he very likely did not experience much disappointment over the results.

More credence can be given to the explanation that he was unhappy with the diminishing opportunities in his profession, or his lack of success in his law practice, whatever the case may have been.[86] One old account explained that Stanford once lost a case in Port Washington before a "tired and irritable" judge, Hopewell Coxe, whom the young attorney had the misfortune to lecture on how to decide a case being argued. This angered Coxe, who then decided against Stanford's client, whereupon "Stanford threw down his law books in utter disgust, with an expression emphasized by a Texas adjective, to the effect that he would never . . . try another case in Washington County."[87] If this episode ever occurred, Stanford's impatience with law was more a reflection of his own practical nature, his dislike of theoretical or legal niceties, than upon the judge's disposition.

Mrs. Stanford's biographer would not have it that Stanford's legal practice was dwindling, and she stated that at the time of the fire his practice was still growing steadily. The disaster discouraged him no end, she said, but ironically the deciding factor was the theft of a load of firewood on the very night of the fire. Although this loss was trivial compared to that of his library and other personal effects, it was the last straw, according to this writer, and they concluded that Port Washington was not to be their abiding place.[88]

Much has been written about the factors driving the Stanfords from Port Washington, but the forces attracting them to the West have been largely ignored. Stanford's brothers had been attracted to California by gold, with its promises of instant wealth, and he, too, like many another adventurous young man in that day, found the gold fever irresistible and was drawn to the diggings in California. Stanford had been considering a move to California even before the fire, and he probably would have gone eventually without this catastrophe. His brother Thomas had said just two months earlier: "Judging from what you have written home, I expect to see you in California in the spring."[89]

At any rate, the fire definitely settled matters in the minds of the Stanfords. With little hope of collecting the $2,000 owed him on various accounts, the unhappy lawyer was obliged to depend once again upon his parents for financial support. He wrote that it was with great reluctance that he must again lean upon them.[90]

Leland was disposed to travel directly to California by the overland route, and it would have undoubtedly been better for them if they had, in terms of avoiding their later separation, but Jane was so strongly opposed to this that he abandoned the idea and decided to return to Albany and then sail from New York. They sold their possessions in Port Washington, a twenty-acre parcel of land received in lieu of a legal fee, his property on Franklin

Street, and several lots on or near Washington Street, and returned home.[91] After two years of marriage and four years of practicing law, Stanford was worse off financially than when he began. But the lure of California, with its seemingly limitless flow of gold, promised new hope and a new life.

In Albany, the Stanfords found Mr. Lathrop strongly opposed to Jane's leaving for the wild, rough life of the Coast until some advance preparation had been made. After discussing the matter with the elder Stanfords and finding them in agreement, it was decided that Leland should first make the trip west and establish a home for Jane before she should undertake the arduous journey. Jane had wanted and expected to go with her husband; she never entertained the thought of remaining behind. But the counsels of the parents prevailed, and Leland, "leaving his wife well-nigh heartbroken, and feeling that she had been very unjustly treated," sailed from New York in June, 1852, to find a new home and build another life in an even greater west than that in which they had pioneered together for the past two years.[92]

1. Stanford dropped his first name and thereafter went by Leland, the maiden name of a paternal great-grandmother. Arthur Willis Stanford, *Stanford Genealogy, Comprising the Descendants of Abner Stanford, the Revolutionary War Soldier* (Yokohama, 1906),14.

2. Leland was the fifth of eight children, only six of whom survived childhood. His only sister, Elvira (1815-1816), died in infancy before he was born, and a younger brother, Jerome Bonaparte, lived from 1829-1838. His older brothers were Josiah (1817-1890), Charles (1819-1885), and Asa Phillips (1821-1903). Junior to him were DeWitt Clinton (1826-1862) and Thomas Welton (1832-1918). Stanford, *Genealogy,* 26, 53-55.

3. Several family trees of Leland Stanford, varying in degree of detail, are in the Stanford papers.

4. George T. Clark, *Leland Stanford* (Stanford, 1931), 7.

5. Stanford, *Genealogy,* 11-12.

6. Hubert Howe Bancroft, *History of the Life of Leland Stanford, a Character Study* (Oakland, 1952), 3. This biography was originally prepared for inclusion in Bancroft's *Chronicles of the Builders of the Commonwealth* (San Francisco, 1891). It is uncritical, often unreliable, and very impressionistic, but there are signs that much of the factual material was furnished by Stanford himself. Because of a rift between Stanford and Bancroft, it was omitted from the *Chronicles.*

7. George R. Howell and Jonathan Tenney, ed., *History of the County of Albany, New York, from 1609 to 1886* (New York, 1886), 934-935. Also, see Stanford, *Genealogy,* 14.

8. According to the *Albany Directory,* in Clark, *Stanford,* 8. Tradition has it that Stanford entertained General LaFayette in 1825. Stanford, *Genealogy,* 26.

9. Benjamin Silliman, *Remarks Made on a Short Tour between Hartford and Quebec in the Autumn of 1819* (New Haven, 1820, second edition, 1824, used here), 63.

10. James Parton, *et al. Men of Progress* (New York, 1870-1871), 229. The chapter on Stanford was reprinted anonymously in the *California Mail Bag,* V(August, 1874), i-xiii, and again in W. S. Smyth, *First Fifty Years of Cazenovia Seminary, 1825-1875* (Cazenovia, 1877).

11. Bancroft, *Stanford,* 3. Elm Grove farm stood on a rise of ground just west of the present New York Central underpass, on the road linking Albany and Schenectady. It was razed in the early 1950's as a fire hazard and is used for a golf course at the present time. Albany *Times-Union,* August 25, 1963.

12. There are over thirty bound Stanford Family Scrapbooks on the life and career of Leland Stanford preserved in the Stanford Collection, Stanford University. They contain thousands of newspaper clippings, most of which are identified and dated, but some are not. Henceforth this set will be abbreviated SFS. Unidentified newspaper clipping, SFS, XXII, 2.

13. Unidentified newspaper clipping, SFS, XVIII, 67.

14. *Stephen Van Rensselaer Manor,* Ledger A2, Folio 820 in the New York State Library, in Clark, *Stanford,* 10. *Albany County Book of Deeds,* cited in Clark, "The Romance that Founded Stanford," *Stanford Illustrated Review,* XXX (1929), 461.

15. Stanford to his mother, May 25, 1862.

16. Bancroft, *Stanford,* 4.

17. San Francisco *Chronicle,* June 21, 1893.

18. Bancroft, *Stanford,* 4.

19. Anonymous, "Leland Stanford," *California Mail Bag,* I(1871), 1.

20. Bancroft, *Stanford,* 5.

21. *Ibid.,* 4.

22. Parton, 230. Anonymous, "Leland Stanford," *California Mail Bag,* V(1874), iii.

23. John W. Barber and Henry Howe, *Historical Collections of the State of New York* (New York, 1842), 377.

24. Stanford to his father, May 21, 1841. Anonymous, *Catalogue of the Officers and Students of Clinton Liberal Institute* (Utica, 1844), 5.

25. Helen N. Rudd, *A Century of Schools in Clinton* (Clinton, 1964), 10. Grover Cleveland, Clinton's most famous student, attended the Institute in 1851. Allan Nevins, *Grover Cleveland* (New York, 1934), 18-19.

26. *Clinton Catalogue,* 12.

27. *Ibid.,* 11.

28. Stanford to his father, January 7, 1843.

29. Stanford to Charles, January 29, 1843.

30. *Clinton Catalogue,* 12.

31. Stanford to Charles, January 25, 1844.

32. *Ibid.*

33. Smyth, *Cazenovia Seminary,* 115.

34. Stanford to Philip, April 13, 1844.

35. Smyth, *Cazenovia Seminary,* 32.

36. Stanford to Philip, February 23, 1844.

37. *Ibid.*

38. Stanford to Charles, January 25, 1844.

39. Stanford to Philip, February 23, 1844.

40. Stanford to his father, March 10, 1844.

41. Stanford to DeWitt, February 29, 1844.

42. *Ibid.*

43. *Ibid.*

44. Parton, *Men of Progress,* 231.

45. Stanford to Philip, April 13, 1844.

46. Stanford to DeWitt, January 25, 1845.

47. Stanford to Charles, March 24, 1844. Stanford to Charles, April 30, 1844. Stanford to Philip, October 11, 1844. Stanford to Charles, December 1, 1844.

48. Stanford to Charles, March 24, 1844.

49. Stanford to Philip, April 13, 1844.

50. Stanford to Philip, October 11, 1844.

51. Stanford to DeWitt, January 25, 1845.

52. *Ibid.* Stanford remembered Cazenovia in his later philanthropies; among his many gifts to the school was a life-size portrait of himself which was placed in the school chapel.

53. Albert Shaw, "Leland Stanford," *Review of Reviews,* August, 1893, 158.

54. San Francisco *City Argus,* n.d., 1888, in Stanford papers, box 6, folder 66. Oakland *Enquirer,* June 21, 1893.

55. Albert Shaw, "Leland Stanford," *Review of Reviews,* August, 1893, 159. Albany *Journal,* January 25, 1888, in San Francisco *City Argus,* n.d., SFS, XIX, 6 and unidentified newspaper clipping, SFS, XVI, 7.

56. Port Washington *Democrat,* October 19, 1848. Clark, *Stanford,* 36.

57. Bertha Berner, *Mrs. Leland Stanford, An Intimate Account* (Stanford, 1934), 6.

58. Bancroft, *Stanford,* 7.

59. Sheboygan *Press,* December 24, 1959. Certificate of Admission to the Bar, signed by Jerome R. Brigham, Clerk of the Wisconsin Supreme Court.

60. Milwaukee *Journal,* May 23, 1895.

61. Sheboygan *Press,* April 30, 1950.

62. Milwaukee *Sentinel,* November 11, 1848, in Clark, *Stanford,* 38. C. W. Butterfield. *History of Washington and Ozaukee Counties* (Chicago, 1881), 330.

63. Butterfield, *History,* 745. Milwaukee *Journal,* May 23, 1895.

64. Stanford to Thomas Welton, January 5, 1850, and December 20, 1851.

65. For a number of years the Post Office Department persisted in calling Port Washington after the name of the county in which it was located—Ozaukee.

66. Sheboygan *Press,* November 24, 1947. His interest in the Masons continued after he left Wisconsin: on January 11, 1854, he joined the lodge in Michigan City, California, when it was organized. John Whicher, *Masonic Beginnings in California and Hawaii* (1931), 73. Stanford's initiation and Masonic degrees are discussed in a brief and factually inaccurate biographical sketch in Louis W. Bridgman, "Leland Stanford and Port Washington," *Wisconsin Freemason,* XII (November, 1955), 5-6. Mrs. A. H. Barr, of the Ozaukee County Historical Society, to Port Washington *Pilot,* February 11, 1965.

67. *California Spirit of the Times,* April 7, 1888.

68. Pamphlet in Stanford papers. The ball was discussed years later in the Port Washington *Star,* February 18, 1922.

69. Butterfield, *History,* 509.

70. Milwaukee *Journal,* May 23, 1895.

71. *Ibid.*

72. Berner, *Mrs. Stanford,* 1, 5, 9.

73. *Ibid.*

74. Stanford to Hannah Clark, June 20, 1850.

75. Albany *Argus,* October 1, 1850, in Clark, *Stanford,* 41. Jane's family was one of the most respected in Albany; her father was a successful merchant in that city. See Bancroft, *Stanford,* 7 ff., for a sketch of the history of the Lathrop family. Clark, *Stanford,* 42.

76. *California Spirit of the Times,* April 7, 1888.

77. Milwaukee *Journal,* May 23, 1895.

78. Mrs. Barr to Port Washington *Pilot,* July 2, 1964.

79. Milwaukee *Daily Sentinel,* March 18, 1852. In Clark, *Stanford,* 45. Milwaukee Journal, May 23, 1895. In October, 1851, Leland Stanford signed a petition as a property owner to get the town to improve Franklin Street. Mrs. Barr to Port Washington *Pilot,* February 11, 1965.

80. Port Washington *Pilot,* December 12, 1964. Mrs. Barr, in her letter of February 11, 1965, denied that Stanford's law office had been burned. Perhaps this difference is due to confusing Stanford's Main Street property, which might or might not have burned, with his Franklin Street office, which did burn.

81. *California Spirit of the Times,* April 7, 1888.

82. Editorial by Fred Horn, Port Washington contemporary of Stanford and editor of the Cedarburg *News,* January 21, 1885. Butterfield, *History,* 324, 353.

83. Port Washington *Pilot,* July 2, 1964. Sheboygan *Press,* November 24, 1947.

84. Sheboygan *Press,* December 24, 1959.

85. Arthur R. Boerner, "Early Letters of Theodore E. R. Hartwig, Cedarburg's Physician and Surgeon," *Wisconsin Magazine of History,* XXIX(1946), 347-356, 348 quoted.

86. Mrs. Barr to Port Washington *Pilot,* February 11, 1965.

87. Butterfield, *History,* 544.

88. Berner, *Mrs. Stanford,* 7.

89. Thomas Welton to Stanford, February 17, 1852.

90. Stanford to parents, April 1, 1852.

91. Milwaukee *Journal,* May 23, 1895. Mrs. Barr to Port Washington *Pilot,* February 11, 1965.

92. The next three years were as trying for Jane as for her husband. She was in almost constant attendance upon her father, who was gravely ill during most of this time, and, what was worse, she was the subject of much cruel gossip for having been "abandoned" by her husband. Bancroft, *Stanford,* 11-12.

CHAPTER II

SUCCESSFUL BUSINESSMAN AND UNSUCCESSFUL

POLITICIAN, 1852-1860

Leland Stanford followed his brothers to California, but since they had already broken ground, he was not faced with the necessity of making a totally new beginning. Josiah had moved west three years before, and Charles and DeWitt had followed in 1850. Thomas and Philip sailed from New York in February, 1852, just a few weeks before Leland made up his mind to join the masses pouring westward.

Josiah tried his hand first at panning gold, but abandoned this for the financial security of selling to others who would do the actual mining. In his second year in California he opened a store in the Sacramento County town of Mormon Island. DeWitt was later made manager of this prospering store, while the elder brother extended his business ventures elsewhere.

In 1851 Josiah and Charles closed a store they owned together; Charles then returned to Albany, where, among his other business and political activities, he served as the New York purchasing agent for his brothers' various stores.[1] DeWitt wrote home that he would liked to have gone with Charles, but that he had not yet made his pile.[2] Meanwhile, the store that DeWitt was managing was now owned on equal terms by himself, Charles, Josiah, and Chauncey Peck, a friend.

As the Stanford brothers prospered in their various projects, they remained enthusiastic about the long-range prospects of their adopted home. DeWitt wished that more of their friends would join them so they could carry on business on a grand scale with one large company; he predicted that three stores could be opened within five miles of his with sufficient volume to net $10,000 per year each.[3] In the fall of 1851 Josiah completely remodeled the Mormon Island store to make it larger and more comfortable. DeWitt was confident that it would make far more money in the future than it had in the past, and lamented that Charles had gone home when he did, since, he asserted: "There never will be another California to make money in."[4]

Thomas and Philip had no sooner landed in the Golden State than they threw in with their brothers in business.[5] Josiah and Philip soon opened a

Stanford Library

STANFORD'S STORE in Cold Springs.

store together in Sacramento. Leland followed in June, 1852, by way of the isthmus of Nicaragua, and arrived in San Francisco on July 12, after thirty-eight days of travel. He journeyed to Sacramento a few days later, and spent a month in the capital before deciding definitely to stay there. Leland preferred a small business all his own to tying up with his brothers, and went so far as to make an offer on a piece of land, but the deal fell through. Rather than pressing the matter, he moved on to the Eldorado County town of Cold Springs, a central business point about halfway between Placerville and Coloma.[6]

After his unpleasant experiences as an attorney in Wisconsin, with all the financial uncertainties, hair-splitting technicalities, boring details, and petty-fogging legalities, to which his practical nature objected, Stanford never again considered the legal profession. He had mistaken his vocation, and was intelligent enough to realize it in time to make a change to another line of work. Yet his education and professional experiences were far from wasted; as a businessman, he could put to use the wide knowledge gained over the past several years. His training had given him a good understanding of contracts and of the laws governing the purchase or sale of all kinds of property; he had learned about banking, how to borrow and lend money, and he had learned how to incorporate businesses and form joint stock companies. In short, his training and experience were preparation for a business career; this, with his natural aptitude for organization and administration, made him an instant success in the business world which he now entered.

In Cold Springs, Stanford formed a partnership with an old friend, Captain Nicholas T. "Nick" Smith, who years later would become a treasurer of Stanford's Southern Pacific Railroad. Their Cold Springs store was owned in part by Stanford's brothers; Thomas Welton later called it one of the Stanford Brothers branches.[7] But when gold diggings began falling off and miners started moving away, business fell off precipitously; thus, in the spring of 1853, when a better opportunity presented itself in the Placer County town of Michigan City, later known as Michigan Bluff, Stanford moved there and opened a store. He and Smith had made a good move. The prospects of success for a miner were very promising; in point of mineral wealth, it was described as beyond comparison with any other area between the American and Yuba rivers.[8]

In one short year Michigan City grew from a settlement of six houses and thirty people to a town of 2,000 people and 250 houses. This burgeoning community contained two banks, three express offices, five attorneys, four physicians, a watch maker, ten carpenters, three blacksmith shops, two machine shops, five restaurants, six hotels, four bakeries, ten general stores, eleven clothing stores, a drugstore, and a bookstore.[9] It also had four "gambling saloons" doing business and a church under construction. Michigan City was a typical fast-growing mining town, and Leland Stanford shared its ever-increasing wealth as one of several general merchandisers.

While operating this store, the thirty-year-old Stanford traveled a great deal among the miners, taking orders and supplying them with goods. He now tipped the scales at over 200 pounds, and was a man of great physical strength. He worked himself hard and drove his own eight- and ten-horse teams through the rough mining country, but his experience was a far cry from that depicted in a poem by David Starr Jordan, in which Stanford supposedly drove a grocer's cart:

> He kept a miners' store — a stock in trade
> Of Odds and ends of all sorts. He was then
> A sturdy fellow, full of schemes and plans,
> But sticking like a bull-dog, once they're made.
>
>
> For I have seen him on his grocer's cart,
> Driving along here on the rough red roads
> That ran through Placer County east and west
> From Clipper Gap to Lone Star and beyond,
> From Yuba Canyon down to Placerville.[10]

Not even poetic license could justify this romanticized version of Stanford's business activities. To make things worse, it was impossible for him to have driven his teams and heavy wagons from the Clipper Gap of the poem, since the Clipper Gap station was not built until later placed on the Central Pacific line.[11]

The young businessman soon won the respect of his fellow townspeople, for he was shortly made justice of the peace, the only elective office he held in

California before his later governorship.[12] Stanford was educated far above the average California immigrant, and this, plus his reputation as a man of sound and fair judgment, more than qualified him for this position of trust. He afterwards enjoyed an enviable reputation among the townspeople and his fellow businessmen; one acquaintance remembered him long after his Michigan City days as a kind and charitable man who often lent a hand to strangers as well as friends during the many crises brought on by fire and illness.[13]

In May, 1855, Stanford received word that his father-in-law had died. He immediately sold his share in the store, resigned his justiceship, and in June sailed home to Albany. If he were merely planning to get Jane and come back to California, this closing out of all business and social ties does not make sense. According to Mrs. Stanford's secretary, he had no intention of going back to California; rather, he planned to open a business in Albany. But once there, he found his wife determined to live elsewhere. She had suffered keenly because a number of people considered her a deserted wife, and she proposed that they return to California.[14]

They returned to California that fall, and moved into a hotel in Sacramento until they could find a suitable house.[15] They bought the Sacramento store from Josiah and Philip, who then moved to San Francisco to manage their recently acquired Pacific Oil works.[16] Leland continued to operate under the familiar name "Stanford Brothers," though he was the sole owner until 1858, when he formed a partnership with David Meeker. Thereafter, until the new partner withdrew a year later, the business was called "Stanford Brothers and Meeker."[17]

The original Stanford Brothers store was at 56 and 58 K Street; it was later located at 224 and 226 K. In the fall of 1856 Stanford moved into a new fireproof building at the southeast corner of Front and L. This impressive structure, which measured 42 by 150 feet, cost him $14,000.[18] He had told his parents that his business was doing well, but few suspected just how prosperous it was. He also assured them that he and Jane were living quite comfortably and had all the things they needed and most of what they wanted, and then confessed that both of them were "fond of the substantial."[19]

On July 22, 1857, while the Stanfords were quartered securely in their new fireproof building, the town of Michigan City was devastated by fire. In a single hour most of the town was destroyed, including Leland's former store, though the myth persists in a number of forms that this building escaped the holocaust.[20] Twice within five years buildings which had housed his businesses were burned to the ground, and for the second time in as many years there occurred the amazing spectacle of a total resurrection from the ashes. After he became a millionaire and a figure of national prominence, his Michigan City property and that in Port Washington were exhumed, dusted off, and converted into historical shrines.

Most of Stanford's Sacramento business was in tools for miners. It has been estimated that he amassed a tidy fortune of nearly a half million dollars grubstaking miners who were down on their luck.[21] Most of this fortune was made on the Lincoln mine in Amador County. In 1859 the company which owned and worked this mine mismanaged it into bankruptcy, and Stanford, as a major creditor, received seventy-six out of a total of ninety-three shares of the company's stock. He was disposed to unload the Amador stock for whatever he could salvage from his investment, but Robert C. Downs, one of the former owners of the mine, persuaded him that it had great potential and that with proper management it could be made to pay. Stanford accepted this challenge. He let Downs manage the mine, and agreed to pay him a handsome salary and give him a one-third interest in it if he could make good on this boast. In his first year Downs brought in profits amounting to $15,000, and in 1861 Stanford turned over to him twenty-nine ninety-thirds interest in the property. He reneged on the full one-third share because this would have left him just short of a controlling majority of the stock, and Downs waived all claim to the additional two shares.[22] In times of financial trouble Stanford borrowed heavily from Downs, and at one time owed him $90,000. Stanford's profits from this mine, known later as the "Union Quartz property," increased steadily over the next several years. This income made it possible for him to participate in the building of the Central Pacific Railroad.[23] In 1872 the mine was sold for $400,000.[24]

Stanford's mining activities were not limited to the Amador mine. Gold was discovered in Bodie in 1859, and the following year a mining district was organized there. During the next two years lack of capital forced a number of the original locators to sell out, and many claims were consolidated into the Bodie Consolidated Mining Company, a new corporation with a capital stock of $1,000,000. Leland Stanford, either because of debts owed him or by purchasing his way in — it is unclear which — was elected president of this corporation.[25]

II

While busily engaged in his expanding businesses, Stanford became more and more interested in politics.[26] In 1856 he helped organize the Republican party in California; and, as a successful businessman educated far above the general level of California immigrants and an articulate though not brilliant speaker, with experience as a practicing attorney, he inevitably succeeded to leadership in the ranks of the new party. His training in law and his participation in local government were excellent preparation for his later political career, which got its real start in the late 1850's.

In the excitement of the postwar decade of the fifties and the gold rush that continued to attract thousands of immigrants, California assumed an important place in national counsels. That state's early politics cannot be understood apart from national issues. The contest there between proslavery and antislavery forces was waged with unrelenting determination.[27] Democrats in California were deeply and bitterly split into two hostile camps, the proslavery forces of the William Gwin faction and the antislavery group led by David C. Broderick. The death of Broderick in 1859 in a duel with Judge David S. Terry illustrates the extremes to which this rivalry was sometimes carried.

California bypassed the territorial stage as it entered upon statehood. When the Golden State was admitted to the Union by the thirty-first Congress as the thirty-first state, in 1850, following a year of unprecedented stampeding westward by all classes of people in search of fortunes, there existed a political vacuum in the new state that Eastern and Southern politicians struggled to fill. Since immigrants from the East and North tended to devote themselves more completely to the amassing of fortunes so as to return to their former homes, and therefore remained somewhat aloof from public affairs, Southerners soon came to dominate state politics. Though it was true that many had left their home states as a result of widespread defeat at the hands of the Whigs in 1848, it was patently unfair to characterize Southern leaders who had migrated in large numbers to the Golden State and subsequently came to control state politics as "broken-down politicians" who had "outlived their usefulness at home" and who were now little more than "frequenters of gambling saloons and election conventions."[28] The editor of the New York *Herald* charged, for example, that when President Taylor was elected, "all the democratic politicians of the United States were thrown out of employment; and gold being discovered simultaneously in California, they went off there."[29]

Many politicians and lawyers were attracted by the prospects of statehood and the wealth of litigation in the mines, but it was difficult to interest the average miner in politics. Most of them, from North and South alike, were more concerned with making their fortunes and returning to the States than taking part in government. These transients, who numbered half the population of San Francisco in 1850, were not anxious to settle down and shoulder civic burdens.

Even before the gold rush had subsided, however, the character of California immigrants had undergone something of a change; more farmers, mechanics, and laboring men were finding their way to the bonanza state. Yet as late as the election of 1852, one miner, most likely reflecting the sentiment of a great number of his class, said that he did not take the slightest interest in politics, and in the middle of political excitement, and speeches on all sides, he did not care at all who was elected president. After all, he said: "Money is what we all want and came for, and when we get it and return we will then perhaps look out for our country and see that she is not ruined."[30]

The Southerners who poured into California during this period were generally Democrats, and more often than not defenders of slavery. A San Francisco attorney lamented that California had been in bonds to the slave power "since the hour of its birth."[31] And when a Whig postmaster assumed his duties in San Francisco, following Taylor's election in 1848, his predecessor, a loyal Democrat, was scarcely able to restrain the people of San Francisco from holding indignation meetings and expressing their feelings against the administration of General Taylor.[32] In this state of affairs, the Whig party, which was becoming more and more Free Soil in composition, and in many instances outright abolitionist, had little chance of success in California. It nominated candidates for Congress and for clerk of the state Supreme Court as early as 1854, but suffered overwhelming defeat at the polls and disbanded immediately afterwards.

Except for Governor John Neely Johnson's American party victory in 1855, the Democrats ruled California from 1850-1862; especially successful were the LeCompton, or proslavery elements. The ascendancy of this group has been attributed to a number of factors. First, the Northerners, though at all times in the majority, did not contest the leadership of the Southerners. Second, the Northerners wanted to avoid introducing sectional strife into California politics, which of course had been sectional even before statehood. Finally, the Southerners in California were the "ablest politicians in the field."[33]

Owing to the irresistible strength of the Democrats in California politics, the newly organized Republican party grew slowly and painfully. A former state superintendent of education said that Virginians and Tennesseans, trained to the stump at home, were "ready on all occasions to run a primary meeting, a convention or a canvass," and he noted that there was scarcely a mining camp in the state which did not have at least one leading local politician from these states.[34] Republicans were caustically denounced by them as abolitionists, and had their meetings broken up by proslavery mobs.[35]

Republicans as well as Democrats were divided over which course to pursue with regard to slavery, but this does not mean that their programs were identical. The Democrats were generally divided over whether to contain slavery or to allow it to spread, while Republicans differed over whether to contain it or abolish it. One delegate to the Republican state convention in 1856 expressed unwavering support for Fremont and the Pacific railroad, but would have nothing to do with either abolitionism or slavery. So far as slavery was concerned, he said: "Let it remain on one side of the Mason and Dixon line and we will stay on the other."[36] Other Republicans believed that their party existed primarily as an antislavery organization.

Leland Stanford possessed strong antislavery convictions that he traced to Dr. Francis Wayland's *Moral Philosophy*, which he had read in school. Believing that the rights of men were an "inalienable endowment of their

Creator," he regarded as a gross inconsistency preaching about free government and at the same time upholding doctrines by which slavery was per-
petuated.[37] Yet the power of his convictions never got the better of him; as a
former Free Soil Whig, he opposed slavery in principle, but he never became
an abolitionist.

The incipient Republican party of California started out with few ad-
herents. Among its leading figures were Charles Crocker, Collis P. Huntington, Edwin B. Crocker, and Mark Hopkins, all of whom were destined to
work together in the building of the Republican party in the fifties and the
Pacific railroad in the sixties. They occasionally met in Sacramento and discussed politics. Besides these few prominent figures, the members of the party
could be counted on one's fingers.[38]

The severe opposition encountered by the fledgling Republican party
was described as "more vindictive and bitter than ever assailed any political
organization that ever existed in the United States."[39] Under such circumstances it took unusual courage to associate with the new party, which was
fast becoming more and more abolitionist, regardless of disclaimers to the
contrary. Stanford was early recognized as one of the party's most promising
young men and he soon became one of its leaders, but it was an overstatement
to say, as someone did, that "from the very first hour of its organization he
was chosen as its leader."[40]

E. B. Crocker, as president of the Republican Club, convened one of the
group's first meetings, on April 18, 1856, in front of the Orleans Hotel in
Sacramento. The meeting opened without incident, but before long the
speakers were interrupted by hecklers in the crowd who rushed at the
speaker's stand, overturned it, and broke up the meeting.[41] A few days later
the Sacramento *Union* expressed its regret that a noisy minority could disrupt
the gathering, when a large majority was willing to hear what the Republicans
had to say. But it nevertheless came out against the emergence at that time of
the Republican party, arguing that this would inject sectionalism into California politics.[42] The editor apparently had forgotten that California politics
had always been sectional.

The new party held its first state convention in Sacramento on April 30,
1856. Thirteen counties were represented by a total of 125 delegates who
poured into the capital, over half of them from San Francisco and Sacramento. Twelve delegates were chosen to represent California at the national convention in Philadelphia.[43]

The next party convention was held in Sacramento on August 27 to
choose a slate of presidential electors. Leland Stanford was one of the delegates at this convention, but he was not elected to the central committee.[44]
This convention dutifully endorsed the national platform and took a strong
stand in favor of the much discussed Pacific railroad project, widely regarded
among Republicans as the most important issue of the day.[45] To avoid unnecessary conflict with the proslavery population of the state, the convention

went on record against any kind of interference where slavery already existed. Stanford endorsed this action. Though personally averse to slavery, as has been pointed out, he was not "prepared to repudiate the claims of the south to their right to hold slaves under the constitution."[46]

On the following day a Sacramento editor condemned this meeting as a "convention of nigger worshipers," and warned the people of California about allowing the "dangerous fanaticism" of abolitionism to rear its ugly head among them. He challenged what he called the "national men" to unite to save California from Black Republican abolitionism.[47]

Stanford participated in several major political rallies during the campaign of 1856, and served on one occasion as vice-president of a meeting featuring E. D. Baker as the chief speaker, but his flourishing business prevented him from spending as much time as he would have liked on the presidential election.[48] As events turned out, John C. Fremont, the Republican nominee for president, ran third in California, trailing both James Buchanan and Millard Fillmore.

The following year Stanford had another try at politics as a candidate for local office when he was nominated in April for the position of alderman of Sacramento's First Ward, but he suffered an overwhelming defeat when he proved unable to attract more than 87 of the 3,068 votes cast.[49] In July, 1857, he was selected as a delegate to the Republican County Convention, where he was then elected delegate to the state convention, which would meet in Sacramento to choose a slate of Republican candidates for statewide office. Stanford was defeated in a bid for the lieutenant-governorship, but was nominated for state treasurer, indicating again that his leadership among California Republicans was still not top-level.[50] He was not optimistic about victory; in his acceptance speech he confessed that he did not know what chance there was for his election, but he thought that the Republican ticket might succeed.[51]

The Republican party had its hands full taking on the more numerous Democrats, but to make things worse the Know-Nothing party insisted on putting a slate of candidates in the field, which practically assured the Democrats of success.[52] A number of Republicans hoped that the Americans would unite with them and help defeat the Democrats, but these two parties had little in common except their mutual enemies, the Democrats, so hopes of fusion were dashed. In fact, American party nativism was for political reasons repugnant to Democrats and Republicans alike. Three-eighths of the residents of California were foreign born, and a considerable number were Catholic, so it would have been impossible for a party to have opposed successfully both foreigners and Catholics.[53]

When the Americans persisted in running a full ticket of their own and refused to support the Republicans, the latter charged them with being tools of the Southern Democrats. The editor of the San Francisco *California Chronicle* believed that the only reason the Americans put forth a ticket was to insure the election of Democrat John B. Weller, by keeping former Fillmore men from voting for Stanly, the Republican nominee. The editor of the San Francisco *Alta California* agreed.[54]

On election day, September 3, 1857, most of the Republican ticket ran a poor second; Weller was elected governor, with 53,000 votes to Republican Edward Stanly's 21,000, while George W. Bowie, the American candidate, was close behind the Republican, with 19,000.[55] Unable to outpoll either the Democrat or the American, Stanford ran third in a field of three; the Democratic victor got 58,000, the American 19,000, and the Republican somewhat less than 17,000.[56] In neither case could the Republican candidate have won even with all the American vote; despite this, Stanly condemned them for helping the common enemy, and called them "Know Nothing Democrats."[57]

Undaunted by this series of reversals, Stanford remained loyal to the party, and was numbered among those attending the county and state Republican conventions in Sacramento on August 4 and 5, 1858, being one of the vice-presidents of the state convention. He was at one time in the running for the nomination as state controller, but withdrew.[58]

On June 7, 1859, Stanford answered an invitation to speak to the Republican County Convention in Sacramento. In a forceful presentation of his views, he set the stage for the coming campaign by calling upon all anti-LeCompton Democrats to support the Republican party. He was confident that when antislavery Democrats realized that there could be only two parties in the state, the Republicans and the proslavery Democrats, they would unite with the Republicans. Stanford sought to allay fears of Democrats and Republicans alike that a Republican administration might seek to interfere with local, domestic issues in the states, particularly slavery. He assured his audience that Republicans were the true conservatives and would uphold the doctrine of popular sovereignty: "We are all well satisfied with the doctrine of non-intervention, and we do not desire our rights to be frittered away by any judicial or executive interference."[59]

The Republicans who met in convention on June 8, 1859, were badly divided on how best to combat the pro-Southern Democrats in the state, and anticipated almost certain defeat in the fall contest. Many of David C. Broderick's anti-LeCompton Democrats favored fusion with the Republicans, and many Republicans wanted to unite with the anti-LeCompton forces.[60] Unable to decide on a strategy that would satisfy everyone in their party, and thus faced with overwhelming odds against victory, Republicans entered the lists weakly without even a contest for the gubernatorial nomination. Six names were presented to the convention for this position, but all except Stanford, who was chairman of the Sacramento County Central Committee, were withdrawn immediately.[61] When the "silver-tongued" E. D. Baker withdrew his own name, he asked the convention to give Stanford a unanimous nomination by acclamation.[62] This was done, and Stanford accepted, proving himself the only one willing to submit to almost certain defeat.[63] The Sacramento *Union* publicly recognized Stanford's outstanding qualities for the office of governor, and characterized him as "a man of sound judgment, handsome talents, extensive business experience, and a citizen without reproach."[64]

The Republican nominee was as pessimistic in his acceptance speech as he had been in 1857; never had a man seemed less confident of victory than he: "Were I an aspiring man, seeking political station, I might hesitate about allowing myself to be placed in this position. But I have no political aspirations; I am content to be a humble citizen."[65] But he was unwilling to let go unheeded the popular demand for his services, and he pledged himself to battle for "the cause of the white man — the cause of free labor, of justice and of equal rights." Stanford gladly accepted the Republican platform, which affirmed his party's Free Soil heritage, and said that he was unalterably opposed to the introduction of slavery into territory now free. He made a bid for the support of Democrats of both persuasions, as well as of Republicans, by disassociating himself from abolitionism or even racial liberalism. He said he had no desire to infringe upon the rights of Negroes, but he was nevertheless in favor of free white American citizens: "I prefer the white man to the negro as an inhabitant of our country."[66]

Stanford again pledged his support to the building of a transcontinental railroad, and very cleverly explained that it should follow the route mapped out by immigrants into California; in other words, it should follow the central path, not the southern. After offering to campaign and speak to people across the state if his services were desired, he sat down.

He kept his promise to carry the campaign of 1859 to the people, and joined Baker and Frederick P. Tracy on July 8 in addressing a large crowd at the San Francisco Music Hall.[67] His speech was little more than a reaffirmation of the provisions of the Republican state platform. He attributed high taxes and the heavy state debt to Democratic administration mismanagement, and reminded his audience that the interests of California would best be served by the Republican party. He recommended building a Pacific railroad, a project that would strengthen the bonds of union, provide employment for the nation's surplus labor, and give homes and land to those who had neither. He again pledged his support to the principles of Free Soilism, though he personally opposed the "peculiar institution," and endorsed popular sovereignty in the territories, as opposed to the argument that popular sovereignty applied only after statehood had been granted.

Stanford closed with a long appeal to anti-LeCompton Democrats to unite with the Republicans in order to insure the defeat of the slave power in California politics. He asserted that the railroad was the great issue on which they could and should fuse, and called upon the free Democrats to join the Republicans in creating what would amount to a "railroad party."[68]

A week later Stanford and Baker addressed a large crowd at the Metropolitan Theater in Sacramento. Baker was the star attraction at the meeting, so Stanford spoke first. His speech was substantially the same as that delivered earlier at the San Francisco Music Hall, but he delineated in great detail some of the arguments presented there. Repeating that state interests were naturally tied to national interests, he asked voters from all parties to consider both aspects of the plat-forms they planned to support in the election and the views of the candidates for whom they were going to vote. The great national and state question which was "prominent above all others," he said, was the railroad project. He than traced in some detail the reasons why slave interests, the masters of the Democratic party and the Buchanan administration, were opposed to this project: it struck at the heart of slavery by carrying westward into new unsettled territories free farmers and free laborers who would oppose the introduction of slave labor. Moreover, slaveholders realized that they must expand their area of control or die by atrophy.

There were, Stanford further noted, other aspects of the Repub-lican platform that were beneficial to the state and the nation as a whole which were believed by slaveholders to be inimical to their in-terests. The Homestead bill, which Republicans favored and Demo-crats opposed, would provide lands for settlers who would tend to be antislavery. At the root of all Democratic opposition to Republican programs, then, was the interest of the slaveholder.

Stanford stressed again that the Republican party was funda-mentally conservative, and reassured the slave interests that the new party was in favor of popular sovereignty, a doctrine that would carry the battle if allowed to meet face to face those who wanted to extend slavery. He was confident that most people moving into new areas would oppose slavery, and would tend to support the Republican cause. Yet, he vowed that his party would not act in defiance of the Constitution and make a head-on assault on the peculiar institution.

Stanford closed the speech with one of his apologies for being neither a good orator nor a "seeker after office." He said that if he were a politician or a seeker of office he would probably make a more complete canvass of the state, but as it was, being a businessman, he could not spare the time for an extended campaign; he would simply state his views and look to the good sense of California voters to recognize what was best for themselves, their state, and their country, and vote for him and the Republican ticket.[69]

Tracy and Stanford together made an extended tour of the mining towns, and spent the greater part of the next two months going by mule or horse-drawn stagecoach throughout the hinterland. Generally this team of political prospectors traveled without fanfare. One newspaper correspondent reported from Placerville that very little notice was given to their coming; but Stanford drew a large crowd, and his speech was generally approved by the miners and residents, as was evidenced by frequent applause. He added that Stanford's exposition of the differences between the two parties as to policies and aims was excellent, and that he had "won golden opinions for himself and his cause."[70]

Stanford even received praise from some of the opposition press for his abilities as a campaigner and for his moderation. On July 22 he spoke at Georgetown, later known as Auburn. The Auburn *Placer Herald*, which supported Milton S. Latham for governor, reported that a fairly good-sized crowd, mostly Democrats, turned out to hear Stanford's speech. There were only thirty Republicans in the town.[71] Stanford held his crowd well, though he was not an exceptionally good orator, "a fact patent to all who heard him." And although very critical of the national Democratic administration, he was "mild and courteous" in his presentation.

On the other hand, Democrats believed that Stanford did betray strong sectional prejudices. He insisted that the "slave power" was behind every act of the Democratic party. According to the *Placer Herald*, Stanford felt that the Republicans and Broderickites differed only in name and organization, yet he charged the Republicans to remain faithful to their own party and reject fusion at all costs, since the Broderick forces were interested primarily in their man, not in principles. He challenged Broderick Democrats to join the Republican party for the advancement of the doctrines they held in common. Though Tracy and Stanford were well received everywhere they went, their presence embarrassed fusionist forces who insisted that Republicans should join the Broderick Democrats. Tracy described their meetings in Marysville, North San Juan, and Quincy as triumphs, but conceded that others amounted to nothing. He even regretted that they had gone to Gibsonville on August 19, since there were almost no Republicans there.[72]

Another town rather thinly populated with Republicans — there were only three there — was Downieville, where the team of Stanford and Tracy planned an address for the 18th of August. At dinner one of the Republicans urged them to forgo their talks that night, fearing that the solidly Democratic town might react violently to them. He and his compatriots, he said, hardly dare show themselves. Undaunted, Stanford and Tracy searched out the other two Republicans, though their dinner partner managed to slip away undetected, and they held their "rally."[73]

The Democrats, "in the spirit of fun and fair play," assured the Republicans that they could hold their meeting without fear of interference, and one even offered to preside. As it turned out, a Republican presided and Tracy and Stanford had their say. Tracy's speech, which focused on the sectional question as it involved California, was the highlight of the meeting. He said that the North and South were divided in opinion, sentiment, religion, mind, heart, and soul on this matter of slavery. Instead of following the moderate position that Stanford had generally espoused, he denounced the institution of slavery, and said that civilization should no longer tolerate the holding of human beings as slaves. In words that must have smacked of revolution, Tracy said that if the South did not voluntarily give up slavery it should be compelled to do so. He proclaimed that the Negro was the neighbor of the white man, and, as a creature of God, was entitled to God's gift of "liberty of thought, liberty of conscience, liberty of body." Though they did not agree with him, it was reported that the 3,000 miners in the audience were held spellbound by his oratory and the strangeness of his doctrines.[74]

There is some evidence that the Republicans at no time expected to win the 1859 elections, but were merely trying to hold their fledgling party together for the presidential contest of 1860.[75] There were three candidates for governor: Leland Stanford, John Curry, the Free-Soil or Douglas Democrat, and Milton S. Latham, "regular" Democrat. It was rumored that Stanford at the last minute would withdraw and give his support to Curry.[76] He denied being a party to any such plans and insisted that there should be but two parties in the state, and one of them should be the Republican. Although Republicans and anti-LeCompton Democrats agreed in their opposition to the slave power, his was not a "one idea" party; so long as it was committed to the construction of the Pacific railroad, to the Homestead bill, and to the preservation of public lands for actual settlers, it should not impair its organization and advance Democrats that were opposed to all Republican planks but one. He again challenged the Free Soil Democrats to unite with the Republicans.[77]

On election day, September 7, 1859, the Republicans were completely routed, and Stanford presented the sad spectacle of again running third in a field of three. In round numbers, Latham captured

62,000 votes, Curry 31,000, and Stanford a mere 10,000.[78] But Stanford never regretted his decision to keep the Republican party organization intact.

Stanford was a delegate to the Republican Convention which met in Sacramento on February 22, 1860, to select delegates to the national convention in Chicago. On the recommendation of Charles Crocker, Stanford and Tracy were placed on the California delegation.[79] Stanford, still lacking in confidence, told the Sacramento convention that it was possible that the electoral vote for California might go to the Republican candidate. He attributed past losses to Democratic misrepresentation; Republicans were misunderstood, misrepresented, and maligned by those who opposed the Pacific railroad, the Homestead bill, and the distribution of public lands to actual settlers. In closing, Stanford explained what he regarded as his role as a Republican delegate to Chicago. First, he was not committed in advance to any one candidate. He believed that California Republicans were trusting him to vote for whichever candidate would best serve Republican principles for the next four years. He drew applause from the audience when he said that at this time he strongly believed that man to be William H. Seward.[80]

On April 5, seven of the eight delegates sailed from San Francisco on the *Golden Age*.[81] Stanford, who was not among them, was scheduled to leave on the next steamer, but he failed to sail at that time too. Many biographical sketches of Stanford err in having him in attendance at the Chicago convention.[82] In a letter to his parents, two weeks later, he explained that business pressures, especially the need for assisting his brothers in San Francisco, made it impossible to leave at that time. He was still more interested in business than politics, and in the same letter home hinted at the prospects of opening yet another store. In a letter written from Sacramento one day before the Chicago convention opened, he said: "I would have liked much to have been home and cast the first vote in convention for Mr. Seward, as I would have done if there."[83]

California Republicans had given their undivided support to Seward, so when news came on June 8, three weeks after the convention met, that Lincoln had been nominated, the editor of the San Francisco *Alta California* said that the public mind was wholly unprepared for this news, and that it gave the Republican leaders of the state a severe shock. Most of them had supported Seward and had expected him to win, yet the journalist acknowledged that Lincoln was a very strong candidate.[84] All this is not meant to imply that Republicans were greatly disappointed over the nomination of Lincoln, though they were surprised. Tracy wrote that the delegation remained loyal to Seward as its first choice, though not instructed to do so, and very gladly accepted Lincoln as the second choice when their favorite was defeated.[85]

On June 20, 1860, a Republican convention met in Sacramento to nominate presidential electors. Although Stanford was not a delegate, he presided over a meeting that same evening to ratify the nomination of Lincoln and Hamlin as the party's standard bearers. Throughout the campaign he travelled widely, speaking for the Republican ticket. He and one of the state's electors, William H. Weeks, began stumping in Yreka on October 1 and worked their way southward, speaking every day except Sunday, and ended their campaign on November 3 in Amador County.[86]

The year 1860 saw the organization of "Wide Awake" Clubs among the Republicans across the country; this movement was especially popular in California.[87] Uniformed party faithfuls marched in parades bearing pickets and torches. One torch light procession, which far eclipsed in numbers any other demonstration at the capital during the campaign, marched through many of the principal streets, and concentrated in front of the St. George Hotel, where the meeting came to order by the appointment of Leland Stanford to the chair.[88]

Republicans were no more hopeful of victory in 1860 than they had been in earlier elections. In fact, the chairman of their delegation in Chicago had described themselves as a small delegation from a state they could not hope to carry.[89] Election day was November 6, and as usual the Republicans in California received a minority of the votes cast — about 39,000 out of 120,000, or 32 percent, but, owing to an almost even split between the Democratic factions, the Republicans were able to carry the state. Lincoln polled 39,000, Douglas 38,000, Breckinridge 34,000, and Bell 7,000.[90] Thus the Republican party of California got its first taste of victory; and even though it was at the national level, it gave hope for the future. Stanford, unable to capture the victory wreath for himself, played a conspicuous role in building the party that shared in Lincoln's triumph, and in so doing made his own political future secure.

---

1.   Next to Leland, Charles became the most successful businessman among the Stanford brothers. Before going to California he had been a contractor in New York. Howell and Tenney, *History of Albany,* 459. As a railroad contractor he had assisted in the building of a number of Eastern roads. Stanford, *Genealogy,* 54. This account, at variance with some, has him returning to Albany in 1854. He represented Albany County in the New York Assembly from 1864-1865 and in the State Senate from 1866-1869. Howell and Munsell, *History of Schenectady,* 160 and 198. He later became one of Schenectady's greatest real estate

owners. In 1865 he launched the Schenectady *Daily Union* and later made his brother Thomas one of its managing editors. *History of Schenectady,* 139. In 1859 he and two of his brothers, DeWitt and Thomas, established a large commercial house in Australia which served as an outlet for their oil. DeWitt died in Melbourne in 1862. Unidentified newspaper clipping, SFS, X, 38. See historical sketch of the Stanford Brothers oil enterprises and other business interests in Gerald T. White, *Formative Years in the Far West, A History of the Stanford Oil Company of California and its Predecessors through 1919* (New York, 1962), 14-20, 39, 96.

2.   DeWitt to Philip, October 10, 1851.

3.   *Ibid.*

4.   DeWitt to parents, October 27, 1851.

5.   Thomas to parents, April 17, 1852.

6.   *Stanford Illustrated Review,* XXX(June, 1923). Bancroft, *Stanford,* 13.

7.   *Bankers' Magazine of Australasia,* April 8, 1901, in Clark, *Stanford,* 51, 55. J. M. Bassett, later Stanford's private secretary, said that two of Stanford's brothers set him up in business in El Dorado County. Daggett, *Southern Pacific,* 11. Stanford testimony, p. 2,616, in *Testimony Taken by the United States Railway Commission,* 1887, in *Senate Executive Document* 51, 50 Cong., 1 Sess. In 1887 President Cleveland appointed a commission to investigate railroads that had received government assistance. The testimony taken, the report of the commissioners, and the President's message to Congress when he presented the *Report* are all reprinted in nine volumes as *Senate Ex. Doc.* 51, above. The nine volumes are bound in five, with the *Report* in Volume II. Since the pagination is continuous no volume numbers will be given here. Hereafter, this testimony will be abbreviated *Pacific Railway Commission* or *Report, Pacific Railway Commission.*

8.   Auburn *Placer Herald,* April 9, 1853, in Clark, *Stanford,* 57.

9.   *Ibid.,* February 18, 1854, in *ibid.,* 58-59.

10. David Starr Jordan, "On the North Fork, the Keeper of the Toll Gate Speaks of Leland Stanford." First published in the *Stanford Sequoia,* March, 1918. Reprinted in part in the *Stanford Illustrated Review,* XXIV (June, 1923).

11. Boutwell Dunlap, "Some Facts Concerning Leland Stanford and His Contemporaries in Placer County," *Calif. Hist. Soc. Quar.,* II (1923), 203.

12. Auburn *Placer Herald,* June 9, 1855, in *ibid.* Nick Smith later said that Stanford never had a decision appealed to a higher court. Berner, *Mrs. Stanford,* 9.

13. C. B. Herran interview, in Merced *Star,* October 30, 1890, reprinted in Washington [D.C.] *National View,* February 7, 1891.

14. This suggests that the actual reason for Jane's staying behind was to care for her ailing father. Her biographer stated explicitly that this was the reason. Berner, *Mrs. Stanford,* 8, 10.

15. *Ibid.,* 11.

16. Bancroft, *Stanford,* 15.

17. The *Sacramento Directory* of 1858 ran a full-page advertisement reading "Stanford Brothers and Meeker, Importers and Wholesale Dealers." Reprinted in *Stanford Illustrated Review*, XXIV(June, 1923). *Pacific Railway Commission*, 2,616. Stanford testimony.

18. Sacramento *California Times*, November 14, 1856. Quoted in Carroll D. Hall and Hero E. Rensch, *Old Sacramento* (Sacramento, 1958), II, 22.

19. Stanford to parents, May 4, 1856.

20. Sacramento *Union*, July 24, 1857. The only near-contemporary testimony that Stanford's property did not burn in this conflagration was in a Sacramento *Union* biographical sketch of him as the Republican gubernatorial nominee, issue of June 21, 1861. See San Francisco *Examiner*, October 2, 1927. Yet there is no doubt that the present Michigan Bluff, situated high on the brow of a hill overlooking the middle fork of the American River, is not even located where Michigan City was; it was a half mile further down the mountain. This confusion of towns and the story that Stanford's building still stands are based on the testimony of an old resident who was positive that he recalled a Stanford family and children there (Sacramento *Bee*, June 14, 1939). Leland and Jane had no children until 1868, but his cousins, Elijah and Lyman, who later lived in Michigan Bluff, did (Lyman Stanford was listed in the *Sacramento County Directory* as a merchant in Michigan Bluff. Sacramento *Bee*, June 14, 1939. This "cousin" explanation is now generally accepted. Oakland *Tribune*, May 16, 1943). Undoubtedly, this witness confused Leland and his less-famous cousins. As a clincher, a report of the damage after the fire listed an $8,000 loss for E. L. Stanford, a wholesale and retail grocer (Sacramento *Union*, July 24, 1857).

Stanford's California boosters have outstripped his Wisconsin admirers in their enthusiasm for preserving what they insist on calling the "Stanford building." The Placer County Chamber of Commerce bought the buildings thought to have been his store and home in order to maintain them as memorials (Palo Alto *Times*, September 26, 1927). Not to be topped in their display of loyalty to the memory of their founder, Stanford University alumni in 1927 bought the "Stanford home" and made a "pilgrimage" to it, at the end of which they placed a bronze tablet on the house (San Jose *Mercury Herald*, September 26, 1927).

Alumni have generally accepted as fact the old legend that the venerated frame building once belonged to Stanford, but many people lacking their emotional ties also persist in recognizing it as the original. *Stanford Illustrated Review*, XXIV(June, 1923). A San Francisco editor wrote an article on "Leland Stanford's First Residence in California," and even published a picture of the building in case there remained any doubting Thomases (San Francisco *Chronicle*, September 20, 1903, January 11, 1928). The owner of the Santa Cruz *Sentinel* corrected the mistaken editorial, but to no avail; the myth persisted in spite of his debunking (Santa Cruz *Sentinel*, editorial reprinted in Palo Alto *Times*, September 25, 1903).

Stanford's nephew, Jerome B. Stanford, later described the erroneous accounts of his famous uncle's Michigan Bluff property as "more highly spiced" than "fairy tale concoctions." Believing that there was no harm in "giving romance a jolt once in a while," he challenged newspaper reports that were "surrounded with an aura of romance," especially the story of the "little gray home that Leland Stanford built for his bride." It was easy to trace the sources of such errors: "Californians cherish the memory of the pioneers of their state and have been, and still are doing, all they can to keep alive the names of the men who have made California what it is today" (Palo Alto *Times*, April 27, 1928).

21. Bancroft, *Stanford*, 14.

22. W. E. Downs, son of Robert C. Downs, to unidentified correspondent, August 12, 1929, in Clark, *Stanford*, 69-70.

23. Oakland *Tribune*, December 2, 1945.

24. Downs to unidentified correspondent, August 12, 1929.

25. Rodman W. Paul, *California Gold: The Beginning of Mining in the Far West* (Cambridge, Mass., 1947), 280. Grant H. Smith, "Bodie; The Last of the Old-Time Mining Camps," *Calif. Hist. Soc. Quar.*, IV(1925), 64-80.

26. Casper T. Hopkins, "The California Recollections of Caspar T. Hopkins," *Calif. Hist. Soc. Quar.*, XXVI(1947), 181.

27. San Francisco *Argonaut*, August 29, 1885, in Clark, *Stanford*, 75-76.

28. Bancroft, *Stanford*, 8.

29. Quoted in San Francisco *Alta California*, July 16, 1856.

30. Earl Pomeroy, "California, 1846-1860: Politics of a Representative Frontier State," *Calif. Hist. Soc. Quar.*, XXXII(1953), 295-296.

31. Oscar L. Shafter to his sister, Laurette Ransom, September 19, 1856, in Flora H. Loughead, ed., *Life, Diary, and Letters of Oscar Lovell Shafter* (San Francisco, 1915), 186.

32. John W. Geary, Democratic postmaster, to his wife, July 21, 1849, in Clifford M. Drury, "John White Geary and his Brother Edward," *Calif. Hist. Soc. Quar.*, XX(1941), 13.

33. Josiah Royce, California, *From the Conquest in 1846 to the Second Vigilance Committee in San Francisco* (New York, 1948 edition, first published in Boston, 1886), 180-181.

34. Oscar Penn Fitzgerald, *California Sketches, New and Old* (Nashville, 1897), 256.

35. Theodore H. Hittell, *History of California* (San Francisco, 1897), IV, 193.

36. Sacramento *California Daily Times*, August 28, 1856, in Clark, *Stanford*, 72.

37. San Francisco *Argonaut*, November 27, 1886, in Clark, *Stanford*, 73.

38. Cornelius Cole, *Memoirs of Cornelius Cole* (New York, 1908), 112-113.

39. San Francisco *Argonaut*, August 29, 1885, in Clark, *Stanford*, 75.

40. *Ibid.*

41. Sacramento *Union*, April 21, 1856.

42. *Ibid.*

43. Clark, *Stanford*, 77.

44. *Ibid.*, 78.

45. Shafter to his father, July 20, 1856, in Loughead, *Life of Shafter*, 182.

46. Bancroft, *Stanford*, 16.

47. Sacramento *State Journal*, August 28, 1856, in Clark, *Stanford*, 78.

48. Republican state convention in Sacramento, August 27, 1856. Meeting in Forrest Theater in October, in Clark, *Stanford*, 78-79.

49. Sacramento *Union*, April 8, 1857.

50. Winfield J. Davis, *History of Political Conventions in California, 1849-1892* (Sacramento, 1893), 76.

51. Sacramento *Union*, July 10, 1857.

52. Peyton Hurt, "The Rise and Fall of the 'Know Nothings' in California," *Calif. Hist. Soc. Quar.*, IX(1930), 115.

53. *Eighth Census of the United States*, 1860, I, 34, Table 5.

    Know Nothings in California appreciated this and "practically abandoned the nativistic doctrines of their national organization." They declared in favor of "universal religious toleration" and directed their antiforeign animus not at the numerous Orientals and Latins, but against the Irish and Germans, who, unlike the former, took active part in the political life of the state. Their modification of the national platform was so sweeping that Hurt concluded that "genuine Know Nothingism did not exist in California." " 'Know Nothings' in California," 117-118.

54. Both papers were quoted in the Sacramento *Union*, August 22, 1857.

55. Davis, *Political Conventions*, 84.

56. *State Register and Year Book of Facts* (San Francisco, 1859), 186-187.

57. Sacramento *Union*, September 11, 1857.

58. Davis, *Political Conventions*, 93-94.

59. Sacramento *Union*, June 8, 1859.

60. Davis, *Political Conventions*, 97.

61. Sacramento *Union*, June 9, July 7, 1859.

62. *Ibid.*, June 16, 1889.

63. Davis, *Political Conventions*, 99.

64. Sacramento *Union*, June 9, 1859.

65. *Ibid.*

66. Davis, *Political Conventions*, 98.

67. Sacramento *Union*, July 9, 1859. Cornelius Cole later described Baker and Tracy as two of the most powerful orators ever produced in this country. Comparing Tracy to Demosthenes and Baker to Cicero, he called them the Paul and Barnabas of the Republican party. *Memoirs*, 112.

68. Sacramento *Union*, July 11, 1859.

69. *Ibid.,* July 15, 1859. It is impossible to retrace all of Stanford's and Tracy's steps during the campaign, but the major stops on their itinerary were San Francisco, July 8; Sacramento, July 13; Placerville, July 20; Coloma, July 21; Georgetown (Auburn), July 22; Forest Hill, July 27; Michigan Bluff, July 28; Iowa Hill, July 29; Folsom, July 30; Michigan Bar, August 13; Marysville, August 15; Nevada City, August 16; North San Juan, August 17; Downieville, August 18; Gibsonville, August 19; and Quincy, August 20.

70. Sacramento *Union,* July 22, 1859.

71. Auburn *Placer Herald,* July 30, 1859. Bancroft, *Stanford,* 18.

72. Frederick P. Tracy to unidentified correspondent, August 22, 1859. Bancroft, *Stanford,* 18.

73. Bancroft, *Stanford,* 21.

74. *Ibid.*

75. Stanford admitted as much two years later: "I looked forward to the contest of 1860, but I felt that we ought to keep up an organization for that time, and it was for that reason that I strenuously resisted a surrender of the party." Speech before the Republican State Convention, June 19, 1861. Sacramento *Union,* June 20, 1861.

76. William P. Jones to Stanford, August 10, 1859, in Sacramento *Union,* August 15, 1859.

77. Stanford to Jones, August 13, 1859, in *ibid.*

78. Davis, *Political Conventions,* 108.

79. Sacramento *Union,* February 23, 1860. The delegates originally appointed were Frederick P. Tracy, Charles Watrous, D. W. Cheesman, D. J. Staples, A. A. Sargent, Sam Bell, R. N. Mattheson, and Leland Stanford. The alternates were James R. McDonald, J. C. Hinckley, and John P. Zane. Milton H. Shutes, "Republican Nominating Convention of 1860," *Calif. Hist. Soc. Quar.,* XXVII (1948), 97.

80. San Francisco *Daily Times,* March 2, 1860.

81. *Ibid.,* April 5, 1860. The Sacramento *Union,* April 6, 1860, reprinted a mistaken report by the Sacramento *Bee* that all were aboard.

82. Among them are: Bancroft, *Stanford,* 23. Shutes, "Republican Nominating Convention," 97. Parton, *Men of Progress,* 234. Palo Alto *Times,* September 26, 1927: "He had gone to Chicago as a delegate to the convention that nominated Lincoln for the presidency." San Francisco *Chronicle,* September 20, 1903: "He was sent as a delegate to the Republican National Convention at Chicago. There he established a firm friendship with Abraham Lincoln and went on to Washington as his guest." Rockwell D. Hunt, *California's Stately Hall of Fame* (Stockton, 1950), 284; "In 1860 he went as a delegate to the famous Republican National Convention at Chicago, where he earnestly worked for the nomination of Abraham Lincoln and became a trusted friend of the new national leader."

83. Stanford to parents, May 4, 1860. If there still remained reason for the continued belief that Stanford attended the convention, it ought to have been dis-

pelled by the letter which Tracy wrote to the California State Central Committee informing them that since Stanford and R. N. Mattheson had been absent, they had filled the vacancies by the appointment of alternates J. C. Hinckley and James R. McDonald (Tracy to Barnaby W. Hathaway, May 30, 1860, in Shutes, "Republican Nominating Convention," 99. Official list of delegates is in Murat Halstead, *Caucuses of 1860: A History of the National Political Conventions* (Columbus, 1860), 127).

84. San Francisco *Alta California*, June 11, 1860. Democrats must have been equally surprised (All eight California delegates were loyal to Seward on every ballot. Horace Greeley and John F. Cleveland, comp., *A Political Text-Book for 1860: Comprising a Brief View of Presidential Nominations and Elections* (New York, 1860), 27-28). The Sacramento *Union*, which had endorsed the Union Democrat Stephen A. Douglas, conceded that Lincoln was a good candidate, of unblemished private character, but found it hard to take him seriously as a presidential candidate (Sacramento *Union*, June 11, 1860). The San Francisco *Chronicle* remained confident that the state was essentially and strongly Democratic and would reject "black Republicanism" (San Francisco *Chronicle*, May 19, 1860). The Democratic editor of the San Francisco *Herald* was delighted with the nomination of Lincoln and rejoiced at the prospect of an easy victory over such a ticket; the team of Lincoln and Hannibal Hamlin left no doubt that the Democrats would win (San Francisco *Daily Herald and Mirror*, June 11, 1860). The San Francisco *Bulletin* reprinted a letter from a disgruntled Republican who grumbled about the nomination of the relatively unknown man from Illinois and then said: "So now I have had my growl out, I shall go off and work for the ticket. Hurrah for—what's that man's name?— Abraham Lincoln!" (San Francisco *Bulletin*, June 15, 1860). The editor of the *Bulletin* was satisfied that since both "Northern" candidates favored a transcontinental railroad, which was the most important issue facing the state, it would make little difference to the state whether Lincoln or Douglas was elected (*Ibid.*, June 11, 1860).

85. Tracy to Hathaway, May 30, 1860.

86. Clark, *Stanford*, 93-94.

87. Davis, *Political Conventions*, 126.

88. Sacramento *Union*, September 26, 1860.

89. Tracy to Hathaway, May 30, 1860.

90. Edward Stanwood, *A History of the Presidency* (Boston, 1916), I, 297.

CHAPTER III

CIVIL WAR GOVERNOR OF CALIFORNIA

Following the narrow Republican victory in California, Stanford sailed to the East in January, 1861, to participate in the distribution of Pacific patronage.[1] He was one of a committee of three selected to advise the new president on California appointments, and was consulted on how best to preserve peace in California and insure that state's loyalty to the Union.[2]

Stanford's motives in returning to the East are not at all clear now. It was thought that he simply made a political trip in order to meet with President-elect Lincoln, but Stanford's private secretary, Herbert C. Nash, later confused the whole affair by stating that his employer had no intention of returning to California.[3] Like many gold seekers, Stanford had been lured to the Coast in search of wealth and had realized his ambitions by accumulating at least a quarter of a million dollars by 1861. He returned to Albany, according to Nash, with the intention of settling down in the home of his boyhood dreams.

It was later explained by Stanford that he had stayed out of the state for patriotic reasons — in order to hasten the erosion of party lines. If his name did not come forward for governor in 1861, he reasoned, it would be easier for another Republican without his own widely known partisan identification to emerge as a fusion candidate.[4] This explanation was given just after Stanford re-entered California's political arena, and was obviously intended to satisfy the public as to why he had left and had remained away for five months, without letting it appear that he had abandoned the state. It was also designed to make him appear more Unionist and less Republican. Nash's account does not answer as many questions as it raises, but Stanford's explanation should probably be discounted too.

Meanwhile, back in California, the Republican victory in 1860 served as a fillip to party aspirations for the upcoming 1861 gubernatorial contest. Stanford's friends began grooming him as a possible candidate for either the United States Senate or the governorship.[5] Philip wrote him in the East that the political mood of California had altered considerably following the attack

LELAND STANFORD, official governor's portrait.

on Fort Sumter, and that Union sentiment was already fast eroding party lines. Since the major issue was now Unionism versus Secessionism, rather than Republicans versus Democrats, Philip believed that his brother now had the best chance ever of winning the governor's chair as a Union candidate.[6] Leland confided to Philip that even if the parties had remained unchanged he would have "desired a nomination," but now that the welfare of the nation rested squarely upon the shoulders of those loyal to the Union, doing anything short of fighting for the preservation of California as a Union state would be a dereliction of duty. Above all, he wanted the people of California to elect strong Unionist officials who would support the Lincoln administration.

Stanford viewed the conflict facing the nation as a struggle between democratic and aristocratic forces. The issue, he thought, was of infinitely greater significance than the welfare of any particular party, and he said he was willing to withdraw from active political life and devote his time and talents to campaigning for the principles of Republicanism, if this would guarantee the victory of these doctrines. Yet in his mind there was no substantial difference between Unionism and Republicanism. He told Philip that he would leave immediately for home.[7] In view of Nash's interpretation of Stanford's motives, it is interesting that he spoke of California as home.

On June 3 Stanford arrived in San Francisco, and three days later was given the unanimous endorsement of the Sacramento County Republican Convention as its choice for governor. The resolution to endorse him, which was presented by E. B. Crocker, lavished praise upon him as a "long tried, true, and faithful Republican."[8]

Two weeks later, when the Republican State Convention met in Sacramento, three names were placed in running for the state's highest office: Timothy Guy Phelps, D. J. Staples, and Leland Stanford. Each addressed the convention. When Stanford's turn came he reminded the delegates that he had twice been a candidate for higher office, once for the governorship, but that he had not sought the nomination either time. He had accepted the call of the party both times because of his devotion to its principles, but this time it was different: he was now actively seeking the nomination. Liberty, he said, was at stake, and whatever the convention's decision, he would continue to support "true Republicanism and true democracy." In what was for him an unprecedented display of egalitarianism, he proclaimed: "I believe in the people; I believe in the Democracy; I believe in the elevation of the masses."

Stanford then recalled his efforts in 1859 to maintain the Republican party intact and how he would not agree to fusion with the Douglas Democrats. The party's victory in California in 1860, he claimed, proved that he had been right all along. He then repeated publicly that his extended absence from the state in the first half of the year was designed to encourage the emergence of a new leader who would serve as a fusion candidate, but that he had discovered upon returning to the state that a number of people still thought that he was the best man for the job. He was now giving in to the importunities of his friends. He closed his speech by assuring the delegates that he would support whomever they nominated.[9]

Stanford's hurried trip back to California and his active solicitation of support for the gubernatorial nomination do not square in all particulars with the later story that upon hearing in Washington that he was being considered for governor he immediately wrote withdrawing his name.[10] According to this account he withdrew his name, but since his friends did not publish the letter he was disappointed to find on his return from the capital that his nomination was a foregone conclusion.[11] In the first place, Stanford's "offer" to withdraw was not a withdrawal. There is no indication that Philip was to take it as such or that it was to be published. It is possible that his active part in the founding of the Republican party, his strong adherence to Republican principles and to the Lincoln administration, as well as his two previous defeats, made him realize that he would not make a good fusion candidate, or that he might lose to a Union Democrat if he were nominated again. But his letter to Philip, in which he expressed an interest in being nominated, his return to California, and his political activities after landing all suggest that he was not thinking of withdrawing. And his acceptance of the nomination in 1859, when there was almost no chance of victory, weakens the argument that he would avoid a fight for fear of losing it.

Stanford was clearly the convention's choice for the Republican nomination. He had participated in county and state conventions since the organization of the party, had proved an able campaigner, and had repeatedly demonstrated a willingness to battle against overwhelming odds, which, according to F. F. Low, was the paramount factor in his being selected.[12] He was nominated on the first ballot, receiving 197 of the 325 votes cast.[13] In a brief acceptance speech he merely reiterated what he had earlier told the convention, adding that he would "leave no honorable means untried" to secure victory for the Republican ticket.[14]

A much-rumored fusion of the Republicans and Union Democrats never materialized, and three candidates took the field: John Conness for the Free-Soil Democrats, John R. McConnell as the choice of the Buchanan, or pro-South, Democrats, and Leland Stanford, Republican. Though there was no formal fusion, many Union, Conness, or Douglas Democrats, as they were called in various places, supported the Republicans as the surest way of guaranteeing a Union victory.

The Sacramento *Union*, which earlier had opposed the formation of the Republican party, now praised Stanford as one of the capital city's "most substantial, reliable and able merchants."[15] He was a man of common sense, sound judgment, and integrity, and the editor predicted that he would be well-received in the campaign, because, among other things, he was an ordinary speaker with no pretensions to brilliancy. The editor of this newspaper was confident that if Stanford was elected he would place the interests of the state above all else; the candidate's wealth would place him above all temptations to use the office for personal aggrandizement.

On June 29, Stanford briefly addressed a ratification convention in San Francisco, stating that there was no well-defined party issue within the state.[16] He promised to eliminate whatever abuses might be found to exist in the state's government, and said that if elected he would devote himself to running the state economically. But Unionism was the paramount issue before the voters, and they had to realize that the federal government could be sustained in its "holy cause" of saving the Union only if a Republican administration was elected. Stanford recognized no substaintial difference between Republicans and Douglas Democrats, or between Republicans and many of the people who had supported the Breckinridge faction in the election of 1860, before secession and Civil War had defined the issue concretely. Now he called for a polarization of political opinion and challenged all Unionists of whatever former political persuasion to support him and his party.

Stanford launched his campaign by asking Cornelius Cole to accompany him on a tour of the state. Cole's support was sought in order to attract the support of antislavery Democrats, for he had been one a short time before. These two men got to know each other very well from their extended travels, and Cole came to the conclusion that Stanford was "a man of broad views concerning public affairs, and an independent thinker."[17]

This team of political partners travelled widely through the mining districts and almost every night addressed large audiences made up in good part of Democrats.[18] Some Republican measures, such as the Pacific railroad project, were already generally accepted by the miners, and others were "frequently greeted with cordial approval."[19] One of the best attended and most successful rallies of the campaign was at Folsom. A special train loaded with men and women from Sacramento went out to hear the brass band, witness the giant bonfire, and hear Stanford and others speak. Stanford again stressed national issues, but he spent more time than usual calling for much needed state reforms. In one of the strongest statements ever leveled at the Democratic party in California, he attributed corruption in government to the character of the men in power, and asserted that social and political conditions in the state had been such that "bad men" had "foisted themselves into power in that party." These Democratic politicians, many of whom were totally unfit for the high positions they held, had used their authority to corrupt and demoralize society. Stanford commended the Republican party as having the advantage of never having been corrupted by power!

The Republican candidate told his Folsom audience that the issues before them were the greatest ever faced by an electorate; they involved not only the destiny of their own government and personal welfare, but that of generations to come. In an unusual display of hyperbole, he said that the civil liberties for people all over the world were at stake and self-government itself was threatened. The Civil War, this struggle between aristocracy and democracy, had "important bearing upon the future welfare of humanity." He closed his passionate speech with an appeal to the audience for its undivided moral and political support against "rebels and traitors," asserting that this was the only way to overturn the Southerners who were determined to ruin the nation if they could not rule it.[20]

Stanford's message began taking hold everywhere in the state. Californians of all persuasions came to recognize that the issues of 1861 transcended partisan loyalties. One independent journalist of San Francisco came to the conclusion that the success of the McConnell ticket "would be tantamount to a declaration of war by California against the General Government," and predicted that a pro-Southern victory would be followed by open hostilities within the state.[21] By the end of August, he was giving Stanford daily endorsement in his editorial columns.[22]

Two weeks after the Folsom meeting Stanford spoke in Santa Rosa, where most people were, in the words of a contemporary, "decidedly unfriendly to the new party and its candidates." The Republican candidate was impressive in personal appearance; his large frame and swarthy complexion, this observer noted, gave him "something of the plain, rugged features of the frontiersman," and he was received "respectfully, but not enthusiastically."

In a dignified manner and in a "melodious and pleasant" voice, Stanford addressed the assembly on all the major issues of the campaign: the Pacific railroad, the necessity for a public school system, and the need for keeping the public domain open to actual settlers rather than speculators, and he again stressed that the Republican party was Unionist, that it was pledged to sustain the national administration at Washington. It was reported that Stanford's "plain, straightforward speech and manner" won him the confidence of a number of people at this meeting.[23]

As the gubernatorial campaign progressed, it became increasingly clear that Stanford was running ahead of the other contenders, owing largely to the fact that Unionists of all parties were coming to regard him as the only hope for keeping California loyal. One northern California Republican editor boasted that he received letters daily from the central and northern parts of the state from Unionists expressing their choice of Stanford "as the representative of the only uncontaminated and thoroughly reliable Union organization in the State."[24] He believed that only Stanford's election could keep California from following Missouri's lead, where a civil war was precipitated by the state's "traitorous governor." This editor praised the pro-Union sentiment of most Democrats in the state, and reminded them that a vote for Stanford was not so much a vote to elect Republicans as to defeat secessionists.

Stanford received a welcome but totally unexpected boost when in early September twenty-five prominent Sacramento Democrats endorsed him. Fearful of the consequences of a divided Unionist vote, they supported Stanford on the ground that he was the stronger of the two Union candidates, and in an open letter signed by all twenty-five, they recommended that their friends and fellow citizens follow their example.[25]

The voters went to the polls on September 4 and again gave the combined Democratic forces a majority, but this time the Republican candidate picked up a plurality: Standford polled 56,000 votes, McConnell 33,000, and Conness 31,000.[26] It was a clear victory for the combined Unionist forces, who captured seventy-three percent of the total vote, and a not-so clear triumph, though still a triumph, for the Republicans. Stanford carried a majority of the state's forty-six counties, twenty-six to McConnell's seventeen, and only three for Conness. Preference for Unionist candidates was also reflected in the composition of the new legislature. The Senate would now include seventeen Republicans, sixteen Union Democrats, and seven McConnell Democrats. Republicans were relatively more successful in the Assembly, where they elected forty-one, while the Union Democrats captured twenty-nine seats to only ten for the "secessionists."[27]

The Sacramento *Union* enjoined Stanford and his running mates to remember what their victory meant. Californians had voted for Unionism, not Republicanism.[28] In the same vein the Republican editor of the Marysville *Appeal* wrote:

> Stanford is undoubtedly elected Governor by a large plurality, if not a majority of the whole vote, probably leading his ticket by several thousands. This is a victory of the Union sentiment, not of a party. It is the triumph of patriotism, not of Democracy or Republicanism. Let no bigoted partisan anywhere claim that it is aught else, but remember that it is due to the generous self-sacrifice of men of various organizations, who feared that the division of the Union forces would give the State to the common enemy.[29]

The governor-elect did recognize this, and when the telegraph was completed to California in October he wired President Lincoln that Californians in their recent endorsement at the polls had shown that they held civil liberty and union above all else.[30]

II

Opinion was divided on what effect Stanford's election had on keeping California in the Union. Those who believed that the state had been on the verge of secession regarded it as a death blow to separationists' schemes. Fears that California would secede had led to considerable Union agitation in the months preceding the election. A gigantic pro-Union demonstration was held in San Francisco on May 11. Conspicuous by his absence was Governor George Downey, a LeCompton Democrat who felt that the only way to preserve the Union was by compromise and respect for the constitutional rights of all sections. He later summed up his attitude toward the war as follows: "I did not then believe, nor do I now, that an aggressive war should be waged upon any section of the Confederacy, nor do I believe that this Union can be preserved by a coercive policy."[31]

Not all those against remaining in the Union wanted to join the Confederacy. Some Californians felt that the state should pursue a totally independent course and create a Pacific republic. As early as January, 1860, Governor John B. Weller predicted that if the fanaticism then raging across the nation should succeed in destroying the Union, California would go it alone and establish "upon the shores of the Pacific" a mighty union that might in the end "prove the greatest of all."[32] Even before the Confederates fired on Fort Sumter, a California Congressman urged the creation of a West Coast republic far greater in area than the state of California. He wrote a friend that it was advisable and desirable for the people of California, Oregon, New Mexico, Washington, and Utah to "seek refuge for themselves from the blighting effects of disunion and civil war, by retiring and establishing a prosperous, happy, and successful republic on the Pacific."[33] A colleague from Sonora agreed.[34] For what it is worth, both of these Representatives were Democrats, and both were born in slave states.

The editor of the Sacramento *Union* stoutly maintained there was no essential difference between out-and-out secessionists and schemers who advocated a Pacific republic. The latter, he said, knowing it was impossible to coax California into throwing in her lot with the rebellious states, and yet determined to realize this goal at all costs, merely pretended to favor neutrality between the North and the South and plotted to use their proposed republic as a means of effecting secession. He challenged all Unionists to be on the alert against this ill-concealed form of disunionism as much as they would outright sucession.[35] Cornelius Cole agreed that the proponents of a Pacific republic were actually seeking "virtual secession."[36] One secessionist later confessed that there was a well-organized and secret secessionist group of thirty zealots, each of whom was to form a fighting force of 100 men, determined to seize control of the state and convert it into a Pacific republic as a preliminary step to union with the Confederacy.[37]

Some people argued later that the secessionists never at any time had the slightest chance of realizing their ambitions in California, and that fears of secession and the creation of an independent nation on the Coast were nothing more than Republican chimeras designed to rally Unionist support to their cause. One proponent of this interpretation said that Stanford's election "added nothing to the security of the State against secession, for the time had passed when the sympathizers of the Confederates could do anything to disturb the loyal attitude of California towards the Union."[38] A distinguished historian believed that there was never any danger of California's seceding, and that "such a thing as setting up a new and independent government was

California Historical Society
UNION RALLY in San Francisco, 1861.

no more contemplated than joining and making common cause with the south."[39]

There never was any danger of California's seceding from the Union. The overwhelming majority of its people were loyal Unionists; in fact, less than eleven percent of the state's population in 1860 came from states that later broke away.[40] When the evidence is considered, Stanford's election appears not so much a mandate to do what he could to keep California in the Union as a demonstration of the fact that the vast majority of the voters had already made up their minds on the question and were voting for a candidate whose views best reflected theirs.

III

Inauguration day, the tenth of January, 1862, was ushered in by the greatest and most devastating flood thus far in the state's history.[41] Water covered farms all over the state, rushing "through the rugged canyons of Siskiyou, and over the vine-clad plains of Los Angeles. Mines were washed out, farms were left desolate, and bridges and roads from one end of the state to the other were destroyed."[42] One story had it that the governor-elect and his party were forced to travel from their homes to the Capitol in boats.[43] Everyone who could left the city, and even the Stanfords were forced to abandon their Sacramento mansion.[44]

Stanford delivered his inaugural address in the Assembly chambers before a joint session of the legislature. He promised to work for the promotion of the intellectual, scientific, moral, and agricultural improvement of the state.[45] He insisted that land titles be guaranteed to actual settlers and that speculators no longer be allowed to dispossess those who had occupied and improved government lands. In one of the strongest statements he ever made against the Chinese, the new governor proposed discouraging by every legitimate means the settlement of the Golden State by "an inferior race," and lamented that Asia continued to send the dregs of her society to California. As important as was the settlement of California's vast territory, he said, more important still was the character of its settlers. He predicted that unless something was done to curtail this influx of undesirables there would eventually be a clash between them as they moved eastward and the superior races moved westward.

Stanford hoped to promote the overall economic prosperity of California by converting San Francisco into a great world steamship port. This was important to California's prosperity, but nothing was more essential than the building of a transcontinental railroad. Stanford, who was also president of the Central Pacific Railroad, believed the task could be accomplished by private funds, but said that federal land grants and credits were indispensable to its success.

Recognizing that Nevada would someday be a wealthy and prosperous state, and that the needs of her people could be supplied only by a railroad, Stanford proposed that construction be initiated as soon as possible. The first link in the transcontinental road should be from California to Nevada, since the thriving territory to the east was then dependent upon California for supplies. Furthermore, the Civil War made such a road a military necessity.

The war itself occupied half of Stanford's message, yet nothing in any way new appeared in his remarks. The war was caused, he emphasized, repeating what he had said many times before, by aristocratic elements in the Democratic party, and could have been prevented if the people of the South had really understood the motives of the Republicans. He closed with an appeal to all Union forces to unite and defeat the "traitors" who were attempting to disrupt the nation.

The inaugural ball was a gala affair, especially so for the Stanfords because of their guests from the East. Stanford's mother was there and so were his wife's mother, sister, and brother Henry. The new governor opened the ball "with a mother on each arm."[46]

Four days after the inaugural ceremonies the legislature adjourned for more than a week, hoping that the flood waters would subside, and then it reconvened in San Francisco, on January 24. Many Sacramento residents resented this move; they had always felt unsure of the permanent location of the seat of government and now feared losing it altogether. The editor of the Sacramento *Union* wrote that Governor Stanford had left for San Francisco, and that "his furniture was seen heading in the same direction."[47] This was evidence enough that he had "abandoned the Capital and followed the Legislature in its discreditable retreat to the Bay City." The whole affair was a "cowardly haste to leave a prostrated city." The editor of the Marysville *Appeal*, the foremost Republican organ of the state, defended Stanford's temporary move, recognizing that he was loyal to the interests of Sacramento.[48] After all, his home and business were in the city, and he had protested against the move to San Francisco on the ground that it was impolitic and might embarrass the new administration.[49] The *Union* editor rejected this explanation, noting that since Stanford had recently sold out his wholesale grocery business, and was now interested only in the oil and camphene business of Stanford Brothers, his interests would not have been impaired by remaining in the city.[50] After the floods, the governor and legislature returned to Sacramento and all was quiet again.

During his two-year tenure as governor, Stanford did much to augment the state's defenses. He completely reorganized the state militia, building it into a fighting force of over 8,000 men, and arranged with the Secretary of War to have arms sent to California so that it might be properly equipped.[51] Concern for the defense of the San Francisco harbor led him to recommend that the legislature request federal protection; this body's "earnest representations" paid off, and an ironclad vessel was sent to San Francisco.[52] Additional fortifications and water batteries were planned later for the shoreline.[53]

No quota of troops was ever assigned California, owing to its distance from the front, but several calls went out from the Secretary of War for California soldiers.[54] Stanford offered more troops than were requested; all in all 16,000 men enlisted in various voluntary organizations, and many helped the state of Massachusetts meet her quota by joining that state's military draft.[55] Others enlisted among the eight companies raised by the Territory of Washington. California volunteers served as guards on the overland mail and accepted garrison duty in a number of areas, thus releasing regular troops to fight at the front.

Governor Stanford worked closely on occasion with Thomas Starr King, the pastor of the First Unitarian Church in San Francisco, one of the outstanding California spokesmen for the Union cause. King toured the state raising funds for the United States Sanitary Commission, an organization that cared for wounded soldiers. His success is reflected in the fact that one-fourth of all funds raised in the nation came from California.[56] In response to King's appeals, Stanford accepted the chairmanship of a committee to canvass Sacramento city and county raising money for this "patriotic fund."[57]

The California legislature of 1862 passed a number of important and far-reaching laws. In long range effect possibly none was more significant than that which provided for the formation of corporations to manage savings and investments.[58] This was the forerunner of California's whole system of banks and lending institutions. Another legislative milestone of considerable significance was an act signed by the governor on May 2, 1862, establishing the California State Normal School, the successor of Minns' Evening Normal School and the forerunner of San Jose State College, the first of a long line of state-supported colleges.[59]

One of the most important achievements of the 1862 legislature was its encouragement of agriculture and manufacturing by paying bonuses for new industries, including flax, hemp, cotton, raw silk, hops, tobacco, and sorghum.[60] On September 26, 1863, addressing the tenth annual fair of the State Agricultural Society, at Sacramento, Stanford praised agriculture as the source of man's greatest happiness and as an art of the highest order.[61] He endorsed the bonus law in glowing terms and proposed that the premiums offered to encourage these enterprises be increased and that the payments be extended to apples, peaches, plums, butter, beef, pork, raisins, figs, nuts, and wines.

Several amendments to the state constitution were adopted by the people in the general election of September 3, 1862. These included one making the sessions of the legislature biennial and increasing the terms of Assemblymen from one to two years and senatorial and gubernatorial terms from two years to four.

With few exceptions, Stanford and the California legislature worked together harmoniously. What could have been a perfect record of compatibility was first marred by the legislature's refusal to confirm three of Stanford's appointees to office.[62] There was nothing lacking in their credentials or questionable about their public or private morality, so it must be assumed that opposition to them was partisan.[63] Stanford vetoed only five out of over 430 bills passed by the 1862 legislature, and in only one case did the lawmakers override his negative. This law provided for the transfer of money from the Swamp Land Fund to the General Fund. The General Fund, out of which legislators received their pay, was exhausted, so they were forced either to go without pay, pass an additional revenue bill, or transfer excess funds from one account to another. They chose the last, but the governor disapproved.[64]

Stanford kept his promise to lower the state debt, and in his first year in office the General Fund had a surplus of $91,000.[65] In the second year alone the state debt was reduced almost $800,000, over eleven percent of its total amount; at this rate the obligation would have been paid off in eleven years.[66] In order to retire the debt inherited from his predecessors, Stanford called for a tax increase and a pay-as-you-go policy for the future.[67] By the time his term was up, he had cut the state debt in half, because "economy, retrenchment, and reform were severely practiced in all public offices."[68]

Although busy with official duties, business affairs, and railroad matters, Stanford never neglected to write his recently widowed mother. At the end of his first year in office he sent her a modest appraisal of his administration, expressing confidence that he had made no intentional errors and wishing that he was worthier of the office. He told her that the recent death of his father had greatly weakened his political ambitions; but for this, he would probably have run for the Senate in the fall of 1862. But he was still primarily a business man, even while occupying the gubernatorial chair; he boasted that business prospects were never so bright, and remarked on his valuable Amador mine.[69]

Some of his letters home give valuable insights into his inner feelings, especially his religious beliefs. Following his father's death, he wrote his mother that he and Jane talked daily of her loneliness. They were very happy that she had Charles so near in this time of bereavement. Stanford had not the least doubt of an after-life, and he was confident that nothing could console his mother as well as her Christian faith, for which he was grateful. Though he loved his father dearly, he was happy for him that he had gone to a better world, where there was rest for the weary.[70]

Stanford's faith was reflected as well in his Thanksgiving Day Proclamation of 1862. He reminded his fellow citizens that they had much to be thankful for, and enjoined them to go to their places of worship and engage in acts of devotion that God might continue favoring them with His blessings.[71]

At the beginning of his second year in office, Stanford reiterated his opposition to the heavy Chinese influx, and proposed that a tax be levied upon the Orientals in order to discourage immigration without completely prohibiting it.[72] A recently-enacted California tax had been declared unconstitutional on the ground that it prohibited Chinese immigration, so the Governor challenged the legislature to use its ingenuity in finding a legal way to limit this undesirable flow of Orientals.[73] They could not become citizens and therefore were unable to enjoy the benefits of free men. They could avoid this political injustice, he said, by not coming to California. Further remarks indicated that he was motivated less by altruism toward the Chinese and a desire to keep them from becoming second-class citizens than by anti-Oriental bias. California law viewed the Chinese, in fact all Asiatics, as inferior people, and Stanford feared that the presence of more of them in California — the population of the state was already one-sixth Chinese — would discourage the coming to the state of "desirable citizens," whom he called the "higher and more enterprising and labor-creating class."

In his message of January, 1863, to the California lawmakers, the governor purposely avoided making extended remarks concerning the Pacific railroad. He conceded "motives of a personal character," an allusion to the fact that he was president of the Central Pacific Railroad Company, but he did not refrain from taking a stand on the question of taxing mines, another area in which he was involved. He opposed as impolitic and superfluous the taxing of mining claims, and argued that such a tax would reduce the incentive to work mines of doubtful or of little value.[74] The proposal to tax mines was dropped.[75]

The 1863 legislature was almost entirely Unionist; of the total membership of 120 there were ninety-five Republicans, fourteen anti-Administration Union Democrats, and eleven secessionist Democrats. One of the first acts of this legislature was to adopt a resolution endorsing Lincoln's Emancipation Proclamation.[76] Laws were passed making it a misdemeanor to display a rebel flag, making the fitting of ships to be used against the United States a capital offense, and making the undermining of the Union cause a misdemeanor. Public servants in some positions were required to take a loyalty oath.[77] Stanford approved two laws removing restrictions on Negroes and mulattoes, who had been forbidden to testify in courts when a white person was involved, but Asian disabilities were left intact.[78]

Governor Stanford got along with the legislature in 1863 even better than he had the previous year, vetoing only one out of more than 530 bills passed in the four-month session. He explained in his veto message that he did not disagree with this bill, a proposal to fund the Mendocino County debt, but that the residents of Mendocino were not themselves agreed on it. Furthermore, one branch of the state legislature had requested its return, since another bill had already been proposed that included the matter treated in it.[79]

Stanford later recalled that he almost vetoed the Specific Contract Bill presented him by the 1863 legislature. During the Civil War, greenbacks had been used to pay off indebtedness incurred before they were issued. In California this was expecially distressing, because, as a state producing gold and silver, it transacted its financial affairs in nondepreciating specie. The result was that many creditors were paid back with money worth far less than they were owed, sometimes as little as sixty percent of the face value of the loan.[80] The legislature of 1863 sought to eliminate this inequity by passing a law which would specify in writing the kind of money or currency acceptable in payment, but Stanford disapproved. He argued in his veto message that it was the duty of Californians to support the government by accepting its money at par. He never sent the veto to the legislature because he learned that the government was discriminating between its paper and gold in paying employees at the navy yard on Mare Island. If the government could not keep its money at par, he was helpless in trying to sustain it. He tore up his veto message and signed the bill, which he said in itself was fair, since it provided only for carrying out a contract according to agreement.[81]

In early 1863 Stanford again found himself involved in a question of depreciated paper currency. A year and a half earlier, in August, 1861, Congress had passed a direct tax to help finance the war, and had assigned a quota to each state. Stanford on several occasions had recommended that this additional burden be accepted cheerfully as the state's contribution to the preservation of the Union.[82] But on September 30, 1862, when California State Treasurer D. R. Ashley paid part of California's quota to D. W. Cheesman, assistant treasurer of the United States, the payment was made in legal tender worth slightly less than the same amount in specie. In January, 1863, Ashley offered more paper as payment for the balance, but this time Cheesman rejected it and complained to Stanford that Californians were paying their taxes into the Federal Tax Fund in specie, but the quota, which was to be paid out of the Fund, was being paid with greenbacks. He strongly objected to this speculation at the expense of the federal government.[83]

Stanford agreed with Cheesman's assessment, and protested to both houses of the legislature, declaring Ashley's act illegal and maintaining that the state should not force upon the government depreciated currency which had been issued reluctantly for the purpose of suppressing an "unholy rebellion."[84] Earlier, when the first payment had been made, he had sent a letter of apology to Cheesman, assuring him that Californians had no intention of benefiting themselves at the expense of the federal government and promising that he would protest against this substitution of paper for coin.[85] A special committee was formed for the purpose of investigating this payment, and on April 15, 1863, the Assembly adopted a resolution censuring Ashley for his actions.[86] But the payment in paper money stood.

Stanford continued to object to the widespread boycott of legal tender notes by a number of Californians. He warned that besides the "higher, holier, and nobler question of patriotism," they must face the economic consequences of their actions. While California alone held to a gold and silver standard, Eastern states were profiting from the circulation of millions of dollars in legitimate paper currency which stimulated their "productive energies" and developed their wealth. Stanford chided those who rejected legal tender for presuming to place themselves above the central government in deciding what should and should not be received as money. If all states had "discredited and refused to receive the currency so provided," disastrous consequences to the Union would have ensued.[87]

IV

As Civil War governor of California and dispenser of California patronage, Stanford worked closely with President Lincoln. As early as April, 1861, before his election to the gubernatorial chair, he wrote Lincoln, underlining the endorsement another California Republican had made of a party regular for political preferment, stating that the man in question was a "very staunch and reliable Republican." Stanford asked that the President give him a "respectable position worthy of his status in the party."[88] This letter was followed months later by a military telegram, stating: "Should a vacancy occur in the office of U. S. Circuit Judge for California myself & friends wish to be consulted about the appointment."[89] And in the summer of 1862 Stanford wrote to Lincoln expressing his hope that the President would see to it that the unidentified mission to Washington of a Mr. S. B. Bell be successful.[90] Nor did Stanford's attempts to influence the President cease with the crossing of state boundaries. In the fall of 1863 he wired Lincoln: "Will the President withhold the appointment of a District Judge for the territory of Nevada until the people of the territory may be heard. This is important."[91]

A critic of Stanford and two other "radical Republicans" claimed that Stanford's intention was to appoint Gordon N. Mott, a Californian sympathetic to them, to the position "in the hope that California mining interests would be more secure."[92]

V

Stanford was elected governor on a combined Republican and Union Democratic ticket, but when it came to political affairs, after his victory as before, he remained staunchly Republican. In 1862 his strong partisanship cost him considerable embarrassment and possibly significant loss of support. In that year there was only one state office vacant, that of state superintendent of education. Lieutenant-governor Chellis and others wanted to call a nominating convention in order to select a candidate, but others preferred to leave the selection to the State Central Committee. Chellis, wanting an "unmistakable enunciation" of the people on "patriotic, political and party principles and policy," wrote Stanford asking his views on the matter.[93]

The governor replied immediately, indicating that he favored holding a convention, and in the same letter challenged the Chellis group to retain intact the Republican organization within the state. He then invited Union Democrats to support them.[94] All this seemed to indicate that the projected convention was to be Republican, otherwise why the specific invitation to Democrats to join in? Rather than meeting this question head-on, in replying to critics of his position, he addressed himself to a related but different matter; he wrote at length on the necessity of having the people of the state express themselves on all political issues in convention, but this he could have arranged without calling for a Republican convention. Stanford proceeded to deliver more partisan remarks that would soon rise up to plague him. He described party organizations as the only way the people had of showing their preferences, and repeated again his oft-made assertion that the Republican party alone was the organizational spokesman for the preservation of the Union. Then, to make matters worse, he launched into a bitter denunciation of the Democratic party. All this sounded inconsistent to those Democrats who had supported him as a Unionist rather than a Republican. It was enough to cause some embarrassment as well to fellow Republicans. The San Francisco correspondent of the Sacramento *Union* wrote his editors that some of these "petty chiefs" took the governor at his word when he said that all men ought to unite under the Union banner, but they were forced to blush for him when he thrust "the name of his own party directly ahead of all his Union exhortation."[95]

Stanford thus appeared unable to bury the party hatchet even for the duration of the war. Consequently, many of his Union Democratic supporters of 1861 decided that he was not the best man to succeed himself the next year.

John Conness, a strong anti-LeCompton Democrat who had favored the bipartisan Union label as the best way of saving the nation, now came to question the advisability of this bipartisanship. Just over a month after Stanford's statement, Conness wrote:

> I have been willing and desirous that the true, loyal and patriotic people of California should, until this war was ended, constitute one party for the great purpose of maintaining the Government; and I have done no act inconsistent with such an end. It belonged to the party in power to have promoted and secured so desirable an object; but I regret to say that the efforts of their leaders have been confined to adroit movements to add to their party numbers and partisan strength.[96]

Against Stanford's wishes, the Republicans and Union Democrats in the legislature met and resolved that the state committees of both parties should call a "Union Administration Convention." It assembled in the capital on June 17, 1862.[97] Even Stanford came around to accepting it and denied ever calling for a "Straight Republican Convention," but admitted that no assembly could be too straight Republican in principle to suit him. He accepted the appellation "Union Administration" on the ground that names were of little consequence except insofar as they gave "expression to the character of the party."[98] Another reason for his acquiescence was that the Union Administration party would simply be the Republican party supported by Union Democrats, which, after all, was the same group that had elected him governor. This arrangement constituted a fusion of Union Democrats with the Republican party, a combination he had long sought, for in his mind there was no difference between Unionists, the national administration, and Republicans. In fact, he described the favorable results of the 1862 elections as a "triumphant and overwhelming victory in favor of the Union and the National Administration."[99]

Being the last California governor to serve a two-year term, Stanford's tenure was due to expire in December, 1863. Much ink has been spilled over the reasons that he was not considered for reelection. His supporters generally argued that he could have had reelection for the asking, but that he preferred to retire from public life in order to devote more time to the building of the Central Pacific Railroad.[100] Yet he had been president of the Central Pacific and governor of California concurrently for two years without serious difficulty.

Stanford did not offer himself for renomination in 1863, but not for the reason generally given. He avoided the contest because he knew he had no chance of winning. In the year or so before the question of selecting a gubernatorial nominee for the Union forces had to be faced, Stanford and John Conness had worked together smoothly in the Unionist cause. Conness took active part in the formation of a number of Union leagues that denied "for the present all partisan interests and former political ties."[101] Stanford and Conness both participated in the formation of the Sacramento Union League and made public addresses from the same platform, with Stanford abjuring partisan politics and urging all voters regardless of party to support Lincoln.[102]

Stanford's political downfall, if it can be called that, appeared inevitable after the Union County Convention that met in Sacramento on June 3, 1863. Robert Robinson, a Stanford supporter, introduced a resolution calling for the county delegates chosen at this time to cast their votes for Stanford when they went to the state convention. This move prompted William B. Carr, a Conness man, to move that the delegates to the state convention be instructed to vote for Frederick Low of San Francisco. To the surprise of a great number of people who had taken it for granted that a majority of the convention would be for Stanford, the resolution endorsing Low carried by a vote of fifty-three to thirty-seven.[103] The editor of the Sacramento *Union* chided the followers of Stanford for their colossal blunder in introducing his name at this time and for being so overly confident that they made no extra efforts to secure a majority of the convention until it was too late.[104] It was evident to him that the Low forces had a well-worked-out plan going for them and that they followed it without a slip.

The disaster foreshadowed at the county convention fully materialized when the state Unionist Convention met in Sacramento on June 17. Conness, who was accused of political bossism, was able to get his slate of delegates elected.[105] Low and Aaron A. Sargent vied for the nomination, and Low was the easy victor on the first ballot, outdistancing Stanford's man 176 to 94.[106] Stanford's attorney-general, F. M. Pixley, managed to get the floor and deliver a ringing condemnation of the way the Conness forces had steamrolled their way through the convention. He reminded the delegates that the Union Democrats, the "junior members" of the fusion which won the state from the seceders in 1861, brought in only a third of the votes needed. He excoriated them for passing over Stanford, the state's "faithful Chief Magistrate" of two years. Pixley claimed that it had been his intention of withdrawing the name of Stanford from the lists after he was renominated so that he could retire gracefully from public life, but now the governor was denied that privilege. Pixley reminded the convention of Stanford's loyalty to party and cause for the past six years, calling him a Spartacus who on bended knee had beaten back the hosts of the Democracy: "This is the man whom I sought to withdraw from public life, that we might let him out easy, not with disgrace, but like a gentleman, a statesman and an honest man, as he is."[107]

Struck to the quick by Pixley's speech, the convention unanimously adopted a resolution praising Stanford's administration as good, honest, energetic, and fair. But this was merely a sop to the Stanford forces; it did nothing to change what had happened. Pixley's intended withdrawal of Stanford's name was little more than a face-saving device for the Governor; the evidence points to the fact that he could not have won if he had tried. In fact, on June 2, the day before Low's victory, Stanford hinted in a letter to his friend Sargent that he might withdraw his name rather than be the object of abuse at the convention. He complained that the San Francisco *Bulletin* and "kindred sheets" were preparing an attack on him and his administration. Stanford spoke in this same letter of a proposed change that might have placed them both in an awkward position, evidently alluding to his withdrawal in favor of Sargent.[108]

The editor of the San Francisco *Bulletin*, who had promised to make life uneasy for Stanford, in no way endorsed the political machinations of John Conness, whom he condemned as a man struggling to attain despotic powers over the people of California.[109] He said the Sacramento convention at which "petty politicians" had attached themselves to Conness and had instructed their delegates to vote for Low was "so bald a case of fraud upon the voters that about a third of the convention retired in disgust."[110]

All the opponents of the national and state administrations and of the war held a "Fusion Democratic Convention" in Sacramento on July 8 and nominated John Downey for governor. This convention expressed a strong desire to preserve the Union intact, but censured the Lincoln administration for its disregard of the rights of states.

The campaign itself was short, lasting only two weeks, but was no less heated for this, and in the end resulted in a lopsided victory for the Unionist ticket. On September 2 the people of California gave Low 64,000 votes, 20,000 more than Downey received.[111]

In his last annual message, on December 9, Stanford expressed satisfaction with his administration, stressing the fact that the state's finances were in much better shape than when he had assumed office, evidence itself of a number of improvements in the way he governed over that of previous administrations. The out-going governor sat out the 1863 campaign and never manifested any animus toward Low for sidetracking him at the last moment. Stanford appeared happy and relieved on December 10 as he turned over the reins of power to his successor and again became a private citizen.[112]

1. Sacramento *Union,* June 21, 1861.

2. The others were E. D. Baker and John Satterlee. New York *Herald,* March 31, 1861, quoted in Elijah R. Kennedy, *The Contest for California in 1861* (Boston, 1912), 205. Bancroft, *Stanford,* 23.

3. John M. Stillman, acting president of Stanford University, made this known in 1904, address printed in pamphlet entitled *Military Order of the Loyal Legion of the United States* (San Francisco, November 29, 1904), 14.

4. Speech before Republican state convention in Sacramento, June 19, 1861. Sacramento *Union,* June 20, 1861.

5. *Ibid.,* January 21, 1861.

6. Philip to Stanford, April, 1861, no date given.

7. Stanford to Philip, May 5, 1861.

8. Sacramento *Union,* June 6, 1861.

9. *Ibid.,* June 20, 1861.

10. Parton, *Men of Progress,* 235.

11. Maggie McClure to Boutwell Dunlap, April 30, 1923.

12. Frederick F. Low, "Political Affairs," p. 32, in unpublished interview, 1883, Low papers.

13. Davis, *Political Conventions,* 176. Sacramento *Union,* June 20, 1861.

14. Sacramento *Union,* June 10, 1861.

15. *Ibid.*

16. *Ibid.,* July 3, 1861.

17. Cole, *Memoirs,* 135-136.

18. *Ibid.,* 135. The itinerary included Yreka, July 30; Fort Jones, July 31; Trinity Center, August 1; Weaverville,August 2; Shasta, August 3; Red Bluff, August 5; Oroville, August 6; Marysville, August 7; La Porte, August 8; Downieville, August 9; North San Juan, August 10; Timbuctoo, August 12; Nevada City, August 13; Grass Valley, August 14; Dutch Flat, August 15; Iowa Hill, August 16; Michigan Bluff, August 17; Folsom, August 19; Coloma, August 20; Placerville, August 21; Jackson, August 22; Angels Camp, August 23; Columbia, August 24; Sonora, August 26; Stockton, August 27; Pacheco and Benicia, August 28; Suisun, August 29; Napa, August 30; Santa Rosa, August 31; Petaluma, September 2. There were no speeches on August 4, 11, 18, 25, and September 1, all of which were Sundays.

19. Cole, *Memoirs,* 135.

20. Sacramento *Union,* August 21, 1861.

21. San Francisco *Bulletin,* August 26, 1861.

22. *Ibid.,* August 30, 31, 1861.

23. William W. Morrow, "The Founders of the University," Founders' Day address, March 9, 1914, published in *Leland Stanford Junior University Publications,* Trustees' Series (Stanford, 1914), XXV, 15-16, 27-28.

24. Marysville *Appeal,* August 28-September 1, 1861.

25. Sacramento *Union,* September 2, 1861.

26. Davis, *Political Conventions,*180. California *Senate Journal,* 1862, 94.

27. Sacramento *Union,* September 6, 1861.

28. *Ibid.*

29. Marysville *Appeal,* September 5, 1861, quoted in *ibid.*

30. Clark, *Stanford,* 112.

31. Downey to Sacramento *Union,* May 13, 1861.

32. Annual Message, January 9, 1860, in California *Senate Journal,* 1860, 36-70, and *Assembly Journal,* 1860, 40-74.

33. Congressman John C. Burch to Charles R. Street, November 22, 1860, in San Francisco *Herald,* January 3, 1861.

34. Congressman Charles L. Scott to Charles Lindley, Chairman of the Democratic State Committee, December 21, 1860, in *ibid.,* January 17, 1861.

35. Sacramento Union, February 8, April 25, 1861.

36. Cole, *Memoirs,* 142.

37. Asbury Harpending, *Great Diamond Hoax and Other Stirring Incidents in the Life of Asbury Harpending* (San Francisco, 1913), 25-39.

38. James J. Ayers, *Gold and Sunshine: Reminiscences of Early California* (Boston, 1922), 197. For evidence that the Confederate minority in California never posed a threat to the stability of that state's loyalty to the Union, see Benjamin F. Gilbert, "The Confederate Minority in California," *Calif. Hist. Soc. Quar.,* XX (1941), 154-170, and, by the same author, "California and the Civil War: A Bibliographical Essay," *ibid.,* XL (1961), 289-307. See also Leo P. Kibby, "California, the Civil War, and the Indian Problem: An Account of California's Participation in the Great Conflict," *Jour. of the West,* IV (1965), 183-209 and 377-410. Kibby concludes that secessionists were ineffective in California, and shows why.

39. Hittell, *History,* IV, 284. According to Harpending's account, General Albert Sidney Johnston, whose loyalty some suspected, was faithful to the Union and in fact played an important part in preventing an organized revolt against the government. *Great Diamond Hoax,* 32-39. In agreement, Clarence C. Clendenen concluded that the conspiracy to force California into the Confederacy was "scotched" by Johnston. "A Confederate Spy in California: A Curious Incident of the Civil War," *So. Calif. Quar.,* XLV (1963), 219-233. General E. V. Sumner, Johnston's successor, believed that most Californians were loyal, but that there was a small but zealous band of secessionists hard at work trying to create a Pacific republic as a half-way house between the Union and the Confederacy. Sumner to Col. E. D. Townsend, April 28, 1861, in *War of the Rebellion* (Washington, 1897), Series I, Vol. L, Part I, p. 472. A recent study has shown that Southern sympathizers were active in southern California. Harry H. Goldman, "Southern Sympathy in Southern California, 1860-1865," *Jour. of the West,* IV (1965), 577-586.

40. Walton Bean, *California, An Interpretive History* (New York, 1968), 178.

41. Sacramento *Union,* January 11, 1862.

42. First Annual Message, January 7, 1863, in California *Senate Journal,* 1863, 27-48, and *Assembly Journal,* 1863, 34-56.

43. Maggie McClure to Boutwell Dunlap, April 30, 1923.

44. Ella Sterling Mighels, "A Memory of the Governor," *Grizzly Bear*, X(February, 1912), 5, in Caroline Wenzel, "Finding Facts about the Stanfords in the California State Library," *Calif. Hist. Soc. Quar.*, XIX(1940), 251.

45. Inaugural Address, in California *Senate Journal*, 1862, 98-102, and *Assembly Journal*, 1862, 98-102.·

46. Berner, *Mrs. Stanford*, 13. Mrs. Stanford's widowed mother came to live with them in their Sacramento home and died there on February 25, 1873. Sacramento *Union*, February 26, 1873.

47. Sacramento *Union*, January 25, 1862.

48. Description of Marysville *Appeal* in Sacramento *Union*, May 13, 1861.

49. Marysville *Appeal*, quoted in Sacramento *Union*, February 15, 1862.

50. Sacramento *Union*, January 29, 1862.

51. Second Annual Message, December 9, 1863, in California *Senate Journal*, 1863-1864, 21-41, and *Assembly Journal*, 1863-1864, 47-67.

52. First Annual Message.

53. Second Annual Message.

54. Secretary of War Simon Cameron to Governor John G. Downey, July 24, 1861, in Richard H. Orton, *Records of California Men in the War of the Rebellion, 1861-1867* (Sacramento, 1890), 12. Cameron to Downey, August 14, 1890, *ibid.* Downey to Gen. E. V. Sumner, August 28, 1861, *ibid.*, 28.

55. Stanford to H. J. Teel, September, 1862, no date given. Orton, *Records*, 5.

56. Charles J. Stille, *History of the United States Sanitary Commission*. Philadelphia, 1866), 541-549.

57. Sacramento *Union*, September 26, 1862.

58. California *Statutes*, 1862, 199-205.

59. H. Brett Melendy and Benjamin F. Gilbert, *Governors of California* (Georgetown, Calif., 1965), 126.

60. California *Statutes*, 1862, 415-419.

61. In *California Spirit of the Times and Underwriters' Journal*, January 2, 1885.

62. California *Senate Journal*, 1862, 194-360.

63. Sacramento *Union*, March 11, 1862.

64. California *Senate Journal*, 1862, 355-358. Those vetoed were Senate bills 152 (overridden, *Statutes*, 1862, 56), 227, 372, 428, and Assembly bill 290. *Senate Journal*, 1862, 782-786, and *Assembly Journal*, 1862, 881-885.

65. First Annual Message.

66. Second Annual Message. Sacramento *Union*, December 10, 1863.

67. First Annual Message.

68. San Francisco *City Argus*, January 24, 1885.

69. Stanford to his mother, December 14, 1862.

70. Stanford to his mother, 1862, no date given, and December 24, 1865.

71. Thanksgiving Day Proclamation, November, 1862.

72. First Annual Message.

73. California *Supreme Court Reports,* 1862, 534-535.

74. First Annual Message.

75. Second Annual Message.

76. California *Senate Journal,* 1863, 23, and *Assembly Journal,* 1863, 84.

77. California *Statutes,* 1863, 350, 490, 566, 727, 755.

78. *Ibid.,* 60, 69.

79. California *Senate Journal,* 1863, 596-600, and *Assembly Journal,* 1863, 868-873. Veto message for Senate bill 43 in *Senate Journal,* 1863, 220.

80. Hittell, *History,* IV, 346.

81. *Congressional Record,* 51 Cong., 2 Sess., 667-668.

82. Inaugural Address.

83. D. W. Cheesman to Stanford, January 3, 1863, and January 5, 1863.

84. Message to California Legislature, January 8, 1863, in *Appendix* to journals of both houses of the legislature.

85. Stanford to Cheesman, October 6, 1862, in *Appendix* to First Annual Message, *Senate Journal,* 1863, 50, and *Assembly Journal,* 1863, 58.

86. California *Assembly Journal,* 1863, 610.

87. Second Annual Message.

88. Stanford to Lincoln, April 5, 1861.

89. Stanford to Lincoln, February 25, 1862.

90. Stanford to Lincoln, June 25, 1862.

91. Stanford to Lincoln, September 7, 1863.

92. Petition in favor of Gordon Mott, no date given, in Application Papers of the Justice Department, No. 16, in National Archives, quoted in Vincent G. Tegeder, "Lincoln and the Territorial Patronage: The Ascendancy of the Radicals in the West," *Miss. Vall. Hist. Rev.,* XXXV(1948-1949), 86.

93. Chellis *et al* to Stanford, April 6, 1862, in Sacramento *Union,* April 12, 1862.

94. Stanford to Chellis *et al,* April 9, 1862, in *ibid.*

95. Sacramento *Union,* April 24, 1862.

96. John Conness to unidentified resident of Shasta, May 11, 1862, in Sacramento *Union,* May 27, 1862.

97. Sacramento *Union,* June 17, 1862.

98. Stanford to William H. Rogers, August 2, 1862, as copied from Placerville *News* and reprinted in Sacramento *Union*, August 23, 1862.

99. Telegram from Stanford to Lincoln, September 7, 1862.

100. Parton, *Men of Progress*, 227.

101. Resolution adopted by Sacramento Union League, reprinted in Clark, *Stanford*, 153.

102. Sacramento *Union*, April 20, 1863.

103. *Ibid.*, June 4, 1863.

104. *Ibid.*

105. Bancroft, *History*, VII, 303.

106. Davis, *Political Conventions*, 195.

107. Sacramento *Union*, June 20, 1863.

108. Stanford to Aaron A. Sargent, June 2, 1863.

109. San Francisco *Bulletin*, June 5, 1863.

110. *Ibid.*, June 6, 1863. From June 5 until after the convention on June 17 the *Bulletin* printed daily anti-Conness editorials.

111. Davis, *Political Conventions*, 201.

112. F. F. Low, "Political Affairs," 34. Low papers.

CHAPTER IV

THE GREAT TRAIN RACE

In a certain sense the fifteen-mile-long Albany and Schenectady railroad, built with the help of Josiah Stanford, was a section of the 3,000-mile transcontinental completed in 1869. By several interesting twists of fate the young man who had spent many a day watching that construction, later, as governor of California, shoveled the first earth beginning construction of the nation's first transcontinental and still later, as president of the Central Pacific, saw the completion of the project. This incomparable undertaking did not end in 1869, nor did it begin in 1863, for decades of dreams, plans, and frustrations on the part of California railroad enthusiasts made the triumphant success at Promontory Point a possibility.

When California joined the Union in 1850 as a state, it was separated from the rest of the nation by wild, formidable territory occupied by Indians and covered with mountains, deserts, or windswept plains. Travelers to the new state came either by steamer and then across the Panama or Nicaragua route, or by wagon, horseback, or foot across the continent. By the late fifties the Butterfield Mail stage line had cut the cross-country trip to three to four weeks, about the same time as it took by steamer.

Horace Greeley, accustomed to the luxury travel enjoyed by Easterners, early recognized how imperative was the need for a transcontinental railroad. After journeying to California in 1859 over the new Salt Lake route, he became a confirmed proponent of the much-discussed Pacific railroad project. Such a road would strengthen the nation, cement the Union, and act as a fillip to America's industry, prosperity, and wealth.[1]

Long before serious agitation began for the construction of a Pacific railroad, a battle had been waged to get a wagon road built to the thirty-first state.[2] Since the 1830's, Californians had battled for such a road, and finally, on March 3, 1853, Congress appropriated money to finance a study of several proposed routes. A quarrel soon broke out between proponents of a southern route and those who favored a northern one. Residents of Los

Angeles and San Diego were pleased with the prospects of a road cutting across the southern part of the nation, and argued that since this route would be free of snow most of the time it would be easier and less expensive to build and maintain.[3] But people in San Francisco, Sacramento, and the various mining districts of central California were determined that the road should cross the middle of the country.[4]

Secretary of War Jefferson Davis preferred the southern route, but President Franklin Pierce, a confirmed enemy of internal improvements at federal expense, was opposed to any federal appropriation for such a project.[5] Californians, nevertheless, continued to press for a Pacific wagon road and railroad, and on December 12, 1854, an "Atlantic and Pacific Railroad" meeting was called at the Music Hall in San Francisco.[6] A committee of twenty-five prominent business and transportation men was selected to study the feasibility of building a wagon road across the Sierra Nevada to the Carson Valley. Dr. P. M. Wozencraft of San Francisco was appointed chairman and was instructed to draw up and present to the state legislature resolutions calling for the building of a Pacific railroad.

At the next meeting of this "Emigrant Road Committee," on December 28, 1854, resolutions were adopted which called for a transcontinental railroad, the immediate building of a wagon road from the Mississippi River to the California state line, and the appropriation of money by the state legislature for building and maintaining a wagon road to connect with the federal road.[7]

In his annual message of January 5, 1855, Governor John Bigler endorsed these resolutions, and residents of Marysville, Sacramento, Placerville, and Shasta joined him and the San Franciscans in calling for a railroad or wagon road.[8] The legislature promptly passed the required legislation, which was praised as the "harbinger" of a railroad to the Pacific.[9] On January 16, 1855, the Emigrant Road Committee met with a number of influential men, including Governor Bigler, and decided to incorporate as the "Pacific Emigrant Society." This Society would promote the settlement of California, publish information about the best routes into the state, provide rescue services for stranded emigrant parties, protect emigrants against Indians, and campaign for a wagon road or railroad across the continent.[10] A series of privately financed surveys of a route for the proposed road was next made, and in late 1855, after a good route had been found, bids were accepted for construction of the road.[11]

At this juncture opposition to the proposed road began to make itself felt.[12] Owners of vessels operating out of San Francisco were against it because they stood to lose a considerable portion of the $1,200,000 paid annually by the United States government to deliver mail along the East and West Coasts.[13] To make matters worse, the law of April 28, 1855, which authorized the construction of this road, was declared unconstitutional by a San Francisco judge, and the state Supreme Court upheld his decision.[14]

This opposition did not dampen interest in a road across California, and when a riot in Panama City on April 15, 1856, left two dozen Americans dead and scores injured, meetings were called in several California towns to subscribe the necessary funds for building a road from Big Tree to Carson Valley. Citizens of Calaveras and Stockton joined in the project, and as soon as enough money had been raised to begin construction, a contract was let.[15]

The road between Murphys and Carson Valley was completed in August, and throughout the rest of 1856 and the year following most immigrants into California followed this route.[16] Other towns, meanwhile, began discussing the possibilities of additional roads into the Carson Valley, and competition among them led to another series of surveys for alternate routes.[17]

California's agitation for a wagon road moved again to the national level after January, 1856, when the Missouri and California Overland Mail and Transportation Company was incorporated in St. Louis. Residents of San Francisco, Sacramento, Marysville, and Placerville held mass meetings to dramatize their support, and 75,000 San Franciscans sent a petition to Congress requesting that a road be built between Missouri and California; the California legislature sent a memorial underlining this request.[18]

United States Senator John B. Weller of California presented these petitions to the upper house, accompanied by a bill to provide for the construction of a "military road" from Missouri to California.[19] The Senate subsequently passed the bill, but it died in the House.[20] Legislation later provided for the building of such an artery from Fort Ridgeley, Minnesota, to South Pass and another from Fort Kearney via South Pass to the eastern boundary of California near Honey Lake.[21]

This government action prompted Californians living near Honey Lake to consider building a road of their own to meet that to be constructed by the government.[22] The California legislature adopted a measure allowing the supervisors of Sacramento and Eldorado to place before the people of their counties a proposed appropriation of $25,000 from each county treasury to build a wagon road from Sacramento to the Carson Valley.[23] These appropriations were approved and immediate steps were taken to get the project started; on June 28, 1858, a contract was let to William M. Cary and A. M. Johnson, who agreed to complete the construction by September 30.[24] It was not finished until November, 1858, but mail had already begun flowing over this "central route," demonstrating once and for all that a highway over the Sierras was both possible and practicable.[25]

II

Until Theodore D. Judah appeared on the scene with his irrepressible obsession for a transcontinental railroad, the widely-discussed California railway projects never materialized.[26] In 1853, when a group of Californians organized the Sacramento Valley Railroad, to run from Sacramento to the rich mining areas of the Sierras, they chose Judah, a well-known New York railroad engineer, as chief engineer.[27] He made a preliminary survey of the terrain between Sacramento and Mormon Island and quickly surveyed and staked out this route.[28] Grading of the roadbed began in February, 1855, and within a week 500 men were at work on the project. But this early California railroad never extended beyond Folsom.[29]

Between the time Judah left the Sacramento Valley Railroad until he became involved in the Pacific Railroad Convention in San Francisco, in 1859, he worked for a number of short roads in California.[30] He lobbied in three sessions of Congress for the Pacific railroad, and in 1857 distributed to members of Congress a pamphlet explaining the need for this road.[31] He argued that wealthy capitalists had not built a Pacific railroad because of lack of confidence, and this in turn he traced to the fact that no survey had yet been made that would allow them a proper basis for making a realistic estimate of the cost. A mere $200,000 outlay for this survey, he said, would result in a road worth $150,000,000, financed without government assistance.

Judah lobbied skillfully, but sectional deadlock prevented any success on his part. By early 1859 it was apparent that the state would have to take the initiative. On April 5 the California legislature called a railroad convention in San Francisco for September 20, 1859, to consider Congressional refusal to act on the Pacific railroad project and to adopt whatever measures were necessary to get the project moving.[32]

Judah, who soon became one of the convention's leading figures, insisted that the convention take up the question of surveying the proposed route before memorializing Congress on the matter. His attitude on financing the project had changed, and he now believed that the convention should seek the assistance of the federal government.[33] After much debate, the convention resolved in favor of the central route for the transcontinental railroad, and petitioned Congress to grant lands through which the railroad would pass, guarantee the interest on the railroad's bonds, and refund duties paid on iron used in the construction of the road.[34] It adopted resolutions endorsing the building of a railroad from San Francisco eastward and another from the Columbia River or Puget Sound eastward, to meet at some point on the way to the Missouri River. The California road was to run from San Francisco to San Jose and then eastward through Stockton and from there over whatever route the legislature designated.[35]

Judah was sent to Washington to present these resolutions to Congress. Once there, he prepared a bill and sent it to California for approval, but, for a number of reasons, his bill never reached the floor of Congress. The work of the Pacific Railroad Convention thus came to nothing.[36] Judah was convinced by this that the only way to force Congress to make a move was to begin actual construction on the railroad, and the fall of 1860 found him hard at work in the Sierras surveying a number of possible routes for his proposed road. He and Dr. Daniel W. Strong, a Dutch Flat druggist, together made a reconnaissance of the Donner Pass, or Dutch Flat route, which Judah decided was the best available.

Judah's next move was to find subscribers for capital stock so he could incorporate his "Central Pacific Railroad," and he then wrote a pamphlet to win him the needed support.[37] Meanwhile, Dr. Strong carried the subscription drive to the people of a number of small towns, where he was very successful. With great optimism Judah took his subscription campaign to San Francisco, only to meet a series of reversals in that city.[38] Rebuffed there, he went to Sacramento and called a meeting of people who had some interest in the project.[39] Among those present were Collis P. Huntington and Mark Hopkins, partners in a prosperous hardware business, Charles Crocker, another successful Sacramento merchant, and Leland Stanford.[40]

These men decided to provide Judah with sufficient funds to make additional surveys and explorations.[41] Everyone present subscribed stock in the new railroad company, and on April 30, 1861, Mark Hopkins, the treasurer, called a stockholder's organizational meeting. On June 28, the company was incorporated as the "Central Pacific Railroad of California." The capital stock of the company was fixed at $8,500,000, divided into 8,500 shares at $100 each. Most of the promised subscribers soon lost faith and dropped out, so that the new project got underway with a mere 1,580 shares sold, on which ten percent had been paid down.

Leland Stanford, already one of Sacramento's most prosperous merchants, who had just been nominated for the governorship by the Republican party, was made president. Huntington became vice-president, though he thought he should have had first place. Hopkins became secretary, and Judah the chief engineer. The directorship of the company included Charles Crocker, Lucius A. Booth, James Bailey, D. W. Strong, and Charles Marsh.[42] Stanford, Huntington, Hopkins, Crocker, Judah, and Bailey each subscribed 150 shares of the company's stock, at $100 per share.[43]

The size of the fortunes of Stanford, Huntington, Crocker, and Hopkins is largely a matter of conjecture; by existing standards they were no doubt very wealthy, but when it came to financing a project as vast as the western link of a transcontinental railroad, they could handle just the bare preliminaries. Huntington later estimated that at the inception of the road their combined assets were approximately $1,000,000; other estimates were considerably lower, closer to the assessed value of their properties in 1861, which was $118,000.[44]

The next move for the Central Pacific was to win recognition from Congress and the necessary appropriations. In October, 1861, Judah was accredited the railroad's agent to Congress to work toward these ends. This time his efforts were successful. Following the secession of the South, with its strong opposition to any but a southern route for the transcontinental rail-

Southern Pacific

COLLIS P. HUNTINGTON.

Bancroft Library

MARK HOPKINS.

Bancroft Library

CHARLES CROCKER.

Author's Collection

LELAND STANFORD.

road, the Pacific railroad bill was passed. The Civil War served to point up the need for a "military" road to tie California closely to the Union and to make defense of the distant state possible. On May 6, 1862, the bill passed the House of Representatives 79 to 49; on June 20 it passed the Senate 35 to 5; and on July 1 President Lincoln signed it into law. It provided for the building of the Union Pacific Railroad westward from the Missouri River and the Central Pacific eastward from the Pacific Coast near San Francisco or the navigable waters of the Sacramento River to the California-Nevada state line.[45] Federal funds were to be made available after forty miles of track had been laid. First mortgage bonds of six percent for thirty years would be issued by the government: $16,000 per mile for track laid in flat country, $48,000 per mile in the high mountains, and $32,000 per mile in the foothills or areas between mountain ranges.

Besides the government bonds made available — in the form of a loan, not a subsidy — ten alternate sections of land for the total length of the road

ARTIST'S CONCEPTION of the Sacramento meeting on June 28, 1861, when the Pacific Railroad's articles of incorporation were drawn up. Stanford is standing in the center. Seated at the table are, left to right, Mark Hopkins, Charles Crocker, and Collis P. Huntington. To Stanford's right is Theodore D. Judah and to his left is E. B. Crocker. Other likenesses depicted in the group are James Bailey, L. A. Booth, Daniel W. Strong, and Charles Marsh, all original directors.

Stanford Library

were given outright to the railroads. There is serious question of the wisdom of giving these public lands, especially since they did not directly help finance the construction of the transcontinental, and would not be worth anything for years after its completion.

III

Stanford had long been interested in the Pacific railroad, and as a delegate to the Republican convention on August 27, 1856, he endorsed the national platform, which called for the building of such a road. When he accepted his party's nomination for governor in 1859 he favored the central route for the railroad.[46] Stanford endorsed the projected Pacific railroad in almost every campaign speech of the gubernatorial race of 1861, and as governor he continued to speak of the blessings that the railroad would confer upon the state, once it was completed.

Despite Stanford's support of the railroad there was no hint until he was chosen its president that he would be involved personally in the ownership or building of it. He was introduced to the Pacific railroad question by Sacramento businessman James Bailey, who had learned of Judah's discovery of a suitable route through the mountains. Stanford first consulted Huntington and Hopkins about discussing the matter with Judah, and the more they talked of it the more they liked the idea. Crocker then came in, completing the famous Central Pacific team.[47]

Stanford's first interest in the railroad was probably owing to his interest in capturing the business of the thriving territory of Nevada. In his inaugural address, as he accepted the governorship of California, he called attention to the fact that Nevada supplies had to be bought in California. The platform adopted by the convention which nominated him had called for a speedy completion of a Pacific railroad, but that portion of the railroad linking California and Nevada had greater importance to Californians at the time than did the completion of the whole transcontinental. Awareness of the riches of the Nevada mountains was manifested as early as 1860, when he wrote his parents that there was a great deal of excitement in Sacramento about the gold and silver discoveries on the eastern side of the Sierra Nevada Mountains.[48] Stanford early recognized that if a transcontinental train's only competition were ox and mule teams on a wagon road, he and his associates could afford to build a railroad on the promise of the Nevada trade alone.[49]

In the fall of 1861 the Central Pacific associates organized the Dutch Flat and Donner Lake Wagon Road Company, owned exclusively by Stanford, Crocker (who was president), Huntington, Hopkins, E. L. Bradley, and D. W. Strong.[50] This road would allow them to cash in on the enormous profits of the mining areas while the railroad was being built; it would also facilitate the movement of supplies needed in the construction of the railroad.

Stanford's nomination for the governorship was in part owing to his railroad views, and his appointment to the presidency of the Central Pacific barely a week and a half later was not just a coincidence: as governor he could do much to encourage the building of the railroad, and as the president of the railroad he could see to it that its affairs were guaranteed or protected by the government. In September, 1861, just before Stanford was elected governor, Judah said that political talk so occupied everyone that he could not scare up any immediate interest in the railroad project, but the road, he said, needed Stanford in the governor's chair. As he expressed it: "A good deal depends upon the election of Stanford, for the prestige of electing a Republican ticket will go a great way toward getting us what we want."[51]

Judah's railroad bill was no sooner through Congress than work on the Central Pacific was begun. Contractors forced up prices by bidding against each other for labor, quarreled among themselves, did not finish their sections in consecutive order, and were not subject to control by the Board of Directors.[52] To mitigate these problems, Charles Crocker resigned from the Central Pacific directorate in the fall of 1862 and took charge of the construction. His company, supposedly a one-man organization, was given a contract to grade the first section of road, from Sacramento to Newcastle.

Ceremonies commemorating the beginning of construction were held on January 8, 1863. Governor Stanford promised there would be no delay in linking the two oceans by bonds of iron, and predicted that the railroad would bring the state unbounded prosperity.[53] Two wagons loaded with earth were then drawn up to the speaker's rostrum and Stanford began pitching dirt for the railroad's embankment.

The railroad's directorate comprised a number of strong personalities who regarded themselves as first in importance, making a clash inevitable. Judah, for example, referred to the Central Pacific as his "little road;" he complained that Huntington's influence was too great and that Stanford, who was personally "all right," was too much under the influence of those who were not.[54] In the summer of 1863 Judah tried to get control of the railroad by purchasing the stock owned by those of whom he disapproved. He told his friend Strong that if the parties now managing did not change some of their opinions there would be a radical change in the management of the company.[55] En route to the East to discuss his plans with interested financiers, he contracted a tropical fever and died on November 2, one week after arriving in New York. Despite his differences with his associates, at the time of his death he was still the chief engineer of the railroad.[56]

Even if Judah's tragic and premature death had not intervened, the story of the building of the Central Pacific Railroad would probably not have been much different. Stronger men than he lost their nerve before the transcontinental railroad was finished and bowed out. By 1863 Stanford, Huntington, Crocker, and Hopkins were in virtual control by themselves, each having gravitated into that position for which he was best qualified. With a letter of introduction to President Lincoln, written by Stanford, telling the President that the entire state of California would "feel a deep interest" in the success of his mission, Huntington, the group's master at financial affairs, left for New York in the fall of 1861 as the company's financial and purchasing agent. In addition, he was to use his influence to steer favorable legislation through Congress.[57] Hopkins, the oldest of the four associates, became treasurer and office manager. Crocker, one of Sacramento's most successful dry goods merchants, was given the job of managing the actual construction of the road. And Stanford, widely trusted by political friend and foe, was to employ his political influence where it could best be used for gaining popular, political, and financial support for the railroad.

At times Stanford was regarded as little more than a figurehead or front office public relations expert for the more aggressive Huntington, who preferred to manipulate events behind the scenes, but his driving force, his influence on legislation and finances, and his services while president of the railroad would indicate that he was much more important than this view concedes. He was never at any time a lackey or an obsequious follower of his vice-president. As president, Stanford's major task was to oversee legislation as it related to the Pacific railroad, and, during his last year as governor, "President Stanford promoted, the California legislature passed, and Governor Stanford signed seven acts of benevolence toward the Central Pacific."[58] In an age when "conflict of interest" had not yet become an obsession with watchdogs of public morality, few suspected him of unethical action. After all, he had won the election on a platform promising that his administration would do everything it could to build the railroad. He was selected by people who wanted and expected a transcontinental railroad built.

Stanford personally lobbied on the floor of the legislature to get a half-million-dollar subsidy passed, and was accused of cajoling senators into voting for the measure. Despite talk of its being unconstitutional, he used all the political influence he had to get it past the legislature, and his signature as governor then made it law.[59] However, not a cent was ever given the railroad under this law.

The federal government's loan to the Central Pacific was to be $48,000 per mile from a point 150 miles westward from the Sierra Nevada. Where these mountains began was largely a matter of definition, and Stanford had written Lincoln, who was given the task of defining it, asking what kind of evidence was needed to fix the western base.[60] Meanwhile, California state geologist J. D. Whitney selected the Arcade Creek, just seven miles from Sacramento, and a little over twenty miles farther west than generally accepted, as the point where there was a perceptible rise in elevation.[61] The State Surveyor-General, J. F. Houghton, agreed, but E. F. Beale, United States Surveyor-General for California, thought the line should have been fixed farther east, about halfway between Sacramento and Folsom.[62] Stanford accepted Whitney's recommendation. Thus it was shown that the Central

Pacific associates could move mountains, but there is some evidence that Judah disapproved of this "relocation" of the foothills, though Stanford denied that there was any ill feeling over it and said that in the last analysis President Lincoln established the line.[63]

With the government backing the project, the company became sanguine about its prospects, expecting that its stock would be gobbled up like hot cakes, but these expectations were soon disappointed. When no stampede for stocks developed, a meeting was called to analyze the situation.[64] Following a short exhortation by Stanford, prominent citizens of each district of the capital city were assigned the job of canvassing for subscriptions, which Stanford hoped would amount to a million dollars.[65] The campaign was then carried to San Francisco, but the results were the same; only a dozen or so shares were purchased there.[66] San Francisco capitalists did not want to risk money in a venture that promised no returns for several years. Money was so scarce that they could lend all they had available at good interest and immediate returns; moreover, many of them still questioned the feasibility of a railroad over the Sierra Nevada.[67] To make things worse, under the laws of California, stockholders in any corporation were personally responsible for its debts.

In 1863 the California legislature passed a law authorizing Sacramento, Placer, and San Francisco counties to issue bonds in payment for stock in the Central Pacific Railroad, subject to the approval of the citizens of these counties.[68] Just before San Franciscans went to the polls to vote on the measure, Governor Stanford wrote an open letter reminding them of the advantages to the state as a whole and to San Francisco in particular. He gently rebuffed them for contributing neither their time nor their money to the railroad, and reminded them that the Central Pacific had made San Francisco its terminus; because of this, $800,000 in federal funds would go to the San Jose-San Francisco road as part of the transcontinental system, and the city of San Francisco owned one-third of the stock in this road.[69]

Sacramento immediately subscribed its $300,000 worth, as did Placer its $250,000. San Franciscans passed the bond subscription by an overwhelming two to one vote, over powerful opposition, but a taxpayer's suit brought by a member of the San Francisco Board of Supervisors led to a temporary injunction halting payment of the $600,000.[70] The fall of 1863 saw Stanford trying desperately to borrow money in San Francisco, on one occasion offering interest of one percent per month and $40,000 in first mortgage railroad bonds for a short-term loan of $20,000.[71]

Opposition to the Central Pacific came from a number of San Francisco horse-power companies which were threatened with the loss of the lucrative Washoe mining business; among them were Wells Fargo, the California Stage Company, and the Overland Stage.[72] The Sacramento Valley Railway and certain enterprises with near-monopoly businesses also fought it, including the Pacific Steamship Mail Company, the California Navigation Company, various clipper ship owners, telegraph companies that feared the effects of the telegraph line that the Central Pacific was to string as it built westward, and the Sitka Ice Company, which could not compete with cheaper ice from the Sierra mountain lakes.[73]

In January, 1864, the San Francisco Board of Supervisors sent a committee to Sacramento to examine the books of the company in which their city was to invest, but Stanford refused to allow this, and admitted that an examination of the books would injure the company's public image.[74] One of the supervisors said that Crocker told him that they refused to let anyone see the books because the railroad company had been "carrying elections."[75]

When the San Francisco supervisors refused to purchase the railroad stock, the Central Pacific brought suit against the city's mayor, auditor, and treasurer. The case was ultimately appealed to the state Supreme Court, where the railroad won, but not before the dragged-out litigation had done the company serious damage.[76] A series of witnesses for the defense testified that Leland Stanford had not limited his influence in the 1863 election to mere letter writing; they personally saw his brother Philip, a heavy stockholder in the Central Pacific, purchase votes at the polls. One saw him drive up to the polls in the Ninth Ward and throw handfuls of money into the street. A crowd scrambled for the money and promptly marched off to vote for the railroad subscription. Another saw him at the First, Third, Ninth, and Tenth Wards throwing money from his wagon. Others said that he showed up at every poll in the city. One witness said that at the Fourth Ward there was a crowd of people shouting against the railroad proposition, but Stanford threw them a considerable sum of money in five and twenty dollar gold pieces, saying, "Now go to work for the railroad." The same people then began shouting in favor of the railroad proposition.[77]

Arguing that the Central Pacific Railroad had bribed enough people to get a majority of the votes, the defense attorneys asked the state Supreme Court to nullify the 1863 election.[78] The Central Pacific shrugged off the whole series of charges as "too absurd . . . too insulting to the people to require any formal refutation."[79] It won the case, but the supervisors still refused to give in. Fearful that the city would lose its investment in what promised to be a nonpaying enterprise, they arranged a compromise which allowed the city to turn over $400,000 of its gold bonds to the railroad instead of purchasing $600,000 worth of stock, but since the road later made money and its stocks soared in value, this move cost the city millions in railroad securities.[80]

IV

The Central Pacific began laying track in October, 1863, and in the following spring was ready for business.[81] In early June, 1864, the railroad was opened to Newcastle, thirty-one miles from the capital city, which remained the terminus for about a year. The prices of building materials were sky high, owing to Civil War inflation and the fact that all materials except ties and timber had to be shipped from the East, either around South America or across the isthmus of Nicaragua.[82]

Several more financial snags developed. For one, according to the terms of the Pacific Railroad Act of 1862, the government held the railroad's first mortgage bonds, and few capitalists were willing to invest in second mortgage bonds in an undertaking considered risky even for first mortgage holders. A new act was passed in 1864 which greatly liberalized the terms of the 1862 law. Now only twenty-five miles of track had to be laid per year instead of fifty, the number of alternate sections of land awarded to the railroad was doubled, the time for the building of the first fifty miles was extended one year, and, most important of all, bonds issued to the public would be first mortgage bonds, with government bonds now becoming second mortgage.[83] Still, Central Pacific bonds would not sell at anywhere near par, and the associates were fortunate to get seventy-five percent of face value.[84] They were unable to purchase on credit the rails for the first fifty miles of road until they put up their personal securities and guaranteed that as private individuals they would pay the interest on these securities for a ten-year period.[85] If they had not gambled everything in accepting these terms, there would have been no railroad, at least not then.

Meanwhile, the California act of 1863 providing a half million dollar subsidy was superseded in April, 1864, by a law which provided that the state would guarantee the interest on railroad bonds at seven percent for twenty years, to the extent of $1,500,000.[86] This act, like that of 1863, was opposed as unconstitutional, but under it the railroad did receive some assistance from the state. Stanford admitted that the associates at the time were at the end of their "tether" and that without his help they could never have built the road.[87]

Further problems followed the opening of the Dutch Flat Road, in June, 1864, which called down the wrath of the railroad's enemies. They charged that the associates had never intended to build a transcontinental and that they were planning to build the line only as far as Dutch Flat, where their wagon road began, and stop there. The opposition published a 128-page tract entitled *The Great Dutch Flat Swindle: The City of San Francisco Demands Justice*, which included every conceivable antirailroad argument.[88]

The associates encountered an unexpected attack upon themselves when the Nevada constitutional convention assembled in the summer of 1864. As in California, Nevada toll road operators and staging interests were against having the Central Pacific make off with their profits; though not opposed to a railroad coming into Nevada, they did not want the Central Pacific "monopoly." The provision written into the projected constitution which called for an appropriation of $3,000,000 in bonds to the first railroad building from navigable rivers on the Pacific to the California-Nevada state line prompted the Central Pacific associates to act. Not wanting a competing railroad covering

THE GREAT

DUTCH FLAT

SWINDLE!!

The City of San Francisco

DEMANDS JUSTICE!!

THE MATTER IN CONTROVERSY, AND THE PRESENT STATE OF THE QUESTION.

AN ADDRESS

To the Board of Supervisors, Officers and People of San Francisco.

Author's Collection

TITLE PAGE of famous 1864 antirailroad pamphlet.

the same ground, and faced with greater difficulty in selling railroad bonds if the public thought that another road might be built, Stanford went to Carson City, and on July 13, 1864, addressed the convention. He stressed the financial difficulties of the Pacific railroad project and pointed out that it was almost impossible to sell railroad securities.[89] Rather than aiding in the building of a railroad into Nevada, the proposed subsidy would hinder it by suggesting that the Central Pacific route was not the best. Members of the convention insisted that they did not want two roads, but simply wanted a road built as quickly as possible. Due to Stanford's influence, the proposed appropriation was stricken out.[90]

Nevada opponents of the Central Pacific took up the battle again when the first session of their legislature convened the following winter. In the interim, two railroads had been organized which, if built and linked together, would stretch from Folsom to the state line. Resolutions were again introduced in both houses of the Nevada legislature instructing their Congressmen to support measures to give federal assistance to the first road reaching the state line.[91] Stanford complained to the Nevada Senate about the resolutions, but this time did not exert himself to keep them from being adopted.[92]

A recent California Supreme Court decision upholding the appropriation act of 1864 made Central Pacific bonds as good as state bonds, and gave the associates enough security that the Nevada threat no longer appeared so important.[93] Within a few days the railroad advertised for 5,000 laborers for "constant and permanent work."[94] A labor shortage caused in part by the Comstock drain on manpower induced a reluctant Charles Crocker to employ Chinese laborers, but they worked so well that from late 1864 on, the railroad hired between two and three thousand of these "celestials."[95] It was reported that they could do almost as much work as white men and were far more reliable, since they were not heavy drinkers, did not join labor unions, and did not strike for higher pay.[96] Once construction was in full swing, the Central Pacific kept an average of 8,000 Chinese laborers on the payroll.[97]

Another event auguring well for the Central Pacific's financial future occurred on April 5, 1865, when the California Supreme Court forced the city of San Francisco to issue the $400,000 in city bonds. The money was needed, but not as critically as it had been two years earlier. Stanford later said that if it had not been for the delay in getting these funds the Central Pacific would have met the Union Pacific at Cheyenne instead of Promontory.[98]

Construction continued without interruption throughout 1865 and 1866. Money was coming in from government bonds at seventy-five percent of face value, while Central Pacific bonds were selling at fifty-five to sixty-five percent.[99] Stanford, meanwhile, established an office in his brothers' store in San Francisco, and made it his center of operations for political, financial, and business operations. He worked at getting the best available equipment into the field, and actually purchased and delivered to the construction site a newly-invented steam drilling machine, but he met resistance from J. H.

Southern Pacific

THE CENTRAL PACIFIC'S FIRST LOCOMOTIVE.

Southern Pacific

CISCO IN 1866 with railroad construction still in progress.

Strobridge, the construction superintendent.[100] Strobridge, because of Crocker's support, usually got his way when there was a disagreement.[101]

Record snowfalls in the winters of 1866-67 and 1867-68 put a brake to the fast laying of track to which the associates had become accustomed. To avoid laying off men, they hauled building materials over the mountains in advance of construction; if they had not kept building they would not have received federal funds.[102] Building continued, though on occasion the camps were destroyed by snowslides and men were killed.[103] To keep the project moving, Stanford decided to cover the construction area with snow sheds, the first of which had been built in the summer of 1867; by 1869 thirty-seven miles of sheds had been built, at a cost of over $2,000,000.[104]

With railroad construction moving slowly, government money was held up. Because of this the associates decided to place Central Pacific bonds on the London market. Stanford arranged to have Milton S. Latham, a prominent San Francisco banker, wined and dined on a tour of the road to Donner Lake; Latham's influence was necessary if negotiations with the Morgan financial firm to oversee the project on the London market were to prove successful.[105] Stanford collected a number of letters of recommendation from San Francisco bankers and financial houses to use in his promotion of bonds on the foreign market.[106] He was kept busy raising money to keep the track moving, and told Hopkins on one occasion that since it would be some time before there would be any government money coming in, he had been "looking around" in San Francisco for money.[107] At one point he borrowed $60,000 from the financial house of Davidson and Company, an agent of the noted Rothschild organization.[108]

When in 1867 the associates again ran out of money they organized the Contract and Finance Company, a $5,000,000 corporation designed to attract the outside capital which Crocker's company had failed to get.[109] This organization was the Central Pacific's counterpart of the Union Pacific's Credit Mobilier. Stanford claimed credit for the idea of organizing the company, although Crocker was made president.[110] But when this organization failed to attract investors, Stanford, Huntington, Hopkins, and the two Crockers divided the company's shares equally among themselves.[111] Stanford then submitted to the company a contract for the building of the rest of the Central Pacific, and he and the three other directors present awarded the contract to their own company.[112] The company agreed to complete the road, build depots, roundhouses, turntables, and station-houses, and furnish the Central Pacific all necessary equipment, including cars, engines, tools, and machinery. It was to be paid a flat rate per mile for building the road, half in cash and half in Central Pacific securities.[113]

For the lifetime of the Contract and Finance Company, the five associates continued to hold all its stock as well as the bulk of that in the Central Pacific Railroad. This was a very profitable arrangement to all concerned:

Contracts between the finance company and the railroad company were . . . made by the associates in one capacity, with themselves in another capacity. . . . The funds of the Contract and Finance Company, over and above the sums received from the Central Pacific, were derived from loans to the company by its stockholders and not from payments on the stock subscribed. There is no evidence that Hopkins, Stanford, Huntington, or either of the Crockers paid a cent in cash on their subscriptions. Instead, they gave their notes. To provide the Contract and Finance Company with funds they deposited money . . . paying interest on their notes, and receiving credit for interest on their balances, each partner as a rule putting in all the funds which he could spare, and having an individual account kept of his transactions. The Contract and Finance Company was, therefore, always heavily in debt, although the debt was owed to its own stockholders. The advantages of this arrangement would seem to be two: first, that it concealed effectively the profits which the company was making; and second, that it did not limit any stockholder to a proportionate share in the burdens and gains of the undertaking.[114]

The antirailroad editor of the San Francisco *Bulletin* condemned this practice of allowing the Central Pacific associates to let contracts to themselves under a different name as the "most vicious system of railroad building ever introduced into the United States," far worse even than that of the Credit Mobilier.[115]

Under the Contract and Finance Company, railroad construction progressed rapidly; it even accelerated the building of the western end of the transcontinental by taking over the construction of the Western Pacific.[116] In 1869 the partners awarded the contract for building the San Francisco Bay Railroad, which extended from Goat Island to a junction with the Western Pacific, to their own construction company, and in the same year both of these roads were consolidated into the Central Pacific system.[117]

V

As president of the Central Pacific, Stanford took upon himself a variety of management problems, from getting equipment to arranging finances. After 1867 he concentrated on expanding the system by the purchase of other roads and finding a deep water terminus so he could cash in on the lucrative commerce with Asia. He and his associates fixed their sights upon Goat Island, or Yerba Buena, in San Francisco Bay as the terminus of the Central Pacific, as an alternative to the circuitous Sacramento, Stockton, San Jose, San Francisco route.[118] It was the failure of the Western Pacific and the San Francisco and San Jose railroads to complete the road between San Francisco and Sacramento that prompted the associates to consider Goat Island. San Francisco and Oakland opposed the idea, since each hoped to become the terminus of the transcontinental. The city fathers of Oakland made a bid for the terminus, but Stanford made it clear that he would be looking for a *quid pro quo* before a decision was made. He suggested that the city improve its waterfront by building wharves and facilities for handling railroad traffic.[119]

Goat Island had been set aside for military use; therefore it would take an act of Congress to release it. The editor of the Sacramento *Union* fought the project, fearful that all commerce from the Orient would land at the Island and that the Central Pacific would gain control of all the business of the interior of the state, bypassing not only San Francisco, but Sacramento's lucrative river trade.[120] He was elated in 1870 when he could report that the measure had been defeated in the House of Representatives.[121]

It was inevitable that the associates would become involved at times in political machinations, if they were to build the transcontinental railroad; with bills to be put through the state legislature and Congress, they could not operate in a political vacuum. But Stanford insisted that they tried to avoid politics except where self-defense was involved.[122]

For a number of years Cornelius Cole provided needed support in the House of Representatives as a member of the Select Committee of the Pacific Railroad. Many of the amendments of the 1862 and 1864 railroad acts were suggested by Huntington, who was the associate's political arm in the nation's capital, but it was Cole who actually introduced them into Congress and helped get them passed.[123] The conscientious Congressman, feeling as he did that it was inappropriate for him to hold financial interests in the road, sold twenty-five shares of Central Pacific stock to Stanford for less than $4,000, stock later worth several times that amount.[124]

The associates and Cole later fell out on the Goat Island issue. Cole charged that they had become greedy as a result of government assistance during the war, and now had no legitimate reason for demanding the land. In response to appeals by hundreds of San Franciscans, he now opposed the railroad request.[125] The associates were not about to let Cole's action go unchallenged, and Stanford said that if nothing else could be done about the matter, he intended to "spike his battery," but he never explained what this meant.[126]

VI

In 1862 the Western Pacific Railroad Company had been organized to build from San Francisco to Sacramento by way of San Jose and Stockton.[127] The railroad act of 1862 had given the associates authority to build this road, but, doubting that it would ever be profitable, since it would have to compete with the steamship traffic on the Sacramento River, they gave up the franchise to the newly-created Western Pacific.[128] They also wanted to avoid a battle with the San Jose-San Francisco interests, who had already begun building into San Francisco over the only available route. By disposing of this section of the transcontinental system they could mitigate opposition to their "monopoly" and still retain exclusive control over everything to the east of Sacramento, most important of all, the Nevada trade.[129]

In April and May of 1867 Stanford and E. B. Crocker, the railroad's attorney, tried to regain the Western Pacific and a number of other short lines that were needed if they were to control the California railroad business. Much of Stanford's time during the next few months was spent raising money to buy the Western Pacific.[130] There was also strong feeling in favor of buying the San Jose and San Francisco, which its owners allegedly did not know how to manage, and thus acquire control over the whole transcontinental system through the state.[131]

Charles Crocker was reluctant to purchase the Western Pacific, and Hopkins was unwilling to sign the agreement until Huntington agreed. Stanford was piqued with his two associates for dragging their feet and he let them know of his displeasure. He had agreed to buy the Western Pacific, contingent upon the approval of his associates, but never suspecting that one of them might hold back, he had proceeded with the negotiations.[132] E. B. Crocker, known affectionately as "Judge," wrote Hopkins that he would be "terribly mortified" to have all his labors brought to nothing because he and his brother Charles opposed it.[133] As for himself, he was *decidedly* in favor of buying the Western Pacific, which was not only the "butt end of all the lines," but would bring with it a "big slice" of government bonds. Stanford, meanwhile, waited impatiently and anxiously for Huntington's reply, fearful that the delay would cause the Western Pacific owners to change their minds.[134] The Judge implored Hopkins to approve the deal so that it could be consummated, and even pledged that he and Stanford would buy him and Charles out if Huntington did not approve.[135] Stanford wrote the Judge that the two of them were honor bound to consummate the deal even if the other three associates did not like their so-called "outside operation," and said he was going ahead with the purchase by himself if necessary.[136]

In late April, 1867, Hopkins and Crocker gave their consent, and Huntington appears to have approved at that time, if the Western Pacific could be bought without a money transfer, which it was.[137] Stanford was named president of the newly-organized Western Pacific, with his associates and his brother Philip on the Board of Directors.[138] Stanford's paramountcy in this purchase is reflected in the fact that for years afterward the Western Pacific was called "the Governor's Road."[139]

Stanford kept prodding the Judge not to neglect the Western Pacific, now that they controlled it again, reminding him that the road ought to be pushed forward as fast as possible.[140] Meanwhile, the Central Pacific president not only kept a close eye on the progress of the transcontinental, but incorporated into the Central Pacific system a number of other roads, among them the Southern Pacific Railroad, which had been organized in 1865 by local San Francisco citizens. This road was to run from San Francisco to San

CENTRAL
PACIFIC RAILROAD
OPEN TO CISCO,
93 MILES FROM SACRAMENTO,
FOR FREIGHT AND PASSENGERS.

Trains leave **Sacramento** DAILY, (Sundays excepted) connecting at **Cisco** with Stages of the PIONEER STAGE CO. for **Virginia City, Austin,** and all parts of **Nevada.** Also, connect with the OVERLAND MAIL STAGES for **Great Salt Lake City** and all parts of **Utah** and **Montana Territories.** The Stages of the PIONEER STAGE CO. connect at **Hunter's,** on **Truckee River,** with

HILL BEACHEY'S LINE

To **Ruby City** and **Silver City, Owyhee.** Also, **Boise City, Idaho City, Placerville, Centreville,** and all parts of **Idaho Territory.**

THIS EXTENSION OF THE

CENTRAL PACIFIC RAILROAD,

In connection with the New Wagon Roads now open, *via* **Humboldt River,** will enable Passengers between **Idaho Territory, Owyhee** and **California,** to make the trip **IN FOUR DAYS,** being much less time than by any other route, and one-half the time formerly consumed *via* the Columbia River. Also, at much less risk and expense.

LELAND STANFORD, Prest. C. P. R. R. Co.

CHARLES CROCKER, Supt. C. P. R. R. Co.

SACRAMENTO, SEPTEMBER 1, 1867.

Southern Pacific

EARLY CENTRAL PACIFIC POSTER.

Diego and then to the Arizona border, and in 1866 it was authorized to connect with a southern transcontinental.[141]

From 1865 until 1868 the Southern Pacific existed in name only, but on April 4, 1868, it opened negotiations to purchase the San Francisco and San Jose Railroad. This transaction was to cost $2,770,000 and was to be completed before December 31, 1870.[142] At this juncture the Central Pacific took notice, and Stanford wrote the Judge in early 1869 that the Central Pacific must name the directors of the Southern Pacific.[143] He later explained:

> We early saw that if that line of railroad was completed . . . all the valleys of the State would be open to it and it would be a very serious competitor of the Central Pacific. So we tried to control it, and we have succeeded in controlling it; and the consequence is, that it has never been operated to the prejudice of the Central Pacific.[144]

It is not clear exactly when the Central Pacific got control of the Southern Pacific, but in the spring of 1868 the San Francisco *Bulletin* started a rumor that the Central Pacific associates had already acquired both the San Francisco and San Jose and the Southern Pacific.[145] The next day the same paper printed a letter from Stanford denying this. Timothy G. Phelps, president of the Southern Pacific, also denied it.[146] The *Bulletin* may have been wrong about the date of the transaction, but the evidence is strong that the Southern Pacific fell under the control of the Central Pacific some time between March and September, 1868. Two years later, on October 12, 1870, the consolidation of the Southern Pacific into the Central Pacific became a matter of record when the Southern Pacific, the San Francisco and San Jose, the Santa Clara and Pajaro Valley Railroad, and the California Southern were organized into the Southern Pacific Railroad of California.[147]

On March 28, 1868, the legislature gave the Terminal Central Pacific Railway Company title to a plot of submerged tideland in San Francisco Bay for the purpose of building drawbridges to Goat Island and for the construction of depot and commercial facilities at the western terminus of the transcontinental railroad.[148] The Terminal Central was later bought out by the Central Pacific.On September 25, 1868, the San Francisco Bay Railroad Company was organized to construct a road from Goat Island to connect with the Western Pacific. The five associates were the principal stockholders, with Stanford president and E. B. Crocker vice-president.[149] A year later, as noted earlier, the Contract and Finance Company was given the contract to complete the line.[150]

VII

During the building of the Central Pacific, Stanford traveled to Salt Lake City five times to help encourage Crocker and his workers to outrun the Union Pacific to the lucrative business of that city. He personally negotiated with Mormon Church President Brigham Young for laborers to build the road. Young was also supplying workers to the Union Pacific. Stanford apparently had full power to let out contracts, and he not only negotiated contracts with the Mormons who lived near the construction sites, but signed with construction companies.[151]

On each of these journeys he watched the construction project carefully and offered advice freely on how best to continue at a record-breaking pace. He even advised in areas of responsibility belonging to Crocker, such as how many men and horses should be working on a project, when and how grading should be done, and how far beyond the base of supplies it was or was not safe to work.[152] In spite of continued progress, Stanford was depressed over the advance of the Union Pacific, which threatened to beat the Central Pacific into Salt Lake City, and he complained that if Crocker had stayed out on the line pushing materials faster there would have been more progress.[153]

In October of 1868 the Central Pacific filed a map with the Secretary of the Interior showing its proposed route of the last section of the transcontinental railroad, and on October 28 this route was approved.[154] Stanford interpreted this as meaning that the government would recognize only that road which built on this line; thus, if the Union Pacific built by them on another line, the Central Pacific line would have to be recognized.[155] Huntington wanted either to force the Union Pacific to build on this line or to stop its construction altogether, but Stanford spelled out *his* strategy as follows: "Now my idea is and has been that if our theory is sound that the accepted line is the only Pacific R. R. line, then let the U. P. work off it and when they want to draw bonds on their line raise the question."[156] To further this scheme, he tried his best to keep the route secret; nothing was to be done to let the Union Pacific know for certain too far in advance which route the Central Pacific was planning to use.

In one of his many trips to the construction site, Stanford discovered that the Union Pacific line was going to be very near that of the Central Pacific; in places they would be within a hundred feet of one another.[157] Neither road had purchased a right of way through farms in the area, so Stanford, cautioning Hopkins that he had kept this question "entirely still," set about cornering the needed passage. To keep the Union Pacific from moving too far into what he now regarded as Central Pacific territory, Stanford decided to block its progress by land purchase, buying, if necessary, the right of way through every farm in the valley through which the road had to be laid. He wrote to the Judge: "I think I may conclude to buy in some

Southern Pacific

WESTWARD BOUND COVERED WAGONS meet special Central Pacific train headed for ceremonies at Promontory, May 8, 1869.

Stanford Library

COMPLETION OF THE TRANSCONTINENTAL, May 10, 1869. Mr. and Mrs. Stanford in the center.

proper person's name some land between here and the mouth of the Weber over which the Union Pacific cannot avoid passing."[158]

Stanford came to realize the inadvisability of getting himself too much involved in these purchases. In his place he began sending Mormon Bishop West, a partner in a Salt Lake City construction company, to survey farms across which the road must pass, and commissioned him to secure a 100-foot right of way through the whole area.[159] This would be the key to victory if a showdown with the Union Pacific became necessary. Later, if the Union Pacific tried to get authorization to build into this territory he would be in a position to assert that the Central Pacific tract was the only Pacific railroad route allowable and that all others would have to keep off its right of way.[160]

Stanford's strategy of letting the Union Pacific lay tracks on which it could not collect backfired. When the government commission certified for payment a section of Union Pacific road that had not even been built, he conceded defeat.[161] The roads were rushing toward each other at the rate of almost twenty miles a day, with little serious thought as to where they might meet; in fact, the two companies graded over 100 miles of parallel road-bed.[162] Awakening to the possibility that they might build past each other and both claim federal funds for the same section, they decided on a junction, and on April 10, 1869, Congress ratified this agreement, which called for the two roads to meet at or near Ogden, Utah.[163]

On May 10, near Ogden, the two railroads were linked into one great transcontinental highway. Stanford, the only one of the Central Pacific associates present at the event, led an entourage of California notables, while from the East came Thomas C. Durant and other high officers of the Union Pacific. The Central Pacific's "Jupiter," wood-burning engine number 60, and the Union's coal-burner number 119 were drawn up cowcatcher to cowcatcher opposite the last gap in the transcontinental line.[164] Stanford was stationed on the north side of the track and Durant on the south, each armed with a silver sledge for tapping the spikes into holes already drilled for the purpose. To complete the telegraph lines paralleling the railroads and to symbolize the linking of the two sections of the nation, one end of a telegraph wire was wound around Stanford's hammer and the other end connected to an iron spike. Though both men missed as they tapped at the preset spikes in predrilled holes, they were finally driven home and then removed to be replaced by some made of more conventional materials.

Stanford wired the Central Pacific office the simple message, "Last spike driven."[165] In what was one of the greatest understatements ever made on the celebration that followed, Stanford later said: "We were exceedingly relieved when we got through and we 'jollified' a little."[166] There followed speeches, music, and the readings of congratulatory telegrams. Even poets were inspired by the august scene, for Bret Harte wrote:

What was it the engines said,
Pilots touching—head to head.

. . . .

Said the engine from the west;
"I am from Sierra's crest,
And if altitude's the test,
Well, I reckon, it's confessed,
That I've done my level best."
Said the engine from the east:
"Those who work best talk the least.

. . . .

Let those folks with champagne stuffing,
Not their engines, do the puffing."[67]

An invitation from over 150 of Sacramento's outstanding citizens and businessmen was sent to the directors of the Central Pacific inviting them to a great public dinner in their honor in the capital city on September 28.[168] The feast came off as planned with the directors in their places, and, as to be expected, Stanford was called upon to make a speech. He honored the guests with a short message, but Huntington, who was also invited to speak, declined. Thus with champagne, celebrations, and happy speeches, the completion of the transcontinental line was heralded; one era had passed, another was on the horizon.

1. Horace Greeley to New York *Tribune*, October 20, 1859, in Horace Greeley, *Overland Journey from New York to San Francisco* (New York, 1860), 368-386.

2. The following synopsis of the building of the first wagon road from California to the Carson Valley and of early agitation for a transcontinental road is based largely upon Chester L. White, "Surmounting the Sierras," *Calif. Hist. Soc. Quar.*, VII(1928), 3-19.

3. *Southern California Weekly*, April 25, 1855, in *ibid.*, 3.

4. San Francisco *Alta California*, April 16, 1855.

5. New York *Times*, January 4, 1855.

6. San Francisco *Alta California*, December 12, 1854.

7. *Ibid.*, December 29, 1854.

8. California *Senate Journal*, 1855, 23-58. *Assembly Journal*, 1855, 22-57. Sacramento *Union*, January 6, 20, 30, February 20, 1855.

9. California *Senate Journal*, 1855, 663-669. California *Statutes*, 1855, 180-181. Sacramento *Union*, June 15, 1855.

10. White, "Surmounting the Sierras," 6.

11. *Ibid.*, 7-9. San Francisco *Alta California*, December 30, 1855.

12. San Francisco *Alta California*, November 3, 1855.

13. New York *Times*, November 21, 1853.

14. Sacramento *Union*, May 1, 1856. California *Supreme Court Reports*, VI (1856), 499-506.

15. Sacramento *Union*, May 9, June 8, 10, 18, 26, 1856. For an account of this riot, see Horace Bell, *Reminiscences of a Ranger* (Los Angeles, 1881), 378ff.

16. Sacramento *Union*, August 27, 1856. White, "Surmounting the Sierras," 13.

17. Sacramento *Union*, November 17, 1856. White, "Surmounting the Sierras," 13-15.

18. Sacramento *Union*, March 28, 29, April 2, 4, 8, May 1, 1856. San Francisco *Alta California*, April 19, 1856.

19. *Congressional Globe*, 34 Cong., 1 Sess., 1,297.

20. *Ibid.*, 1,485 (Senate), and 2,187-2,188 (House).

21. *Ibid.*, 3 Sess., 401. United States *Statutes*, 1856, 27, 162.

22. Sacramento *Union*, May 2, 4, 5, 7, 11, 13, 27, 28, 1857.

23. California *Statutes*, 1857, 272-273.

24. Sacramento *Union*, May 8, 13, 1857; June 29, November 30, 1858.

25. *Ibid.*, July 21, December 3, 1858.

26. For a good summary of early movements for a Pacific railroad, see R. S. Cotterill, "Early Agitation for a Pacific Railroad, 1845-1850," *Miss. Valley Hist. Rev.*, V (1918-1919), 396-414. Also, see Lewis H. Haney, *A Congressional History of Railways in the United States, 1850-1887* (Madison, 1910), 49-64.

27. *Articles of Association and Estimates of Receipts* (New York, 1853), in *Pamphlets on California Railroads*, VII, no. 6, in Bancroft Library, quoted in Carl I. Wheat, "A Sketch of the Life of Theodore D. Judah," *Calif. Hist. Soc. Quar.*, IV(1925), 221.

28. Theodore D. Judah, *Report of the Chief Engineer on the Preliminary Surveys and Future Business of the Sacramento Valley Railroad*, May 30, 1854, a twenty-four page pamphlet in *California Railroad Pamphlets*, VII, no. 3, in Bancroft Library.

29. Sacramento *Union*, February 9, 1855. San Francisco *Alta California*, February 17, 1855. The Sacramento Valley Railroad was incorporated in 1853, but the Union Plank Walk, Rail Track, and Wharf Company Railroad was the first to be completed. Its wooden rails were in use in January, 1855. Lynwood Carranco and Mrs. Eugene Fountain, "California's First Railroad: The Union Plank Walk, Rail Track, and Wharf Company Railroad," *Jour. of the West*, III (1964), 243-256.

30. Wheat, "Judah," 226-227.

31. Theodore D. Judah, *Report to the Executive Committee of the Pacific Railroad Convention of 1859,* in Sacramento *Union,* July 25, 1860. T. D. Judah, *A Practical Plan for Building the Pacific Railroad* (San Francisco, 1857), *California Railroad Pamphlets,* VII, no. 6.

32. California *Statutes,* 1859, 391. Harry J. Carman and Charles H. Mueller, "The Contract and Finance Company and the Central Pacific Railroad," *Miss. Valley Hist. Rev.,* XIV(1927), 327.

33. Hittell, *History,* IV, 453-456. Judah to Sacramento *Union,* printed in *Union,* September 26, 1859.

34. Sacramento *Union,* September 22, 26, 1859.

35. Wheat, "Judah," 236-237.

36. Sacramento *Union,* October 19, 1859. Pacific Railroad Convention Minutes, in *ibid.,* February 7-11, 1860.

37. California *Statutes,* 1853, 99. Theodore D. Judah, *Central Pacific Railroad Company of California* (San Francisco, 1860), an eighteen-page pamphlet, in Wheat, "Judah," 242.

38. Charles C. Goodwin, *As I Remember Them* (Salt Lake City, 1913), 33.

39. Cole, *Memoirs,* 148.

40. Strong said that there were at least thirty. *Pacific Railroad Convention,* 2,841. Strong testimony.

41. *Ibid.,* 2,618. Stanford testimony.

42. *Ibid.,* 2,824. Daniel W. Strong testimony.

43. *Articles of Association of the Central Pacific Railroad of California,* attached as Schedule A, in *Pamphlets on California Railroads,* VIII, no. 9, Bancroft Library, as quoted in Wheat, "Judah," 246.

44. *Pacific Railway Commission,* 3,774. Huntington testimony. Bancroft, *History,* VII, 545 note. Daggett, *Southern Pacific,* 22, note 3.

45. *Congressional Globe,* 37 Cong., 2 Sess., 1,971 (House) and 2,840 (Senate). United States *Statutes,* XII, 1862, 489.

46. Sacramento *Union,* June 9, 1859.

47. *Pacific Railway Commission,* 2,617-2,618. Stanford testimony.

48. Stanford to parents, May 4, 1860.

49. *Pacific Railway Commission,* 2,617-2,618. Stanford testimony.

50. *Ibid.,* 2,927.

51. Judah to Strong, September 2, 1861, in *Pacific Railway Commission,* 2,964. Strong testimony.

52. *Pacific Railway Commission,* 3,769. Huntington testimony; and 2,621. Stanford testimony.

53. Sacramento *Union,* January 9, 1863.

54. Judah to Strong, September 2, 1861, July 10, 1863, in *Pacific Railway Commission,* 2,964 and 2,966. Strong testimony.

55. Judah to Strong, September 9, 1863, *ibid.,* 2,967.

56. Stanford to Nevada Legislature, January 12, 1865, in *Statement Made to Senate Committee of Nevada Legislature* (Sacramento, 1865), pamphlet 4 in *Central Pacific Railroad Pamphlets.*

57. Stanford to Lincoln, November 29, 1861.

58. Neill C. Wilson and Frank J. Taylor, *Southern Pacific* (New York, 1952), 40. Bancroft, *History,* VII, 555-556.

59. Sacramento *Union,* April 25, 1863. "Political Affairs," p. 36, Low manuscript.

60. Stanford to Lincoln, September 29, 1862.

61. *Pacific Railway Commission,* 3,680. Crocker testimony.

62. Houghton to Stanford, June 29, 1863, in *ibid.,* 3,570. Beale to Stanford, April 30, 1863, in *ibid.,* 3,569.

63. *Ibid.,* 2,958. Stanford testimony. Whitney to Stanford, March 23, 1863, in *ibid.,* 3,568-3,569. Miller testimony. *Ibid.,* 2,849, 2,861. Strong testimony. *Ibid.,* 2,958. Stanford testimony. Lincoln to unidentified correspondent, January 12, 1864, in Stanford papers.

64. Sacramento *Union,* October 16, 1862.

65. Clark, *Stanford,* 182.

66. *Pacific Railway Commission,* 3,421. Marcus D. Boruck testimony. Nor did increasing the authorized stock issue to $20,000,000 in 1864 and to $100,000,000 in 1868 attract capital.

67. *Ibid.,* 2,464. Stanford testimony.

68. California *Statutes,* 1863, 145 (Placer), 380 (San Francisco), and 447-451 (Sacramento).

69. San Francisco *Alta California,* May 15, 1863.

70. Years later Placer County brought an unsuccessful suit against the Central Pacific to recover its share of profits proportional to the subscription. It wanted 1,000,000 acres of land and $15,000,000. In 1870 Placer and Sacramento counties, and afterward Santa Clara, sold their bonds back to the Central Pacific associates. As the value of the stock rose, the directors made a vigorous attempt to get it all back. San Francisco *Bulletin,* June 25, 1872.

71. Stanford to President and Directors of the Merchants Insurance Company of San Francisco, August 1, 1863.

72. Hittell, *History,* IV, 474-475.

73. San Francisco *Bulletin,* June 3, 1893. Special Historical and Commercial Edition. Edwin L. Sabin, *Building of the Pacific Railway* (Philadelphia, 1919), 56-58.

74. *The Great Dutch Flat Swindle, An Address to the Board of Supervisors, Officers, and People of San Francisco* (San Francisco, 1864), 85.

75. *Ibid.,* 4-5.

76. *Pacific Railway Commission,* 2,620. Stanford testimony. California *Supreme Court Reports,* 1864, 25, 518.

77. *Dutch Flat Swindle,* 89-115.

78. *Ibid.,* 60. The legal arguments are found on pages seventeen to eighty-three of this tract. For a point-by-point defense against the charges expressed here, see the thirty-five-page reply, *The Pacific Railroad: A Defense Against its Enemies* (San Francisco, December, 1864), written by "A Friend to the Pacific Railroad."

79. *A Defense Against its Enemies,* 12.

80. California *Statutes,* 1863-1864, 388.

81. Sacramento *Union,* March 26, April 25, 1864.

82. Sabin, *Pacific Railway,* 98.

83. United States *Statutes,* 1863-1865, XIII, 356-365. This act and the one it superseded authorized the Central Pacific to build only to the California-Nevada state line. In 1866 Huntington used his influence to get the act amended so that he and his partners could build eastward until they met the Union Pacific. Bancroft, *History,* VII, 551-552.

84. *Pacific Railway Commission,* 3,493-3,494. Darius O. Mills testimony.

85. Daggett, *Southern Pacific,* 24.

86. California *Statutes,* 1863-1864, 344-346.

87. Frederick Low manuscript, "Political Affairs," 37.

88. *Dutch Flat Swindle,* 122.

89. *Speech of Honorable Leland Stanford in the Constitutional Convention of Nevada, July 13, 1864* (San Francisco, 1865).

90. Nevada Legislature of the next year, statement made by DeLong, in Clark, *Stanford,* 210.

91. Nevada *Statutes,* 1864-1865. First session of the legislature.

92. Stanford to Nevada Senate Committee, January 12, 1865, in *Statement Made to the Senate Committee of the Nevada Legislature* (Sacramento, January 14, 1865), 2-3, in *Central Pacific Railroad Pamphlets,* Volume I, no. 4.

93. California *Supreme Court Reports,* 1864-1865, XXVII, 175-228. Sacramento *Union,* January 3, 1865.

94. Sacramento *Union,* January 7, 1865.

95. *Pacific Railway Commission,* 3,660. Crocker testimony. See George Kraus, "Chinese Laborers and the Construction of the Central Pacific," *Utah Hist. Quar.,* XXXVII (1969), 41-57.

96. E. B. Crocker to Cole, April 12, 1865, in Clark, *Stanford,* 215.

97. *Pacific Railway Commission,* 3,140. Strobridge testimony.

98. *Ibid.,* 3,611. Stanford testimony.

99. *Ibid.,* 2,731. Stanford testimony.

100. Stanford to Hopkins, April 1, 1867.

101. E. B. Crocker to Hopkins, April 1, 1867, in Clark, *Stanford,* 221.

102. Stanford to Hopkins, February 5, 1867.

103. *Pacific Railway Commission,* 3,150. Strobridge testimony.

104. Arthur Brown, Superintendent of Bridges and Buildings, to Stanford, July 25, 1887, in *ibid.,* 2,581-2,582. Stanford testimony. Bancroft, *Stanford,* 40. Clark, *Stanford,* 224. Daggett, *Southern Pacific,* 67.

105. Stanford to Hopkins, April 5, 1867.

106. Stanford to Hopkins, April 16, 1867.

107. Stanford to Hopkins, May 17, 1867.

108. Stanford to Hopkins, April 10, 1867.

109. *Pacific Railway Commission,* 2,624, 2,637-2,638. Stanford testimony.

110. *Ibid.,* 2,636, 2,638.

111. *Ibid.,* 3,661. Crocker testimony.

112. *Ibid.,* 3,062, 3,436-3,437. Miller testimony.

113. *Ibid.,* 3,062.

114. Daggett, *Southern Pacific,* 77-78.

115. San Francisco *Bulletin,* June 25, 1872.

116. *Report, Pacific Railway Commission,* 76.

117. *Ibid.*

118. San Francisco *Bulletin,* June 14, 1860.

119. Stanford to Oakland City Council, December 23, 1867, in Sacramento *Union,* May 15, 1868.

120. Sacramento *Union,* July 23, 1868.

121. *Ibid.,* June 18, 1870.

122. Stanford to Sacramento *Union,* March 13, 1865.

123. Cole, *Memoirs,* 180. E. B. Crocker to Cole, April 12, 1865, in *ibid.,* 182-184.

124. *Ibid.,* 149.

125. *Ibid.,* 266-267.

126. Stanford to Hopkins, May 30, 1867.

127. Sacramento *Union,* December 22, 1862.

128. *Pacific Railway Commission,* 12.

129. Bancroft, *History,* VII, 577.

130. Stanford to Hopkins, August 10, 1867.

131. E. B. Crocker to Hopkins, March 29, 1867.

132. Stanford to Hopkins, April 12, 1867.

133. E. B. Crocker to Hopkins, April 12, 1867. Hopkins had been appointed to the California Supreme Court by Stanford while the latter was governor. He served as Central Pacific counsel while on the court.

134. Stanford to Hopkins, April 19, 1867.

135. E. B. Crocker to Hopkins, April 19, 1867.

136. Stanford to E. B. Crocker, April 22, 1867.

137. E. B. Crocker to Hopkins, April 29, 1867.

138. E. B. Crocker to Hopkins, June 8, 1867.

139. Alban N. Towne to Mrs. Jane Stanford, June 17, 1895.

140. Stanford to E. B. Crocker, December 8, 1868.

141. United States *Statutes,* 1865-1867, XIV, 292-299.

142. *In Annual Report of the Southern Pacific Company,* year ending December 31, 1869. Submitted to California Secretary of State and now located in California State Archives, Sacramento.

143. Stanford to E. B. Crocker, January 3, 1869.

144. *Pacific Railway Commission,* 2,803. Stanford testimony.

145. San Francisco *Bulletin,* March 5, 1868.

146. Stanford to San Francisco *Bulletin,* March 6, 1868. Phelps to San Francisco *Bulletin,* March 6, 1868, printed in *Bulletin,* March 8, 1868.

147. Daggett, *Southern Pacific,* 120-124.

148. California *Statutes,* 1867-1868, 473-475.

149. *Report, Pacific Railway Commission,* 76.

150. *Ibid.*

151. Stanford to Hopkins, June 9, November 21, 1868.

152. Stanford to Hopkins, November 1, 1868.

153. Stanford to Hopkins, November 8, December 4, 1868. Stanford and Crocker spent considerable time together at the front, and no matter what the hardships, they willingly endured them with the workers. They often slept on flat cars, wrapped in buffalo hides, and found themselves covered with snow in the morning. Railroad engineers later recalled these incidents, and said they very much endeared them to the workers (Brotherhood of Locomotive Engineers, *Stanford Eulogy.* Berner, *Mrs. Stanford,* 13-14). In this and other ways the president of the Central Pacific showed his regard for his help; it was the beginning of a long line of favorable labor relations for him. He won the reputation of being the man to see if one felt wronged in any way. The Railroad Brotherhood recorded an instance when, following a conference with railroad officers, the brotherhood members were invited to Stanford's Palo Alto home for further consultation (*Eulogy*). He

won their undying affection a number of years later when he insisted that if proposed wage cuts were carried out, the officers of the company should cut theirs first. All remained intact (Archibald Treat, "The Stanfords and their Golden Key," unpublished manuscript (San Francisco, 1937), 28).

154. Clark, *Stanford*, 247.

155. Stanford to Hopkins, December 13, 1868.

156. *Ibid.*

157. Stanford to Hopkins, December 1, 1868.

158. Stanford to E. B. Crocker, December 8, 1868.

159. Stanford to Hopkins, December 10, 1868.

160. Stanford to Hopkins, December 1, 4, 1868.

161. Stanford to Hopkins, January 15, 1869.

162. *Pacific Railway Commission,* 3,039. Miller testimony.

163. United States *Statutes,* 1869-1871, XVI, 56.

164. Oscar O. Winther, *Transportation Frontier* (New York, 1964), 114. Durant of the Union Pacific also missed, and the spike was finally "driven" home by General Jack Casement, head of Union Pacific construction. Lucius Beebe, *The Central Pacific and the Southern Pacific Railroads* (Berkeley, 1963), 114-115, describes in colorful detail the celebrations of the day. The best and most complete reconstruction of the day's activities is found in J. N. Bowman, "Driving the Last Spike at Promontory, 1869," *Calif. Hist. Soc. Quar.,* XXVI(1957), 97-106, 263-274. This oft-told story was chronicled in the Sacramento *Union,* May 10, 1869. It has been ably retold by Sabin, *Pacific Railway,* and John P. Davis, *The Union Pacific* (Chicago, 1894), 152-156. Gerald M. Best, "Rendezvous at Promontory: The 'Jupiter' and No. 119," *Utah Hist. Quar.* XXXVII (1969), 69-75.

165. Stanford to Central Pacific office, May 10, 1869.

166. *Pacific Railway Commission,* 2,773. Stanford testimony.

167. Zoeth S. Eldredge, *History of California* (New York, 1915) IV, 298.

168. Sacramento *State Capitol Reporter,* September 27, 1869.

CHAPTER V

RAILROAD MAGNATE: MILEAGE AND MONEY

The completion of the transcontinental railroad in May, 1869, was barely a beginning in the railroad careers of Stanford and his associates, little more than a first step in terms of the near-monopoly of railroad transportation they would later develop in California and much of the Southwest. That they worked assiduously to create a railroad monopoly does not necessarily imply any personal or collective unethical behavior on their part; monopoly as such was not generally condemned unless it was detrimental to the public as a whole.

As a railroad tycoon Stanford was confronted by a host of problems in the two decades following the driving of the last spike. He was responsible with Huntington for expanding their railroad empire into a second, southern transcontinental by new construction and consolidation with old roads, and he had to find the money that their railroad empire needed. Shortage of funds was a constant and crucial problem which took years to overcome. Stanford also had primary responsibility for coping with a steadily-rising public, journalistic, and political opposition to the Central and Southern Pacific railroads. These roads were increasingly regarded as cancers on the body politic or depicted as octopus-like monsters which stretched their greedy arms into every area of California's economic and political life. The associates' railroads, everyone knew, charged fraudulently high freight and passenger rates, and were in some way responsible for all the social ills of the Golden State.

Even before completion of the transcontinental, the Central Pacific partners began extending their holdings and influence, when they took steps to reduce potential competition by acquiring the California Pacific, which ran from Sacramento to Vallejo.[1] This line cut fifty miles off the trip to San Francisco and reduced the travel time ninety minutes from the Central Pacific's circuitous route through Stockton. Some Central Pacific passengers made it a regular practice to get off in Sacramento and change to the California Pacific, sacrificing the difference in cost for the savings in time.[2] The California Pacific had become a serious competitor, and when it was rumored

HO! FOR CALIFORNIA!!

THE LABORER'S PARADISE!!

Salubrious Climate, Fertile Soil, Large Labor Returns.

NO SEVERE WINTERS, NO LOST TIME, NO BLIGHT OR INSECT PESTS.

Daily Trains from Boston, New York, Philadelphia, Baltimore, Chicago, St. Louis, Om ·ha and Intermediate Points, for San Francisco.

EMIGRANT TICKETS AT LOW RATES.

Choice from nearly every Variety of Farming, Fruit, Grazing and Timber Lands.

The Central Pacific Railroad Co.

now offer, in sections, adjacent to their Railroad lines in **CALIFORNIA, NEVADA** and **UTAH**, a large body of Land, most of which is well adapted to cultivation, and offer unequaled advantages for settlement or investment.

IN CALIFORNIA the lands lying on each side of the main line of the Central Pacific Railroad extend from the navigable waters of the Sacramento, above the Bay of San Francisco, across the broadest and most populous portion of the Sacramento Valley and both slopes of the Sierra Nevada Mountains. They are diversified in soil, climate and conditions—embr.cing the semi-tropical productions in the lower valleys—corresponding with those of Spain, Italy, and the shores of the Mediterranean—the vine, orchard and grain lands of the foot-hills corresponding with those of France, Germany and Austria—and the timber lands of the mountain slopes corresponding with those of Maine, Sweden, Norway, etc. This central portion of California is already noted for the excellence of its wheat, grapes, pears, cherries, strawberries, small fruits and garden vegetables generally, *and to the ease with which they c·n be grown to dimensions and perfection unattainable elsewhere.* The lands in this be.t. purchased of the Company, have resulted in gratifying success to the settlers. Wheat can safely lie in the field till threshed and shipped, and the fruit trees are not troubled by insects or blight.

Along the CALIFORNIA and OREGON BRANCH, in the renowned Valley of the Sacramento, extending from the centre to the northern boundary of the State, the Company also offer a choice selection, with the same general characteristics. This valley is at present the seat of the most successful culture of small grains (wheat, barley, oats, etc.), in the country, and also offers unrivaled facilities for extensive and profitable sheep and stock gr zing. The whole comprises *some of the Best Land in California.*

IN NEVADA the main line of the Central Pacific Railroad occupies the Truckee and Humboldt Valleys, the larest and best settled in the State, at a short distance from numerous and important mining regions, whose yield of the precious metals is estimated at from fifteen to twenty million dollars annually. The lands of the Company are so situated as to command these markets for their produce. Wherever the proper cultivation has been applied, these lands have yielded good crops of cereals and esculents.

IN UTAH, in the great Salt Lake and contiguous valleys, where the Mormons have so successfully demonstrated the fertility of the soil and the healthfulness of the climate, the Company have also good land.

TITLE, PATENT DIRECT FROM THE UNITED STATES GOVERNMENT.

These lands will be sold in quantities and on terms to suit. Immigrants, colonists and capitalists, who desire to acquire indestructible real property, certain to advance in value, will be benefited by an examination. Pamphlets, maps, etc., will be furnished by application to

B. B. REDDING, Land Commissioner Central Pacific Railroad Co.,

SAN FRANCISCO, CAL.

ALONG THE ROUTE OF THE SOUTHERN PACIFIC RAILROAD.

The undersigned has been authorized by the Southern Pacific Railroad Company of California, to offer, in conjunction with the above, a vast extent of land, among the best in the southern half of the State, situated on both sides of the line of their road, now building, extending from the Bay of San Francisco to San Jose, southwardly to the Colorado River (700 miles). This grant covers some of the best lands in the coast and valley counties, of the southern half of California, including the far-famed wheat lands of the Contra Costa, San Joaquin, Tulare, Kern River and other valleys. Wine-making, orcharding, tobacco, cotton and fibrous plant-raising, and sheep and cattle husbandry, are extensively and successfully carried on there.

Parties desiring information relative to large tracts can apply at the Offices of the Southern Pacific Railroad Company,

No. 9 Nassau Street, New York, and

Cor. Fourth and Townsend Sts., San Francisco, California.

C. P. HUNTINGTON.

Southern Pacific

COLONIST POSTER issued by Central Pacific in the early 1870s.

that it was planning to move into the San Joaquin Valley and possibly extend its line eastward to Ogden, the Central Pacific associates were prompted to action.[3]

They wanted to purchase the California Pacific, but lacked sufficient capital. The next best thing to ownership was control, and this they got by an agreement of July 13, 1871, by supplying the road with desperately-needed money. The California Pacific had been plagued by financial difficulties from its inception and by 1871 was barely able to remain solvent. In exchange for ready cash, the Central Pacific was given a majority of the seats on the Board of Directors, and, indicative of how thoroughly the associates had succeeded in their move to gain control of the road, on August 10 Stanford was elected president.[4] Hopkins had already been made treasurer. In September the Central Pacific took full charge of the company and moved its offices from San Francisco to Sacramento.[5] The next year Stanford, Huntington, and Hopkins were given sweeping powers as "general agents" in the newly-acquired company.[6]

In January, 1868, the Central Pacific gained control of the California and Oregon Railroad and the Marysville Railroad, the two of which were then consolidated into a new company which operated under the name of the first, with Stanford as president.[7] In the fall of the same year, the San Francisco, Stockton, and Alameda merged with the San Francisco and Alameda Railroad. By 1869 the four Central Pacific associates had already acquired the Southern Pacific, with Huntington as president and Stanford vice-president, reversing their customary roles.[8] Charles Crocker later became president and held the position until 1885.[9] No further consolidations of any significance were arranged until November 2, 1869, when the San Francisco Bay Railroad was incorporated into the Western Pacific, and in the following month, when the Yuba Railroad joined the California and Oregon.

On June 23, 1870, the Central Pacific and the Western Pacific were joined into one system, with Stanford president of both roads. Six days later, the San Francisco and Oakland and the San Francisco and Alameda linked up to become the San Francisco, Oakland, and Alameda Railroad Company.[10] In August of the same year, the Central Pacific acquired under its own name the California and Oregon and the San Joaquin Valley Railroad, with Stanford as president, besides the San Francisco, Oakland, and Alameda.[11]

To guarantee their planned extension of the Southern Pacific, the associates had to keep other railroads out of their territory. The threat of invasion by another road loomed large in 1871 when Congress passed the Texas railroad bill, providing for a southern transcontinental.[12] President Thomas Scott of the Pennsylvania Railroad, also president of the Texas Pacific, planned to purchase roads on both ends and fill in the system by new construction; in California he hoped to acquire the San Diego and Gila road, which had been organized in 1854 and later incorporated into the Memphis,

El Paso, and Pacific Railroad.[13] But before the newly-named Texas and Pacific was started, the panic of 1873 halted all construction. And when its managers tried in 1874 to win federal assistance, they encountered fierce opposition from the Central Pacific associates, who, in 1871, had been granted the right to build from San Francisco to the Colorado River, there to connect with the Texas and Pacific.[14] Charles Crocker later said that he and his associates had fought for this right in order to keep the Texas and Pacific out of California, knowing that if that road crossed the Colorado "Tom Scott was bound to scalp the Central Pacific."[15]

At this point Scott decided to push his road across the state into San Diego, but the Southern Pacific managers, meanwhile, had made plans to build south from San Gorgonio Pass and then to Yuma; there was even talk of building the Southern Pacific to the Gulf of Mexico and shipping cargo from there to the East Coast.[16] If Scott had built to San Diego through the same pass, the two roads would have run parallel, but Standford decided to fight the Scott forces for control of the Southwest. He announced plans to build the Southern Pacific through Yuma into Texas in order to protect California from Scott, explaining: "Had Tom Scott built his road to the Pacific he would have taken from us our best prospective traffic and carried it east. . . . He would have given San Francisco a blow from which she would never have recovered."[17]

II

The completion of the transcontinental and subsequent expansion of their system did not cause the associates to lose sight of the Goat Island project. In the winter of 1872 Huntington again attempted to force through Congress legislation that would allow them to purchase the Island. As he stepped up the pressure in Washington for the Goat Island transfer, Californians flooded Congress with critical telegrams, which proved very damaging to the Central Pacific's cause.[18] Meanwhile, on March 16, 1872, a mass meeting of citizens convened in San Francisco to protest giving Goat Island to the railroad and formed a Committee of One Hundred to spearhead the opposition.[19] Mayor William Alvord was chairman. The Committee prepared a detailed statement of arguments against the Goat Island project and accompanied it with a number of military and scientific reports and the official correspondence of Mayor Alvord and Governor Newton Booth.[20] A commission was then appointed to go to Washington to present the city's case before Congress.

The Committee of One Hundred also set its sights on the Central Pacific's "monopoly" of California railroad transportation, and listed twenty-four railroads that the associates had acquired. According to the Committee, the roads they did not own in northern California numbered only five and totaled a mere fifty-nine and a half miles.[21] To show the excessive holdings of the Central Pacific system and Stanford's personal possessions, the Committee listed him as part owner with Huntington and Hopkins of over two dozen railroads, ferries, and steamboats.[22]

Stanford welcomed any workable solution to the Goat Island problem, and had earlier accepted with certain conditions a proposal by some San Franciscans that the Central Pacific terminal be built in Mission Bay, the area between the China Basin and Seventh Street.[23] They had promised the railroad a $3,000,000 loan of six percent city bonds payable in twenty years if their plan was accepted.[24] The legislature of 1868-1869 had authorized the Board of Tide Land Commissioners to convey to the Central and Southern Pacific railroads thirty acres of land each in Mission Bay for $100 per acre.[25] According to this plan, the Central Pacific was to bridge the bay and run its track into San Francisco east of the San Bruno mountains. But this was not enough land for adequate terminal facilities, Stanford insisted. Other restrictions on the distance that must be kept between the terminus and the water made it virtually impossible to come to terms.[26] Nevertheless, he was willing to accept the San Francisco plan, with two conditions: the San Francisco terminal would be one of two — Oakland's would not be discontinued — and the city must remove its restriction keeping the railroads 300 feet from the water.[27] When this "Ravenswood project," as it was called, after the point where the railroad was to bridge the bay, later failed, Stanford placed the blame on six men who had material interests at stake, but he was assured by a member of Congress that he could have had the necessary legislation for the Goat Island project for a bribe of $10,000.[28]

During the dispute Stanford telegraphed the Mayor and Board of Supervisors that the transfer of terminal facilities from Oakland to Goat Island would bring business closer to San Francisco. He denied their charge that the railroad would injure the harbor, and promised that if they accepted his proposal business for the Tulare and San Joaquin valleys would be sent through San Francisco.[29] Stanford next wrote the spokesmen for the Committee of One Hundred, refuting point by point every objection they had expressed.[30] First, they were wrong in thinking that San Francisco had ever given the railroad any land, and he strenuously denied any obligation to build his terminal in the city. He assured them, as he had the Mayor and Board of Supervisors, that the railroad would guarantee against any damage to the bay, and reiterated that the welfare of San Francisco depended upon the railroad's having a terminal on the island.

Stanford was surprised that the railroad's offer of $10,000,000 in improvements to the bay was rejected by the San Franciscans. He attributed this country's loss of traffic to the Suez Canal and around the capes to the shortsightedness of these men. He and his associates rejected as patently absurd the argument that a rival city that would eclipse San Francisco would be created on the island.[31]

Much of the opposition to the Goat Island project came from the Terminal Pacific Railroad Company, so, to ease pressure in this quarter, the associates bought it out.[32] They paid an inflated price of $250,000 in order to gain control of the whole route along the Straits of Carquinez.[33]

On April 24, 1872, Aaron A. Sargent and others forced the Goat Island bill through the House of Representatives.[34] Huntington tried to persuade President Grant to support the measure in the Senate, where he feared defeat, but the Chief Executive preferred to wait until after the fall elections.[35] Consequently, the bill never came before the upper house that session, and in the next it never got beyond a hearing before the Senate Committee on Military Affairs. The Goat Island project was dead.

One San Francisco editor recognized the inconsistencies among the various opposition groups and with biting sarcasm described the *imbroglio* between the city fathers of San Francisco and the Central Pacific Railroad as follows:

> We want you to come into this city; you shan't come into the city. You shall not have Goat Island, you must build a bridge; you shan't build a bridge, for that would ruin the harbor; a bridge *shall* be built anyhow. You shan't have Mission Bay. You shall have Mission Bay, if you will give guarantees; we don't believe in your guarantees; we will subscribe $15,000,000 to build another road; we are willing to make any proposition; but you must propose first. . . . It is a great deal on the principle of
> You shall and you shan't
> I will and I won't;
> You'll be damned if you do,
> And I'll be damned if I don't.[36]

III

In 1870 the Southern Pacific had only the eighty-mile stretch of road between San Francisco and Gilroy open. Seven years later it had completed over 700 miles, and in 1877 it reached the California and Arizona boundary. Construction on the Southern Pacific of Arizona began in earnest in 1879 and within a year had a total of almost 300 miles of track laid.Two years later it joined the Texas and Pacific to form the second transcontinental.[37]

As the Southern Pacific continued its inexorable drive up and down the state and into every town of any importance, there was only occasional resistance worthy of notice. Leland Stanford generally played his role of public relations expert with commendable skill, but when the road pushed into the Mussel Slough area of present-day King's County, disaster struck. No other event contributed more to the already rapid deterioration of the railroad's image than did the Mussel Slough tragedy of 1880.

The Mussel Slough district, now called the Lucerne Valley, was fast filling up in the 1870's with settlers who never bothered to purchase the government lands they squatted upon, lands on which for years the Southern Pacific had tried to secure federal patents.[38] Its efforts had succeeded only in alarming the squatters, but railroad managers sought to allay their fears by assuring them that if their company got possession of the land it would be sold for the customary price of $2.50 per acre, without regard to improvements.[39] In 1877 the Southern Pacific finally got the long-sought lands.[40]

In response to a rumor that the railroad intended to charge more than $2.50 per acre, a Settlers' Land League was formed at Hanford, on April 12,1878, composed of several hundred farmers pledged not to pay a higher price.[41] But the prices the railroad eventually demanded ranged from eleven to forty dollars per acre, depending upon location and improvements.[42] This announcement prompted sporadic violence against the property of the Southern Pacific and its agents. The impossibility under the circumstances for new owners to take possession of their lands caused Crocker and Stanford to seek ejectment judgments against the settlers.[43] In early 1879, when twenty-four suits for damages and ejectment were decided in favor of the railroad, the farmers appealed unsuccessfully to the Circuit Court. They then petitioned the United States Senate for guarantees that their homes and farms would be made secure, and in another meeting resolved that they would resist by force all attempts to dislodge them. On March 4, 1879, 300 people, some of them determined to "make trouble" if they did not win their fight with the railroad, met in the farming town of Hanford to protest the ejectment decisions. They organized five military companies of sixty men each to cope with any eventuality.[44] The settlers recognized the railroad's legal right to the land, according to the decision of the United States Circuit Court, but felt that they had a moral right to it, based on earlier railroad promises. As one writer defined the issue: "The company fought for its property; the settler, for his home."[45]

In early 1880 the farmers tried to negotiate with Charles Crocker, president of the Southern Pacific. Failing in this, they sent a committee to appeal to Stanford.[46] There followed a conference that was reportedly marked by "a mutual spirit of concession and compromise," which resulted in an understanding that Stanford would personally visit the valley and confer with the settlers to find an amicable solution to the dispute.[47] On the basis of this agreement, some ill-advised friends of Stanford, without his knowledge, started a rumor without foundation in fact that Crocker was the cause of the Mussel Slough troubles and that Stanford had begged him to be lenient with the farmers.[48] At any rate, the committee reported that Stanford had agreed to stay all legal proceedings until the matter had been investigated further. On March 11, he arrived in Hanford to see firsthand the land under dispute and hear the farmers' complaints.[49] The settlers were satisfied that as a result of

Stanford's interest there would be "fair concessions on the part of the rail-road."[50] A San Francisco reporter said that Stanford seemed willing to compromise with the settlers, and was sure he would make liberal concessions.[51]

Hopes for a peaceful settlement were dashed on April 10, 1880, when Daniel Parkhurst, a Southern Pacific land agent, came to Hanford to handle the sale of railroad lands at the inflated prices. The settlers advised him for his own safety to leave town, and accused Stanford of bad faith.[52] Stanford was squeezed by both sides in the dispute: pressure was applied not only by the squatters, but by people who had bought and were unable to occupy lands on which the settlers had built.[53]

The railroad finally insisted that a United States marshal deliver eviction notices.[54] Southern Pacific authorities said they did everything within their power to avoid conflict, and had not directed that new purchasers be placed in possession of disputed lands until the United States Circuit Court had declared the settlers in wrongful possession and until the time for appeal to the United States Supreme Court had expired.[55]

When accused of duplicity, and insincerity, Stanford insisted that the Settlers' League had violated their agreement by filing appeals on ejectment cases that had gone against them.[56] Faced with defeat at every turn, the committee agreed to meet the railroad price halfway, but Stanford, for some unexplained reason, refused. His sudden change in attitude has often been attributed to Huntington's unwillingness to compromise.[57] According to this interpretation, Stanford was inclined toward leniency, but he toughened his stand because of his partner's intransigence. If this were true, Huntington's attitude must have changed since the mid-seventies and would have to change again by the early nineties. After similar problems with squatters at the earlier date, he wrote Hopkins:

> It occurs to me that some arrangement might be come to with these squatters as to the amount they shall pay the company when it is decided they are on its lands. If it is possible, get them to agree on something, even less than their value, so as to avoid litigation.[58]

Always the practical man, Huntington added: "Just now we cannot afford to have any more enemies in Congress from the Pacific Coast." Following further problems with squatters after he became president of the Southern Pacific system, Huntington told his nephew Henry, his first assistant, that the government's lax land policies were more to blame for squatters' trespasses than was the greed or dishonesty of the settlers themselves.

> The settlers do not seem to be to blame in going on and occupying the lands as they did. . . . I hope you will be very careful that the railroad company does not charge them for their improvements, but lets them have the

land at the same price that the company would have sold them for before they were occupied.[59]

For whatever reason, a tough line was followed, and on May 11, 1880, a United States marshal and a railroad agent armed with a Circuit Court writ ordering the settlers off the land attempted to dispossess some of the farmers. A gun fight broke out which left eight men dead or dying; everyone shot eventually died.[60] Seven settlers were indicted for obstructing an officer of the law in execution of his duties, and five were convicted and imprisoned for their part in the fray.[61] The other farmers moved away or paid the railroad's price.[62] From that day the Southern Pacific continued downward in public esteem at an accelerated rate. Antirailroad activity in the state became a powerful force in California politics for the next thirty years, with Mussel Slough as a rallying cry of the enemies of the Southern Pacific.[63]

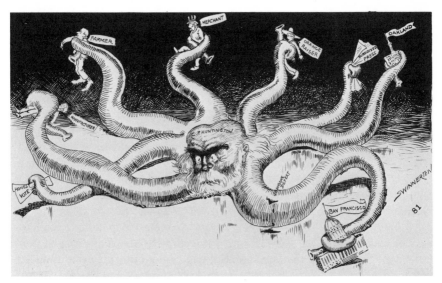

C. P. HUNTINGTON depicted as an octopus.

IV

There took place in the fall of 1884 one of the most far-reaching railroad alignments ever made, as the Central Pacific system, the Southern Pacific of California, and a number of shorter roads extending eastward as far as New Orleans, including the Southern Pacific companies of Arizona and New Mexico, were leased to a new holding company, the Southern Pacific of Kentucky.[64] Huntington incorporated the company in Kentucky so that California lawsuits could be handled in federal rather than state courts.[65] When asked why he and his partners had gone to Kentucky for a charter, Stanford explained, candidly: "To get a charter that was favorable — that would allow us to lease all the roads in the country."[66] He said they needed to keep up with other railroads, twelve of which were forming a through line to New Orleans.

An 1880 arrangement leasing the Southern Pacific of California to the Central Pacific for five years had given the associates a fixed profit off their Southern Pacific holdings, but by 1884 the economic prospects of the road looked so bright that they became dissatisfied with the old arrangement.[67] A key factor in their decision to reorganize was that Central Pacific stock was selling so well that they no longer held a majority of it; in fact, their combined holdings amounted to less than thirty percent, whereas as late as 1885 almost all the Southern Pacific stock was still owned by the three associates and the Hopkins estate.[68] Another reason for the change was that while the Central Pacific had now lost much of its mining business in Nevada, the Southern Pacific was just getting to the place where it would be able to cash in on the lucrative transcontinental business. Another important consideration was that the Southern Pacific had become so large and its interests so varied that the smaller Central Pacific could no longer control it.[69]

After a series of protracted and unfruitful meetings, the associates tossed into Stanford's lap the responsibility for devising a workable plan of consolidation. His scheme as finally adopted provided that the Southern Pacific of Kentucky would issue $100,000,000 in capital stock; it would lease the Southern Pacific railroads of California, Arizona, and New Mexico for ninety-nine years, from February 10, 1885; and it would lease the Central Pacific for ninety-nine years for annual rents of from $1,200,000 to $3,600,000, depending upon its earnings. The new system already controlled almost 5,000 miles of track, but Huntington was not satisfied; he wanted to include some of his own Eastern holdings to give them control of a coast-to-coast line, but Stanford and Crocker, more conservative than he in the business of empire building, were against incorporating any roads east of New Orleans.[70] Stanford by the late seventies had begun branching out into such extra-railroad activities as horseracing and winemaking and did not wish to tie up all his money in railroad construction and consolidation.

At a directors' meeting, on February 18, 1885, Stanford was named president of the new company; Huntington and Crocker were made first and second vice-presidents; and Timothy Hopkins, Mark Hopkins' foster son, became treasurer.[71]

For years after the completion of the transcontinental, the cost of financing new construction and of maintaining and operating the system continued to be a problem. The associates were slow in realizing any substantial profits from the road itself. The first real money they made came from their various construction companies, the earliest of which was the Crocker organization. But the profits from this firm were insignificant compared to the fortunes piled up under its successor, the Contract and Finance Company. This company built over 550 miles of road, for which it received in excess of $47,000,000, half in gold and half in stock, amounting to $86,000 per mile.[72]

Governor Low later told historian H. H. Bancroft that the real story of the Contract and Finance Company could never be told, because of what he termed "inside workings." No one on the outside could get to the inside, and those on the inside who knew the truth would never tell.[73] Low was right: no accurate account of the cost of building the Central Pacific Railroad can now be made, since the fifteen volumes of the Crocker Company and Contract and Finance Company books were destroyed. Who destroyed them and what was the exact reason may never be known. Daniel Yost, Stanford's private secretary, said that the last time he saw the books Mark Hopkins was packing them for the company's move from Sacramento to San Francisco.[74] Charles Crocker said that Hopkins had probably destroyed the books, thinking them not worth keeping.[75] Hopkins, of course, was now dead and could not deny or explain the actions attributed to him.

The 1887 Pacific Railway Commissioners were convinced that the construction of the road cost far less than the amount paid to the companies working on it. After investigating the Central Pacific's finances, they concluded:

> Putting all these facts together — the existence of a strong motive on the part of Stanford, Huntington, Hopkins and Crocker to suppress the books; the impossibility of accounting for their disappearance, except in pursuance of the act or direction of one of these four persons; the evidence of Yost that he saw Hopkins engaged in packing the books in boxes; the evidence of John Miller of their sudden disappearance, and the statement of Mr. Crocker connecting their disappearance with Mark Hopkins — it is impossible to avoid the conclusion that the suppression of these books has been intentional and willful.[76]

The total cost of the Central Pacific Railroad from Sacramento to Promontory, about 737 miles, could not have exceeded $36,000,000. For this the railroad received in par terms approximately $38,500,000 in land grants and government bonds, all of which were worth far less than their face value. But even Stanford conceded that the $54,000,000 in Central Pacific stock received by the Contract and Finance Company was in time clear profit.[77] Stanford, Huntington, Hopkins, and the Crocker brothers were equal co-owners of this company, and each received $13,000,000 in Central Pacific stock from it when it was later dissolved.[78] With these kinds of profits described in the company books, it is not surprising that they were "lost."

In October, 1869, a few months after the Central Pacific was completed, the four associates, as directors and principal stockholders of the San Francisco Bay Railroad, awarded to themselves as directors and sole owners of the Contract and Finance Company a contract to build the balance of the line from San Francisco to San Jose.[79] In addition to the main part of the Central Pacific-Union Pacific system, their companies built a number of branch lines. Since these roads paid their construction bills in stock, the associates naturally came into ownership or control of them. It was in this way that they became the chief stockholders in the San Joaquin Valley Railroad and the California and Oregon road.[80]

After a notorious government suit in 1870, and the notoriety of the Credit Mobilier affair in 1873, the Contract and Finance Company was dissolved.[81] Its successor, the Western Development Company, was organized with capital stock of $5,000,000. For some unexplained reason, its ownership was concealed from the public. The principal stockholders were Stanford, Huntington, Crocker, Hopkins, and David Colton, but their stock was registered in the names of five other people.[82] During its brief lifetime, this company did a few repair and construction jobs for the Central Pacific, and it built over 400 miles of railroad for the Southern Pacific.[83] However, its connections with the Central Pacific were more open than they were with the Contract and Finance Company. The Central Pacific and Western Development offices were in the same San Francisco building, at the corner of Fourth and Townsend.[84] The Western and its successors even used the Central Pacific as a bank, depositing and withdrawing money as needed.[85] Crocker later complained that they were always borrowing money from the Central Pacific.[86] The Western Development Company bought all the construction materials owned by the Contract and Finance Company, and then took over that company's contracts with the Southern Pacific, though its operations were broader in scope than those of its predecessor. The Western Development Company engaged in manufacturing, mining, banking, and construction, as well as a number of less important activities; it even built the private residences in San Francisco of Stanford, Crocker, and Hopkins.[87]

Following Hopkins' death in 1878, his widow refused to participate in new construction, so the three remaining associates decided to close shop on the Western Development Company. It was replaced on November 4, 1878, by the Pacific Improvement Company, which performed largely the same services as had the Western.[88] The company was owned at first by Stanford, Huntington, and Crocker, but Mrs. Hopkins later had a change of heart and came in.[89] In 1883 the remaining construction equipment was sold to the Central Pacific Railroad, and the Pacific Improvement Company was superseded by the Southern Development Company, whose organization was much the same as that of the first three companies through which the associates worked. Unlike its predecessors, the Pacific Improvement Company was not dissolved. It owned a great deal of real estate and property in California and New York, stocks and bonds in a number of railroad companies, and stock in the Oakland Waterfront Company, and continued a valuable financial plum until well into the twentieth century.[90] As late as the summer of 1887 Stanford still owned $1,250,000 in Pacific Improvement stock.[91]

It was difficult for Stanford and his associates to keep straight whether they were operating as officers of the railroad or of one of their construction companies. In many cases they merely took money out of one pocket and placed it in another, though the amount somehow grew with each transaction. The construction companies received railroad bonds in payment for services, bonds that had no saleable value at the time, and therefore were not a genuine source of income. The only money these companies received came from the Central Pacific or from the associates themselves and was recorded not as stock subscription payments but as loans, which paid from six to ten percent interest.[92] The contributions thus received by the Western Development Company amounted to over $3,000,000 by 1877 and $11,000,000 by 1878.[93]

At times the associates themselves borrowed money from the Central Pacific and left it recorded on the books by replacing it with "cash tags" which were listed as money. Cash tags were kept by the company treasurer when there was a constant demand made on a certain fund, until the demand was satisfied, at which time one voucher or receipt was issued. This was a common business practice, but was subject to abuse, since it allowed one to borrow what amounted to interest-free loans.[94]

Because of lost or destroyed records, as well as poor bookkeeping, it is now impossible to determine how much the associates made from their construction companies or their railroad securities. Their salaries were substantial, but not nearly enough to add up to the fortunes they amassed. Most of the key officers of the road received $10,000 per year, with the exception of Huntington, who got $12,500 a year for the vice-presidency and another $35,000 for being the company's financial agent and attorney, a total of $47,500.[95]

When Hopkins died in 1878 he was worth at least $19,000,000, and in 1889 Crocker's fortune was estimated at over $24,000,000.[96] Stanford's probably amounted to $30,000,000, and Huntington's over $40,000,000. In the summer of 1887 Stanford said he owned $3,200,000 in Central Pacific stock besides securities, in a dozen or so other companies.[97] It must be remembered that much of this money was in Southern Pacific stock and California real estate, neither of which was saleable at anything approaching face value.

At first few people begrudged the Central Pacific associates the money borrowed from the government, since it was generally believed that the high cost of construction during the Civil War had taken most of it. Only in absolute terms did the 8,453,694 acres received from the national government, valued in excess of $10,500,000 if it could have been sold at the current minimum, together with the almost $28,000,000 in government bonds, look like a windfall. But all this changed in the seventies, when some Central Pacific stockholders demanded that Congress make a complete investigation into the financial affairs of the railroad.[98] In 1870 several threats of lawsuits were made against Stanford and his partners and a few were actually filed. Several minority stockholders in the railroad sued them for voting themselves valuable contracts which were then paid in company stock, thus giving them even greater control over the road.[99] To silence these critics, the associates bought up a number of shares at inflated prices of from $400 to $1,000 per share.[100]

V

It was largely in response to complaints and suits like these that Congress in March, 1887, directed President Cleveland to appoint a Pacific Railway Commission to investigate all Western railroads receiving federal land grants and loans. On April 15, the commission was appointed, and there was launched one of the most grueling railroad investigations ever conducted, in which scores of witnesses in several cities across the country were subjected to unrelenting interrogation by the committee.[101] Every major character in the building or management of the Central Pacific and Southern Pacific railroads was eventually subjected to an almost inquisitional probing into his personal and business affairs.

The Commission decided that the associates had made excessive profits from their railroad interests; Crocker, for example, had been paid almost twice what it cost to build some sections of the railroad, and even though he claimed that he had no partners in his company, a railroad official admitted it was composed of Charles Crocker, Stanford, Huntington, Hopkins, and Ed Miller.[102] Whether a formal partnership existed between the associates or not, there was "an explicit understanding that they should share equally" in profits from construction, repairs, branch lines, leases, express business, and the sale of materials and coal.[103]

If it was true, as seems likely, that Stanford was part owner of the Crocker Construction Company, he was not entirely truthful in telling the Pacific Railway Commissioners that he did not profit from the proceeds of that company.[104] He admitted that Crocker turned over to the Contract and Finance Company all railroad stock received for his construction costs, and this company was owned by him and his associates. This stock had a par value of $14,000,000, though the market value was far less; in fact, Crocker claimed that he gave the stock to the Contract and Finance Company because it was worthless.[105]

The investigating Commission concluded that the associates had made on construction contracts alone over $100,000,000 in stocks and in excess of $5,000,000 in bonds. Furthermore, they cleared $12,000,000 in gold and $52,000,000 in stock on the government-aided construction of the Central and Western Pacific railroads. Besides this, they spent or allowed their agents to spend almost $5,000,000, "without requiring any sufficient vouchers disclosing the purpose to which they were applied." The investigators concluded: "On the face of the books the barren fact appears that Leland Stanford and C. P. Huntington have taken from the assets of this company, over which they had absolute control, the sum aforesaid of $4,818,355.67."[106]

A detailed study of the finances of the whole Central Pacific network showed that this railroad and its subsidiaries cost $58,000,000 to build, but since $120,000,000 was paid in bonds, stocks, and cash, there was an excess of $62,000,000. Most of this was clear profit, the Commissioners decided, and was paid entirely to Stanford, Huntington, Hopkins, and Crocker, "voted to themselves by their own votes." As if this were not enough, similar profits were taken from leased roads.[107] The Commissioners failed, however, to distinguish between real money and inflated stock values.

The Commissioners struck at the Central Pacific associates for the "many instances of the exercise of the power of their votes as directors in determining . . . contracts beneficial to themselves," and condemned in all cases the practice of awarding contracts to companies in which the directors had a personal interest.[108]

> It seems to be the general belief that the present weak condition of the Central Pacific Railroad Company is due to the fact that the contract with Crocker & Co., and the contract with the Contract and Finance Company, and the contracts with the Western Development Company, and the contracts with Pacific Improvement Company have drained the company of its its resources; that certain individuals have procured to be issued to themselves enormous quantities of stock and bonds of this company, and have paid dividends on the stock, and have made the interest charge on the bonds exceedingly heavy, and that the origin of its difficulties lies there entirely, and nowhere else.[109]

The Commissioners conceded that Stanford and his partners had received little money from government lands and railroad bonds during the first few years, but insisted that they had made sizeable profits later, not only from their ownership of the construction companies, but from operating their various roads. They showed profits up to 1870 of almost $2,500,000; from 1870-1873 over $6,500,000; and over $52,500,000 from 1874 to 1884. This was not gross income, but profits, money left after operating expenses, taxes, and interest on loans had been paid. Between 1874 and 1884 over $34,000,000 was distributed to stockholders in dividends, and since Stanford, Huntington, Hopkins, and Crocker were virtually the only stockholders during most of this time, "nearly the entire amount of dividends declared during these years was therefore received by those four persons." The investigating body concluded: "The distribution of this vast sum of money to these four persons, whose stock represented substantially no contribution whatever to the actual value of the railroad, was most improvident, and was in plain disregard of the obligations incurred by the company to the United States."[110]

As of December 31, 1886, the Central Pacific had piled up a total public and government liability of almost $172,000,000.[111] Until this time there had been no effort made to retire the high government loans, which led the Commissioners to charge that the Central Pacific as well as other bond-aided companies had defrauded the government of its advances as well as the shippers of a large proportion of their cash.[112] In a searing condemnation of the financial and political operations of the government-assisted companies, they stated:

> The aided companies combined with others to tax the communities which they served, and they forced the consuming classes in all sections of the country to contribute to the payment of interest and dividend upon the ficti-tious capital which they had created. They increased the cost of living. They laid proprietary claim to the traffic of large sections of the country. They squandered millions of their money to "protect" their territorial claims, while expending other millions in encroachments upon the territory claimed by other companies. They constituted themselves the arbiters of trade. They attempted to dictate the channels that trade should follow and fixed rates of transportation that were extortionate. They charged all that the traffic would bear, and appropriated a share of the profits of every industry by charging the greater part of the difference between the actual cost of produc-tion and the price of the article in the market. They discriminated between individuals, between localities, and between articles.They favored particular individuals and companies. They destroyed possible competitors, and they built up particular localities to the injury of other localities, until matters had reached such a pass, that no man dared engage in any business in which transportation largely entered without first soliciting and obtaining the per-mission of a railroad manager. They departed from their legitimate sphere as common carriers and engaged in mining articles for transportation over their own lines. They exerted a terrorism over merchants and over com-munities, thus interfering with the lawful pursuits of the people. They par-ticipated in election contests. By secret cuts and violent and rapid fluctua-tions in rates they menaced business, paralyzed capital, and retarded investment and development.[113]

VI

Congressional and state investigating committees could discover vast fortunes that the associates had piled up, but those on the inside had another story to tell. Huntington in early 1870 complained that earnings from the Central Pacific barely paid interest on their various accounts and that there was hardly enough left to cover maintenance and routine improvements.[114]

He later testified that Central Pacific stock in the early seventies would not have sold for five cents on the dollar.[115] In corroboration, one California capitalist told the 1887 Railway Commission that when the road was first completed he would not have taken its stock as a gift if he had to be responsible for its debts.[116]

In his March 10, 1873, "Paint Shop" speech, Stanford pointed out that the completion of the Central Pacific Railroad seven years ahead of schedule was saving the federal treasury $7,000,000 per year,but its cost of construction was fifty percent higher than it would have been if the road had not been completed until 1876.[117] He showed too that at current discounts the amount of money received from the federal government when reduced to gold coin would not have carried the road over the mountains, let alone build it to Ogden. Besides that, the government had received far more in securities for its loans than required, since the Central Pacific had put up its entire railroad system rather than just the original transcontinental.

Because of forced discounts, the company realized only sixty cents on the dollar in gold on the government bonds; therefore only about $16,000,000 was received from government bonds for the building of the whole Central Pacific line.[118] But the Pacific Railway Commissioners, who listed the values at par, rejected the railroad's suggestion that the government loan be reduced to the gold or saleable value. They expressed some doubt that government bonds had been discounted, and argued that even if they had, the government debt to the public for these bonds had to be repaid at par.[119] Stanford insisted that in calculating the railroad's debt they ought to take into account the fact that the railroad was paying interest on $20,000,000 which it never received.[120]

As late as 1885 some people believed that Stanford and his partners were on the verge of bankruptcy, owing largely to the fact that the Southern Pacific and Northern Pacific were cutting into their business.[121] Even the Pacific Railway Commissioners, as hostile as they were, conceded that Central Pacific profits dropped considerably after 1883.[122] But Stanford assured the public that there was nothing fundamentally wrong with the soundness of the Central Pacific operation that caused a current decline in prices, and said that the road had not and would not suffer from business taken by the other roads.[123]

At one time or another all the associates despaired of their railroad involvements and financial difficulties and wanted to get out of the business with whatever they could. In 1871 Charles Crocker actually made the break. He and his brother sold out for $1,800,000, accepting $600,000 in notes from each of the remaining partners and retaining a large block of interest-bearing Central Pacific securities, with par value of about $3,500,000.

In 1871 even Huntington, the financial genius upon whose shoulders most of the burden of raising money for the Central Pacific rested, decided that he had had enough and tried to sell out. From this period through the financial panic of 1873 he did his best to unload his railroad securities and retire from the field.[124] When the panic of that year was at its worst, Huntington found it impossible to borrow a cent; only by the greatest of financial wizardry was he able to keep the Central Pacific afloat during the panic.[125] He was like a man demented as he rushed about the East seeking ways of keeping the Central Pacific from following a number of other roads into bankruptcy.[126] As late as 1875 Huntington reported that Southern Pacific bonds could not be sold, and he and his close friend and partner Mark Hopkins offered their Central Pacific and Southern Pacific holdings together for $33,000,000 to any prospective buyer, particularly a number of San Francisco's leading bankers, but the debt of the road scared these people off.[127] Huntington wrote Hopkins that he knew of no reason for wearing himself out for more money, even if it amounted to untold millions, and in the fall of 1872 he said: "The more I think of it I am inclined to the opinion that we had better close out our R. R. interests."[128] A month later he solicited Hopkins' and Stanford's views on the best way of selling out.[129]

Crocker later gave failing health as his reason for retiring. His brother had actually broken down under the strain.[130] The Crockers were so anxious to get out that they were willing to sell their stock for thirteen cents on the dollar, but with that Hopkins said that the Crockers were in a much better financial position than any of the partners who were going to stay in.[131] Charles Crocker then spent the better part of two years traveling abroad, but when the Panic of 1873 struck, his former partners could not make good on their notes. In September, 1873, he showed up at Huntington's office demanding his money or to be let back in. For payment of $100,000 to each of his former partners he reassumed his place among them on equal terms.[132]

By 1873 Huntington and Hopkins were even trying to unload the Central Pacific. Huntington worked out a plan for forcing the price up: he and Hopkins would offer to sell low, but Stanford was to hold firm for par; this ruse was to make it appear that the stock was more valuable than it actually was, thereby making it possible for all of them to get out at par.[133] Huntington and Hopkins were willing to sell for twenty cents on the dollar, and they offered San Francisco capitalist D. O. Mills eighty percent of the Central Pacific for $20,000,000.[134] Stanford was to retain possession of the other twenty percent, but Mills, believing that the property was still overpriced, broke off negotiations.

While Stanford on occasion had wearied of railroad business, during the seventies, when his partners were one by one suffering fits of mental as well as financial depression and trying to make the break, he had no interest in selling. Nor did he want them to get out. Huntington complained to Hopkins that Stanford had talked to Mills about purchasing the Huntington-Hopkins interests, but most likely not in a way that would have encouraged Mills to act.[135] He did not blame Stanford for not wanting to sell out, adding that if he had someone growing up to take his place he too would have stayed in, an allusion to the fact that Stanford had an heir to take up his railroad interests.[136] But the financial panic of 1873 ended all hopes of getting out of the railroad business. In a series of letters to California, Huntington spelled out in great detail the effects of the crisis upon all railroads: no investor trusted them, and money was impossible to get from any source.

The finances of the road were so critical that at times Stanford and his partners communicated in code, to keep others from knowing what was going on. Stanford on one occasion telegraphed Hopkins: "Have advised Lion [Huntington] of sand [one] lava [hundred] kid [and] shield [twenty] rival [thousand] baker [coming] ash [by] bark [mail]."[137] Two days later he was happy to report: "Jack [have] Savoy [deposited] with belloc freres lamb [for] west [L. von Hoffman Company] sand [one] bag [hundred] kid [and] sink [thirty] rival [thousand] naked [gold]."[138] At other times, Huntington could plead in plain English: "Impossible to borrow a dollar here except with stock or bonds sold on N.Y. Stock Board. You must send 25,000 a day."[139] Scores of roads went bankrupt and into receivership, but this never happened to either the Central Pacific or the Southern Pacific.[140]

VII

The decade from the mid-eighties to the mid-nineties ended an era in the growth and finances of the Southern Pacific Railroad. From 1881 to 1884 the Central Pacific associates' railroad empire had grown in leaps and bounds, by construction and consolidation, but there was very little significant extension after the new leasing arrangement of the Southern Pacific Company of Kentucky had been worked out. By the late 1880's, in fact, there was almost no new construction being done anywhere in the Southwest. The associates would continue to strengthen their positions in the Southern Pacific and would build new feeder lines from the main lines to the various byways along it, but by 1890 growth of the system had all but halted.

In 1895 the thirty year government securities lent to build the Central would be due. Before the eighties the road had not done anything toward repaying this debt, and it was widely believed the railroad had no intention of ever repaying it. Stanford had told Huntington that it was clear that instead of the Southern Pacific owing the government, the government was actually in debt to the company, for all the money it had saved the treasury. "I think we ought to take that position," he confided, "and decline to make any offer of future payment."[141] In 1887, in his report to Congress following the Congressional investigation of the Pacific railroads, Cleveland said that nobody really expected the debt to be paid. He said that even considering the public importance of the Pacific railroads, there had been a "reckless and unguarded appropriation of the public funds and the public domain." [142] The minority report of the Pacific Railway Commission recommended that the charters of the roads be forfeited and that a receiver be appointed to work out a system whereby the government would be repaid, but on the first of February, 1899, the government and the Southern Pacific Railroad resolved the whole problem of the debt owed the government, when settlement was made for over $58,000,000 in principal and interest.[143]

---

1. Daggett, *Southern Pacific*, 107.

2. *Pacific Railway Commission*, 3,613. Stanford testimony.

3. *Ibid.*, 3,628-3,629. San Francisco *Bulletin*, November 29, 1869.

4. Daggett, *Southern Pacific*, 110-111.

5. *Ibid.*, 111. See statement by Milton S. Latham, San Francisco *Chronicle*, August 16, 1874.

6. Daggett, *Southern Pacific*, 115.

7. For a complete list of consolidations, see *Pacific Railway Commission*, 2,497-2,498, and 2,783. Stanford testimony. Also, Daggett, *Southern Pacific*, 125ff.

8. Daggett, *Southern Pacific*, 123. Wilson and Taylor, *Southern Pacific*, 48.

9. San Francisco *Alta California*, August 15, 1888.

10. In addition to the empire created by these consolidations and purchases, the Central Pacific leased a number of railroads, including the Berkeley Branch, the Northern Railway, the Stockton and Copperopolis, the San Pablo and Tulare, the Amador Branch, the California Pacific, the Southern Pacific of Arizona, the Southern Pacific of New Mexico, the Los Angeles and San Diego, and the Los Angeles and Independence railroads. *Pacific Railway Commission*, 2,498.

11. *Pacific Railway Commission*, 2,783.

12. The story of the subsequent conflict is ably told by Lewis B. Lesley, "A Southern Transcontinental Railroad into California: Texas and Pacific versus Southern Pacific, 1865 to 1885," *Pac. Hist. Rev.,* V(1936), 52-60. Also, see Ralph N. Traxler, "Collis P. Huntington and the Texas and Pacific Railroad Land Grants," *New Mex. Hist. Rev.*, XXXIV (1959), 117-133.

13. Lesley, "Southern Transcontinental," 52-53.

14. United States *Statutes*, XVI, 1871, 579.

15. *Pacific Railway Commission*, 3,683. Crocker testimony.

16. Stanford to Frank Pixley, August 22, 1882.

17. San Francisco *Chronicle*, May 19, 1875. In southern California the press was divided over the battle between the Central Pacific and Texas Pacific. The Los Angeles *Republican* favored Scott over Stanford, but the Los Angeles *Star* favored Stanford. In Los Angeles *Star*, September 20, 1877.

18. Huntington to Hopkins, March11, 1872.

19. San Francisco *Bulletin*, March 18, 1872. SFS, XXVI, contains hundreds of newspaper clippings from California papers on both sides of the Goat Island dispute.

20. *Appeal to the California Delegation in Congress upon the Goat Island Grant to the Central Pacific R. R. Company* (San Francisco, 1872). This fifty-nine page pamphlet is generally called *The Goat Island Grant.*

21. *Ibid.*, 49-50.

22. *Ibid.*, Among them the Central Pacific, Western Pacific, San Francisco and San Jose, Southern Pacific, Pajaro Branch, San Jose and Oakland, San Francisco and Oakland, San Francisco and Alameda, Market Street (in San Francisco), Potrero and Bay View, Sacramento Valley, Placerville and Sacramento Valley, Stockton and Copperopolis, Stockton and Visalia, San Joaquin Valley, California Pacific, Marysville Branch, Napa Valley, California Central, California and Oregon, San Francisco and North Pacific, San Pablo and Tulare Valley railroads, the California Steam Navigation Company, the Oakland Ferry, the Alameda Ferry, and a number of Vallejo steamboats. At about this time, several meetings were held in San Francisco to raise subscriptions for a projected Atlantic and Pacific railroad, a transcontinental that would parallel the Central Pacific. San Francisco *Alta California*, July 2, 14, 1872. San Francisco *Bulletin*, July 13, 22, 31, 1872.

Stock certificates in the Stanford collection show that his holdings were broader and more substantial than his critics realized. In 1868 he owned 1,000 shares in the Contract and Finance Company, at $100 per share (by 1873 this had increased to 2,500 shares); in 1869 he had 50 shares in the Capital Woolen Mills at $100 per share, and one share in the Orleans Hills Vinicultural Association, worth $200; in 1872 he held 490 shares of Mission Bay Bridge Company stock at $100 each; in 1874 he had 20 shares in the Riverside Hotel and Turnpike Company, worth $100 each; 40 shares in 1875 in the Gilmore Angora Goat Breeding Association, at $100 each, and 100 shares in the Cornell Watch Company at $100 each; in 1877 his holdings in the Colorado Steam Navigation Company amounted to 1,111 shares at $100; in 1879 he owned 60 shares of Capital Savings Bank of Sacramento stock at $100 per share; in 1881 he had 9,750 shares in the Southern Development Company, at $100 each; and in 1883 he owned 200 shares in the Pacific Steam Agricultural Company, at $100 each.

23. San Francisco *Bulletin*, June 25, 1872.

24. E. L. Sullivan *et al* to Stanford, December 18, 1871, in San Francisco *Alta California*, December 28, 1871.

25. San Francisco *Bulletin*, May 21, 1872.

26. The editor of the San Francisco *Examiner*, March 21, 1872, was in favor of making more land available and of easing the restrictions. Other papers, for example, the San Francisco *California Farmer*, July 17, 1873, ridiculed the antirailroad press and the Committee of 100, and spoke at length on the commercial advantages of the railroad. The Sacramento *Record*, August 5, 1873, agreed.

27. Stanford to E. L. Sullivan, *et al*, December 21, 1871, in San Francisco *Alta California*, December 28, 1871.

28. Stanford testimony before United States Senate Subcommittee on Military Affairs, February 17, 1873, in Clark *Stanford*, 320. *Pacific Railway Commission*, 3,170-3,171. Stanford testimony.

29. Stanford telegram to Alvord, *et al*, reprinted in San Francisco *Chronicle*, March 12, 1872.

30. Stanford to A. Wheeler, Secretary of the Committee of One Hundred, April 26, 1872, in San Francisco *Alta California*, April 28, 1872, and in *California Mail Bag*, V (1874), 110-112.

31. Huntington to Stanford, April 26, 1872. Others pretended to fear that Stanford was planning to build a town north of Oakland, force up the value of real estate, and then sell lots to Congressmen and Europeans. San Francisco *Call*, May 15, 1872. On this, see also San Francisco *Alta California*, May 12, 1872.

32. San Francisco *Alta California*, March 19, 1872.

33. Senate Committee on Military Affairs, January 18, 1873, in Clark, *Stanford*, 325.

34. *Cong. Globe*, 42 Cong., 2 Sess., 2,739. San Francisco *Bulletin*, May 3, 1872.

35. San Francisco *Chronicle*, May 21, 1872.

36. *California Spirit of the Times*, April 13, 1872.

37. By 1877 the Central Pacific-Southern Pacific system, which Stanford considered one organization, controlled eighty-five percent of California's railroads (Huntington to Colton, December 10, 1874 and May 28, 1875, in *Ellen M. Colton versus Leland Stanford, et al*, 1,615-1,616 and 1,643-1,644. Hereafter cited as *Colton Case*. Huntington to Colton, May 28, 1875, in *Pacific Railway Commission*, 3,720. Huntington testimony). The combination itself was divided into five parts: the original Central Pacific, with the Western Pacific, the San Francisco, Oakland, and Alameda Railroad, the San Joaquin Valley Railroad, and the California and Oregon included; the California Pacific; the Northern Railway; the Northern Division of the Southern Pacific, from San Francisco to Tres Pinos; and the Southern Division of the Southern Pacific. The associates could not have afforded to buy all these roads if they had wanted, but as it was this proved unnecessary: a combination of the right leases and control of key stock put them in charge of all the roads. Nevertheless, by the late seventies they had become owners together of all or a majority of the stock in each of these companies. In most cases there had been no money transaction. Ownership came by their being shareholders and owners of the various construction companies that built, repaired, or maintained the roads (Daggett, *Southern Pacific*, 140-142).

38. One of the best accounts of the events leading up to the Mussel Slough tragedy and the battle itself is in Wallace Smith, *Garden of the Sun* (Fresno, n.d.), 259-290.

39. *Railroad Lands in California, Nevada, and Utah* (San Francisco, January 1, 1875), 17. See also, *The Struggle of the Mussel Slough Settlers for their Homes* (Visalia, 1880). James Lorin Brown, *The Mussel Slough Tragedy* (Fresno, 1958), and, by the same author, "More Fictional Memorials to Mussel Slough," *Pac. Hist. Rev.,* XXVI (1957), 373-377.

40. Irving McKee, "Notable Memorials to Mussel Slough," *Pac. Hist. Rev.,* XVII(1948), 20. Also, see William C. McKinney, "The Mussel Slough Episode, a Chapter in the Settlement of the San Joaquin Valley, 1865-1880." Unpublished M. A. thesis (University of California, Berkeley, 1948).

41. Cerinda W. Evans, *Collis Potter Huntington* (2 vols., Newport News, 1954), I, 291.

42. *Memorial and Biographical History of the Counties of Fresno, Tulare, and Kern, California* (Chicago, 1892), 166, quoted in Evans, *Huntington,* I, 290. Smith, *Garden,* 266.

43. Crocker to Huntington, November 30, 1878, in Evans, *Huntington,* I, 291-292.

44. Sacramento *Union,* March 5, 1879. McKee, "Notable Memorials," 21.

45. Smith, *Garden,* 260.

46. San Francisco *Morning Call,* May 13, 1880.

47. Sacramento *Record-Union,* March 12, 1880.

48. Stockton *Mail,* April 12, 1890.

49. McKee, "Notable Memorials," 21. Smith, *Garden,* 268.

50. McKee, "Notable Memorials," 21.

51. San Francisco *Morning Call,* March 12, 1880.

52. San Francisco *Morning Call,* December 4, 1880. Sacramento *Record-Union,* May 11, 1880.

53. Mills D. Hartt to Stanford, May 5, 1880, in *ibid.,* May 13, 1880.

54. Jerome Madden, Southern Pacific Land Agent, to Hartt, May 8, 1880, in *ibid.,* May 13, 1880. Hartt, generally considered a tool of the railroad, was one of those killed in the ensuing battle. *Ibid.,* May 14, 1880, and Sacramento *Record-Union,* May 14, 1880.

55. Sacramento *Record-Union,* May 13, 1880.

56. *Struggle of the Mussel Slough Settlers,* 26-29, in McKee, "Notable Memorials," 21.

57. James L. Brown, *Mussel Slough,* 58. Bean, *California,* 227.

58. Huntington to Hopkins, April 10, 1876, in Evans, *Huntington,* I, 289-290.

59. Huntington to Henry E. Huntington, October 19, 1893, in *ibid.,* I, 295.

60. San Francisco *Morning Call,* May 12, 13, 1880. Sacramento *Record-Union,* May 12, 13, 1880.

61. For a summary of the trial and the trial judge's charge to the jury, see Sacramento *Record-Union,* January 22, 1881, and San Francisco *Morning Call,* December 2, 1880.

62. There followed one of the most bizarre imprisonments on record. At the San Jose jail, where they were sent for eight months, they were given the key to the front door and allowed to attend church and lodge meetings in town. One prisoner, owing to ill health, was allowed to live in San Jose so long as he reported daily to the jail. A recently-married settler brought his wife with him and they honeymooned in jail. The other married men were joined by their wives and children and were given three rooms over the jail for keeping house. The one bachelor among them married the jailer's daughter.

When released, the convicts were escorted to the city limits by the San Jose municipal band and were made guests of honor at a huge barbecue on the city. Upon their return to Hanford they were welcomed by 3,000 people celebrating their homecoming. The journey home was made by wagon, not railroad! Smith, *Garden,* 285-287.

63. For fictionalized versions of this tragedy, see Josiah Royce, *The Feud of Oldfield Creek: A Novel of California Life* (Boston, 1887), and Frank Norris, *The Octopus* (1901).

64. *United States versus Southern Pacific,* 655. Timothy Hopkins testimony, in Daggett, *Southern Pacific,* 146. The charter of this new holding company is in Haney, *Congressional History, 1850-1887,* 134-137.

65. Daggett, *Southern Pacific,* 151.

66. *Pacific Railway Commission,* 2,809. Stanford testimony.

67. A copy of this lease is in *House Executive Document* 60, 49 Cong., 1 Sess., p. 2 (Serial 2,398).

68. Daggett, *Southern Pacific,* 146-148. Mark Hopkins died in 1878. *Pacific Railway Commission,* 2,825. Stanford testimony.

69. *Pacific Railway Commission,* 3,616. Stanford testimony.

70. Daggett, *Southern Pacific,* 149. Grodinsky, *Railway Strategy,* 299. Central Pacific, 1,254 miles; Northern Railway, 153; San Pablo and Tulare, 46; Berkeley Branch, 3; California Pacific, 115; Stockton and Copperopolis, 49; Amador Branch, 27; Southern Pacific of California, 552; Southern Pacific of Arizona, 384; Southern Pacific of New Mexico, 167; Galveston, Harrisburg and San Antonio, 936; Mexican International, 171; Texas and New Orleans, 105; Louisiana Western, 112; Louisiana and Texas, 281; Sabine and East Texas, 104; Los Angeles and San Diego, 27; Los Angeles and Independence, 16; and Southern Pacific of California, Northern Division, 202. *Travelers' Official Guide,* June, 1885, in Clark, *Stanford,* 339-340.

71. Wilson and Taylor, *Southern Pacific,* 103.

72. *Pacific Railway Commission,* 3,061-3,063. Edward H. Miller, Jr., testimony.

73. Cited in Clark, *Stanford,* x.

74. *Pacific Railway Commission,* 2,712-2,713. Daniel Z. Yost testimony.

75. *Ibid.*, 3,664-3,665. Charles Crocker testimony.

76. *Report, Pacific Railway Commission,* 74.

77. *Pacific Railway Commission,* 2,669-2,670. Stanford testimony.

78. *Ibid.,* 2,648-2,656.

79. *Report, Pacific Railway Commission,* 76.

80. *Ibid.,* 13, 17-19. *Pacific Railway Commission,* 3,674. Charles Crocker testimony. *Report, Pacific Railway Commission,* 81.

81. *Pacific Railway Commission,* 2,655-2,658. Stanford testimony.

82. *Ibid.,* 2,671-2,672. Douty testimony. See *Colton Case,* 5,475-5,477.

83. *Pacific Railway Commission,* 3,671. Charles Crocker testimony. 2,658. Stanford testimony.

84. *Ibid.,* 2,673. Douty testimony.

85. *Ibid.,* 2,679.

86. Crocker to Huntington, February 21, 1882, in Grodinsky, *Railway Strategy,* 209.

87. *Pacific Railway Commission,* 2,672-2,673. Douty testimony. Daggett, *Southern Pacific,* 132.

88. *Pacific Railway Commission,* 2,658-2,662. Stanford testimony.

89. *Ibid.,* 2,672. Douty testimony.

90. Daggett, *Southern Pacific,* 134.

91. *Pacific Railway Commission,* 2,662. Stanford testimony. Edwin T. Coman, Jr., in an excellent article entitled "Sidelights on the Investment Policies of Stanford, Huntington, Hopkins, and Crocker," *Bulletin of the Business Historical Society,* XVI(1942), 85-89, identifies the broad and extensive investments of the Pacific Improvement Company. His source of information was a recently-acquired set of the company's records, including 279 ledgers, journals, and minute books, 42 cases of correspondence, and 150 drawers of vouchers dealing with subsidiary companies. This collection is now housed in the Jackson Library, Graduate School of Business, Stanford University.

92. Daggett, *Southern Pacific,* 136-137.

93. *Ibid.,* 137. *Pacific Railway Commission,* 2,832. Stanford testimony.

94. *Pacific Railway Commission,* 3,022. Charles F. Crocker testimony; 3,027. Elisha S. Miller testimony. *Colton Case,* 9,669-9,673. Charles Crocker testimony.

95. *Pacific Railway Commission,* 2,500-2,501. Stanford testimony.

96. Daggett, *Southern Pacific,* 138. San Francisco *Examiner,* October 8, 1889. See Eldredge, *History,* IV, 303, for estimates of their fortunes.

97. California Pacific, 24,755 shares; Southern Pacific Company, 82,587; Southern Pacific of Kentucky, 150,233; Stockton and Copperopolis, 586; Berkeley Branch, 231; Amador Branch, 1,560; Los Angeles and San Diego,

370; California and Oregon, San Joaquin Valley, San Francisco, Oakland, Alameda, and Western Pacific (He could not remember how much Central Pacific stock he exchanged for these holdings when they were consolidated.); Wells Fargo, 86; Occidental and Oriental Steamship Company (of which he was president), 9,995; Western Development Company, 10,000; Pacific Improvement Company, 12,500; Ione Coal and Iron Company, 8,000; and Rocky Mountain Coal and Iron Company, 1,817. *Pacific Railway Commission*, 2,492-2,493, 2,657. Stanford testimony.

98. *Congressional Record*, 44 Cong., 1 Sess., 3,064, and 44 Cong., 2 Sess., 1,073.

99. *Report, Pacific Railway Commission*, 73.

100. *Ibid.* San Francisco *Bulletin*, January 4, 1873.

101. *Report, Pacific Railway Commission*, 3.

102. *Pacific Railway Commission*, 3,501-3,512. Richard F. Stevens testimony; 2,865 and 3,641. Daniel W. Strong and Charles Crocker testimony.

103. Carman and Mueller, "Contract and Finance Company," 338.

104. *Pacific Railway Commission*, 2,636, 2,648-2,649. Stanford testimony.

105. *Ibid.*, 3,651, 3,661. Charles Crocker testimony.

106. *Report, Pacific Railway Commission*, 84, 138-139.

107. *Ibid.*, 81-82.

108. *Ibid.*, 82-83.

109. *Pacific Railway Commission*, 2,630.

110. *Report, Pacific Railway Commission*, 87-88.

111. *Ibid.*, 147.

112. Carman and Mueller, "Contract and Finance Company," 340, note 69 for payment of these notes.

113. *Report, Pacific Railway Commission*, 141.

114. Huntington to Stanford, January 4, 1870, in Grodinsky, *Railway Strategy*, 3.

115. Quoted in Grodinsky, *Railway Strategy*, 3.

116. *Pacific Railway Commission*, 2,394. Alfred A. Cohen testimony.

117. Sacramento *Record*, March 11, 1873. *Pacific Railway Commission*, 2,465. Stanford testimony.

118. Sacramento *Record*, September 13, 1873.

119. *Report, Pacific Railway Commission*, 91.

120. *Pacific Railway Commission*, 2,526. Stanford testimony.

121. Ellen M. Colton, in *California Spirit of the Times*, October 10, 1885.

122. *Report, Pacific Railway Commission*, 90.

123. Boston *Transcript*, May 21, 1883, in Grodinsky, *Railway Strategy*, 214, 225.

124. Grodinsky, *Railway Strategy,* 30.

125. *Ibid.,* 50, Table II.

126. *Ibid.,* 40-55, for a careful analysis of Huntington's activities during this crisis.

127. Huntington to Colton, May 3, 1875, in Grodinsky, *Railway Strategy,* 61. Wilson and Taylor, *Southern Pacific,* 51.

128. Huntington to Hopkins, December 5, 1871, August 23, 1872.

129. Huntington to Hopkins, September 14, 1872.

130. *Pacific Railway Commission,* 3,658. Charles Crocker testimony.

131. *Ibid.,* 3,782. Stanford testimony. Hopkins to Huntington, October 17, 1872, in Wilson and Taylor, *Southern Pacific,* 94, and Clark, *Stanford,* 327.

132. Huntington to Hopkins, September 26, 1873.

133. Huntington to Stanford, February 28, 1873. Huntington to Hopkins, March 1, 1873.

134. *Pacific Railway Commission,* 2,782. Stanford testimony. *Ibid.,* 3,496-3,500. Darius O. Mills testimony.

135. Huntington to Hopkins, January 23, 1872.

136. Huntington to Hopkins, March 27, 1872.

137. Stanford telegram to Hopkins, October 1, 1873.

138. Stanford telegram to Hopkins, October 3, 1873.

139. Huntington telegram to Stanford, October 25, 1873.

140. Huntington to Hopkins, September 18, 19, 27, October 11, November 11, 24, December 31, 1873.

141. Stanford telegram to Huntington, September 23, 1887.

142. *Report, Pacific Railway Commission,* iii.

143. *House Executive Document* 238, 55 Cong., 3 Sess. (Serial 3,812).

CHAPTER VI

RAILROAD MAGNATE: POLITICS AND POLEMICS

As the Southern Pacific system grew larger and its managers wealthier, the image of the railroad as an octopus and its owners as corrupters of legislatures grew apace. Antirailroad feeling spread like wildfire, and California politics began to focus more and more upon railroad affairs, especially ways of regulating rates by state legislation. The associates at times found their railroad enterprises assailed by most of the California press, by a number of adverse politicians, sometimes by well-intentioned citizens who misunderstood their motives, and by special interest groups, such as farmers who wanted cheaper rates and blamed the railroad for all their difficulties.

Political manipulation was the irregularity most often charged against the associates. Their enemies then as later discovered that their political power "extended through bought politicians and bought newspapers into the legislatures, regulatory bodies, town and country government, and frequently the courts."[1]

From 1864 to 1889, according to H. H. Bancroft, there was not a single year in which the affairs of the Central and Southern Pacific companies were not the subject of investigation by either the state or the national government.[2] This may have been an exaggeration, but investigations increased in number and as they did they became more critical and more antirailroad. Stanford and his partners were constantly beset by court actions, political attacks, and regulatory bills; because of this, legal and political defense became as much a part of railroading as the building of sheds against the avalanching mountain snows.[3] As the railroad managers lost the public's sympathy, they were more and more regarded as aristocratic and autocratic. Some people believed any kind of political influence exercised by railroads was wrong, *ipso facto*; others were more willing to discriminate between the kinds of influence, rejecting some, accepting others.

There were a number of ways by which the Central Pacific associates tried to improve their image. Public appearances by men like Stanford helped a great deal; letter writing campaigns and newspaper advertisements were also helpful, so long as money was not used to purchase support beyond honest advertising. But there exists an area of grey between these devices that is difficult to recognize and avoid, leading the editor of the Sacramento *Union* to charge on one occasion that one of the managers of the Central Pacific tried to bribe him to support "one of their wicked schemes to snatch property from the State."[4]

Another means the associates adopted of looking out for their economic and political interests was to retain a corps of influential attorneys, but this practice too was subject to serious abuse; it could lead to the buying of influential members of the community, since they were often public figures. A common, almost universal, means of winning the good will of politicians was to give them free railroad passes.

A third way the railroad partners had of safeguarding their interests was to be well represented in the state legislature any time key legislation was pending; in fact, it was a regular practice in most legislatures to allow railroad representatives to testify before committees. This system too was subject to abuse, for it was a short step from keeping an eye on legislation to getting a hand in it. Lobbying in Washington was another means of bringing influence to bear where it could best help the cause, but it too could lead to bribery.

Another means of influencing legislation was the outright purchase of votes; because of its very nature, little is known for certain about how often this was done or how successful it was. Huntington spoke frequently of the possibility of using this kind of leverage, though not in a way that would prove that he did it himself. For example, he wrote David Colton on one occasion that the Southern Pacific could not get a certain piece of legislation passed without paying more for it than it was worth.[5] Huntington had handled railroad politics in the East since the death of Judah, and he told H. H. Bancroft, with only slight exaggeration, that he went to Washington in 1866 and got the votes needed to modify the Pacific railroad act to allow him to build to the Union Pacific line rather than just to the California boundary. He later boasted that he was able to do this without the use of a single dollar for purchasing votes.[6]

Stanford was responsible for looking after the Central Pacific's political affairs in California, but he said he was not acting as president of the railroad when he did so.[7] Railroad involvement in politics was justified on the ground that the managers of the road could and should take part in politics as private citizens; what was good for private citizens was of course good for the public, and what was good for the public was good for the railroad, and vice versa. Hopkins agreed, and averred that railroad intervention was generally prompted by self defense rather than by a desire to get special legislative considerations: "As a company, our rule heretofore in political affairs has been to take no part, except where an enemy endeavors to obtain position with intent to do us harm, then self interest induces us to oppose."[8] Stanford corroborated Hopkins' statement that anytime the railroad was involved in politics it was for the purpose of preventing confiscation of its property.[9]

Crocker added his weight to his partners' argument that railroad politics were defensive, limited entirely to opposing harmful legislation. He conceded that the road had lobbied for financial assistance in order to complete its construction, but afterward he and his associates had withdrawn from the political arena, except when their enemies tried to damage their interests.[10]

II

The first major political threat to the Central Pacific after the completion of the transcontinental was the election in 1871 of Governor Newton Booth, an antirailroad candidate to whom Stanford had sold his Sacramento business, in 1861, the year he was elected governor. Booth was supported by the powerful Sacramento *Union*, which had suddenly become an enemy of the railroad. The election followed two exceptionally dry winters which had done considerable damage to California agriculture. The railroad was blamed for the farmers' problems because of their disappointed expectations of universal and permanent prosperity once it was built. When this prosperity did not materialize, it was allegedly the fault of the road for having promised it. The convention that nominated Booth declared that subsidizing railroads or other private corporations with public land or money was contrary to principles of sound government; such subsidies led to gross corruption and abuse and were an invasion of the rights of the taxpayers.[11]

With Booth's nomination the Sacramento *Union* exulted that the railroad had been virtually driven out of politics.[12] Rumors that the owners of the Central Pacific were going to abandon Sacramento and move to San Francisco because of this defeat prompted hundreds of Sacramento businessmen to pledge their support to the railroad and disavow any support of the *Union*.[13] But it was clear by now that the associates had to do something about this journal, for its opposition had begun to threaten their securities on the eastern market. Their first move was to purchase a rival newspaper, the Sacramento *Record*. In March, 1872, when Huntington wrote Hopkins recommending that they put a first-class man in as editor and business manager of the *Record*, it was clear that the Central Pacific was in control.[14]

In early 1873 the Central Pacific and the *Union* again clashed, this time over a municipal election in Sacramento, where a seat on the city council was at stake. The *Union* supported James McCleery and opposed Horace Adams, whom it termed the railroad candidate. The city was inflamed over this contest, and workmen in various railroad shops invited Stanford and Hopkins to address them on the issues and candidates.[15] At noon on March 10, an audience numbering almost 2,000 began crowding into the cleanly swept paint room in the Sacramento railroad shop.[16] Seats were provided down front for ladies and their escorts, and a small platform was constructed for the speakers, with the stars and stripes floating above. Stanford and Hopkins were greeted with hearty cheers as they came in and took their seats.

Stanford, in the clearest expression made to date of his ideas on the relationship of the railroad to politics, insisted that as individuals he and his associates had not only the right but the duty to take part in politics. He ridiculed those who believed that he and others, his audience included, should be disfranchised because they worked for a railroad. He had no intention of pushing a railroad candidate, and he had not even talked with Horace Adams, the so-called railroad man. Stanford assured his audience that he had never made a deal in his life for political favors in exchange for railroad support.

The Central Pacific president reminded the workmen and newspaper reporters present that he, like they, had the right to use whatever legitimate influence he possessed to get his ideas accepted. In fact, he and his associates were being criticized by newspaper editors for doing the same thing that they were doing. "These men are constantly putting up men for office, not because they are good men, but because they avow their intention to do a damage to the railroad, to cripple its resources, and we defend ourselves."

For whatever reason, and perhaps Stanford's lucid defense of "railroad politics" was one of them, the following day Horace Adams was elected by a decisive margin. But the Booth-Sacramento *Union* forces did not surrender. They continued to press the antirailroad issue throughout the crisis year of 1873. Booth, capitalizing upon the economic upheavals that were sweeping the nation and widespread interest in the Granger movement, came out as the champion of the Patrons of Husbandry. As Booth stormed over the state for independent legislators who would support him once elected to office, Stanford's charge that he was actually running for the Senate rather than trying to benefit the state by destroying the Central Pacific monopoly was lent considerable credence.

During the summer of 1873 the editor of the Sacramento *Union* continued to insist that the key issue in the election was the candidates' stand on the railroad. In one editorial he wrote: "The taxpayers' call for a primary election today, signed as it is by over four hundred and fifty leading Republicans and as many leading Democrats, will either force the Republican convention to nominate good and true enemies of the Central Pacific Railway Company or defeat that party."[17] Governor Booth echoed this sentiment the following month. At the same time, a San Francisco editor complained that the railroad controlled the machinery of both parties.[18]

As a result of continuing opposition to the railroad and dissatisfaction among a number of workmen because their work force had been cut back, Stanford and Hopkins again addressed their employees. Stanford entered the paint shop a second time, dressed in white, and was "rapturously applauded" by over 2,000 people who had turned out to hear him.[19] This turned out to be the bitterest anti-Booth speech ever heard.[20] Enemies of the railroad had charged that the jobs were cut off in retaliation for the workers' part in the election on September 3, when many antirailroad politicans were elected, but Stanford emphatically denied this. He avowed the right of every work-man to vote as he pleased, and drew hearty applause when he said that most of them probably voted the way he had. Stanford explained then that the general recession sweeping the nation had made it necessary to cut back the work force temporarily.[21]

Stanford summarized the political and financial history of the company, and went on to delineate the benefits accruing to the state and to the people of California as a result of the railroad. All one had to do to see the beneficial aspects of the road, he said, was to turn back the calendar to 1860 and com-pare the state now to what it was then.[22]

Lastly, the former governor turned his attention to matters more at hand, Newton Booth. He ridiculed Booth's recent charge that three men in the Central Pacific organization were ruling 200,000 Californians. This was an insult to the citizens of the state; if they would allow themselves to be ruled by any group of men or corporation, Stanford said, he would not re-gard them very highly, but Californians were not of that character. Booth was merely using the railroad as a scapegoat for all the ills of the state and as a hobby horse for riding into the United States Senate. He said that if Booth's speech had been made by anyone other than a state governor, it would have been regarded as the ravings of a madman.

Contrary to Booth's repeated charge that the Central Pacific associates were monopolists, Stanford insisted that the railroad had been a destroyer of monopolies, including those of the Pacific Steamer Company, the Western Union Telegraph, and the Sitka Ice Company. If the railroad were to dis-appear, prices on every service and product sold in the state would skyrocket. Stanford charged that Booth was an entirely negative candidate; he opposed railroads, state university appropriations, and the use of public funds for the establishment of common schools. In short, he was opposed to everything good, but was in favor of nothing. Stanford said that he preferred a positive candidate to a negative man, and challenged his audience and the many newspapermen there to find a single thing that Newton Booth had ever done for the state.

Having "paid his respects" to Governor Booth, Stanford sat down. Cheering prevailed throughout the shop for several minutes and did not die down until he returned to the rostrum and again thanked the audience for its patience and enthusiasm.[23]

In general, Huntington approved of the speeches by Stanford and Hopkins. He wrote Hopkins that he intended to change a few things that would sound better in New York and then publish them.[24]

III

In late 1873 the San Francisco Chamber of Commerce drew up a bill on railroad rates and fares which it proposed to support in the legislature, and sent Stanford a number of questions on the topics under discussion, to get his ideas on them and to hear what objections the railroad had, if any, to its policies on rates.[25] The opening remarks of his reply left no doubt how he felt about state regulation of railroads: "To me it seems that the only proper legislation on this subject is that of the total abolition of any fixed rates by law."[26] In an exposition of the classical doctrine of *laissez faire*, he argued that the free market was the best regulatory device: excess profits would attract competition, and competition would lower profits. He warned the committee that the end result of control was ownership; the two were inseparable. He denied the state the power to destroy the value of property by regulatory legislation, and attributed the current depression in America to loss of foreign confidence in the integrity of the American market, caused by "injudicious agitation" in and out of legislatures upon railroad property. If legislatures would mind their proper business, confidence and prosperity would return.

Despite the efforts of Stanford and his associates, Governor Booth was elected to the Senate. The same legislature that elected him then turned its energies to antirailroad legislation. A state Senate committee was appointed to study a series of regulatory bills.[27] Stanford wrote an open letter to the committee explaining the adverse effects the proposed measures would have, arguing that present railroad policy and rates were beneficial to the people of California, and that any change in the laws regulating fares or rates would be detrimental to them as well as to the railroad.[28] He claimed that the people of the state were saving over $15,000,000 per year by railroad service over what they would pay for any other form of transportation.

Stanford argued, illogically, that the huge bonded indebtedness to the government was evidence that the railroad was not reaping the wild profits imagined by its enemies. This indebtedness was incurred, he insisted, upon the railroad's belief that the laws which brought the company into existence would not be altered to its detriment. Passage of the proposed legislation would deprive investors of part of the money they had placed in railroad securities. If the property of investors could be condemned in this way, other investors would be afraid of placing their money in the railroad in the future. There would then be no more lines built unless the state assumed ownership and construction costs.

Stanford said that California railroad rates were the lowest in the world. Because of this, many railroads in the state were not yet on a paying basis, and even fewer were paying dividends. These roads would be hurt most by regulatory legislation, since the main road in the state and almost the only one showing profits was the Central Pacific, to which state legislation would not apply. A thorough investigation would show that the alleged abuses of the railroads in California were imaginary, Stanford predicted, but he willingly offered to correct any malpractices that the committee might uncover.

The California Assembly tried to pass strong regulatory measures, but the Senate countered with a moderate bill reducing some rates and providing a commission that was to arbitrate differences between the public and the railroads. When the Assembly rejected the Senate bill, there was no legislation of any kind adopted.[29]

Meanwhile, relations with the Sacramento *Union* had become unbearable. From being a close friend of the railroad during the sixties, this paper had become its most dangerous enemy. It is uncertain why the *Union* editor underwent such a drastic change in policy. His explanation was that the railroad had become an irresponsible force that was doing much damage to the state of California, and that he was defending the public by fighting it. Others, on the other hand, traced his pique to the fact that the Central Pacific gave its printing jobs to a competitor.[30] In any event, the war between the Central Pacific and the *Union* editor began in earnest in early February, 1868, when he endorsed a bill pending in the legislature designed to reduce railroad rates, and it did not end until seven years later.

In the fall of 1874, when one of the three Sacramento *Union* partners decided to retire, it was announced that the paper would be sold. If it were not sold before December 21, it was to go on auction. No buyers appeared, so it was sold on December 28 for a paltry $65,000. Only a few years earlier it had been one of the wealthiest and most widely-read papers in the state, but now it was in serious financial straits. A Nevada City editor said that there had hardly been a home or a miner's camp in the state without the *Union*, until it commenced a "crusade against Stanford & Co., and a determined effort to destroy the Republican party."[31] According to this editor, the people of California supported the *Union* in its fight against the railroad until they discovered that the quarrel was a personal matter having nothing to do with public issues or policy. At this point subscriptions began to fall off. Another cause for its decline, he said, was that it now had two very able competitors, the Sacramento *Record*, owned by the Central Pacific Railroad, and the Sacramento *Bee*.

On February 20, 1875, the *Union* announced that its issue of that day would be the last published under the present proprietors. At the same time the editor of the *Record* represented the sale of the *Union* as a merger with his paper.[32] The former owners of the Sacramento journal disavowed any intention to merge with the enemy, and published a letter explaining that when they sold out they expected their paper to continue as an independent journal.[33] Huntington, however, referred to the transaction as the purchase of the *Union*, and was pleased with the way the competitive sheet had been silenced.[34] From then on they were one paper, the Sacramento *Record-Union*.

Throughout the seventies Stanford showed less and less interest in railroad politics, and in 1875 said that he was so absorbed in business affairs that he was no longer interested in politics of any kind. Even if he had been, he did not have the time. When Stanford was asked to comment on the allegation that he controlled the politics of the state, he simply denied the charge, admitting that when the railroad was young he and his associates had to demand protective legislation, but since that necessity no longer existed, they wanted only justice — their legal rights — with no special favors. When asked if he was indifferent to politics, especially to an upcoming election, he pointed out that he was a Republican, but added: "I have no personal preferences; I am taking no part in the election. I never talk politics and I seldom think about them."[35]

Stanford was shaken out of this indifference to political affairs in the spring of 1876 when Santa Clara County Assemblyman Lawrence Archer introduced a bill to the legislature that would have imposed stringent regulations upon the Central Pacific Railroad.[36] A. N. Towne said that at least three divisions of the Central Pacific could not afford to operate under its provisions.[37] A San Francisco editor predicted that the Archer bill would be calamitous to the state's prosperity and would suspend operation of a number of short railroads.[38] He reminded his readers that the Central Pacific had been one of California's greatest bonanzas, and insisted that the associates, the greatest railroad builders of the age, had rendered incalculable service to California and the nation.[39]

The associates, meanwhile, were not going to take this bill without a show of resistance. They treated a number of Assemblymen and their friends to a trip from the capital city to Truckee. The honored guests were given the best cars available, including the personal cars of Stanford and his partners. Food, drink, and after-dinner cigars of the finest quality were free to all. After a sleigh trip to a small lake and a day of ice skating, the merrymakers returned home.[40]

Despite these overtures, the bill passed the Assembly sixty-six to eight. The partners then turned their attention to the state Senate, where the bill was killed, though there is no evidence that they employed any unusual influence. There was some suggestion of bribery in the following legislature, however, as shown in a December, 1877, letter Colton wrote Huntington: "I do not think *this* legislature will hurt us very much, for we looked at these matters in advance, but if we had not looked after the Senate, they would try to steal all we have before their adjournment."[41]

State investigations were expensive and annoying, but as it was they presented little danger to the railroads. In 1874, for example, an Assembly committee used an investigation into the charge that public officials were not getting railroad passes they were entitled to as an occasion for a fishing trip into railroad practices, even inquiring into details of the organization of the Central Pacific system.[42] Nothing came of this.

The California legislature failed on several occasions to adopt regulatory measures, but in 1876 a bill was passed creating a State Board of Transportation Commissioners. It was hoped that this board would function as a regulatory body by investigating alleged discriminations and prohibiting such practices.[43] It proved ineffective and in 1878 was replaced by a one-man commission which was as much a failure as its predecessor.[44]

The watchdogs of railroad morality did not give up easily, and in 1879, when a new state constitution was written, they provided for three railroad commissioners, each elected from a different district within the state. Not one of the first three commissioners, J. S. Cone, C. J. Beerstecher, and George B. Stoneman, paid much attention to the problem of regulating railroads. Cone had long been a friend of Stanford and of many other railroad men. In at least one case he actually negotiated with Stanford over a proposed passenger and freight schedule, rather than merely enforcing the new rates.[45] It was never proven that any of these commissioners ever received direct bribes from the railroad, but favors they accepted from the associates leave little doubt that it was bribery in all but name.[46]

A legislative committee investigating the relationship of the three men to the Central Pacific concluded that some of them made a great deal of money from special railroad favors. Stanford was directly involved. The committee reported that Commissioner Cone "sacrificed the best interests of the State through personal friendship for Governor Stanford, and in return therefore received favors from him."[47] Moreover: "Commissioner Beerstecher's conduct admits of no other explanation than that he was bribed, and that in the opinion of this committee Commissioners Cone and Beerstecher acted in the interests of the railroad corporations rather than the people."[48]

One result of this investigation and the committee's subsequent exposé was that from then on any time the Central or Southern Pacific railroads were not sufficiently controlled by the state, it was believed that they owned the railroad commissioners. This allegation was easier to maintain than that they owned the legislature or controlled the state's political conventions.

Exceptions to the rule that Stanford avoided politics were generally reactions to specific threats to the railroad empire that he and his associates had built, as in 1878-1879, when the new state constitution required that railroads operating in more than one county in the state pay higher taxes than short lines operating entirely within one county. As a result of this, from 1880 to 1888 the associates paid taxes of $100 per mile above the average tax base in fifteen other states.[49] The United States Supreme Court later nullified this tax, but not before the railroad had paid a substantial sum in overpayment.

IV

In 1878, when the legislature was still considering the matter of regulatory legislation, Stanford wrote an open letter to a San Francisco newspaper spelling out again in lucid detail his views on the regulation of corporations. This letter was more than a mere rationalization of Stanford's railroad position; it was a well-reasoned, well-thought-out statement of his economic philosophy. Regulation of corporations was to Stanford a serious break with America's traditional respect for the property rights of the individual, especially the small man who needed cooperation with others in his class to give him the economic leverage needed to protect himself from the wealthy.

Stanford characterized the modern corporation as a most effective economic institution for allowing common people to cooperate in enterprises too big for any of them alone. It constituted "the poor man's absolute defense against the monopoly of the rich." He again went to great lengths to show that corporate ownership was a matter of individual ownership of a part of a big business. Since it was the same as a partnership, except for its greater number of partners, a wrong done to a corporation was a wrong done to individuals. The attacks against corporations that were being heard throughout the country, especially in California, he said, amounted to attacks against private initiative and individualism, and were repugnant to the individualism that had made the American republic great. When the individual is safe, he asserted, "the many cannot be otherwise." In fact, the very basis of civilization was the right of property and the protection of individuals in the fruit of their industry. Stanford rejected regulation of railroads as superfluous, since competition would keep rates as low as possible without government intervention. Repeating one of his favorite doctrines, he said that state regulation would lead ultimately to state ownership.[50]

In Stanford's annual presidential report to the stockholders of the Central Pacific Railroad for the year ending July 1, 1879, he again addressed himself to the much-discussed program of federal regulation. There was no "good foundation in reason," he said, for attempts by either the federal or state government to control the railroads of California. He elaborated upon his earlier assertion that free enterprise, private wealth, individualism, and the rights of labor were threatened by state regulation of the nation's railroads. Realizing that most of the California opposition to his road centered in San Francisco, he focused at length on the benefits to that city derived from railroad transportation. Of all the cities of importance in California, San Francisco was the least likely to be injured by any so-called "railroad monopoly." Her location made it possible to use either the Isthmus of Panama or the Cape, a situation which allowed merchants to dictate the rates they would pay for transcontinental service.

President Stanford told the stockholders that if the state regulated profits, it should also guarantee against loss resulting from such regulation. He then reminded them of a little-appreciated side effect of that article in the new constitution that created a Board of Railroad Commissioners, a body clothed with "great and arbitrary powers." The existing roads in the state were given the right to regulate their own rates, by the railroad act of 1862. If the state moved against this prerogative, he warned, there would be no more railroad construction within the state, for no capitalists could be found so reckless as to make investments where the gross proceeds were regulated by somebody other than those who made the investment. Furthermore, those moving against the railroads would probably bring about a state of affairs just the opposite of what they intended; since the proposed legislation would discourage the building of new roads, it would indirectly benefit the old roads by scaring off competition.

Stanford's remarks on railroad regulation reflected his profound aversion to pure democracy. "Unfortunately," he said, "scarcely was the [United States] constitution adopted when came the declaration that the majority should rule, intensified afterwards in its application by that calamitous declaration that to the victors belonged the spoils." Like the property-oriented conservatives of all ages, Stanford was fearful that democracy meant the end of property and government. He rejected majority rule and endorsed instead a system in which the majority administered but the Constitution ruled. He complained that the Constitution was gradually being eroded by the Granger cases, warehouses cases, various railroad decisions adverse to the roads, and the Thurmond Act, which required that a fund be set aside for retiring the railroad's debt to the central government. All this was leading to two conditions repugnant to American political traditions: communistic distribution of property and absolute control by the majority. This kind of absolutism, with no guarantees of the rights of minorities, he said, had at times been more complete and tyrannical under republican governments than under monarchies. He challenged statesmen to scrutinize carefully the present tendencies to absolutism and return to the civilized government of their political fathers.[51]

The most comprehensive statement of Stanford's economic and political philosophy was made in 1881, in response to a questionnaire from the New York City Chamber of Commerce, addressed to him and other prominent businessmen asking their views on government regulation of business. He elaborated upon ideas often expressed elsewhere, but offered nothing new. Yet the intensity of his arguments and language was such that his ideas assumed a new significance. Rather than merely objecting to regulation, he condemned it as the "direct offspring of robbery and rapine enforced by the hand of might," having "originated in a barbarous age." The regulation of the economy, he said, would lead to the creation of "commissions of espionage" that were contrary to American traditions, ideals, and constitutional principles. The logical conclusion of the Granger cases would be state control, therefore ownership, of all property.[52] State regulation of corporations, not "uncontrolled power of large railroad corporations," was responsible for the growing spirit of communism.[53]

As a good businessman, Stanford believed that the first consideration of railroad managers must be the treasury of their companies; this, after all, is expected of all stockholders. But he disavowed operating at the limit of what the traffic would bear, and he reminded his readers that even if he did regulate rates on this principle he would simply be doing what they all did. This oft-condemned practice in itself was a good thing, because the free market was the best regulator. The principle of gearing rates to a market free of regulation was practiced by all professional men — merchants, manufacturers, lawyers, doctors, and farmers.

Stanford once again repeated his claim that the only time the railroad involved itself in politics was where self protection demanded it. Management and regulation of railroad property, he insisted, should be left entirely in the hands of the railroad owners and managers; the state had no jurisdiction unless it condemned the roads by right of eminent domain and reimbursed the owners for the property thus confiscated.

One year later, in the fall of 1882, editor Frank M. Pixley of the *Argonaut* challenged Stanford to reply to a series of antirailroad charges made by a convention which assembled in San Jose to investigate the railroad and which subsequently recommended substantial reductions in passenger and traffic rates.[54]

In his lengthy reply, Stanford delineated in even greater detail his economic philosophy. The first charge he answered was that the Central Pacific had a monopoly on transportation. He repeated his earlier explanation that the railroad was a destroyer of monopolies; besides, water transportation was present to compete with the railroad, thus keeping its rates as low as possible. Not only would water routes keep railroad rates down, but the railroad had actually brought water rates down. Rates through the Isthmus had dropped from $100 per ton to seventeen dollars per ton as soon as the Southern Pacific system opened. So far as railroad rates being excessive, the rate was only about two cents per ton per mile, less than one-seventh the amount allowable by law.

The next charge was that the government had subsidized the transcontinental railroad and therefore had the authority to regulate it. This Stanford denied, not only on the ground that such regulation was unconstitutional, but that the railroads had not been subsidized by the government. The government had not given money to the railroads; rather, it had lent money, which was to be repaid with interest. The only gift was in land that for a great number of years was worthless. In terms of money saved by having the railroad, even if all the interest on the debts was forfeited, the government and the people of California would come our far ahead.[55]

V

As mentioned, the various railroad investigations by the California legislature had considerable nuisance value, but posed no serious threat to the Southern Pacific partners. The Congressional investigation of 1887 was another matter. The question of finances and fortunes was scrutinized carefully by this commission. One of the persistent questions involved the use of rail-road funds for political influence. Stanford confessed that his company employed a good many agents, but insisted that they were commissioned to work against legislation harmful to the company; they did very little in the way of promoting "affirmative legislation" beneficial to the company.[56] When it came to looking after things in the legislature, he generally handled this.

Stanford was represented by counsel at the Senate hearings, and as the cross examination got hotter, his attorney interjected frequent objections. Several times Stanford refused a direct answer to the question of how much money had been paid to influence legislation.[57] At one point in the interrogation, specifically about the use of money earned by the Dutch Flat wagon road, he became extremely irritated and said that he resented the insinuation that he and his associates had robbed the Pacific railroad by appropriating its money to themselves.[58] In one of his sharpest statements to the Commission, he snapped:

> I have been called all sorts of names by demagogues on the stump and by hostile newspapers, and by enemies of the road, and they have never injured me. At one time I was charged with having a connection with bunko sharps and three-card monte men and gamblers, who were robbing passengers on the railroad. I do not suppose that anybody believed that, but still the charge was made. While I wish to treat the Commission with all courtesy, I do not feel like answering questions suggested by that class of complaints and that class of individuals.[59]

When Stanford was asked if one particular large sum had been used to influence legislation, his counsel, Alfred Cohen, would not allow him to answer, on the ground that the question was designed not to get information, but as "seeking to pander to a public scandal" that was in no way related to the affairs of the committee.[60] Stanford was pressed to answer the question, but he again declined, "under the advice of counsel," to do so, charging that the commission lacked the disinterestedness needed to conduct a fair investigation. "It seems to me more like a prosecution against this company than an investigation," he said, "and perhaps I might add, inquisition."[61]

Stanford told the commission that there had hardly been a session of the legislature from 1863 or 1864 that did not propose legislation hostile to the railroad, and said that because of this a number of railroad attorneys regularly represented the road before legislative committees in Sacramento. He continued: "I must say that I have had many an argument before committees, and had many a talk, too, with the individual members of the legislature on behalf of the company, and I have tried to use all the influence I could in various ways."[62] But he insisted that he had never used any illegitimate influence. When a commissioner asked Stanford to name some lawyers who had attended the legislature with him, he again, "under counsel," refused.[63]

San Francisco City Argus

PRORAILROAD CARTOON of the intentions of the 1887 railroad investigation.

The commissioners asked directly whether or not he had ever corrupted any state legislature or the Congress by buying votes, to which he replied: "I never corrupted a member of the legislature in my life, and I do not know that any of my agents ever did." He stated, further, that he had never made a trip to Washington to exercise political influence there; in fact, he had refused to pay a $10,000 bribe that would have secured the votes needed to get Goat Island when the railroad was interested in it as a terminus.

The chairman of the Commission once again repeated the question about corrupting legislators, and the annoyed Stanford blurted out: "I certainly never corrupted an official in my life, nor attempted to." When the persistent chairman asked the question still another time, Stanford accused him of ungentlemanly behavior. The commissioners then asked whether or not Western Development Company funds had ever been used to influence legislation. Again Stanford declined to answer, but expressed the opinion that he did not believe so.[64]

The investigators then directed their attention to certain unaccounted-for money allegedly used to purchase legislative support. Stanford refused to discuss the matter, but was badgered by the committee into denying that such a thing had happened. The committee then leveled a barrage of questions at him, each naming a specific individual allegedly given railroad money for influence.[65] Again, a series of refusals to answer.

Stanford refused to answer any incriminating questions, but the commissioners did not let him off; they believed his answers were needed for the proper conduct of the investigations, so they petitioned the California Circuit Court to compel him to answer. It was widely feared that a court decision in his favor would annul the execution of the Interstate Commerce Act, passed earlier that year.[66] The court, in fact, did decide in Stanford's favor, and dismissed the petition.[67] The commissioners complained that this made it impossible to make any investigation except with information that would be given willingly, thus precluding intelligent legislation based upon Congressional fact-finding missions.[68] But the decision stood.

No proof of corruption was ever produced that implicated Stanford, but guilt was strongly implied by his evasiveness and refusal to answer questions. The Pacific Railway Commissioners were certain that Stanford and his friends were guilty of bribery and of influencing legislation, even though no proof could be found. With the available testimony and what sketchy evidence they could amass, the commissioners concluded that the Central Pacific Railroad spent over $2,250,000 to influence legislation, money it listed under "general expenses."[69] Of the $5,000,000 earlier reported as taken by the associates, the commissioners reported: "There is no room for doubt that a large portion of this money was used for the purpose of influencing legislation and of preventing the passage of measures deemed to be hostile to the interests of the company, and for the purpose of influencing elections."[70] They said it was impossible to read the Huntington correspondence and his testimony without concluding that he had expended large sums of money in Congress to defeat the passage of railroad bills. The fact that the associates had attempted to conceal some of their financial transactions was in itself evidence of irregularity; their objects must have been illegitimate.

Stanford and his associates were embarrassed by the Pacific Railway Commissioners, but they survived with their railroad empire intact and in fairly good shape. But for another twenty years California politics would continue to focus upon their "octopus." Hopkins had died in 1878 and Crocker in 1888, leaving only Stanford and Huntington of the original Central Pacific managers. More and more Stanford branched out into other interests, even abandoning at times any really active participation in the counsels of the road, having gradually given up to Huntington the primacy that Huntington in many respects had always exercised behind the scenes. With Stanford's entrance into politics in the mid-eighties and the great battle between the two old partners in 1890 that saw Huntington step into the number one office of the Southern Pacific system, another era in the life of Stanford closed, but much of the story of his varied career during the two decades following the completion of the transcontinental in 1869 remains to be told in another context.

1. Wilson and Taylor, *Southern Pacific*, 45.

2. Bancroft, *Stanford*, 61.

3. Wilson and Taylor, *Southern Pacific*, 41.

4. Sacramento *Union*, August 19, 1871.

5. Huntington to Colton, November 9, 1877, in *Colton Case*, 1,802-1,803.

6. Sabin, *Pacific Railway*, 123-124. Though Huntington employed whatever influence he could, he was hardly guilty of "debauching Congress," as one critic later charged him. Myers, *Fortunes*, III, 131. Another enemy of the railroad believed that the associates controlled California politics by manipulating political conventions. According to this interpretation, agitation for the direct primary was a result of this control and was an attempt to break the railroad's stranglehold upon California politics. Franklin Hichborn, "The Party, the Machine, and the Vote: The Story of Cross-filing in California Politics," *Calif. Hist. Soc. Quar.*, XXXVIII (1959), 351-354.

7. Sacramento *Union*, March 13, 1865.

8. Hopkins to unidentified Nevada man, in Clark, *Stanford*, 278.

9. Stanford to Sacramento *Record-Union*, January 20, 1881, printed in edition of January 22, 1881.

10. Quoted in Clark, *Stanford*, 279.

11. Davis, *Political Conventions*, 308.

12. Sacramento *Union*, August 19, 1871.

13. Published in Sacramento *Bee*, August, 1871, in Clark, *Stanford*, 286.

14. Huntington to Hopkins, March 16, 1872, in Clark, *Stanford*, 288.

15. Stanford and Hopkins to Messers. Grow, Stevens, Welch, and others, March 7, 1873, in Sacramento *Record*, March 11, 1873.

16. The whole affair was described in the speech reported in the Sacramento *Record*, March 11, 1873.

17. Sacramento *Union*, July 31, 1873.

18. San Francisco *Alta California*, August 13, 1873. San Francisco *Bulletin*, July 21, 1873.

19. *California Mail Bag*, V (1874), xiv.

20. Reported in Sacramento *Daily Record*, September 13, 1873, and the Sacramento *Weekly Record*, September 19, 1873. Reprinted with correspondent's remarks in *California Mail Bag*, V (1874), xiv-xxiv.

21. Just four days earlier Huntington had written Hopkins that money was "fearfully scarce" in New York; things had not been so bad since the Panic of 1857. Huntington to Hopkins, September 2, 1873.

22. Something like this had already been done, in 1868. Alonzo Delano, under the pseudonym "Old Block," wrote *The Central Pacific Railroad*, or *Forty-nine and Sixty-nine* (San Francisco, 1868), a twenty-three page pamphlet comparing and contrasting Nevada and California before and after the coming of the railroad. Published in *Central Pacific Railroad Pamphlets*, I, no. 10.

23. *California Mail Bag*, V(1874), xxiv.

24. Huntington to Hopkins, September 21, 1873.

25. Caspar T. Hopkins, Chairman of the Committee, to Stanford, November 11, 1873.

26. Stanford to Caspar Hopkins, December 1, 1873.

27. For a thorough treatment of early movements to regulate the Central Pacific Railroad, see Ward M. McAfee, "Local Interests and Railroad Regulation in Nineteenth Century California." Unpublished Ph.D. dissertation (Stanford, 1965), 12-23.

28. Stanford to Committee on Corporations of the California Senate, January 22, 1874, in San Francisco *Bulletin*, January 23, 1874. Also reprinted with a number of pamphlets and proposed laws on state regulation of railroads, in *Railway Rates in California*. This publication fails to identify compiler, place, or date.

29. *Appendix to Journals of the Senate and Assembly*, 20 Sess., VI, 1874.

30. Clark, *Stanford*, 284.

31. Nevada City *Transcript*, December 2, 1874, in Clark, *Stanford*, 304.

32. Sacramento *Record-Union*, February 22, 1875.

33. San Francisco *Bulletin*, February 23, 1875.

34. Huntington to Hopkins, March 18, 1875.

35. San Francisco *Chronicle*, May 19, 1875.

36. Lengthy communications were sent by Stanford to the committees on corporations of both houses of the state legislature, in January, 1876, listing his reasons for opposing regulatory legislation. Reprinted in *Railway Rates in California*.

37. San Francisco *Chronicle*, March 7, 1876.

38. San Francisco *Alta California*, March 5, 1876.

39. *Ibid.*, August 29, 1876.

40. See Sacramento *Record-Union*, February 21, 1876.

41. Colton to Huntington, December 22, 1877, in *Colton Case*, 7,540-7,542.

42. Sacramento *Record*, March 31, 1874.

43. California *Statutes*, 1875-1876, 783-785.

44. *Ibid.*, 1877-1878, 969.

45. Daggett, *Southern Pacific*, 192-194.

46. *Ibid.*, 194-196.

47. *Report on the Committee on Corporations*, 1883, in Daggett, *Southern Pacific*, 197-198.

48. *Ibid.*, 198. McAfee, "Local Interests and Railroad Regulation," 157 ff.

49. Bancroft, *Stanford*, 48.

50. San Francisco *Call*, November 3, 1878.

51. Quoted in Bancroft, *Stanford*, 54.

52. Stanford to New York Chamber of Commerce, January 20, 1881, in Sacramento *Record-Union*, January 22, 1881.

53. Santa Barbara *News-Press*, January 22, 1956.

54. Pixley to Stanford, August 14, 1882, in San Francisco *Argonaut*, August 19, 1882.

55. Stanford to Pixley, August 22, 1882.

56. *Pacific Railway Commission*, 3,162. Stanford testimony. Pixley viewed the commission cynically as a "smelling" committee prompted more by per diem pay and increased recognition than by a desire to root out genuine ills in the economic system. San Francisco *Argonaut*, August 20, 1887.

57. *Pacific Railway Commission*, 2,495.

58. *Ibid.*, 2,928.

59. *Ibid.*, 2,929.

60. *Ibid.*, 3,164.

61. *Ibid.*, 2,793.

62. *Ibid.*, 3,168-3,169. See also 2,720. Yost testimony.

63. *Ibid.*, 3,169. Stanford testimony.

64. *Ibid.*, 3,170-3,172, 3,180.

65. *Ibid.*, 3,185-3,187.

66. Stockton *Mail*, September 16, 1887.

67. *Pacific Railway Commission*, 4,164-4,250. Court decision on 4,250.

68. *Report, Pacific Railway Commission*, 85.

69. *Ibid.*, 144.

70. *Ibid.*, 84.

CHAPTER VII

STANFORD'S RESPONSES TO COMPETITION:

RHETORIC VERSUS REALITY

It was one thing for Stanford and his associates to argue, as they did, on the side of a free-wheeling, *laissez-faire* economic structure in which their railroad empire could operate free of all government constraints, but quite another to tolerate in actual practice ruinous competition when there were ways of destroying or eliminating it, or at the very least of mitigating its injurious influence. They were not at all bothered by the consideration that unrestricted competition was self-defeating, that it led inevitably to monopoly, for the precise reason that they expected to survive the system; yet when their own survival at times seemed threatened, they denied their competitors rights reserved to themselves.

Even before the completion of the transcontinental railroad, the Central Pacific associates were faced with competition from a number of different kinds of businesses. There was a constant threat of a parallel railroad across the country, like the Great Northern, the Northern Pacific, the Texas Pacific, and the Canadian Pacific. The last of these was especially dangerous, for it was subsidized by the British government and was free from the restrictions of the American Interstate Commerce Act passed in 1887.[1] This line was willing to join an American railroad pool, but insisted that it be given special consideration because its circuitous route made it the slowest of the transcontinentals. In 1888 the American roads agreed to its terms and the Canadian line joined a newly-organized pool.[2]

Stanford, complaining that in one year alone his railroad had lost a million dollars in net earnings because of competition from other transcontinental lines, was especially bitter about government grants to the Northern Pacific; this, he insisted, was a violation of the spirit of the grant of assistance to the Central and Union.[3] Government help was designed in the first place to attract investors who would not otherwise have supported the original project, but now those who invested because of this inducement were being injured by competing roads. The Central Pacific president thought it only fair that these investors be reimbursed by the government for all losses sustained because of other assisted roads.[4] They had assumed, with good reason, that the Pacific railroad which they helped finance would be the only government-aided transcontinental and that it would get all the cross-country business.[5] The government had therefore violated the terms of this arrangement when it subsequently aided three other Pacific roads, giving them twice the land grants awarded the Central Pacific. To make matters worse, the lands these roads traversed was in every case more valuable than those through which the Central had had to build.

Stanford was piqued as well by the fact that other government-aided roads had hesitated — in fact had made no move at all — until the Central Pacific had demonstrated the practicability of operating a through road; the Central was a true "pioneer road" and its success alone encouraged others to enter the field.[6] That they were now receiving special consideration from the government after their past timidity was particularly galling.

The Central Pacific associates owned the Southern Pacific of Kentucky, so there was no fear of losing business to this new transcontinental; as it was, the two roads did not even compete. Stanford himself conceded that these two systems together competed with other railroads, but not with each other.[7] John C. Stubbs, general traffic manager of the Southern Pacific, acknowledged that if the Texas Pacific had built the southern transcontinental, there would have been no effective check on free competition, thus creating a rivalry that would have hurt the Central Pacific.[8] Control of the Southern Pacific route was all that saved the Central Pacific from extermination, for competition with the Texas Pacific would have bankrupted the Central Pacific.[9] This conclusion was corroborated by Alban Towne, general manager of the Central Pacific. When asked what would have happened to the Central Pacific if the Southern Pacific had been in hostile hands, he replied:

> I have no doubt that it would have been in the hands of a receiver, for it would not have been able to have earned sufficient money to pay its operating expenses and fixed charges. The competition has been very considerably neutralized by the road having been managed by one head and under one direction.[10]

By design, the Southern Pacific served as a defense for the Central Pacific, as admitted by Charles Crocker, who gave protection of this railroad as the associates' sole reason for building the southern line. Other than for this, he declared: "We had no ambition to build the Southern Pacific Railway."[11] Because every new transcontinental railroad built with government aid hurt their system, he and his partners would have stopped them all if they had been able. He agreed with Stanford that the national government had broken faith with the Central Pacific in assisting other roads and diverting to them business that their company's investors had good reason to depend upon.

It is true that the Southern Pacific did not hurt the Central Pacific associates as far as total personal income was concerned, but it did injure the Central Pacific-Union Pacific system. Charles Francis Adams, president of the Union Pacific, testified in 1887 that the earnings of the Union Pacific had been "enormous" until the Northern Pacific was completed in the mideighties, at about the same time that the Southern Pacific of Kentucky was completed as a transcontinental line.[12] These parallel lines taken together drained annually $4,000,000 worth of business away from his road. But since the Union Pacific was only a portion of a transcontinental, it could not expect the Central Pacific associates to sacrifice their Southern Pacific interests, which they owned outright, for their Central Pacific business; in the latter they owned less than half a company that itself was less than half a transcontinental.

Besides competition from other transcontinentals, the associates were confronted by the prospect of shorter roads paralleling part of theirs over limited sections of their route, such as the California Pacific, the Western Pacific, and the much-talked-about road from Sacramento to Nevada. Loss of business to local roads throughout the state was a danger too, unless they could create a monopoly or extract from these lines voluntary agreements to cooperate in keeping rates up, in other words, sectional pools. Stanford complained a number of times that the California Pacific, which ran from Sacramento to San Francisco, was a "very serious competitor" which injured the Central Pacific "to a very great extent."[13] Both roads felt this competition, and finally the California Pacific managers approached him about buying out their company.

From the beginning, the associates had worked hard to gain control of actual or potential competitors or to negotiate agreements with them to keep prices high enough that no one would be a threat to anyone else. Throughout the 1880's, a series of nationwide railroad pools was organized which lessened the loss of revenue from cut-throat competition, but this means of reducing destructive competition fell apart in 1887.[14] Even at best, pools did not destroy competition; as a Central Pacific manager explained to the Pacific Railway Commissioners, while pools averted rate wars, they did not eliminate competition, which was always present though in a modified form.[15]

One of the nation's greatest railroad pools, the Transcontinental Traffic Association, attempted to prevent competition over the transcontinental lines, but it was dealt a serious blow in January, 1886, when the Atchison, Topeka, and Santa Fe Railroad withdrew, precipitating one of the greatest rate wars of all time.[16]

In early 1887 the Santa Fe management suggested a new pooling arrangement with the Southern Pacific, reserving to itself fifty percent of the railroad business in southern California and twenty-seven percent of that in the northern part of the state. The Southern Pacific rejected this "offer," whereupon the Santa Fe declared all-out war against what it called the "monopoly" of its rival.[17]

When the transcontinental railroad opened for business in the spring of 1869, it cost $130 to travel by rail from Chicago to San Francisco. Four years later first class fare was still $118, and by 1885 had dropped to only $100.[18] The 1887 rate war caused the bottom to fall out of these high fares. The battle rose to a sudden fury in early March, when on the fourth of the month rates from San Francisco to Boston plummeted to forty-seven dollars, those from San Francisco to New York dropped to forty-five dollars, and the fare to Chicago went to thirty-two dollars.[19] The next day these fares were lowered five dollars, five dollars, and seven dollars, respectively.[20]

On the morning of March 6 the two companies determined on a fight to the finish over the cost of traveling from Kansas City to Los Angeles. They opened even at twelve dollars, the Santa Fe dropped to ten, and the Southern Pacific promptly matched it. The would-be interloper then went to eight and again was met by the established enemy. The Southern Pacific then assumed the initiative and dropped its rates to six dollars and then four, and in the early afternoon announced the all time low of one dollar for the 1,800-mile trip from the Missouri River to Los Angeles.[21] These rates quickly bounced back again, but never to the highs of the 1870's; for a year the cost of traveling to California remained less than twenty-five dollars.[22]

The social and economic effects of this rate war are incalculable, as hundred of thousands of people decided there would never be a better opportunity of finding their way to the Golden State, the El Dorado. The Southern Pacific alone carried 120,000 immigrants west in a twelve-month period.[23]

II

The associates on occasion were drawn into nonrailroad businesses in order to stifle competition that was injurious to them, and in a number of instances they bought into different kinds of companies merely to force down prices to themselves. True, this was a case of competition lowering prices, but it was not at all a working of the free market, since they entered businesses in which they had no other interest for the express purpose of allowing themselves to be bought off. As a case in point, they bought the Coos Bay Coal Company to avoid paying high prices for coal, and the result of this purchase was a drop in their cost from eight dollars to four and a half dollars per ton.[24] In another instance, in 1876, they used their own Western Development funds to build a railroad to Ione to develop a coal mine which they had purchased.[25]

Express companies that hauled merchandise between customers and railroads cashed in on a considerable portion of potential railroad profits. Lloyd Tevis, president of Wells Fargo, conceived the idea in 1869 of organizing an express company to compete with the Wells Fargo. He proposed this to Stanford and his associates and "after considerable negotiation" they agreed to form their own company, the Pacific Express.[26] By employing this economic leverage, or legalized blackmail, as the case may be, they eventually forced an agreement out of Wells Fargo that kept their own company out of the express business. It never did any business of its own, and was "substantially" consolidated into Wells Fargo. The deal between the two companies led to a complete reorganization of the established firm, and Stanford and Crocker became directors of the Wells Fargo Express Company.[27]

In exchange for one-third of the total Wells Fargo stock, Stanford, Charles Crocker, and Hopkins dissolved their company, though there was no formal consolidation of the two. But before the stock was transferred to the associates, it was increased from $10,000,000 to $15,000,000, a stock-watering job that was later classed as one of the Central Pacific's most calculated swindles.[28] For its part, the Wells Fargo company was guaranteed the business of the Central Pacific for a period of ten years. Each of these three associates had to put up one-third of a half million dollars, working cash to enable the new Wells Fargo organization to do banking. Thus, for a total cash outlay of only $500,000, they gained control of $5,000,000 in Wells Fargo stock, a tidy swap that proved extremely rewarding.[29]

Later, when queried about the details of the agreement, Stanford was unclear as to its terms, but he recalled that the Wells Fargo company was not given any special consideration; the contract simply guaranteed that no other company would be given special consideration.[30] He was wrong. The agreement reached was based upon the mutual recognition that the Wells Fargo and the Pacific Express would injure each other, and despite Stanford's vagueness, it is clear that Wells Fargo was given a special relationship to the Central Pacific. The terms of agreement acknowledged that the projected Pacific Express company had had an "advantageous" contract with the Central Pacific, and under the new arrangement Wells Fargo was to inherit that company's contract.[31] As it turned out, as late as 1887 Wells Fargo still had a monopoly on the express business for the Central Pacific and the Southern Pacific.[32]

III

The most neglected and consequently the least known of Leland Stanford's many careers is that of president of the Occidental and Oriental Steamship Company. His interest in steam navigation began in the late 1860's and sprang directly from his desire to keep the Central Pacific as free as possible from crippling competition, or effective competition of any kind, for that matter.

Water competition could present almost as great a threat to the Central Pacific as did rail. San Francisco lay at the mouth of the Sacramento and San Joaquin rivers, along which steamboats had long plied their way inland with a substantial commerce to and from the port city. Besides this, the coast-to-coast traffic of steamship companies drew heavily from actual or potential railroad business.

By the late 1860's, the California Steamship Company had gradually won control of most of the inland traffic landing at San Francisco, but in 1869, the year the transcontinental was completed, the company sold its steamers to the Central Pacific, giving the railroad associates a near-monopoly on transportation from Ogden to San Francisco. A few years later, in 1872, the associates bought interest in a number of steamships owned by the California Pacific Railroad Company.[33] Their intention was to destroy competition on the Sacramento River, thereby allowing them to keep railroad rates high.[34] From that time on, the Central Pacific controlled all the water and rail routes from the capital city to the coast; no competition was again tolerated.

Further consolidation of their river-bound competition took place in 1878, when Stanford, his three associates, and David Colton, acting through the Western Development Company, purchased the Colorado River Steam Navigation Company, whose ships started at Yuma, Arizona, and ran up the Colorado River. There was heavy traffic in government supplies along the Colorado for forts and reservations and for the many mines that had opened there, and rather than have a competing firm carry the supplies to be transported to the place where the railroad began, the associates bought this steamship company and thus gained control of the business for the whole distance.[35] In an arrangement that proved extremely rewarding to Stanford and his partners, the Central Pacific managed the steamship company and turned all profits over to the Western Development Company, which they owned.

Once they had weakened or destroyed most of the competition with their coast-to-coast railroad business, the associates turned their eyes to the lucrative Pacific Ocean trade. San Francisco's international trade was far more extensive than that of any other West Coast city, and losing the sea-going business of this city was unthinkable to Stanford and his friends.

In 1847 the Pacific Mail Steamship Company had been organized in New York, and had sent its first steamers around South America in 1848.[36] In 1867 the company initiated a regular transoceanic trade. With the opening of the transcontinental railroad two years later, it was obvious that traffic on the Panama railroad would decline in importance and the need for cooperation between the Pacific Mail and the Central Pacific would become imperative for harmonious travel and transport of goods from the East Coast and the Orient. Together, they shortened the time to China by two weeks, but there was danger that competition rather than cooperation would develop.

No secret was made of the fact that the Central and Union Pacific railroads bought off the Pacific Mail, paying the seagoing competitor over $4,000,000 to maintain high rates. Until 1872 the transcontinental railroads and the Pacific Mail worked together so smoothly that it was rumored, erroneously, as it turned out, that the steamship company had been bought out by the Central Pacific. One San Francisco editor was especially suspicious of what he regarded as a conspiracy to destroy competition, and he informed his readers that there had been some kind of arrangement between Stanford and Company and the Pacific Mail for over a year whereby freight rates had been regulated. He hinted at total amalgamation of the two concerns and publicized the fact that the San Francisco agents of the Pacific Mail had already resigned their positions. This alarmed journalist warned his readers that if Californians were not careful they would have no means of communication with the outside world except through Stanford's railroad, sailing vessels, or oxteams.[37]

In 1873 all of this changed drastically, when Rufus Hatch, the new manager of the Pacific Mail, announced that instead of depositing transoceanic and transcontinental freight from Asia at San Francisco, his company was going to take it directly to Panama, with only a brief stop in San Francisco for the purpose of unloading local freight.[38] The rest would be sent across the Isthmus by railroad and then carried to New York by Pacific Mail steamships. By placing the entire route in the hands of a single company, rates would be lower, even though the service would take slightly longer.[39]

This move forced the Central Pacific associates to act, since their railroad system would have been destroyed by the Pacific Mail's policy. One railroad agent insisted that no profit was possible to the railroads if there were unlimited competition with the Pacific Mail.[40]

The Occidental and Oriental Steamship Company developed out of the ensuing battle. Stanford and his friends organized this company to gain control of a through route to the Orient and to force the Pacific Mail to return to its use of San Francisco as a terminus. The desired result was eventually achieved, as the Pacific Mail agreed to bring its freight to San Francisco and ship a significant portion of it overland by rail.[41] This arrangement gave the Central Pacific eventual control over the Pacific Mail, but this was not the intention; there is no evidence that the associates had any interest in controlling the Pacific Mail, so long as the two companies could cooperate amicably.[42]

But before all this happened, the associates, in November, 1874, organized the Occidental and Oriental, with a capital stock of $10,000,000 divided into 100,000 shares at $100 each.[43] The Union and Central Pacific railroad companies divided the stock almost evenly, with Stanford, Huntington, Crocker, Hopkins, David Colton, and Tevis each holding 9,000 shares.[44]

The rapidly changing membership of the Board of Directors of the Occidental and Oriental Steamship Company was composed of five men, with at least a majority and occasionally all of them from among the Central Pacific group; these actually managed the line.[45] The Union Pacific members never attended board meetings, but they did take an active part in dividing the traffic among the cooperating companies.[46] Stanford, director of the company for the rest of his life, was elected president when the company was first organized. A year later he was succeeded by George H. Bradbury, a former president of the Pacific Mail. Bradbury later resigned and was succeeded by David Colton, on July 24, 1877. When Colton died, in October, 1878, Stanford was again elected president and held the position until his death in 1893.[47] Mark Hopkins, the first treasurer of the company, was succeeded in late 1875 by the London and San Francisco Bank, Ltd. Later the various Central and Southern Pacific construction companies functioned legally as treasurers, but in effect the office was vacant.

Stanford served actively as presiding officer during the first few years of the company's life, when one to five board meetings per year were held, but as he grew older, traveled abroad for longer periods of time, and suffered increasingly from ill health, he gradually withdrew from the actual management of the company. By the late 1880's and early 1890's the directorship had shifted from the old heavyweights like Huntington, Charles Crocker, Sidney Dillon, and Jay Gould to younger Central Pacific officials, including Charles F. Crocker, Timothy Hopkins, F. S. Douty, and W. V. Huntington, with Crocker as vice-president actually presiding over the meetings of the board.[48]

Huntington once suggested to Stanford that the Central Pacific ought to acquire a controlling interest in the Union Pacific, because a single transcontinental line could bargain better with the Pacific Mail, but this scheme never materialized.[49] In February, 1875, a contract was signed by the managers of the Central, the Union, and the Occidental and Oriental, in which they agreed to do everything within their power to recover the trade lost to the Pacific Mail's Panama route. So intent were they at succeeding at this that they were willing to carry ocean trade at railroad rates, which would have meant operating at a loss. According to the terms of this contract, two-thirds of through passenger fares would go to the Occidental and Oriental, while the railroads would divide the other third equally. Freight fares were to be divided equally between the steamship company on the one hand and the two railroads on the other. The Occidental and Oriental was authorized to use without charge the wharves of the Central Pacific Railroad Company.

The financial operations of the Occidental and Oriental leave no doubt that the line was a mere tool of the Central and Union Pacific railroads. In 1877, when the directors of the O and O needed money, they floated a $150,000 loan from the Western Development Company, owned of course by the Central Pacific associates. The promissory note covering the loan was signed by Stanford, Huntington, Hopkins, and Colton.[50]

The Pacific Mail finally accepted the fact that the Occidental and Oriental was going to be a rival line in fact and not a mere paper competitor. Immediate steps toward peace were taken even before war broke out. In February, 1875, the Pacific Mail sold to Lloyd Tevis, an agent of the Central Pacific, below market value, some waterfront property that included sixteen lots, a number of wharves, sheds, warehouses, and coal yards. The suspicious editor of the San Francisco *Bulletin* warned the city again that the Pacific Mail had sold out to the Central Pacific, thereby ending all competition between them. The identity of interests, he said, was "too close to admit of any opposition between the parties." He concluded: "There will be no Occidental line of steamers, nor any other competing line by the procurement of the Central Pacific combination. The transfer of this magnificent property at about half its actual value don't [sic] mean opposition."[51]

The two steamship companies agreed in June, 1875, that each would open a monthly transoceanic passenger service, leaving San Francisco every fifteen days on an alternating basis. Each company was to work closely with the Central and Union Pacific railroads, and then would divide equally the profits for cargo carried by the roads and the Pacific Mail. The railroads, for their part, guaranteed the Pacific Mail 600 tons of freight each month.[52] These arrangements went into effect before the first Occidental and Oriental steamship sailed, and lasted for the lifetime of the new company.

San Francisco wharves were shared by the two companies on an equal basis, but the rumored merger never developed.[53] Nevertheless, by threatening to swing southward into the lucrative Panama trade, the Occidental and Oriental kept the Pacific Mail in line, and gave the railroad men a voice in setting steamship rates between the East and West Coasts. The associates found later that this kind of operation could work both ways, when the Northern Pacific later demanded a subsidy from the Occidental and Oriental for agreeing not to compete with it.[54]

The relations among these companies were not always harmonious, for there were periodic rumors of rate wars.[55] The particulars of an expected battle between the two companies were spelled out in detail in a series of editorials in the San Francisco *Bulletin*, the first of which was entitled "The War between Pacific Mail and the Pacific Railroads."[56] The railroads had canceled their contract with the Pacific Mail in the spring of 1879 and were unwilling to agree to another because of the high subsidy demanded by the steamship company. The Pacific Mail took the initiative in negotiating with the railroads, but when they proved intransigent, it lowered its passenger rates. The Union Pacific shrugged this off, pointing out that the sea-going competitor was already carrying its capacity and that it was almost impossible to get more ships. Because of this, the Pacific Mail could not have hauled more freight and passengers even if the business had been available. There appears to have been considerable whistling in the dark here, for it was generally understood that the railroads were preparing to make sizeable reductions on through rates.[57]

On March 1, 1880, the two companies came to terms. The Pacific Mail won the war, as it wrung from the railroads a five-year contract granting it an increased subsidy, from $60,000 to $110,000 per month.[58] Stanford later claimed that but for its railroad subsidy, the Pacific Mail would have gone bankrupt. When the subsidy ended, with the passage of the Interstate Commerce Act of 1887, the Pacific Mail cut its rates and again became a competitor, but it did not go bankrupt.[59] By that time, Stanford said, its competition was insignificant. The harmful competition was coming from other railroads.[60]

Huntington and Gould got control of the Pacific Mail in March, 1880, and brought that company entirely within the control of the Union-Central railroad system.[61] Still, there was no merger, and the two steamship companies continued to operate separately, though Pacific Mail value of goods shipped between San Francisco and New York dropped sharply and steadily from $70,000,000 in 1869 to $2,300,000 in 1884.[62]

Captain Bradbury, Stanford's successor in the presidency of the Occidental and Oriental, made arrangements in England for the ships that his company needed. Eventually, the *Oceanic, Belgic,* and *Gaelic* were leased from the Oceanic Steam Navigation Company. That most of the Occidental and Oriental's fleet of nine ships were chartered from the White Star Line led one steamship historian to the erroneous conclusion that the Occidental and Oriental belonged to the White Star line.[63] The only American steamship sailed by the Occidental and Oriental was the *San Pablo,* chartered in 1884 from the Pacific Improvement Company. Since the owners of the Pacific Improvement were directors of the Occidental and Oriental, they chartered the ship from themselves.[64]

These were the most modern and most comfortable ships built at the time. The *Oceanic* was completely decked out with all the comforts of a palace: a saloon, library, grand piano, and two fireplaces, and outside staterooms were provided with running water, call bells, and bathing facilities. These ships had between 100 and 200 first-cabin passenger berths.[65]

Initially, the Occidental and Oriental liners sailed from San Francisco in the middle of the month, crossing to Yokohama or Hong Kong and returning by the same route, completing a round trip that took about three months. After 1883 the service was increased to three sailings per month, and the one-way trip from Hong Kong to San Francisco was cut to about three weeks. In 1889 the *Oceanic* set the trans-Pacific record when she steamed into San Francisco only thirteen and a half days out of Yokohama.[66] Three years later Honolulu was added as an occasional port of call, and before the turn of the century became a regular stop on the trans-Pacific trip.[67] Still later, Manila was added.[68]

Until 1896, having been bought off by prominent Japanese steamship companies, the Occidental and Oriental stayed out of the coastwise trade of the Far East, but in that year both the Pacific Mail and the Occidental and Oriental began competing with the Japanese companies in the China-Japan trade.[69]

The cargo trade carried by the Occidental and Oriental was far more profitable than its passenger business, for only about thirty to seventy first class passengers travelled on each ship. Most of these were missionaries, government representatives, naval officers, merchants, and tourists.[70] The Occidental and Oriental proved a profitable enterprise, an unexpected development, as it turned out. When Stanford explained that he and his partners had organized the Occidental and Oriental to force the Pacific Mail to bring its freight to San Francisco, he said that they expected to lose $100,000 per year on their new business venture. But, surprisingly, it had "paid nicely" and had even brought them handsome profits.[71] Charles Francis Adams, made president of the Union Pacific to add respectability to that company, said the Occidental and Oriental had been a source of profit to his road as well.[72] Profits were so good that in 1878 the company began paying dividends, the first of forty-six paid between that year and 1900, with an average of about six percent. The total dividends paid amounted to forty dollars per hundred-dollar share, but since only three dollars per share had ever been paid in, the 1887 dividends amounted to over 200 percent of money actually invested, averaging about sixty percent for the lifetime returns of the company.[73]

Surplus funds accumulated by the Occidental and Oriental were held by the Central Pacific, until it was discovered that some of this money — $150,000 in one case—had been lent interest free to the Western Development Company and the Pacific Improvement Company.[74] This was of dubious honesty, at best, since fifty percent of the money belonged to the Union Pacific. When the managers of this road discovered what was happening, they demanded that their share of the profits be turned over to them at once, thus ending for the Central Pacific partners a very convenient source of ready cash.[75]

A secretary of the Occidental and Oriental admitted that strict records were not kept of such transactions, and that a bookkeeper examining the books of the Occidental and Oriental Steamship Company would not have discovered such loans.[76] Money was "deposited" by the Occidental and Oriental as if the Central Pacific were a bank, and then was withdrawn as needed; no receipts on money so deposited or lent was kept, and for a number of years the Occidental and Oriental did not even have a treasurer.[77]

From 1900 on, the Occidental and Oriental steadily declined, and it went out of business in 1908. The end was signaled by the election of a vice-president and general manager of the Pacific Mail to the presidency of the Occidental and Oriental. The last of the Occidental and Oriental ships were sold by the White Star line to the Pacific Mail. The end was reached when on July 23, 1908, a meeting of the Occidental and Oriental Board of Directors was called and only the secretary showed up.[78]

IV

Stanford's economic philosophy, especially his ideas on the working of the free market, were expressed time and time again over the years, with one unchanging theme, that competition was the best regulator of the market in the railroad business as well as others. Unregulated competition would lower prices by attracting competition if prices or costs got too high. But when it came to implementing these notions of *laissez-faire* capitalism, he and his partners found themselves driven to reducing competition by one means or another.

For a number of years railroad competition had been destroyed or weakened by buying out competing roads and incorporating them into the Central Pacific-Southern Pacific system, and no sooner had the transcontinental railroad been completed than the managers of the Central and Union agreed to maintain rates at a given level without competing against one another.[79] The philosophy of *laissez-faire*, in their thinking, applied only to government controls. Competition could be destroyed from within the system by those involved; it could be avoided by private agreement. The inconsistency of this position never bothered Stanford or his associates; in fact, he admitted later than in certain instances the Central Pacific prospered in the 1870's only because it was able to fix its rates "free of competition," and he complained that when competing lines opened up, the incomes of the Central Pacific and its spur roads fell off.[80] Yet, to be consistent with his earlier arguments, he must have seen that this was merely the working of the natural laws of economics and was therefore good for the economy as a whole; but, instead of this, he and his partners set about to eliminate this "beneficent" competition, whenever possible. In the 1887 railroad investigation, one of the Pacific Railroad Commissioners' strongest criticisms of the Central Pacific associates was that they regularly "destroyed possible competitors," paying out almost $26,000,000 for rebates, subsidies, and pools in order to avoid the competition that Stanford consistently argued was beneficial to the railroads and to the economy as a whole.[81]

The associates wanted *laissez-faire*, but rejected free enterprise; they did not want government regulation, but neither did they desire free competition. They proved themselves "fittest to survive," in terms of contemporary social Darwinism, and therefore rejected public controls. But enemies of their system, and others like it, regarded pools and monopolies and other agreements not to compete as a conspiracy against the public, and the public, the associates discovered, through its representatives in government, was going to insist upon its right to protect itself by forcing competition, or by guaranteeing that competition could exist. This government intervention in the free enterprise system could be regarded as a higher application of the principle of social Darwinism.

1. James O'Meara, "The Union or the Dominion?" *Overland Monthly*, XIV (1889), 419-420.

2. Grodinsky, *Railway Strategy*, 330.

3. *Pacific Railway Commission*, 2,475, 2,752. Stanford testimony.

4. *Ibid.*, 2,752-2,753.

5. Stanford interview with Cincinnati *Inquirer*, February 18, 1887.

6. *Pacific Railway Commission*, 2,757. Stanford testimony.

7. *Ibid.*, 2,823-2,824.

8. *Ibid.*, 3,363. John C. Stubbs testimony.

9. *Ibid.*, 3,389.

10. *Ibid.*, 3,407. Towne testimony.

11. *Ibid.*, 3,683. Crocker testimony.

12. *Ibid.*, 85. Charles Francis Adams testimony.

13. *Ibid.*, 2,795. Stanford testimony.

14. *Ibid.*, 2,573-2,574.

15. *Ibid.*, 3,329. Stubbs testimony.

16. Glenn S. Dumke, *The Boom of the Eighties in Southern California* (San Marino, 1944), 23. See also, Joseph Netz, "The Great Los Angeles Real Estate Boom of 1887," *Annual Publication, Hist. Soc. of So. California*, X (1915), 54-68, especially 56.

17. Dumke, *Boom*, 24.

18. *Ibid.*

19. Los Angeles *Times*, March 5, 1887.

20. *Ibid.*, March 6, 1887.

21. Dumke, *Boom*, 24-25.

22. *Ibid.*, 25.

23. For a florid description of this rate war and its social effects, see Wilson and Taylor, *Southern Pacific*, 86-88.

24. *Pacific Railway Commission*, 2,497. Stanford testimony.

25. *Ibid.*, 2,692.

26. *Ibid.*, 3,119. Tevis testimony.

27. *Ibid.*, 3,114-3,115.

28. This agreement is reprinted in *ibid.*, 3,120. A number of years afterwards, when the Washington [D.C.] *Sun* published a detailed history of what it termed the "frauds and swindles" of the Central Pacific, it included this deal with the Wells

Fargo on its list of railroads "gobbled up" by the associates. Reprinted in San Francisco *Bulletin*, July 21, 1873.

29. According to one witness, the new arrangement was even more beneficial to Wells Fargo; the company had never been a profitable concern until this arrangement with the Central Pacific was made. *Pacific Railway Commission*, 3,118. Tevis testimony.

30. *Ibid.*, 2,921-2,922. Stanford testimony.

31. *Ibid.*, 3,121, for the contract between the Pacific Express Company and the Central Pacific.

32. *Ibid.*, 3,127. Tevis testimony.

33. *Ibid.*, 3,069. Miller testimony.

34. *Ibid.*, 3,070.

35. *Ibid.*, 2,698-2,699. Douty testimony.

36. Will Lawson, *Pacific Steamers* (Glasgow, 1927), 5. See pages 15-28 for a brief history of the Pacific Mail.

37. San Francisco *Bulletin*, December 5, 1872.

38. John Haskell Kemble, "The Big Four at Sea, the History of the Occidental and Oriental Steamship Company," *Huntington Library Quar.*, III (1940), 340.

39. *Pacific Railway Commission*, 3,309. Stubbs testimony.

40. *Ibid.*, 3,349-3,350.

41. *Ibid*, 2,924. Stanford testimony.

42. Edward R. Gundelfinger, "The Pacific Mail Steamship Company, 1847-1917: Its Relations with the Railroads." Unpublished B. A. thesis (University of California, Berkeley, 1917), 39.

43. *Pacific Railway Commission*, 2,924. Stanford testimony.

44. *Ibid.* Also, *Occidental and Oriental Steamship Company Record* (Minutes of the Board of Directors, 1874-1908), 1-5.

45. *O and O Record*, 1.

46. *Pacific Railway Commission*, 2,925. Stanford testimony.

47. *O and O Record*, 47.

48. *Ibid.*, 50, 111.

49. Huntington to Stanford, March 15, 1875. In Grodinsky, *Railway Strategy*, 124.

50. *O and O Record*, 50, meeting of November 21, 1877.

51. San Francisco *Bulletin*, February 12, 1875.

52. Sacramento *Record-Union*, March 4, 9, 1875.

53. San Francisco *Bulletin*, March 30, 1876.

54. Grodinsky, *Railway Strategy*, 262.

55. San Francisco *Bulletin*, July 11, 1879.

56. *Ibid.*, January 31, 1880.

57. *Ibid.*

58. *Ibid.*, March 2, 1880.

59. *Pacific Railway Commission*, 2,929. Stanford testimony.

60. *Ibid.*, 2,930.

61. San Francisco *Bulletin*, March 15, 1880.

62. Joseph Nimmo, Jr., Chief, Bureau of Statistics, Treasury Department, *Report on the Internal Commerce of the United States, 1884*, p. 55, in *House Executive Document* 7, part 2, 48 Cong., 2 Sess., Serial 2,295.

63. Lawson, *Pacific Steamers*, 9. Another classed it as a White Star subsidiary. Eugene Waldo Smith, *Passenger Ships of the World, Past and Present* (Boston, 1963), 728.

64. San Francisco *Alta California*, July 13, 1884.

65. *Ibid.*, June 3, 1875, for a description of the *Oceanic*.

66. San Francisco *Chronicle*, January 2, 1883, August 1, September 3, 1875. San Francisco *Alta California*, November 12, 1889.

67. San Francisco *Chronicle*, January 10, 1892, January 8, 1893, February 22, 1896, December 30, 1897, and December 31, 1898.

68. *Ibid.*, June 7, December 31, 1902, December 31, 1903, and December 27, 1905.

69. *O and O Record*, 29-33, 82-88.

70. Kemble, "Big Four at Sea," 353. O and O passenger lists are in the Pacific Mail Steamship collection at the Huntington Library.

71. *Pacific Railway Commission*, 2,924. Stanford testimony.

72. *Ibid.*, 83. Adams testimony.

73. *O and O Record*, 91-97.

74. *Colton Case*, 1,584-1,587.

75. *Ibid.*, 7,646-7,654.

76. *Ibid.*, 1,573.

77. *Ibid.*, 1,577-1,578.

78. *O and O Record*, 233.

79. *Pacific Railway Commission*, 2,122. Peter B. Shelby testimony.

80. *Ibid.*, 2,849. Stanford testimony.

81. *Report, Pacific Railway Commission*, 141-142.

CHAPTER VIII

COUNTRY SQUIRE

Like many Americans of his century, Leland Stanford was reared on a farm, and remembrances of his boyhood in rural New York never left him; for the rest of his life the farm and the land exerted a strange attraction upon the man. Among his favorite topics of conversation when traveling across the countryside were the nature and quality of the soil, the climate, the seeding of land, and how and when it was best to harvest crops.[1] Stanford was widely regarded as an expert agriculturalist, and following one of his talks at the State Agricultural Society, in 1863, Thomas Starr King described it as the most thoughtful and instructive agricultural address he had ever heard.[2]

It was as a man of the soil that Stanford preferred to be remembered. When a young man working on the New York City directory asked him how he would like his profession listed, this man of many careers asked to be identified as a farmer. Related to his love for the land was his affection for horses; he was never happier than when among his handsome and blooded trotters.[3]

Stanford was bordering on physical and nervous exhaustion when the last spike was driven at Promontory, and his doctor advised him to take a long rest and avoid for a time the cares and pressures of business.[4] Unable to bring himself to even a temporary retirement, he did decide to take up some avocation less strenuous than railroad building. He was always fond of driving a good team, and since this was something he could do without exhausting himself, he took up breeding and training of horses, especially blooded trotters.

In July, 1870, Stanford bought his first race horse, one that had trotted a half mile in the respectable time of 1:12½. Applying his own ideas on how to train trotters, he groomed this horse, Occident, and in 1873 at the California State Fair this prize trotter ran the mile in 2:16¾, matching the world trotting record.[5]

In 1872 Stanford's horses captured the imagination of San Francisco race fans, and about the same time they began to win nationwide recognition. In August he entered Aurora, a product of his Vina stock farm, in a race at the Agricultural Park. Before 2,000 spectators, this fine specimen set the state trotting record.[6] In October of the same year, 6,000 watched in anguish as an eastern horse defeated Stanford's Occident.[7] A nearby newspaper editor rationalized the defeat of the local favorite, saying that the superior California steed was not accustomed to running on a public track.[8]

When the Stanfords moved to San Francisco in 1874, they built a stable on the northeast corner of California and Powell streets, across from their home on the southwest corner. By then the Governor, as he was known to everyone, had acquired several fine horses which he raced through Golden Gate Park with his friend and neighbor, Charles Crocker, who was addicted to fast horses. Timothy Hopkins used to tell the story of how a policeman in Golden Gate Park lost his patience with Stanford's racing about the park and stopped him to remonstrate with him about his fast driving. Stanford, in a playful mood, said, "Officer, you are right. But don't take me this time. Charlie is right behind me—take him instead of me." He smiled, tapped his horse, and drove away, but he broke into a laugh when he looked back and saw that the policeman had indeed stopped Crocker.[9]

Stanford's interest in racing led him at this time to buy some stock in the Bay District Track just north of the Golden Gate Park.

Partly to give his son the appreciation for farm life that he had acquired as a boy and partly to take up serious breeding and training of race horses, as well as find a place for relaxation and escape from the turmoil of city life, Stanford decided to buy a farm. The site he chose was on the Southern Pacific line about thirty miles down the Peninsula from San Francisco. In 1876 he purchased the 650-acre Gordon estate, known as the Mayfield Grange Farm, located on the boundary of San Mateo and Santa Clara counties.[10] In the same year he bought 619 acres from the owner of the large Rancho San Francisco Palo Alto, and 290 acres from the same man's Rancho Rincon de San Francisquito. In 1877 his farm's holdings were enlarged almost 160 acres, and in 1882 Stanford bought 1,400 acres from the eccentric Frenchman Peter Coutts, and got the previous owner's cattle and blooded horses for next to nothing.[11] Ultimately, the farm, which Stanford called Palo Alto, Spanish for "high tree," after an old redwood which stood on the banks of the San Francisquito Creek, grew to over 8,000 acres, located between Mayfield and Menlo Park.

Stanford was a serious student of the anatomy of the horses he bred and trained. Illustrative of his mastery of the subject, once in Paris he examined a $250,000 painting of a running horse done by the famous French master Jean Louis Meissonier, and informed the artist that the horse was depicted incorrectly; if it had run the way represented its back would have been broken. Meissonier was at first unwilling or unable to believe this, but the visiting American finally convinced him by explaining the functioning and relative positions of the parts of a horse in motion, whereupon Meissonier vowed that he would never again paint a horse.[12]

After considerable study of the horse's anatomy, Stanford came to the conclusion that the "mechanical structure," that is, the proportions and positions of the bones and muscles, of trotters and runners was the same.[13] This did not mean that a good runner would necessarily make a good trotter, for, he insisted, fine trotting action and willingness to trot were largely the result of selective breeding and careful training.[14]

Stanford's interest in and assiduous studies of horseflesh made him a creditable authority on the subject, and he became so wrapped up in his avocation that his friends said he would drop business in an instant to talk about horses.[15]

Electioneer, the most successful of Stanford's studs, sired a number of world champion trotters. Stanford noticed Electioneer at Charles Backman's Stony Ford Stud Farm, while on a buying spree to get mares for building up his own stock farm. He casually inquired of a number of experts on fine horseflesh what they thought of Electioneer, and found them all against him. He kept his interest in Electioneer to himself and on the following day when he handed Backman a list of the horses he wanted, the "unfavorable" stallion was on the list.[16] His astonished friends sent up a chorus of disapproval; they could not understand a man of Stanford's sophistication about horses buying one that had "heavy shoulders like a cart horse" and "high hindquarters like a steer."[17] Stanford, who later said that he was willing to pay much more than the asking price, conceded that his purchase did look a little risky, but he paid his $12,000 just the same and took the horse home. He recognized that his reputation as a judge of good horseflesh suffered for some time because of this choice: "The high estimate they had placed on my knowledge of form and breeding was greatly diminished, and should Electioneer fail in the stud there will be ever so many I told you so's."[18]

Most of Stanford's mares were of Hambletonian stock, the same from which Electioneer came. Fearful of the consequences of inbreeding, for the first two or three years he seldom used Electioneer for stud until he had expanded his holding of mares of different lines.[19] Meanwhile, he did breed Electioneer to a number of different kinds of mares for scientific purposes, just to study the offspring. Stanford was pleased with the results, and he was confident that with proper training every one of Electioneer's colts could have done the mile in 2:20 or better.[20] Electioneer himself set no records, having gone lame in 1871 at the age of three; yet, in terms of the number of champion trotters he sired, he was truly the "greatest stallion in the world," and at his death was valued at $200,000.[21]

By 1889 the Palo Alto spread was the largest and best-equipped trotting farm in the world. There were 775 horses, plus yearlings, with eight trainers handling seventy-one colts in training. Stanford was paying at the time approximately $6,500 per month in salaries for the help.[22]

The following year the Palo Alto Stock Farm had over seventy trotters in daily training from a herd of twenty stallions and 300 mares.[23] All in all, over 600 trotters were quartered at the farm and another 400 at the branch farm at Vina. The thoroughbreds numbered about 125 at the peak.[24] One visitor at the farm remarked that Stanford's enterprise was so outstanding that if the next best three stock farms in America were rolled into one they would not equal his farm. Stanford, he judged, was "easily the first trotting horse breeder in the world."[25]

Besides its unsurpassed horses, the farm was provided with a blacksmith shop, a wheelwright shop, and its own feed mill. There were fifty paddocks of three acres each for grazing and enough covered shelter for all the horses.[26] Besides its outstanding qualities as a training farm, it was the most complete horsebreeding establishment in the world.[27] Nowhere had the breeding of trotting horses "on scientific and natural principles" been brought so near a state of perfection as at Palo Alto.[28]

Stanford Library

ELECTIONEER, champion trotting sire of the world. Foaled 1868; died 1890.

In the judgment of Charles Marvin, Stanford's trainer, the owner was the most outstanding asset of all. Marvin said he had never known a better judge of form and conformation for speed than his employer, who instinctively discerned undeveloped merit in animals not recognized by most experts until it was clearly demonstrated. This agreed with another appraisal of Stanford's "horsesense," that he was a "born horseman," one of the "best judges of form" in the business.[29] Marvin said his employer was equally skilled in recognizing the disposition and temperament of horses.

Stanford's trotters were so successful that it is less well known that he became a breeder of outstanding thoroughbred runners as well. He hoped to prove that the key to success in trotting was to infuse thoroughbred blood into trotters, believing, as he did, that the trotter inherited its propensity to trot from the thoroughbred.[30] He had nothing but unstinted praise for English race horses, attributing their success to selective breeding, which in turn had produced "better physical organization, better lungs, arteries, veins and vital machinery throughout than any other of his equine brethren," and he looked to thoroughbred blood for the improvement of all classes of horses, especially the race horses that he developed.[31] When he decided to go into horse raising, it was with the intention of excelling, and he retained this determination.[32]

Another reason Stanford's runners were less well known was that many of them at one time or another ran for other stables. Gorgo, one of his better runners, for example, ran for the Hearst stables.[33]

II

Besides theorizing on the breeding of horses, Stanford conceived a number of original ideas on how best to train young horses to develop the fastest stock. His "Palo Alto system," as it was called, was eminently successful and in time was adopted by a number of other stables. The success of Electioneer's foals was a tribute to its merit; he had not sired a single 2:30 performer all the nine years at Stony Ford, but at Palo Alto he threw one champion after another. One adulatory critic of the Palo Alto system praised it as follows:

> The Palo Alto methods of rearing, educating and training, have been extolled, and quite a number of eastern critics laid a great deal of stress on the part that should be awarded them in the summing up. There is not the least chance to deny its efficacy when champion succeeded champion as the years progressed, and winner after winner carried its colors to the front in hotly contested races.[34]

One of the peculiar features of the Palo Alto system was the special care accorded the brood mares. Every detail for the comfort and care of mares and their foals was looked after. Excellent stables, roomy stalls, and capable attendants were provided and special food prepared.[35] It was reported that Stanford's stables were as quiet and orderly as a church, and that loud talking, swearing, harsh language, scolding, and whipping were not allowed.[36] Posted about the stables were rules forbidding these practices.[37] Stanford once ordered a stable hand dismissed for striking a horse.[38] He later explained: "I make it a rule to employ no man about my stables who loses his temper."[39] Few of Stanford's charges knew the meaning of fear.

Training of colts began almost at birth.[40] Beginning the day with a diet of ground and steamed grain, colts were given daily paddock practice and the best in the way of stalls and sheds.[41] Foals were weaned at five months in pairs in order that they might not grow lonesome because of separation from their mothers. At seven months, after being halter broken, they were put to work in Stanford's "kindergarten," another of his ideas. It was generally believed that colts that young could not be trained to trot, but Stanford disagreed, and in the kindergarten, an oval track about eight feet wide and 315 feet long, he proved that he was right. Colts were turned loose on this track, whose turns were banked like a railroad track, and a trainer was stationed at each end to keep them moving. In this way they soon found their track legs and before long found themselves trotting.

Following the kindergarten initiation, colts were promoted to the breaking stables; there they were bitted and harnessed and driven alongside another horse, first on one side and then on the other. After it was thoroughly "double broke," the yearling was placed in the hands of a trainer and was graduated into Stanford's intensive but careful five-rule training. First, jogging was prohibited absolutely, as a waste of time and energy. Next, the amount of work expected of a horse and the distance it was pushed were determined entirely by the condition of the individual horse. Third, abandoning the usual system of pushing horses at less than their full capacity for long distances, Stanford insisted that they be driven at full speed for shorter runs, which he called his "brush" method. Next, exhaustion was to be avoided at all costs; one of Stanford's cardinal rules was that a horse must always go to the stable with full speed left. He explained his reasons:

> I believe in the supreme effort but I do not believe in keeping that up until the horse is exhausted. Let them go to the limit of their speed but do not let them go so far that they will become exhausted. That principle is the foundation upon which the Palo Alto system is based, and I ascribe the greater part of my success in the trotting world to it.[42]

Last, after a horse had acquired his full speed, its distance was to be increased gradually to that which he was expected to go.

Stanford had an uncanny knack for choosing the right man for the job. This is nowhere better illustrated than in his choice of Charles Marvin as his

KINDERGARTEN TRAINING TRACK for young horses, Palo Alto Stock Farm.

trainer. This selection was one of the keys to Stanford's success at the Palo Alto farm. Marvin, who enjoyed an enviable reputation as both trainer and driver before accepting Stanford's offer, in 1878 joined the farm and soon adapted himself to his employer's unorthodox methods of training. His performance soon won him the position of superintendent of trainers and later superintendent of the whole stock farm. Marvin was a tireless and thoroughly-dedicated trainer. His daily routine left no doubt as to his worth. He ate breakfast each morning before five o'clock, and began the day's work with an inspection of the various stables. At daybreak he began work on the track, where he averaged over fifty miles each day in his sulky. After supper he would go to his office and answer a number of letters, which, with directions for the next day's work, ended a hard long day.[43]

Beginning in 1880, Marvin-trained trotters began setting world records. In that year Electioneer's colt Fred Crocker set the record for two-year-olds, initiating a decade of almost unbroken record-setting for the Stanford stables. The following year Wildflower astonished the racing world by lowering the record for two-year-olds to 2:21, which was never approached again until 1888.[44]

In 1882, the year the thoroughbred department was started, Stanford began entering his horses in the major races in Kentucky and the East, with Marvin doing most of the driving. In the late eighties, his successes began with three outstanding horses, all sired by Electioneer. On October 27, 1888, Stanford's filly Sunol trotted the mile in 2:18, for a new world's record. The following year she set the record for three-year-olds at 2:10½, won the classic for four-year-olds the next year, and in 1891 lowered the world record for five-year-olds to 2:08¼.[45] She not only was the world champion trotter, but was the first horse ever to hold the records simultaneously for two, three, four, and five-year-olds. The year 1891, when Sunol won her last championship race, was the zenith for the Palo Alto farm, as its trotters brought home from the summer campaign every trotting record there was. Sunol brought her owner an estimated $41,000 when she was sold, even before she had run her 1891 record race.[46]

Largely owing to Stanford, by late 1891 California led the world in race horse records.[47] An Eastern editor wrote that the "master mind of Palo Alto" held the trotting records from yearling to five-year-olds.[48] Stanford was the master mind of Palo Alto because only there had thoroughbred blood been consistently tried in trotters, and judged by his gratifying successes, his theory had been proven.[49]

The second of Stanford's outstanding trio was Arion. This fine steed's potential had not yet been realized when he was sold in 1891, but much to the relief of Marvin and Stanford, who came late to appreciate his value, the deal fell through and they were able to retain him. On November 10, 1891, Marvin drove him a mile in 2:10¾, breaking Sunol's record.[50] Eighteen years would pass before this time would be lowered, and then by a horse drawing a technically improved sulky that was rated at four seconds faster than those used in the nineties. Arion's successes raised his price tag to $150,000, the highest price ever paid for a trotter, when Malcolm Forbes of Boston decided that he had to have him.[51] Arion was then regarded as the most remarkable trotting horse of all time.[52]

Stanford's third all-star trotter was Palo Alto, named after the farm where he was foaled, on February 15, 1882. Palo Alto was not raced as a young horse; his first competition came in 1886 when he was pitted against aged horses in a series of nine races in the East, where he surprised everyone by winning eight of the nine. In his next eastern competition, in 1890, he again suffered only one reversal. On November 17, 1891, racing in Stockton, Palo Alto set the world's record for stallions, trotting a mile in 2:08¾. On July 21, 1892, this prize-winning horse died of pneumonia and was buried on the farm in the horse cemetery. His death was lamented as a "national loss."[53]

Sunol, Arion, and Palo Alto were Stanford's luminaries, but he bred and trained a substantial number of world championship holders besides these. His complete record makes an impressive catalog, and several of his records were set outside California.[54] Manzanita's records were made in Cleveland, Ohio, and Lexington, Kentucky. Sunol set records in Cleveland, Buffalo, New York, and Chicago.[55] In Chicago, Palo Alto "trotted the fastest heat ever trotted in a race since the world began."[56] Hinda Rose lowered the record for two-year-olds twice, once in Hartford, Connecticut, and once in Lexington. Arion established a new world mark for three-year-olds at Nashville, Tennessee.

Nine of Stanford's world champion trotters were sired by Electioneer, who died in late 1890, after siring 166 colds that did the mile in 2:30 or less, twelve of them trotting it under 2:15.[58] All but two or three of his records were made while Marvin was in charge of training and was driving.[59]

III

A little-known facet of Stanford's stock farm was a series of experiments that contributed materially toward the creation of the motion picture industry. Stanford had long wondered whether a horse propelled himself by pulling with his forefeet or by pushing with his hindfeet, and had tried to answer this question by measuring the depth of the feet of horses in motion. He also had a theory, rejected by all the authorities, that at some point in its gait a trotter had all four feet off the ground, and he sought some means of proving this to himself and to others. He turned to the use of photography to answer these and a number of related questions, and in 1872 hired an English photographer, Eadweard J. Muybridge, to get a picture, if possible, of Occident with all four feet in the air. Muybridge was currently working on the Pacific Coast for the United States government.[60] Because of technological difficulties growing out of the poor state of the art, Muybridge was unable at that time to get the desired pictures; the briefest exposure possible then was one-twelfth of a second, much too long for recording rapid motion.

In 1877, when Muybridge returned to California after a lengthy absence, they took up the experiment again. Using an exposure time of one one-thousandth of a second, he got a still of Occident that showed an instant in his stride when all four feet were indeed off the ground, substantiating Stanford's theory.[61] It was learned also that the same muscles were used in trotting as in running, something Stanford had long wondered about.[62]

The results of this experiment were so successful that Stanford decided to try another, one that would show every position in a horse's stride. To accomplish this he set up a photo studio alongside the track, and authorized Muybridge to purchase all the equipment needed, regardless of expense.[63] Eventually the bill totaled between $40,000 and $50,000.[64] Stanford reasoned that if one camera could be used to capture a still shot of a horse in motion, so could an indefinite number. He suggested this to Muybridge, and before long they had a whole battery of cameras at work.[65]

By 1878 a studio-workshop had been constructed on the west side of Stanford's private track and all preparations had been completed. Twelve cameras were placed in the building at twenty-one inch intervals, with the double shutters of each pointing toward the track. At Stanford's suggestion, the number of cameras was doubled, and they were placed twelve inches apart. Strings were then stretched across the track which would activate the shutters when the horse hit them.

The cameras so aligned did everything but work. The strings stretched, shrank, jarred the cameras, and frightened the horses.[66] Stanford then assigned one of his railroad engineers, John D. Isaacs, an amateur photographer, the task of creating a stable system that would snap all the shutters closed with no jarring. Isaacs arranged the shutters one above and the other

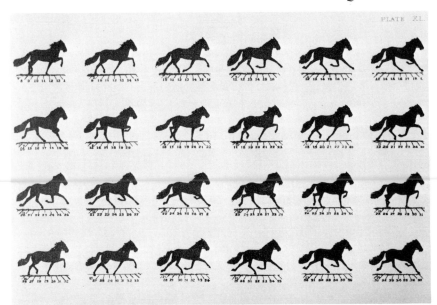

PICTURE OF OCCIDENT showing trotting stride and all four feet off the ground.

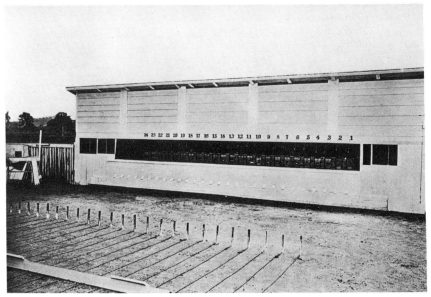

VIEW OF THE 24 CAMERAS IN POSITION.

below the opening through which light was admitted to the lens. They were held by rubber springs, constructed in the form of a ring, with a lifting power of 100 pounds, and were secured by latches which were electronically operated. In order to make the exposures at the proper intervals of time, he constructed a machine with a cylinder having a row of twelve pins arranged spirally. As this cylinder revolved, each pin established a magnetic circuit, with the magnet connected with each of the cameras in succession, and the whole series of exposures was made in the time occupied by a single complete stride of the horse.[67] A wire was then placed across the track so that one wheel of the sulky completed an electric circuit, which activated the cameras.[68] Thus Isaacs built the devices upon which much of Muybridge's later reputation was based.[69]

So much for the camera arrangement. There remained yet the problem of measuring the distance each hoof was from the ground at any given instant. This was solved by building a wooden fence or background about fifty feet long and fifteen feet high which was covered with white muslin and subdivided by heavy black lines into twelve-inch vertical spaces. About eighteen inches out from its base was a board twelve inches high on which were drawn lateral lines four inches apart to show how high the horse raised its foot from the ground. A special rubber roadway was constructed in front of this board, with wires crossing under it every twelve inches. These were so exposed at one edge of the roadway that the wheel of the sulky would depress them as it passed over and each wire would then release the shutter of a camera.[70]

By the summer of 1878 Muybridge had come to see the value of his experiments, and in July copyrighted in his own name a series of pictures of horses in motion. Unfortunately, Stanford raised no objections at that time to Muybridge's claims to originality and ownership; if anything, he encouraged the photographer. Muybridge then devised a crude but effective makeshift projector that would show a series of stills in close succession and in the fall of 1879 the world's first home movies were shown at the Stanfords' home in Palo Alto.[71] Muybridge made about two dozen positives in silhouette and printed them on a large glass disk that revolved so that the pictures passed in rapid succession a slot in front of a projection camera. On the back of his cameras were condensing lenses from which an oxygen light could pass to the screen. The pictures thus shown in motion further verified Stanford's contention that at one point in the stride of a trotter all four feet were off the ground.[72]

In 1879 Muybridge concluded his investigations, and in 1881 he copyrighted under the title *The Attitudes of Animals in Motion* 200 sheets of photographs. In the spring of the same year he turned over to Stanford a bound set of all the pictures he had taken at the farm, accompanied by a letter which said: "Sir: Herewith please find the photographs illustrating *The Attitudes of Animals in Motion*, executed by me according to your instructions, at Palo Alto in 1878 and 1879."[73] This statement proved devasting to

Author's Collection

EADWEARD MUYBRIDGE, photographer who performed Stanford's photographic experiments.

Muybridge when he later assumed credit for the idea of the photographic experiments with horses. Afterwards he said that the whole idea was his and that he won Stanford's cooperation because he needed the latter's farm and horses.[74]

A number of writers traced Stanford's interest in proving that at some point in its stride a trotter has all four feet off the ground to a bet he made with two wealthy Californians, James R. Keene and Frederick MacCrellish. According to this myth—it is no more than that—he backed his opinion with $25,000 cash and hired Muybridge to take instantaneous photographs to prove it. Muybridge experienced considerable difficulty, but finally got the desired pictures confirming Stanford's theory and winning his employer the sizeable stakes.[75]

No one has yet brought any evidence to substiantiate this story, dubbed by one careful student of the problem of romantic "post-mortem press-agent work," and there is considerable reason to question its authenticity.[76] In the first place, in 1872 MacCrellish and Stanford were hardly in a position to be making a friendly wager, even if Stanford were a betting man, which he was not, since the former was using the editorial columns of his paper, the *Alta California*, as a sounding board for his battle against Stanford and his part-ners over the "Goat Island grab."[77] The story also confuses the chronology; in 1872 Muybridge failed to get the pictures he wanted, and from 1875 to 1877 was out of the state, following his acquittal for the murder of his wife's lover.[78]

Even if the general account of how the experiment was initiated were fairly accurate, in its broad outlines, it is highly improbable that such a bet would have still been on five years later.

An even more fanciful version of this episode was invented by Thomas A. Edison, who had Stanford, a "crank" on the subject of trotters, arguing with Muybridge, his guest at the farm, when the famous photographer "con-ceived an ingenious plan to settle the dispute." He immediately set up a series of cameras and snapped a "complete photographic record of the minutest de-tails of a horse in actual motion."[79] Muybridge thus had the satisfaction of using his photographs to win his argument with Stanford, demonstrating that "he had a better eye for trotting horses than Senator Stanford," and putting California on the map as a prominent center of motion picture progress.[80]

Meanwhile, Stanford commissioned his longtime friend Dr. J. D. B. Stillman to organize the results of the photographic experiments and publish them in book form. In 1882 they published the *Horse in Motion*, with Stillman as author and Stanford as publisher. In the preface, which he wrote, Stanford claimed as his the original idea of the experiments:

> I have for a long time entertained the opinion that the accepted theory of the relative positions of the feet of horses in rapid motion was erroneous. I also believed that the camera could be utilized to demonstrate that fact, and by

instantaneous pictures show the actual position of the limbs at each instant of the stride.[81]

He went on to explain that he had then hired Muybridge to carry out his plans. It was not intended that the results should be published, but afterwards, realizing the value and interest to others of these experiments, he asked his friend Stillman to publish them.

The whole history of the experiments, from their conception to completion of the first moving picture, is delineated by Stillman in the appendix to their volume. In it he underscored Stanford's account of the matter, insisting that the original idea of photographing a still of Occidental in motion was Stanford's as well as the decision to expand the experiment to a series of shots capturing the complete stride of the trotter in action.

Stillman's duties on occasion carried him beyond merely publishing the results of another man's experiments. In order to study the whole subject of the locomotive machinery of the horse, he dissected two of Stanford's animals and analyzed the bone and muscle structure.

In the fall of 1881, when the famous French artist Meissonier did Stanford's portrait, he showed some interest in Stanford's photographic experiments, so Stillman and the picture collection were summoned to Paris.[82] The moving pictures, subsequently shown to the most eminent artists, scientists, and literati of Paris, became the latest topic of conversation among the fashionable and learned in the European capital.[83]

The Stanford-Stillman book was published by James R. Osgood and Company of Boston, with the understanding that Stanford would assume all financial liability in the event of loss. Stillman, overly-optimistic about its potential market, ordered the first edition of 2,000 copies run off immediately and then confidently placed an order for a second edition of 3,000 copies. This he lived to regret; too many copies had already been printed, and, to make matters worse, it was priced at ten dollars per copy, placing it out of reach of all but a few. Finally, the name of the photographer was nowhere mentioned on the title page, though Stillman in the appendix did give Muybridge full credit for all the photographs used.[84] Muybridge did not view this as a mere oversight; he believed that his name alone belonged there and that his work had been plagiarized and his copyright violated.

When the publishing house applied for an English copyright, only Stillman's name was mentioned; even Stanford's had been omitted. Stillman insisted that Stanford's name appear, since it was under his authorization that the compiling and writing had been done.[85] Stillman explained to the publisher that all the pictures were taken at the order of Stanford, who paid all the expenses and furnished all the apparatus and material. He insisted, too, that Muybridge gave him the copies from which the plates were made knowing how they were to be used.[86]

A week later Osgood wrote to Stillman asking Stanford to assume all responsibility in the event of a lawsuit by Muybridge, a superfluous move, since Stanford had already agreed to indemnify the company against losses arising out of a Muybridge suit.[87] Muybridge by that time had claimed English as well as American copyright.

As expected, Muybridge brought suit, one against Osgood and another naming Stanford, in which he demanded $50,000 damages.[88] Stanford, confident of victory, showed little concern, knowing it was a simple matter for him to show that Muybridge was merely acting as his agent in the photographic experiments. Muybridge himself had made the mistake of telling others that he at first did not believe it possible to get the pictures that Stanford sought but that Stanford had insisted that he make the attempt.

Stanford attributed Muybridge's claims to vanity: "I think the fame we have given him, has turned his head."[89] In much the same vein, a motion picture historian concluded that it was "in the ardor of his new pride" that Muybridge brought suit against Stanford and that he was a "little dizzy with this sudden acclaim and attention from persons in high station."[90]

In his suit against the publisher, Muybridge sought a court injunction preventing the sale of the book and ordering that all copies on hand be turned over to him.[91] He argued that he owned the copyright on most of the pictures used by Stillman; in fact, Stillman's whole book was little more than commentary and description of his photographs, converted by Stillman and Stanford into "piratical illustrations." The offended photographer conceded Stillman's point that he had given him permission to use the pictures in this way, but insisted that the publication was to have the name Muybridge somewhere in the title.

In its brief, Osgood and Company traced the conception of the photographic experiments to Stanford, and argued that he had employed Muybridge to do his bidding, had supplied the photographer with all necessary supplies, had retained supporting laborers, and had paid the photographer's room and board at the farm. Furthermore, out of good will toward Muybridge, Stanford not only allowed him to take out the disputed copyright in his own name, but had even paid for the copyright fees. Thus Stanford, not Muybridge, was the "equitable owner thereof."

Throughout, Osgood agents stressed the fact that they acted merely as the agent of Stanford in the whole business of publishing the book in question, and that so far as they knew, Stanford was the legal owner of all the materials which they had used.

The attorneys for the defendants petitioned the court to take the deposition of Isaacs, Stanford's engineer who had solved Muybridge's camera problems. Isaacs' testimony destroyed Muybridge's case, and the attorneys for the plaintiff threw up their hands and the cases were dismissed.[92] A number of shopworkers who had seen Isaacs' work on the camera arrangement volunteered their depositions as well. As Isaacs later said: "You know the old employees would fight anyone who was trying to hurt the old Governor."[93] Muybridge lost both suits.

The book never sold well, and in the summer of 1882 Osgood wrote Stillman that the slow sales were a disappointment and that it would take a long time just to get rid of the first edition. The following January the publisher, conceding that they had all overestimated the public demand for the book, lamented that sales had almost stopped.[94] The books that did not sell were remaindered and eventually found their way into the basement of the Stanford mansion in San Francisco, where they were destroyed in the 1906 fire.[95] Apparently Stanford had bought them all.

Stanford had wanted the price of the book kept low to encourage sales, but the cost of publication made this impossible.[96] Like many a disappointed author, he blamed poor publicity for their lack of success; occasionally, he said, he met people who were interested in getting a copy of the book, but were unable to find it in any bookstore.[97] The imbroglio with Osgood became so involved that there was some rumor of a Stanford suit against Osgood, but in late 1883, writing from Paris, Stanford advised against it, at least until his return home. His health was failing—he had "received a little setback"—and his wife was anxious to stay in Europe a bit longer.[98] Stanford said that he preferred to drop the whole affair with Osgood.

Historians of the motion picture business have long acknowledged the Palo Alto stock farm experiments as the beginnings of the industry, but disagreement continues as to whether Stanford or Muybridge should be credited with conceiving the idea. In any case, Muybridge became a celebrity overnight, and, following a private exhibition of what he called his "zoogyroscope," at the San Francisco Art Association, where he gave public lectures every night for a whole week, he was invited to lecture across the United States, on the continent, and in England. In Europe he demonstrated his moving pictures to the best artists and scientists of the day.[99]

Perhaps the greatest long-range significance of the Stanford-Muybridge experiments upon the motion picture industry was that they stimulated work on movies at the Edison laboratory.[100] One historian of the industry stated, poetically: "Daguerre, a Frenchman, rocked the cradle of photography, Muybridge, an Englishman taught it to run, and Edison, an American, gave it wings."[101] Thus Stanford played a significant part in the birth of an industry that changed the face "not merely of a continent but of a planet."[102]

Some writers either play down or neglect altogether Stanford's part; one historian, for example, makes him little more than the photographer's helper.[103] Others give him partial credit, like Fairman Rogers, who, after making a very early zoetrope of galloping horses, said that the idea had already occurred to Stanford and Muybridge, but he too made Stanford the photographer's assistant.[104]

Author's Collection

BRONZE TABLET placed in the inner quad at Stanford University in the presence of many leaders of the motion picture industry.

Another historian, on the other hand, entirely debunked Muybridge's part in the whole affair: "Muybridge . . . had nothing to do with the motion picture at all; and, in truth, but a very small part, if any, in the creative work of the hallowed race horse incident."[105] He attributed the myth of Muybridge's value to a backward reflection of his later fame—fame that rested upon the ideas and inventions of a number of men. This writer believed that the idea that a horse at one point had all his feet off the ground was the "solemn and somewhat lone assertion" of Stanford.[106]

On balance, it seems fair to conclude that Stanford played a more important part in the whole business than he has generally been credited with. He did conceive the idea of getting a picture of Occident with all four feet off the ground, he conceived the idea of placing a series of cameras together to catch the full stride of a horse in motion, he provided all the equipment his photographer would need, and he made a number of helpful suggestions along the way, even going so far as to assign a railroad engineer to the project to assist Muybridge with technical difficulties.[107] To Muybridge was given the responsibility of using his incomparable technological skills to carry out the instructions of his employer.

IV

Stanford's main purpose in continuing his expensive avocation of breeding and training horses was to develop a better horse. With a businessman's sense of values, he recognized the economic promise of an improved horse. Improving the quality of 13,000,000 horses, the number then at work in the United States, made good sense as an economic proposition.[108]

On the stock farm, as in every undertaking where he employed laborers, Stanford enjoyed an enviable record of good relations with his workers. He employed on the average about 150 workers, two-thirds Caucasians and the rest Chinese, and he paid from thirty dollars to $250 per month wages. Workers were boarded by the employer, and Mrs. Stanford, as one of her many philanthropic ventures, established a school for boys and a kindergarten for girls at Menlo Park, where the children of farm hands could attend if the parents wished. Even weekly church services were provided on the farm.[109] Superintendent Charles Marvin said that Stanford was both loved and admired by his employees and that they considered their employer considerate and just.[110] Reminiscent of the Biblical story of the master and the workers in his vineyard, when Stanford discovered on one occasion that the trainers who handled the yearlings were paid less than those handling the older stock, he directed his brother-in-law Ariel Lathrop, his business manager, to increase their pay to the same given the others, explaining: "Those men are entitled to the same wages that the others are getting, because I consider it essential that colts receiving their first handling and education should be in the hands of men just as skillful and competent as the men handling colts further advanced, and I want those men to receive the same pay as the others."[111] When told that he could get better men in Kentucky for less money, Stanford said he was satisfied with the men he had, and insisted that their pay be raised. This was good for employee-employer relations, but it was unorthodox business practice. Stories of Stanford's attempts to mold a happy, contented work force are legion in number, and even if some are exaggerated or apocryphal, the central truth that his relations with his employees were generally cordial is indisputable.

On the whole, the Palo Alto stock farm was a successful business venture. Although it was not started as a place to breed and train horses with an eye to making a profit, Stanford's business manager said that it paid the best returns of his various enterprises. He could have paid his workers less, but his matchless successes at breeding and racing allowed him to reap rich profits without doing so.

As Stanford grew older, especially after the loss of his only son, his sentimental attachment to the stock farm bordered on the unnatural.[112] There he stored mementos of earlier years, among them the first carriage he and his wife ever owned, a "rockaway, cumbrous, sway-backed, old-fashioned" rig that had carried them about Sacramento long before the transcontinental railroad was completed.[113]

In his private stable, Stanford kept the mounted skeleton of Occidental, his first fast horse. No horse was ever killed at the farm except to put it out of pain; and when brood mares grew too old for breeding, they were retired to green pastures and given the same special care as when they were valuable youngsters. It was recorded that Dame Winnie, one of Stanford's favorites, died with a pillow of straw under her head.

The horse that was his special object of affection was Cheatem, his son's pet. When the boy died, this horse was moved from the big barn to the private stables, where he was given his own quarters. His retirement was complete; no duty of any character whatsoever was imposed upon him. At the elder Stanford's death, the sixteen-year-old object of veneration, now turned white, was still eating the choicest grains and rolling in the richest paddocks any horse had probably every enjoyed.[114]

At the end of 1891, Marvin, suddenly, silently, and rather mysteriously, left the Palo Alto farm, accepting a similar position in Franklin, Pennsylvania, and later in Lexington, Kentucky. Neither he nor anyone else ever publicly offered a convincing explanation for this abrupt change after fourteen years with Stanford, but it was generally believed that he left through a misunderstanding with Ariel Lathrop.[115] If this was the case, it was not the first, nor would it be the last time that Stanford would have difficulties with his combination business manager and brother-in-law.

Marvin's leaving marked the beginning of the end for Stanford trotters.[116] When he left, the farm held world's records in seven classes.[117] Two years later Stanford died and the farm continued quickly on its downward path, until in 1903 it was closed as a breeding establishment. Stanford's original intention had thus been denied: "I have so planned that long after I shall have crumbled into dust the breeding establishment founded by me at Palo Alto shall endure."[118]

As late as 1945 a breeding farm was still maintained on the Stanford campus, but today all that remains of the farm's glorious past are a number of the original buildings, those which survived the 1906 earthquake, and a riding school, having about 120 horses in its stables, two dozen owned by the university, the rest privately owned and boarded there.[119]

1. *California Mail Bag*, V (August, 1874), xii.

2. *Ibid.*

3. Bancroft, *Stanford*, 125.

4. New York *Herald*, December 22, 1890. New York *Spirit of the Times*, CXVIII (December 28, 1889), 803.

5. Sacramento *Union*, May 20, 1870. Record set in 1873, in Clark, *Stanford*, 343.

6. Julia C. Altrocchi, *The Spectacular San Franciscans* (New York, 1949), 183. San Francisco *Chronicle*, July 14, 1873.

7. Altrocchi, *San Franciscans*, 183-184.

8. Sausalito *Herald*, quoted in *ibid.*, 184.

9. Archibald Treat, "The Stanfords and their Golden Key," unpublished manuscript (San Francisco, 1937), 23.

10. David Starr Jordan incorrectly dates this purchase in 1870. *Days of a Man*, I, 369. Bertha Berner, whose facts are often unreliable on things that happened before 1884, when she went to work for Mrs. Stanford, confused things even more by making the purchase of the Warm Springs property follow the construction of the San Francisco home. *Mrs. Stanford*, 20. The correct order is: Warm Springs, 1869, San Francisco home built, 1874-1876, and the Gordon estate purchased, 1876.

11. Coutts' real name was Paulin Caperon. Miriam A. de Ford, "Palo Alto's Mysterious Frenchman," *Calif. Hist. Soc. Quar.*, XXXIII (1954), 171, 173. Coutts was said to have been a paymaster during the Franco-Prussian War, and left Paris with a sizeable payroll for French troops. He took the money and his children and their governess to California. There he changed his name, for "political reasons," and with a change in government in France he later returned home. Berner, *Mrs. Stanford*, 53-54.

12. Unidentified newspaper editorial entitled "How Governor Stanford Converted Meissonier, The Great Horse Painter Finds that he has been in error as to the Horse all his Life." Dateline, Paris, June 26, 1881. In Stanford collection.

13. Bancroft, *Stanford*, 126.

14. *Ibid.*

15. Treat, "Golden Key," 7.

16. New York *Herald*, December 22, 1890.

17. *Ibid.* Joseph Cairn Simpson, "Horses of California," *Sunset Magazine*, VII (May, 1901), 12.

18. Simpson, "Horses of California," 14.

19. New York *Herald*, December 22, 1890.

20. *Ibid.*

21. Bancroft, *Stanford*, 138. Simpson, "Horses of California," 14. Albany [New York] *Press*, January, 1891, in SFS, II, 3.

22. New York *Sportsman*, February 9, 1889.

23. Charles Marvin, *Training the Trotting Horse* (New York, 1891), 90, in Clark, *Stanford*, 350.

24. San Francisco *Examiner*, June 21, 1893.

25. Marvin, *Trotting Horse*, 90, in Clark, *Stanford*, 350.

26. Bancroft, *Stanford*, 137.

27. Bancroft, *History*, VII,58, n. 4.

28. Bancroft, *Stanford*, 127.

29. Simpson, "Horses of California," 16.

30. New York *Herald*, December 22, 1890.

31. New York *Spirit of the Times*, CXVIII (December 28, 1889), 803.

32. Bancroft, *Stanford*, 126.

33. New York *Herald*, December 22, 1890.

34. Simpson, "Horses of California," 16.

35. San Francisco *Examiner*, June 21, 1893.

36. Bancroft, *Stanford*, 126.

37. New York *Herald*, December 22, 1890.

38. Treat, "Golden Key," 8.

39. New York *Herald*, December 22, 1890.

40. Bancroft, *History*, VII, 58, n. 4.

41. John S. Hittell, *The Commerce and Industries of the Pacific* (San Francisco, 1882), 272-273.

42. Marvin, *Trotting Horse*, in Clark, *Stanford*, 354.

43. Bancroft, *Stanford*, 137.

44. Unidentified newspaper clipping, SFS, XXV, 7.

45. San Francisco *Examiner*, November 10, 1889.

46. Unidentified newspaper clipping, SFS, XXII, 5. New York *Recorder*, December, 1891, in SFS, XXII, 58.

47. *The Breeder and Sportsman*, November 21, 1891.

48. New York *Herald*, November, 1891, in SFS, XVII, 91.

49. Boston *Courier*, May, 1891, in SFS, II, 81.

50. New York *Spirit of the Times*, October, 1891, in SFS, XVII, 90.

51. New York *World*, January 13, 1892.

52. *Ibid.*

53. [no city] *Spirit of the Times*, clipping in SFS, XXII, 62. San Francisco *Examiner*, July 23, 1892.

54. Yearlings: Hinda Rose, November 5, 1881, 2:36½; Norlaine, November 12, 1887, 2:31½; Bell Bird, October 21, 1891, 2:26¼; and Adbell, September 27, 1894, 2:23. Two-Year-Olds: Fred Crocker, November 20, 1880, 2:25¼; Wildflower, October 22, 1881, 2:21; Sunol, October 27, 1888, 2:18; and Arion, November 10, 1891; 2:10¾. Three-Year-Olds: Hinda Rose, October 10, 1883, 2:19½; Sunol, November 9, 1889, 2:10½; and Arion, November 12, 1892, 2:10½: Four-Year-Olds: Bonita, October 11, 1883, 2:18¾; Sallie Benton, December 13, 1884, 2:17¾; Manzanita, September 3, 1886, 2:16; and Sunol, August 23, 1890, 2:10½. Five-Year-Olds: Sunol, October 20, 1891, 2:08¼. Stallions: Palo Alto, November 17, 1891, 2:08¼. Geldings: Azote, September 5, 1895, 2:04¾. Simpson, "Horses of California," 20. See Bancroft, *Stanford*, 137-139, 141-143, for other notables not mentioned here.

55. Chicago *Tribune*, August 24, 1890.

56. *Ibid.*, August 23, 1890. San Francisco *Examiner*, August 23, 1890.

57. Simpson, "Horses of California," 20.

58. By 1887 Electioneer had sired 294 foals at Palo Alto. Bancroft, *Stanford*, 141. See "Electioneer's Honor Roll," in *Palo Alto Stock Farm Eleventh Annual Catalogue* (San Francisco, 1894), 4-8.

59. Simpson, "Horses of California," 18.

60. Terry Ramsaye, *A Million and One Nights, A History of the Motion Picture* (2 vols., New York, 1926), I, 24ff.

61. San Francisco *Alta California*, August 3, 1877. See this issue for Muybridge letter.

62. New York *Spirit of the Times*, CXVIII (December 28, 1889), 803.

63. J. D. B. Stillman, *Horse in Motion* (Boston, 1882), 124.

64. Ramsaye, *Million and One Nights*, I, 37. San Francisco *Call*, May 5, 1880.

65. Archibald Treat to Howard Tibbitts, Southern Pacific Railroad photographer, January 20, 1936. Ramsaye, *Million and One Nights*, I, 34.

66. Ramsaye, *Million and One Nights*, I, 34.

67. Stillman, *Horse in Motion*, 124ff.

68. *Ibid.*, 124.

69. Ramsaye, *Million and One Nights*, I, 37-39.

70. H. C. Peterson, "The Birthplace of the Motion Picture," *Sunset Magazine*, XXXV (1915), 913. Peterson was Director of the Stanford University Museum. *Scientific American*, XXXIX (October 19, 1878), 241.

71. Eadweard Muybridge, *The Human Figure in Motion* (London, 1901), 7.

72. Treat to Tibbitts, January 20, 1936.

73. Muybridge to Stanford, May 15, 1881, in preface to bound volume of pictures. In Bender Room, Stanford Library.

74. Eadweard Muybridge, *Animal Locomotion* (Philadelphia, 1887), 3. Muybridge, *Animals in Motion*, in Clark, *Stanford*, 370.

75. Leslie Wood, *The Miracle of the Movies* (London, 1947), 67-68. Ramsaye, *Million and One Nights*, I, 22-24.

76. Peterson, "Birthplace," 909-915.

77. Although highly successful with his fast horses, there is no evidence that Stanford ever gambled on them. On one occasion, when Occident won a $2,000 cash prize, awarded by the State Agricultural Society, Stanford returned the winnings to the Society. Edward Curtis, *Two California Sketches: William Watt and Leland Stanford* (San Francisco, 1880), 31.

78. Wood, *Miracle of the Movies*, 67. Ramsaye tells the whole story in considerable detail in *Million and One Nights*, I, 24-33.

79. Quoted in Edward Van Zile, *That Marvel - The Movie* (New York, 1923), 29-30.

80. *Ibid.*, 30.

81. Stillman, *Horse in Motion*, iii.

82. Unidentified newspaper clipping in Stanford collection.

83. *Scientific American Supplement*, XIII (January 28, 1882), 5,058-5,059.

84. Stillman, *Horse in Motion*, 123.

85. Stillman to Osgood, April 10, 1882.

86. *Ibid.*

87. Osgood to Stillman, April 18, 1882.

88. Stanford to Stillman, October 23, 1882.

89. *Ibid.*

90. Ramsaye, *Million and One Nights*, I, 41-42.

91. Transcript of lawsuit *Muybridge* versus *Osgood*, in Stanford collection.

92. Ramsaye, *Million and One Nights*, I, 41. Treat, "Golden Key," 6.

93. Treat, "Golden Key," 6.

94. Osgood to Stillman, January 4, 1883.

95. Peterson, "Birthplace," 914.

96. Stanford to Stillman, July 28, 1882.

97. *Ibid.*, January 5, 1883.

98. *Ibid.*, October 25, 1883.

99. Peterson, "Birthplace," 914. *Scientific American*, XLII (June 5, 1880), 353. San Francisco *Call*, May 5, 1880.

100. Gordon Hendricks, *The Edison Motion Picture Myth* (Berkeley, 1961), 4.

101. Van Zile, *That Marvel*, 28.

102. *Ibid.*, 29.

103. John R. Betts, "The Technological Revolution and the Rise of Sports, 1850-1900," *Miss. Vall. Hist. Rev.*, XL (1953-1954), 249-250.

104. Article in *Art Interchange*, by Fairman Rogers, reprinted in *Scientific American Supplement*, VIII (August 9, 1879), 2,991.

105. Ramsaye, *Million and One Nights*, I, 21.

106. *Ibid.*, 22. Hittell, *Commerce and Industry*, 431.

107. Van Zile, *That Marvel*, 29.

108. New York *Spirit of the Times*, CXVIII (December 28, 1889), 803.

109. Bancroft, *Stanford*, 144.

110. Clark, *Stanford*, 351-352.

111. Quoted in *ibid.*, 352.

112. San Francisco *Examiner*, June 22, 1893.

113. *Ibid.*

114. *Ibid.*

115. New York *Herald*, December, 1891, and Pennsylvania *Leader*, December, 1891, in SFS, XVII, 102, 105.

116. Simpson, "Horses of California," 18-19, for a sketch of his post-Palo Alto career.

117. Robert Bonner telegram to Stanford, October 21, 1891. In Clark, *Stanford*, 361.

118. Minnesota *Tribune*, January, 1892, in SFS, XXII, 49.

119. Tom R. Underwood, ed. *Thoroughbred Racing and Breeding* (New York, 1945), 48.

CHAPTER IX

CALIFORNIA WINE KING

The catholicity of Leland Stanford's interests is nowhere better exemplified than in his endeavors to make California the wine capital of the world. While building and operating the Central Pacific Railroad, serving as president of the Southern Pacific system, sitting in the United States Senate, running the nation's finest stock farm, and busily engaged in founding, constructing, and helping to administer his university, he set himself the task of outdoing French vineyardists in producing the best table wines in the world.

Stanford's first experience with winegrowing came in the early seventies near the resort town of Warm Springs, near San Jose.[1] The town of Warm Springs was originally part of the 9,000-acre Agua Caliente Rancho, granted to Fulgencio and Valentine Higuera by Nicholas Guiterrez in 1836.[2] The springs from which the town derives its name lay about two miles to the east, at an elevation of 350 feet. From them there flowed daily 50,000 gallons of water with a high soda content and a constant temperature of ninety to ninety-eight degrees fahrenheit. The salutary springs were once used by Indians and later by Spanish travelers and visitors.[3]

Sometime around 1850 one Clement Colombet bought 640 acres of land surrounding the springs and opened a hotel.[4] This building had a number of ground floor rooms for bathing, through which the spring waters flowed. One of the springs was channeled into an artificial lake. By 1865 this popular resort had expanded to ten buildings, a large stable, and a winery. The vineyard alone covered seventy-five acres and contained several varieties of choice French grapes.[5]

From 1855 until 1868, Warm Springs was one of the most popular suburban resorts in California, and the names of most of the pioneers and leading families in the state appeared in the register. The hot sulphur water attracted the "fashionable, frivolous, wealthy and leisurely, as well as the invalided," from all portions of the state.[6] Almost 200 of California's "elite" visited the resort daily during the tourist season.[7] The first "grand ball" of the resort's history was given on July 29, 1858, when the lodge was already known as "one of the gayest and most fashionable watering places in the State."[8]

An earthquake in 1868 caused extensive damage to a number of buildings and the hotel was closed. The spa period in Warm Springs history had come to an end.[9] In the following spring, Alfred A. Cohen of Alameda bought the property for about $112,000 and repaired and renovated many of the major buildings, with the intention of reopening the resort.[10] William C. Ralston of the Bank of California became interested in the property and joined Cohen in extending an invitation to Stanford to visit the springs with them. Stanford at once fell in love with the property and offered Cohen twice what he had paid for it. Needless to say, Cohen sold.[11]

Stanford's older brother Josiah moved to Warm Springs in January, 1870, and began operating the farm as a hay, grain, and cattle ranch. The Stanford brothers sold all the grapes produced the first year, but the following year they began experimenting with wine. The gravelly soil, much like that in the best wine districts of France, allowed the vines to send their taproots deep into subsurface water.[12] Starting in 1872 Josiah converted most of the crop into wine, inaugurating a long-range enlargement of the old winery.[13]

BUILDINGS ON THE WARM SPRINGS RANCH.

Weibel Winery

In 1874 Leland Stanford's interest in the Warm Springs property revived. During an epidemic of scarlet fever in San Francisco his wife and son lived at the farm for two months, and he spent the weekends with them. He became very much attached to the place, and was greatly interested in the fine quality of the wines produced there.[14]

Afterward, Stanford bought a home in Menlo Park, where he also raised grapes for wines, but he seems to have preferred Warm Springs. He once suggested to Josiah that they trade homes, but Josiah and his family also preferred Warm Springs, so they stayed. Leland's nephew, Josiah W. Stanford, later surmised that if his father and uncle had exchanged residences Stanford University would have been built in Warm Springs rather than Palo Alto.[15]

In 1876 Stanford's Warm Springs property boasted 100,000 vines, over 60,000 of which were bearing. With this grape crop he was able to produce about 50,000 gallons of wine per year.[16] Besides grapes, the 660-acre farm produced various fruits, including oranges.

Leland gave his brother title to the Warm Springs property in November, 1886, and when Josiah died in early 1890 ownership passed to his son Josiah W. Stanford.[17] During the decade from 1890 to 1900, Josiah W. Stanford developed the place in every way, producing hay, barley, beef, and 250,000 gallons of wine per year. Meanwhile, his Uncle Leland and family continued to visit the resort.[18]

II

Encouraged by his brother Josiah's success, and convinced that California was the world's best wine country, Stanford embarked upon a much more extensive wine enterprise in Tehama County, along the upper Sacramento River.[19] In 1881 he purchased a tract of land near the small town of Vina, and continued to add to his holdings until he owned 55,000 acres of some of the richest land in the state. With a long growing season and almost no chance of frost, this land promised to be what he needed to produce the champion wines he had longed dreamed of making.[20]

Peter Lassen, a Danish immigrant who settled in California in 1840, owned much of what became the Vina ranch. In the mid-1840's, Lassen planted the first wine grapes on the Vina property, and in the early twentieth century his vines were still bearing on the vast Stanford ranch.[21]

Henry Gerke bought a large portion of the Lassen ranch in 1852 and planted a number of choice foreign vines to supplement the domestic varieties planted by the previous owner. He gradually increased his holdings to seventy-five acres, and by 1880, just before Stanford bought the property, Gerke had a wine cellar with a capacity of 100,000 gallons; in a single good year alone he was able to produce 90,000 gallons of wine. His white wine, claret, reisling, angelica, sherry, and brandy were very popular in San Francisco.

The town of Vina was laid out by Gerke, and when the Central Pacific Railroad built a branch to the small town in 1871 the settlement's future was guaranteed. Gerke gradually sold off much of his extensive property, and in 1881 what remained, including the wine business, was purchased by Joseph S. Cone of Red Bluff.[22]

For a number of years Leland Stanford had been interested in the Vina property of Henry Gerke, and in 1881 he began buying his dream ranch.[23] Stanford's agent, Nicholas Smith of the Southern Pacific Railroad Company, made five purchases for him in that year, three of them from Joseph Cone.[24] These purchases subsequently caused much embarrassment to both Cone and Stanford. The 1883 Committee on Corporations publicized the fact that Cone was a state railroad commissioner the year he sold this land to Stanford; moreover, he bought the lands and then resold them immediately at a handsome profit of $100,000.[25] On December 13, 1881, Nicholas Smith deeded to Leland Stanford 9,524 acres for $376,853.[26] The investigating Committee concluded that Cone's wealth was greatly augmented in this case by "extraordinary and unusual facilities afforded by the railroad officers."[27]

The three men involved in the transaction, Cone, Smith, and Stanford, were old friends, and the land deals made may have had no relation at all to the railroad. This of course they could not prove. While any adverse judgment against them on charges of indirect bribery must be based upon a knowledge of their motives, which is impossible to gain, at best such a transaction was of questionable discretion, involving, as it did, a public official.

Between the years 1881-1885, Stanford made fifty additional purchases of land in the surrounding areas.[28] Before he was finished extending his domain he owned all the original Lassen tract, plus more.[29] Of the 55,000 acres he eventually owned, 20,000 were arable; the rest was used for stock grazing.[30]

One of Stanford's purposes in buying the Vina ranch was to retire to the country and spend his declining years working the soil.[31] Living in Sacramento, San Francisco, Palo Alto, or traveling about the continent did not allow him the leisure of living near the land as he wished. Perhaps the whole scheme was a means of returning to his boyhood in rural New York, but whatever the case, his other interests made farm life at Vina an impossibility. Nevertheless, the foundations were laid for a $1,000,000 residence, but the death of Leland Junior in 1884 changed the family plans. The Stanfords stayed at Vina for brief visits, but never resided there or built a home there for themselves. They generally preferred their plush railroad car to the rooms set aside for them in the main ranch house.[32]

Stanford concentrated more and more on developing the farm's wine-producing potential. In 1880, on one of their many trips to Europe, the Stanfords visited some of the world's leading vineyards and wineries. Convinced that the average California wine was better than the average European wine, he decided to produce a wine that was superior to anything Europe could produce. All that was lacking, he thought, was the technical know-how of the European growers and producers.[33] To get the experience and skills needed, he simply "bought" a number of French peasants who were skilled wine workers and brought them to California. By the late eighties there was a sizeable colony of French workers at Vina. They had a large house to themselves, retained their native language and customs, and lived much as they would have in France, except at Vina their wages were much higher.[34]

By the end of January, 1882, Stanford had begun a 1,000-acre extension of the old Gerke vineyard. He ordered the construction of an elaborate irrigation system, hired William H. Smith, the brother of his friend Nick, to manage the new ranch, and set aside $300,000 for immediate improvements.[35]

Stanford began bringing in cuttings from the San Gabriel Valley and added 600,000 vines in 1882 alone. By the end of that year the Vina ranch had 1,000 acres in vines, and was already the largest vineyard in the world, yet in 1883 still another 1,500 acres of vines were added.[36] In 1888 Stanford had a total of 3,575 acres of vines on the Vina ranch, with 2,860,000 vines set out.[37]

The vines that Stanford planted first included Berger, Blaue Elben, Charbonneau, Malvoisie, and Zinfandel.[38] By 1887 the Vina winery was producing over twenty different kinds of wine.[39] By 1890 almost two dozen other varieties had been added at Vina, with the manager's hopes of producing the best table wine in the world now pinned on the Berger grape.[40]

Before 1887 Vina grapes were sold to other companies, but in that year the first were processed and stored on the ranch.[41] By that time most of the Stanford vines were beginning to produce, and output rose rapidly for the next several years; ultimately, they turned out 12,000 tons of grapes per year.[42]

III

With his myriad of other activities, it is no surprise that Stanford took very little direct part in operating his various ranches, especially that at Vina, since he never lived there. He retained his wife's brother Ariel Lathrop as the manager of his vast real estate holdings, and in 1892, when Ariel resigned, his brother Charles G. Lathrop succeeded him. William H. Smith, the general superintendent of the Vina property, was succeeded in 1887 by H. W. McIntyre.

McIntyre's credentials were impeccable, and he was more of a vineyardist than Smith, so his duties were generally narrower in scope. He came to Vina from another winemaking concern to take charge of this particular phase of the Vina operation.[43] He had served for a time as the president of the Grape Growers and Wine Makers Association of California, and had written on the subject of brandy making, on which he was a recognized expert.[44]

IT'S PURE!   THAT'S SURE!

Senator Leland Stanford's

VINA · · · · ·

BRANDY

ITS PURITY A SURETY
OF ITS EXCELLENCE.

Sold by all First-Class Druggists, Grocers and Dealers.

DISTILLERY OFFICE:

819 Market Street, Room 3, - San Francisco.

Author's Collection

1895 POSTER ADVERTISING STANFORD WINES.

Clearly Stanford planned to enter the business of winemaking with all seriousness, and he went to great lengths in his bid to get the best talent possible.

Stanford also saw to it that the whole project was carefully planned to take advantage of the most up-to-date technological advances and scientific knowledge available. Grapevines were set out, spaced eight feet apart, in blocks separated by sixteen-and thirty-two-foot wide alleyways and avenues between the blocks. The irrigation system, with ditches built along these avenues, was the key to success.[45] Across Deer Creek he built a dam which held back the water until it was needed. It was then carried to the vineyards by a series of canals, one of which had a capacity of 80,000 gallons per minute.[46] The various canals on the Vina ranch totaled 150 miles, one-third of which was within the vineyards.[47]

The plant which Stanford built to crush and ferment his grapes and to distill brandy and age wine was one of the finest in the world. In the spring of 1886 he built a completely new winery — crushers, wine pressers, and fermenting vats with a capacity of 500,000 gallons. He made numerous additions to this new plant in 1887.[48] Most important of all the new buildings added was the vast wine cellar, built entirely above ground and constructed so the annual temperature variation was kept within ten degrees.[49] The walls of the wine cellar were thirty inches thick, with the center space reserved exclusively for storage of wines. The floor of the wine cellar, whose capacity in 1891 was 2,000,000 gallons, covered two acres.[50] This cellar, with its brick roof and small, shuttered windows, was praised as the nearest thing to the mountain vaults of European countries that money could build.[51]

So far as construction and vastness were concerned, the Stanford Vina winery was without equal, but, unfortunately, the quality of the wine was proportional neither to the size of the plant nor the effort and cost invested— $9,000,000 by one estimate—as Stanford was soon to learn.[52]

Everything possible was done to make Stanford's wines the best in the world: the plant was the best, the artisans and managers were incomparable, and the actual process of growing grapes and producing wine was watched carefully from the beginning to end. The important step of aging was scrutinized with great care, with no Vina wines marketed less than three years of age.[53] Nothing was overlooked, but nature conspired to defeat Stanford. It soon became obvious that more was needed than money and French peasants even to match the light French wines that Stanford hoped to better. A number of visitors to the Vina ranch who knew something of the conditions conducive to the growing of grapes suitable for dry wines recognized that "both soil and climate" were better adapted to sweet wines than dry.[54] Even Stanford came to acknowledge this, and, as a consequence, he concentrated more and more on producing high quality brandy. His winery's capacity was so great that in distilling five gallons of wine into one gallon of brandy he was still able to produce 1,400 gallons per day.[55] Stanford soon became the "largest distiller of grape brandy on the globe."[56]

Though less than a success, according to his set purpose, Stanford was still unwilling to abandon the project, and in 1888 he purchased a vineyard in Menlo Park to try again. This venture was slightly more successful than that at Vina in producing dry wines, and thenceforth the Vina vineyards were reserved almost exclusively for brandy and sweet wines.[57] By 1890 his entire crop of 1,700,000 gallons of wine was made into brandy, which amounted to ten percent of the entire output of the state of California.[58]

As late as 1892 Stanford sought professional advice on the prospects of moving his Vina winery to Martinez, near the Straits of Carquinez. Conceding that the heat at Vina had beaten him, he wanted to find out whether the Martinez climate was suitable to his purposes.[59]

Stanford's superior brandies won wide praise. One writer said that his was "the finest quality of brandy in the United States."[60] They won several prizes at the Columbian Exposition at Chicago in 1893, where one of his vintages was reported as "by far the best exhibited."[61] And he produced quantities of reasonably good wines, but nothing more than anyone else could have done with his financial resources.

True as it was that Stanford had failed at Vina to produce the world's best table wines, yet the judgment of one critic that "the wines were hardly drinkable" and that Vina was "one of Stanford's mistakes" was neither fair nor accurate.[62] But some have praised his achievements more highly than they deserve. One writer, for example, judged his contribution to the growing of wines inestimable.[63] But Stanford has been justifiably ignored by most historians dealing with the development of wines, since his contributions toward producing better wines or to the technological advancement of the business were nonexistent. While praise was lavished upon him at the Chicago Fair, these laurels were nothing compared to the money and time invested in the project. Probably the only lasting result of his dealings with wines was the creation of a department of viticulture at the University of California at Berkeley, which was an offshoot of his Vina experiments.[64] One student of Stanford's wine business concluded that the Vina ranch will be remembered only as one of the most unusual and expensive hobbies in the history of California.[65] If we add to this the wineries at Warm Springs and Menlo Park, we are forced to agree with such a criticism.

IV

The town of Vina existed primarily to serve the Gerke and later the Stanford ranch. At the peak of its activity it had a population of 1,300, mainly Japanese and Chinese ranch hands. There were two hotels, two grocery stores, five saloons, two livery stables, a post office, a drugstore, a school, and a railroad depot.[66] The town itself was unattractive and run down, and though it was "the heart almost of this largest of the Stanford ranches," Joaquin Miller wrote, "the less said about flat and dirty Vina the better."[67]

The Vina ranch was set aside primarily for horticulture, the growing of grapes, fruits, and nuts, and the making of wine and brandy, but its agricultural operations were extensive.[68] In terms of total acreage, agricultural activities were far greater than winemaking, only 4,000 of the farm's 55,000 acres were devoted to vineyards.

Vina produced a wide variety of fruits, and shipped a crop valued in excess of $175,000 in 1882.[69] Six years later the ranch had over 14,000 fruit-bearing trees, including nectarines, walnuts, figs, plums, pears, apricots, peaches, and oranges, and another 5,000 trees too young as yet to bear.

Besides fruit and grapes, a considerable hay and grain crop was cultivated at Vina. In the late eighties, about 2,500 acres were planted in alfalfa, which was harvested four times each year.[70] The ranch also produced barley and corn; in one season there were 2,000 to 2,500 acres planted in the former, with a crop of 240,000 pounds.[71] There was also some cotton raised, but hardly enough to warrant mention.

By far the greatest amount of land on the Vina ranch, well over 40,000 acres of foothill land that was unfit for anything else, was set aside for grazing.[72] This made it possible to raise over 20,000 sheep, a flock that increased by almost 5,000 head annually.[73] Besides sheep, the Vina ranch had at one time 800 hogs, eighty-six mules, 270 horses, seventy purebred cows, thirty purebred calves and bulls, and 200 other cattle.[74]

The Vina ranch became almost a branch stock farm, an appendage to the Palo Alto farm. A quarter mile race track was constructed there, where much of the preliminary training of young trotters was done.[75] In 1887 Vina housed 125 brood mares and 280 colts.[76] By 1890 the colts had increased in number to 450, most of them sired by Stanford's trotters from the Palo Alto stock farm.

In addition to the equine stock, there was a herd of almost 500 Holstein milk cows at Vina.[77] These cows produced an excess of milk for the market and provided meat for the various Stanford residences around the state. Mrs. Stanford's biographer later wrote that weekly shipments of preserved fruits, mutton, turkey, chickens, eggs, and butter were sent from Vina.[78] The dairy was one of the farm's few paying operations.[79]

The average number of permanent workers on the Vina ranch ran about 200, most of them unmarried Chinese. Seasonal work was a regular part of farm or vineyard work, so there were times when as many as 1,000 temporary hands were employed, generally boys from San Francisco.[80] Stanford's managers, as usual, promoted good relations with their labor force and it was generally agreed that they had their pick of the men available.[81]

Despite widespread opposition to the unpopular Chinese, the Vina ranch continued to employ Orientals, even though the owner sought to protect the ranch's public image by expressing a preference for Caucasians.[82] In 1886 criticism grew to the point that Stanford felt constrained to explain why he used Oriental labor. Addressing himself to the Citizens' Anti-Coolie League of Red Bluff, he insisted that the Chinese in this country were entitled to the same rights and treatment as other foreigners or citizens. He insisted that one's choice of labor should be motivated by his own humanitarianism and self interest, yet he said he was willing to let his convictions go by the board in order to avoid a conflict with the anti-Chinese forces:

> I have my right to dispose of my own property and my own means as suits me best, so long as I obey the laws, if my humanitarianism impels me or my interests incline me to employ Chinese labor. I hold that I have a perfect political right to do so, it being a matter of my own conscience and its dictates. My race prejudice, however, inclines me to my own people, and I am desirous of giving them, on all suitable occasions, the preference. I have, therefore, in harmony with my own inclinations, strengthened by your request, given instructions to my agent to direct that the preference for white labor be carefully exerted.[83]

He later dismissed all Chinese from his vineyards with the explanation that he had become convinced that white laborers were more profitable even at higher wages.[84]

V

In late 1885 Stanford deeded the Vina ranch over to the university which he founded, as a perpetual source of income. He continued to manage it until his death, at which time it fell under the control of the university trustees. The university, however, was disappointed with the Vina property, since it proved to be an unprofitable enterprise.[85]

When Stanford died in 1893, there were over 4,000 acres in vines with 2,500 acres producing, but his wife initiated sweeping changes at Vina, discharging a number of employees and cutting the pay of the rest.[86] The ranch continued to lose more and more money, until David Starr Jordan, the president of Stanford University, complained that the property was plunging the university into debt at the rate of $500 a day.[87]

In addition to the losses sustained or at best the small profits made during the early days of the Vina project, as the century drew to a close the managers had to contend with the growing prohibition movement and serious doubts on the part of university officials that an institution of higher learning should be financed in part or associated with an establishment for the production of alcoholic beverages. Stanford himself had regarded wine drinking as a sure enemy of intemperance; moderation in wine drinking was the best guarantee, he felt, against immoderate use of hard liquors:

If I thought wine-making injurious to the human family I would pull up every vine that I have. The habitual use of wine does away with liquors between meals. In the countries using food wines the people are the most temperate.[88]

In the late nineties, the Vina ranch began paying its own way, though it did not bring in any profits. Gradually, more and more of the land was leased out to farmers, with the ranch getting one-third the income from their crops. The production of wines and brandy was cut back, though Mrs. Stanford favored continuing the making of brandy for medicinal purposes.[89]

In gradual steps the trustees were freed from the original responsibility of maintaining the Vina property, and in 1915-1916 the vineyard was uprooted entirely, bringing to a close another of Stanford's experiments.[90]

The former vineyard was planted in alfalfa and the dairy herd was increased so that gradually Vina took on the aspect of its neighboring farms. In 1919 the bulk of the property was sold to a number of different people, bringing in almost $2,000,000 for the university.[91] In 1950 the same land was purchased by the Pacific Soap Company of Los Angeles and five years later the 580 acres central to the old ranch were bought by Trappist Monks from Kentucky.[92] Six priests and twenty-two brothers moved into their new monastery after rechristening it Our Lady of New Clairvaux.[93] To this day, these monks raise fruits, nuts, alfalfa, wheat, barley, and a herd of Holstein cows, but missing are most reminders of the farm's past as one of California's greatest wineries.

Gone too are the vineyards and winery at Palo Alto. The red brick winery on the Stanford campus was one of the few buildings that survived the 1906 earthquake unscathed. For a time it served as a storage building, a dairy, and a breeder's service facility. In the middle 1960's the Stanford Barn, as it is known, was converted into an international eating house, with a bank and a number of offices included.

The only one of the former Stanford wineries still producing is that at Warm Springs. The nineteenth century saw the Warm Springs winery and vineyards survive a variety of catastrophes: fires, earthquakes, depressions, and numerous changes of ownership.[94] In the early 1920's Frank Kelley of Chicago purchased the Warm Springs property and later sold it to the College of the Holy Names in Oakland, for the purpose of building a girls' college there.[95] Fred Goossen bought it in 1944 with the intention of building a dude ranch, and renamed it the "Hidden Valley Ranch."[96] In 1945 Goossen sold the vineyard to the Weibel Wine Company, which is still in operation, using three of the buildings erected by the Stanford brothers three quarters of a century earlier.[97] The Weibel company now has ninety-seven acres in vines, which with its other holdings produce 800,000 gallons of wine per year.[98] This company has won to date over 300 awards for its high quality wines.[99]

There is still a health resort on the Hidden Valley ranch, with an alcoholic retreat; in fact, Josiah Stanford's home is now a domicile for

Weibel Winery

GRAPES BEING PREPARED FOR WINEMAKING, Warm Springs Ranch.

alcoholics, having no connection with the Weibel Winery, a half mile away! The old lodge building still stands, with a bar, a restaurant, and a dance hall on the main floor.

---

1. Oakland *Tribune,* February 22, 1956.

2. Josiah W. Stanford, Leland's nephew, to Emory E. Smith, October 24, 1932.

3. William Halley, *Centennial Year Book of Alameda County* (Oakland, 1876), 82.

4. Sometimes spelled Columbet.

5. Josiah W. Stanford to Smith, October 24, 1932.

6. Halley, *Centennial,* 133.

7. Oakland *Tribune,* November 14, 1954.

8. Halley, *Centennial,* 133.

9. Oakland *Tribune,* February 22, 1956, for a brief, but not altogether accurate, historical sketch of the Warm Springs ranch.

10. Halley, *Centennial*, 274. Contract of sale was dated September 2, 1869. In Stanford Collection.

11. Josiah W. Stanford to Smith, October 24, 1932. Halley, *Centennial*, 297.

12. Hollister *Free Lance*, May 31, 1962.

13. Josiah W. Stanford to Smith, October 24, 1932.

14. *Ibid.*

15. *Ibid.*

16. Halley, *Centennial*, 485.

17. Josiah W. Stanford to Smith, October 24, 1932.

18. For a florid description of Josiah W. Stanford's life as a country squire, his "charming country seat," and his jaunts between Oakland and Warm Springs by automobile, see Oakland *Inquirer*, August 1, 1900.

19. Irving McKee, "Three Wine-Growing Senators," *California: Magazine of the Pacific*, XXXVII(September, 1947), 15.

20. For an excellent sketch of the original and changing ownership of these lands, see Joseph A. McConnell, Jr., "The Stanford Vina Ranch," Unpublished M.A. thesis (Stanford, 1961), 1-14.

21. John Charles Fremont, *Memoirs of My Life* (Chicago, 1887), 473. Frona Colburn, *Wines and Vines of California* (San Francisco, 1889), 201, in McConnell, "Vina Ranch," 5.

22. *Tehama County Deeds*, Book P, 542-547, in McConnell, "Vina Ranch," 13.

23. *California Spirit of the Times*, January 12, 1884.

24. *Tehama County Records*, Book Q, 294-295, 395-403, in McConnell, "Vina Ranch," 14.

25. *Report on the Committee on Corporations*, 1883. Joseph S. Cone testimony, in Daggett, *Southern Pacific*, 195.

26. *Tehama County Book of Deeds*, Book R, 132. In Alice E. Davis, Clerk and Recorder, County of Tehama, to Guy C. Miller, Palo Alto Public Library, November 28, 1947.

27. *Report on the Committee on Corporations*, 1883, in Daggett, *Southern Pacific*, 197.

28. Elizabeth Gregg, "The History of the Famous Stanford Ranch at Vina, California," *Overland Monthly*, LII(October, 1908), 336. McConnell, "Vina Ranch," 14.

29. *Tehama County Index to Deeds, Grantor and Grantee, 1880-1889*, in McConnell, "Vina Ranch," 15.

30. San Francisco *Examiner*, November 25, 1889, April 6, 1890.

31. Gregg, "Stanford Ranch," 336.

32. Berner, *Mrs. Stanford*, 94. For a detailed description of their car, see San Francisco *Call*, October 17, 1882.

33. *Resources of California,* unidentified clipping on file at the Wine Institute, San Francisco.

34. Gregg, "Stanford Ranch," 337. San Francisco *Examiner,* April 6, 1890.

35. Sacramento *Record-Union,* January 27, 1882.

36. Hittell, *Commerce,* 244. Sacramento *Record-Union,* December 29, 1884.

37. Bancroft, *History of California,* VII, 48n.

38. Hittell, *Commerce,* 244.

39. *Resources of California,* September, 1886, 6. Red Bluff *Sentinel,* December 25, 1887. Josiah at Warm Springs was producing a number of other varieties. *Report on the Sixth Annual Viticultural Convention* (Sacramento, 1888), 214.

40. *Report of the Sixth Annual Viticultural Convention,* 217. San Francisco *Examiner,* April 6, 1890. Red Bluff *Sentinel,* December 25, 1887. *Resources of California,* September, 1886, 6.

41. *California Spirit of the Times,* January 12, 1884. *Report of the Sixth Annual Viticultural Convention,* 217. Gregg dates this change 1886. "Stanford Ranch," 337.

42. Sacramento *Record-Union,* September 23, 1891. Frank G. Carpenter, SFS, III, 121. San Francisco *Examiner,* July 14, 1895.

43. San Francisco *Examiner,* April 6, 1890.

44. *Report on the Fifth Annual Viticultural Convention* (San Francisco, 1887), 1. *Report on the Sixth Annual Viticultural Convention,* 112-128.

45. Red Bluff *Sentinel,* December 25, 1883.

46. *Ibid. Resources of California,* September, 1886, 6.

47. San Francisco *Examiner,* April 6, 1890.

48. *Resources of California,* September, 1886, 6. Red Bluff *Sentinel,* December 25, 1887. San Francisco *Examiner,* April 6, 1890.

49. Red Bluff *Sentinel,* December 25, 1887.

50. Sacramento *Record-Union,* September 28, 1891.

51. Red Bluff *News,* May 30, 1950.

52. Francis Mosher, Jr., "The Stanford Vina Ranch," *Stanford Illustrated Review,* XXXIV(1933), 182.

53. *American Wine Merchant,* VI(1947), clipping on file at the Wine Institute, San Francisco.

54. H. F. Stoll, "The Wineries of Northern California," *Wines and Vines,* XVIII(1937), 3.

55. San Francisco *Examiner,* April 6, 1890. *Pacific Wine and Spirit Review,* XXVII(November 5, 1891), 18.

56. *Pacific Wine and Spirit Review,* XXX(July 6, 1893), 12.

57. *American Wine Merchant,* VI(1947), clipping at Wine Institute.

58. *Pacific Wine and Spirit Review,* XXVII(November 5, 1891), 18.

59. Stanford to Davidson, November 18, 1892, in Davidson papers, Bancroft Library.

60. Sacramento *Record-Union,* September 23, 1891.

61. *Final Report of the California World's Fair Commission* (Sacramento, 1894), 77. Charles A. Wetmore, *Treatise on Wine Production and Special Reports on Wine Examinations,* Appendix B, *The Report of the Board of State Viticultural Commissioners for 1893-1894.* (Sacramento, 1894), 55.

62. Idwall Jones, *Vines in the Sun* (New York, 1959), 146, 148.

63. *American Wine Merchant,* VI(1947), Clipping at Wine Institute.

64. Red Bluff *News,* May 30, July 5, 1955.

65. McConnell, "Vina Ranch," 71.

66. *California Illustrated, A Guide for Tourists and Settlers* (San Francisco, 1891), 107-108. Chico *Record,* February 5, 1948.

67. Sacramento *Record-Union,* July 3, 1886.

68. *Resources of California,* September, 1886, 6.

69. Red Bluff *Sentinel,* December 25, 1883.

70. Sacramento *Record-Union,* April 1, 1887.

71. *Resources of California,* September, 1886, 6. Red Bluff *Sentinel,* December 25, 1883. San Francisco *Examiner,* April 6, 1890.

72. *Resources of California,* September, 1886, 6. San Francisco *Examiner,* April 6, 1890.

73. Red Bluff *Sentinel,* December 25, 1884. Sacramento *Record-Union,* December 29, 1884. San Francisco *Examiner,* April 6, 1890.

74. *Resources of California,* September, 1886, 6. San Francisco *Examiner,* April 6, 1890.

75. Mosher, "Stanford Vina Ranch," 182. Berner, *Mrs. Stanford,* 227.

76. Red Bluff *Sentinel,* December 25, 1887.

77. *Ibid.,* December 25, 1884. San Francisco *Examiner,* April 6, 1890.

78. Berner, *Mrs. Stanford,* 93.

79. San Francisco *Examiner,* July 14, 1895.

80. Sacramento *Record-Union,* July 3, 1886. San Francisco *Examiner,* April 6, 1890.

81. San Francisco *Examiner,* April 6, 1890.

82. *Ibid.*

83. Stanford to Citizens' Anti-Coolie League of Red Bluff, June 15, 1886, in Sacramento *Record-Union,* June 26, 1886.

84. Unidentified newspaper clipping, SFS, XXV, 51.

85. San Francisco *Chronicle,* June 27, 1893. San Francisco *Examiner,* July 14, 1895.

86. Sacramento *Record-Union,* September 23, 1891. San Francisco *Chronicle,* September 2, 7, 1893.

87. David Starr Jordan, *The Days of a Man* (New York, 1922), I, 497-498.

88. San Francisco *Examiner,* November 25, 1889, April 6, 1890.

89. *Ibid.,* July 14, 1895.

90. Chico *Record,* September 29, 1915.

91. *Ibid.,* April 5, 1919.

92. Red Bluff *News,* July 5, 1955. Sacramento *Bee,* July 8, 1955.

93. San Francisco *Examiner,* March 4, 1956. Chico *Enterprise-Record,* June 1, 1955.

94. See Warm Springs article in Los Angeles *Times,* June 17, 1966.

95. Josiah W. Stanford to Smith, October 24, 1932.

96. Oakland *Tribune,* November 14, 1954, August 16, 1959.

97. *Ibid.,* August 16, 1959.

98. Interview with Fred Weibel, Jr., July 1, 1969.

99. Fremont *News Register,* October 2, 1958.

CHAPTER X

THE QUEST FOR CULTURE:

SOCIAL LIFE AND FOREIGN TOURS

A familiar aspect of late-nineteenth-century America was attempts — some successful and some not — of industrial, commercial, and financial *nouveaux riches* to purchase the respect, position, education, and culture denied them by their birthrights. Imitation old-world castles rose on Fifth Avenue and Nob Hill. America's artificial aristocracy fled to Europe for tours and cures, and were followed home by the continent's most expensive art objects and jewelry; everything had its price and American millionaires could eventually name it.

By the late 1860's, despite periodic shortages of cash needed to extend the associates' railroad empire, the Stanfords were financially situated so as to enable them to begin building plush homes, followed by castles and resorts in the following decade. They played host to not only the first families of the nation, but an increasing number of prominent Europeans, and in 1880 they left on the first of five European tours, completing the prescribed quest for culture.

The first five years of marriage were trying for the couple, with a three-year separation and, for Stanford himself, the necessity of making a home wherever he could, often with only a wooden store counter for a bed. His wife rejoined him in 1855, and the two set up housekeeping temporarily in a hotel in Sacramento, until they moved into a small house on Second Street between O and P.[1] Their furnishings were at first crude — Stanford built their tables and chairs out of drygoods boxes and boards — and Mrs. Stanford did all her own housekeeping.[2] This frugality was not an absolute necessity, since they were relatively well off — Mrs. Stanford even retained domestic help one day per week — but it saved them money that could be plowed back into their many business ventures.[3]

Though the young couple entertained often in their small home as their wealth and popularity grew, scarcely any record remains of their first years together in California. But once Stanford was elected governor, all that

STANFORD MANSION IN SACRAMENTO.

changed. On July 11, 1861, following his nomination, but preceding his election, they bought from Shelton C. Fogus for the substantial sum of $8,000 a much larger house of their own at the southeast corner of Eighth and N Streets.[4]

This two-story brick house with its frame addition and brick stable was richly finished inside and out and was located on a lot a quarter of a city block in area, surrounded by all sorts of fruit trees and shrubbery. In 1872 the Stanfords thoroughly renovated their home, adding a third floor and several new wings. When it was completed they were the proud possessors of a forty-four room mansion topped off with a new, stylish mansard roof.[5] The interior evidenced on every hand the owner's railroad interest; even the crystal light shades on a chandelier in the banquet room were etched with designs of a railroad engine.[6]

Once this home was turned into the governor's mansion, it became one of the social. political, and cultural centers not just of Sacramento, but of California, and the Stanfords' banquet table became famous as a center of hospitality. The great, the famous, and the wealthy who visited the West Coast in the sixties and seventies were welcomed there, as on April 24, 1870, when the Stanfords entertained former Secretary of State William Henry Seward as an overnight guest.[7]

California's first lady participated in most of the important social functions of the capital city, and laid down a new rule of etiquette that ladies visiting the capital should call on her first, since she had no way of knowing who of importance was in the city.[8]

Undoubtedly the most brilliant affair ever held at the Stanford mansion was the inaugural ball for Governor Newton Booth, in February, 1872. The party at "Stanford's Palace," given by the "Prince of Central," was attended by most of the 700 people invited. One reporter who was dispatched to cover the gala affair related: "Full dress is the order of the evening, and surely, outside the Courts of Europe, such an array of beauty and such an elaboration of toilets has not been seen." His three-column communication contained an elaborate and florid description of the house and its furnishings, of the guests and their wealth and dress, and of the dinner itself:

> It [the mansion] contains forty-four rooms, all most elaborately and luxuriously furnished. . . . Magnificent and costly furniture in every room; lace curtains of the finest fabric; carpets which receive with noiseless tread the footfall; frescoes beautiful in design and exquisite in artistic perfection, adorn the walls and ceiling. . . . The billiard room and adjacent apartment in which the supper is served present a most inviting appearance. For each guest there are six different wine glasses. The entire service, from napkin-rings to centerpieces, is of solid silver, all being entirely new. There is room for 200 guests at a sitting. . . . Everything is on a scale of unsurpassed magnificence. . . . Church & Clark of Sacramento furnish the music. Seven pieces are stationed in the parlors to the left, which connect with a large hall 30 by 86. The parlors are 20 by 50. The second band is stationed on the lower floor in the hall beneath the main upper hall. This lower hall is also 30 by' 86. This gives, according to our hurried mathematics, 6,000 square feet of space covered with the tireless dancers.[9]

The highest ranking guest entertained at the Stanford mansion was President Rutherford B. Hayes, the first chief executive to visit California while still in office. He came in September, 1880, accompanied by his wife, Secretary of War Alexander Ramsey, and General William T. Sherman. The Hayes procession was given a military escort from the railroad station to J Street, up J to Tenth, down Tenth to N, down N to Eighth; then the procession proceeded past a regiment of soldiers at present arms and turned into the Stanford residence. The streets in all directions were thronged with people cheering Hayes and Sherman. The host met their carriage at the front entrance, led Mrs. Hayes upstairs, and installed her as hostess, in the absence of Mrs. Stanford, who was then in Europe.[10] Stanford reportedly made a most favorable impression upon the chief executive, for he was said to have remarked to his host: "I wish I had known you earlier, I would have been glad to have had you in my cabinet."[11]

Stanford's civic responsibilities during his Sacramento residence extended beyond politics. In 1857 he was one of eighteen charter life members of the Sacramento Library Association and one of the members of the Board of Trustees, each of whom paid $100 for the honor. The Sacramento Public Library, which grew out of this association, was capitalized at $25,000, paid in part by the 100 active members, besides the life members.[12] So many of these association members were Republicans that one detractor regarded the library as a ruse of the recently founded Republican party to appear philanthropic.[13]

The president of the Central Pacific was neither stingy nor munificent with his money or that of his railroad. In 1872, in the interest of improving public relations in that state, he pledged twenty acres of railroad land and $500 cash to a proposed university for the state of Nevada.[14] Two years later, using their own money, he and Charles Crocker assisted the California Academy of Sciences in establishing its first formal museum; the academy was housed for sixteen years in the building they helped buy.[15]

While in Sacramento Leland Stanford found time in his busy schedule as governor, railroad builder, and businessman to attend banquets, travel widely, and take active part in or own part interest in a number of businesses peripheral to his main interests. He and his associate Mark Hopkins headed the Donner Lumber and Boom Company near Lake Tahoe.[16] And even before the railroad was finished, during one of his busiest periods, Stanford helped found the Pacific Mutual Life Insurance Company and he purchased the first policy that the company sold. He served as a board member and was its president until 1877, when the press of other business caused him to resign.[17]

As governor, Stanford even attended on occasion the elaborate balls frequently held in San Francisco to celebrate the visit of foreign ships. One of the greatest welcomes accorded a foreign fleet was in late 1863, when Admiral Popoff, commander of the Russian Pacific Fleet, visited San Francisco. Popoff showed his appreciation for the Bay City's hospitality by giving a banquet on his flagship. Among the many high-ranking military and civilian guests in attendance was Governor Stanford, seated at the head of the table to the left of the admiral.[18]

On December 31, 1866, the former governor was one of the speakers at the "Grand China Mail Banquet" in San Francisco to honor the inauguration of the Pacific Mail's service between the United States and China.[19] This was primarily a "large assemblage of the intelligence and capital of San Francisco," but the Sacramentan conducted much of his business in the Bay metropolis, and very early recognized the value of a possible connection between his railroad and the transoceanic steamship trade.

In their house at Eighth and N, a son was born to the Stanfords on May 14, 1868, after eighteen years of marriage, and Stanford was as proud as any new father twenty years his junior and played the part, as shown in one ancedote related by Mrs. Stanford's biographer:

When the baby was only a few weeks old, Mr. Stanford asked Mrs. Stanford to arrange a dinner party for a group of their particular friends. It was a large party, and when they were seated the waiter brought in a large silver platter with a cover and placed it in the center of the table. Mrs. Stanford was very much surprised, for she had planned nothing of the sort, and also had not seen the platter before. Then Mr. Stanford arose and said, "My friends, I wish now to introduce my son to you." When the cover of the silver dish was lifted, the baby was discovered lying in it on blossoms. He was carried around the table and shown to each guest. He was smiling, and went through his introduction very nicely.[20]

The baby was treated as though he were much more than an ordinary child, and whenever he appeared with his mother in public he was bedecked like a "baby prince;" he was cherished — almost revered — by his parents, and he soon became the center of their lives.[21]

When the Stanfords later moved to San Francisco they left their Sacramento home completely furnished. Mrs. Stanford loved the old house and the city where she had spent so many years, and frequently gave gifts to some worthy cause there. On February 7, 1888, from Washington she authorized her brother, also her husband's business manager, in San Francisco to send a gift of $1,000 to the Protestant Orphan Asylum in Sacramento.[22] Two years later she sent another $1,000 to the mayor to be distributed among the city's charities.[23] The same year she placed a memorial window of stained glass, said to be the most costly memorial in this country or in Europe, in St. Paul's Episcopal Church, and afterwards presented to the Cathedral of the Blessed Sacrament a copy of Raphael's Sistine Madonna.[24] She later contributed toward the purchase of Sutter's Fort for the purpose of preserving it as a historical site.[25]

Except for periodic visits to the capital city, when they lived in their old home, from 1880 until 1900 the Stanford mansion in Sacramento was unoccupied, but for a sole caretaker.[26] On April 18, 1900, before leaving for an extended stay in Europe, Mrs. Stanford gave the house, along with a $75,000 endowment, to the Roman Catholic Diocese of Sacramento.[27] In her deed she designated it the Stanford-Lathrop house.[28] For a number of years it was administered by the Sisters of Mercy as an orphanage and afterwards was converted into a home for girls, run by the Sisters of Social Service.[29] These two orders gradually refurnished the parlors and family dining rooms as they had been in the last century.[30]

When St. Patrick's Orphanage was later built, the Stanford mansion was converted into Sacramento's first settlement house, a place to provide entertainment, rest, instruction, and social service to the men, women, and children of the neighborhood.[31] In 1939 it was restored and renovated as a part of the Golden Empire Centennial.[32]

Stanford Library

LELAND STANFORD, JR.

Stanford Library

MRS. JANE STANFORD.

II

During the building of the Central Pacific Railroad, Stanford's duties as president took him to San Francisco for extended stays, so in 1873 he and his partners moved the general offices there. The following year he moved his family into a rented house at the corner of Pine and Powell streets where they lived while building their own house a block away on the southwest corner of California and Powell, atop Nob Hill, named after the "nabobs" who occupied "castles" on it.[33] The family stables were located just across the intersection, on the northeast corner.

The California Street hill proved attractive to some of Stanford's associates, and in time the Crocker and Hopkins families joined him there. Stanford owned the eastern half of the block bounded by California and Pine and Mason and Powell; Mark Hopkins bought and built on the western end. Both houses faced California Street. Charles Crocker bought the block between California and Sacramento and Taylor and James, about a block and a half away.

In 1874 grading began on the Stanford property, and two years later the house was completed. The architects who designed it were S. C. and C. L. Bugbee. Most of the early work was done by L. D. Mason as the main contractor, but the difficult and detailed woodworking and the frescoing and hardwood finishing were done by the New York firm of Pottier, Stymus, and Garibaldi.[34]

Stanford would not condone the use of any imitations in artistry or materials; the painted ceilings were the work of prominent Italian artists and were put in place by the artists themselves.[35] A local editor, in an article entitled "Stanford's Palace, The Finest Private Residence in America," predicted that when the house was finished and furnished it would be the most elegant private residence in the country.[36] "In the magnificent size of its apartments, the richness of its interior finish, and the splendor of its luxurious appointments," it was a veritable palace, and Jay Cooke's fabulous home, as well as a number of other Eastern mansions, was reputed to be a mere shell compared to it.

Stanford's $2,000,000 home was a fine example of the florid and ornate tastes of the 1870's, and was suited to his hard-earned position among the social elite of the West Coast metropolis. None of the mansions perched on Nob Hill attracted greater attention than this one, described as one of the must luxurious in the world.[37] As the Stanford mansion rose, bay window upon bay window, with marble steps that climbed from California Street to a circular entrance hall, glass-domed, seventy feet aloft, critics of the railroad associates had good grounds for scoffing at their pleas that the railroad was "starving."

The architectural style was Italian, with the bow window as the prevailing feature. The main entrance was a vestibule twelve feet deep and eight feet wide, finished in French walnut and amaranth. The two doors opening onto the porch and main hall were several inches thick and were of solid mahogany and rosewood. As one entered the huge main hall, the sky appeared visible overhead through all three stories, an effect obtained by projecting a great circle of the signs of the zodiac in black mosaic on a white floor through a well in the two floors above into an open amber dome through which sunlight entered the house. All the principal rooms of the mansion opened onto this hall by wide, sliding, double doors, and these rooms in turn were connected to one another by conventional doors.

The various rooms in the house, the India reception room, library, family sitting room, conservatory, dining room, billiard room, picture gallery, Pompeiian reception room, ballroom, cloak room, supper room, bedrooms, and a host of others, fifty in all, were decorated and furnished with the finest furniture and art objects money could buy.[38]

The Stanfords traveled to the East in 1876 to arrange personally for the interior decoration and furnishings for their home. At the Centennial Exposition in Philadelphia, the California millionaire tried to purchase the exhibition of Chinese furniture, only to have the Chinese government insist that he accept it as a gift, in appreciation for his fair treatment of the Chinese in California. For years these pieces of furniture and several rolls of silk brocade furnished the mansion's Chinese room; afterwards, they were placed in the Stanford Museum.[39] To complete their furnishings, the Stanfords brought to San Francisco the finest collection of modern European art works owned by any one west of New York.[40] While on this buying spree, Stanford purchased a prize-winning diamond necklace and other jewels for his wife as an anniversary gift; this was the beginning of a collection that would one day be valued at over $2,000,000.

The Nob Hill "palace" was one of the showplaces of San Francisco, and the owners exhibited it widely by entertaining often and lavishly, playing host to presidents, governors, senators, and Supreme Court justices. General Ulysses S. Grant and President and Mrs. Benjamin Harrison dined there. Congressmen traveling on committee assignments were entertained, as were prominent foreign dignitaries. Leading San Franciscans were welcomed on all gala occasions.

In sharp contrast to these festivities, according to one close and sympathetic writer, "the Stanfords lived simply when alone and spent much of their time alone in the sitting room with members of their two families."[41] Stanford loved his home, and was a charming host, but he often said that the greatest pleasures in life were those around the fireside.[42]

Displays of wealth, whether purposely ostentatious or not, win enemies, and Stanford's case was no exception. It was difficult, under these circumstances, to persuade the community, influential politicians, and the national

Bancroft Library

HOPKINS AND STANFORD MANSIONS in San Francisco.

Stanford Library

INTERIOR OF THE STANFORD MANSION in San Francisco.

government that he and his associates were financially hard pressed. At one of his dinners, when he complained bitterly about the ingratitude of the federal government towards the builders of the Central Pacific Railroad, Justice Stephen J. Field of the United States Supreme Court, one of the guests, reportedly whispered to those sitting near: "One has only to look around him here to see how shamefully these gentlemen have been treated by an ungrateful and ungenerous Government," as with a sweep of his hand he took in "statuary, bric-a-brac, paintings and articles de luxe that were worth hundreds of thousands of dollars."[43]

Following another dinner, Stanford conducted two guests on a personal tour of the various rooms adorned with works of art of the rarest and most costly character. One of them later described what he saw:

> It looked as if the old palaces of Europe had been ransacked of their art and other treasures to embellish the home of an American gentleman. With a feeling of genuine satisfaction he pointed to an immense Sevres vase that stood under a great illuminated candelabra, and told us he had had hard work to get that magnificent work of art for $100,000, and he called upon me to read the inscription inserted in it in gold script characters.

> I read: "*De Marie Antoinette au dernier Marquis de Villette.*" I had no sooner read this inscription than a great howl went up in the street nearby. To my look of inquiry the Governor answered, "Oh, that's nothing unusual. It is Kearney and his crowd. They've adjourned their meeting at the sand-lots so as to give the residents of Nob Hill a taste of their peculiar oratory," and he treated the matter as a joke.

This guest mused on the coincidence between Stanford's position and that of the unfortunate French Queen:

> I said to myself that were I Stanford, I would look upon that beautiful work of art as a "hoodoo," and neutralize whatever evil spell it might possess by donating it to some institution where its power for good or evil would expend itself, not on an individual, but on the general public.[44]

The Stanfords' private railroad car, described as a traveling palace, was also lavishly appointed. It was seventy feet long and twelve feet wide, inside, and contained sixteen feet of storage lockers. It was equipped with a heater, a hot water system, and the most up-to-date Westinghouse airbrakes. The style of the car was modified Queen Anne in architecture, and was furnished with the best carpets and upholstery; its scroll works on the inside were laid in gold and rich colors, and on the outside the name "Stanford" was inscribed. Its total cost was between $20,000 and $25,000.[45]

All the comforts of home were included that were feasible—an eight by twelve parlor, six by ten and six by eight bedrooms, eight by twelve dining room, and a six by seven kitchen. Few families ever saw a home as plush as this palace on wheels, yet a local editor denied any ostentation on the part of the owners, and praised the car as a work of "chaste elegance." It had an exceedingly rich and substantial finish; it had been constructed according to a "refined taste;" and it was totally void of any "gaudy effects."[46]

In San Francisco as in Sacramento, Stanford busied himself with multifarious business and philanthropic enterprises. As railroad men, he and his partners had a special interest in the street car transportation in the city, and as the Clay Street system was being built Stanford directed Henry Root, one of his employees, to "study up and keep informed on that subject," which he did.[47] Stanford soon moved into the cable car business, and on June 14, 1876, a franchise was granted to himself, Crocker, Hopkins, Colton, and others to build a cable railroad on California Street from Kearney to First Avenue.[48] Most of the partners eventually dropped out, feeling that the $350,000 investment needed was too much to get back a nickel at a time, and before long Stanford found himself the owner of 4,750 of the 5,000 outstanding shares of the California Street Railroad Company.[49] He later sold out his interests and quit the business, a move attributed to the fact that two of his appointees in the company, both his personal friends, did not get along well together and were constantly feuding.[50] By getting out, Stanford avoided the necessity of choosing between them or of losing the friendship of either.

The diversity of Stanford's business interests was matched only by his civic and philanthropic concerns. In 1882 he was listed as the honorary president of the "Carnival Association," which included the Ladies' Protection and Relief Society, the French Benevolent Society, the Old Ladies' Home, the San Francisco Female Hospital, the Pacific Dispensary Hospital, and the Little Sisters' Infant Shelter.[51] And when the Ladies' Silk Culture Society of California was incorporated in 1885, it listed Stanford as a member, without specifying whether honorary or active.[52]

III

Stanford bought his Palo Alto farm in the late seventies and began raising horses. Of his many homes, the Palo Alto residence — the old Gordon estate — was his favorite; in fact, the whole family loved the place above all the others. Its background of redwood-covered mountains, its extensive lawns and gardens, and its trees and flowers presented a pleasant and striking contrast to the old-world domicile of San Francisco; to add to its natural beauty, he planted palms from China, cedars from Japan, and various plants from India.[53] It was Stanford's intention to set out every species of tree adaptable to the climate and in one year he added 12,000.[54] He planted there some of his best vineyards, and experimented with various kinds of agricultural and fruit-raising innovations.[55]

In 1888, while traveling in Europe, the Stanfords had extensive additions made to the original Gordon house. They had planned at first to replace the house, but after spending $75,000 just improving the old mansion, they changed their minds.[56] The Gordon house, even with its extensive modifications, was never a fraction as pretentious as the San Francisco home. Yet it was far from plain; the Stanfords furnished it with costly furniture, rugs, and many art objects picked up on their foreign travels.

Stanford built between two rows of trees a beautiful macadamized road from the house to the stock farm. Near the stock farm, on the southern end of the road, lay the trotting track, with the paddocks beyond. Turning right one would pass between two rows of paddocks; turning right again, one would be at the kindergarten track, with a little oblong roof shelter in the middle for observers to stand under.[57] The office of Charles Marvin stood nearby, as did a barber shop, a storehouse, and a mill.

While working at the Central Pacific offices in San Francisco, it was Stanford's custom to leave the busy city on Wednesdays and Saturdays and spend them at Palo Alto. There was an understanding that on these two days he could bring home with him any number of guests without first notifying his wife.[58]

In his later years, as he gradually withdrew from railroad affairs, the Palo Alto home became his haven of rest; on his return from his European travels or from duties in Washington while serving in the Senate, it was his unvarying habit to hurry down to the farm and spend as much time there as business would permit.[59]

Young Leland continued to get the best of everything that money could buy, yet there is no evidence that he was spoiled by the care lavished upon him; his father and mother were parents, not mere benefactors. Collecting things was one of his earliest hobbies, beginning with pine cones at age eight.[60] Later he spent considerable time and money collecting antiquities and art objects, but he was given only small sums of money, and was required to keep close accounts and avoid extravagance. His rooms in San Francisco as well as Palo Alto were converted into miniature museums.

The father disapproved of most toys, but encouraged his son to play with "educational toys," those which would develop any mechanical or artistic bent; he approved of his boy's carpenter's bench, woodcarving tools, stationary engine and small locomotive, and telegraph and telephone instruments.

When Leland playfully built his own train by tying a row of chairs together and sliding them about, Stanford brought a railroad engineer down to the farm and instructed him to build the boy a small railroad. This man dutifully assembled on the beautiful and spacious lawn an unsightly wooden railroad, 200 yards long, with wires, switches, and all the paraphernalia of a real railroad.[61]

Stanford Library

STANFORD HOME on the Palo Alto Farm.

Stanford Library

LELAND JUNIOR'S RAILROAD, Palo Alto Farm.

IV

Stanford had always been a big man, and he was extremely heavy from middle age on; his five-foot ten-inch frame was aptly described as "massive" when he reached 268 pounds. He was a man of imposing appearance, deep chest, large shoulders, and powerful arms, but years of hard work and lack of proper rest, as well as business cares and anxieties, began to take their toll. For years he had slept on store counters or in the open air; he had worked all night countless times, and spent weeks during the building of the railroad sleeping in the open, often on the wet ground. By his mid-fifties Stanford's health was beginning to fail, and his physicians were sure that it was largely owing to his exposure on these various trips.[62] As early as 1878 he began suffering from exhaustion; so bad was it that for a time he gave up all reading, except newspaper headlines, editorials, and telegrams.[63]

Finally surrendering to his wife's importunities, he consulted a doctor, and before long had five of them; it was reported that they nearly killed him by dosing him with quinine, arsenic, and strychnine. Despairing of life, he swore off medicine and returned to Palo Alto. His family physician diagnosed his ailment as "blood poisoning from medicine."[64] Stanford found it impossible to retain any food but chicken broth, and suffered intense nervous spasms, sometimes as many as a hundred a night.

This was Stanford's first serious illness, and he had come to fear for his life, but his doctors' prescription of complete rest went unheeded. Nevertheless, to secure the rest that he needed, in response to his doctor's recommendation he decided on a sea voyage and a tour of Europe. He and his wife first went to New York for the winter of 1879, where he suffered a relapse. He became so engrossed in business one day in his New York office that he neglected to turn the heat on, and was oblivious to the temperature drop; when he prepared to leave for home, he was so stiff he could hardly rise from his chair. That evening he attended a dinner at the home of Secretary of State Hamilton Fish, and on the way home he was taken seriously ill again. The next day his nervous spasms returned, and for thirteen weeks his friends again feared for his life; when they bade him farewell as he left for Europe, some of them never expected to see him alive again.[65]

From 1880 until the summer of 1882, the Stanford entourage, more often than not without the father, followed the typical tour of American aristocracy, touching at the capitals of the major nations of Europe, as well as the principal resort and spa towns. Part of the reason why the Stanfords made the Grand Tour was to broaden their son's education, and such a tour had to be enlightening to an intelligent, alert child, as Leland Junior was; his letters home attest to the education he was receiving.[66]

During the first part of this trip, Mrs. Stanford was ill, and was under the care of physicians in London and Paris; meanwhile, the father and son made a number of excursions together. Then Stanford had to interrupt his pleasure to return home for pressing railroad business; during this time the improved mother and son toured with a valet and maid. They visited Berlin, the Netherlands, Belgium, France, and Italy, always hoping that railroad troubles would allow Stanford to rejoin them.

The son wrote his father about seeing the German Crown Prince, and described a visit to Nice, where they visited a silk factory and saw weavers at work.[67] The Caesars' Palace at Rome was another spectacle that prompted a letter to "papa."[68] While in Rome he and his mother saw a grand review of troops, and then were among 200 received by the Pope. Leland commented on how the Roman Pontiff had placed his hands upon their heads, even though they were not Catholics.[69] The following week they visited Pompeii.[70]

Upon Stanford's return to Europe the reunited family continued its travels. It was during this time that Stanford purchased most of his wife's famous collection of jewels.[71]

Besides visits to the tourist centers, the Stanfords were able to answer many invitations by specific individuals whom they had met at home. On a number of occasions, European travelers to California who were expecting to return to New York to sail for Europe were given passage on the Occidental and Oriental lines to the Orient. In this way Stanford won a number of invitations to Europe.[72]

While visiting Paris in the late fall of 1881, the three had portraits done by some of the greatest artists of France.[73] Stanford's was done by Louis Meissonier, Mrs. Stanford's by Leon Bonnat, and the son's by Carolus Duran. Meissonier was one of the world's greatest painters, but he generally avoided portraits. Yet it was he who proposed doing Stanford's portrait, for two reasons: the friendship that had grown up between them because of their mutual love for horses, and because he reportedly recognized in Stanford's face "the expression of a strong character and certain marked features" which were a "delight to the trained artistic eye."[74] On their next trip, in 1883, Bonnat did portraits of Stanford and the young Leland. The three life size portraits and the smaller Meissonier hang today in the Stanford University Museum.

On this first European trip, the Stanfords visited or at least became acquainted with a number of European health spas and "thermal stations." Mrs. Stanford's letters to her husband in November, 1880, from Berlin and Antwerp showed that she knew some of the German health resorts. In later years, Stanford spent much time "taking the cures" in these resorts, especially at Bad Kissingen, in Bavaria.

The summer of 1882 found the Stanfords back home in Menlo Park, and in the fall and winter of 1882-1883 they leased the Lorillard house on Fifth Avenue in New York City, so they could be near their son as he attended Harvard, and be able to entertain his college friends.[75]

But there was to be one more European tour before he took up his college studies. The elder Stanford's health had continued impaired, and on May 25, 1883, he wrote a friend that he was confined to the house most of the time, weak from the same illness that had plagued him in Palo Alto four years earlier.[76] On May 26, 1883, with no fixed plans or time for returning, the family once again sailed for Europe, on the *Germanic*, reaching London on June 4.[77]

Mrs. Stanford's health had not been good, and her doctors too had advised a therapeutic sea voyage, but in England she worsened, until her condition was described as serious. With both parents ailing, Leland Junior kept up his correspondence home, reporting that "mama" was suffering from an eye inflammation and "papa" was no better than before.[78] In July, he reported them both improved, and the following month the three left for the continent.[79]

In Paris, Mrs. Stanford suffered from fainting spells.[80] She and Leland spent most of August in Havre, where it was felt the sea air would have a salutary effect on her health; afterwards, they pushed on to Paris. Meanwhile, Stanford himself traveled alone, on business, and again spent some time in Bad Kissingen.[81]

The Stanfords were reunited in Florence or Germany—it is unclear where—and visited Hamburg in late September; there they were spectators at military maneuvers.[82] Next they stopped over briefly at Paris, and in October visited Bordeaux, where they observed winemaking, and were given a tour of the wine cellars.[83] Stanford alone visited the Chateau Yquem vineyard, where he watched the vintage in progress.[84]

In November, 1883, the Stanfords, back in Paris again, were taking in the museums, before making a trip to the Near East. They went to Marseilles, stopped at Lyon to visit the silkweavers, and spent two weeks at Nice. At Arles, they visited Roman ruins, and at Marseilles they saw several art galleries and museums.[85]

The party next moved on to Venice for five days, from which Leland wrote home: "Three evenings in succession we took gondolas and hired a boat-load of singers, and had them follow us down the canals and sing under the Rialto."[86] From Venice the travelers journeyed to Vienna, where they spent Christmas; for ten days they remained in the Austrian capital, and went out almost every night, seeing the best opera companies and ballets in Europe.[87]

New Year's Day was passed at Bucharest, and they left for Constantinople on the fifth of January, crossing the half-frozen Danube in an open boat at daybreak. The Turkish capital was the strangest city any of them had ever seen before, according to young Leland.[88] One of the Sultan's aides-de-camp gave them a tour of the national treasury, where they saw diamonds by the bushel, bowls full of emeralds, rubies, and pearls, and carpets covered with gold and precious stones. They were entertained at two palaces.

The thrill of young Leland's life was a day spent on the Bosporus, going from the Golden Horn to the Black Sea, when he was allowed to steer the steamboat. He spent much of the wintry day with the cold wind blowing steam spray in his face. That evening he showed the first signs of his fatal illness.[89]

While in Constantinople, Stanford investigated the possibility of constructing a railroad from that city to the Persian Gulf. The heavy traffic through the Suez Canal had long attracted his attention, taking as it did much of the traffic that otherwise might have gone to his steamship and railroad companies.[90] He observed that much of the trade consisted of fabrics too valuable to be shipped by sea, if there was available a land route, especially a shorter land route.

Rumors of his inquiries in Constantinople reached the Yldez Palace, and the Sultan immediately "requested" an interview with the famous railroad man. Stanford expressed his regrets that he would be unable to make the interview, since he had booked passage on a steamer sailing for Athens the next morning. Word came back from the palace that the steamer would not sail without him.

The pair spent several hours the following afternoon discussing the question of building a railroad from Scutari, opposite the Bosporus from the capital city. Sultan Abdul Hamid asked Stanford to undertake the construction.[91] Stanford agreed to study the matter in depth and give his host an answer within a few days.

For a week Stanford considered the proposal, and then decided that because of his age the undertaking would have been too great; in his communication to the Sultan, declining the offer, he made a number of valuable suggestions in regard to financing and building the road, but he never received a reply. When Herbert C. Nash first published this episode, years later, the projected Euphrates Valley railroad had still not been built.

In January, 1884, the weary party was back in Athens, and, knee-deep in snow, visited the Acropolis. After returning from an expedition to the ruins of the temple of Eleusis, young Leland complained of a sore throat and a headache, but was apparently well the next day, so nothing more was thought of it.

From Athens they crossed the Isthmus of Corinth, and by steamer they traveled to Brindisi, then by train to Naples. During the last leg of this trip Leland was again not well, and continued so for the two weeks they stayed in Naples.[92] The elder Stanford did a great deal of sightseeing in Naples, though his stiffness persisted; meanwhile, both his wife and son were reported as ill from "going it too hard."[93]

From Naples the party traveled to Rome, but Leland's condition grew worse. They moved him to Florence for the more salubrious climate, arriving February 20, where Leland broke into a fever; for three weeks he lay in a darkened room suffering fits of delirium, as the distraught parents stood by helplessly. On March 13, two months short of his sixteenth birthday, he died.

Few people ever experience the success of the Stanfords — wealth, fame, position, adulation were theirs, but influence and wealth were powerless to save their son. They purchased homes, businesses, culture, but this young life, for which they would have gladly exchanged all this, could not be saved. The simple message sent to San Francisco, "Our darling boy went to heaven this morning at half-past seven o'clock after three weeks sickness from typhoid fever," marked the beginning of a new period in their lives, as they entered the depths of despair and emerged with a renewed dedication to humanity that made their earlier philanthropies pale into insignificance by comparison. The loss of their son chastened them and raised them to a higher plane.[94]

1. Caroline Wenzel, "Finding Facts about the Stanfords in the California State Library," *Calif. Hist. Soc. Quar.*, XIX(1940), 249. Berner, *Mrs. Stanford*, 11.

2. Berner, *Mrs. Stanford*, 11.

3. *Ibid.*, 12.

4. Sacramento *Union*, July 12, 1861.

5. Joseph A. Baird, Jr., "Architectural Legacy of Sacramento," *Calif. Hist. Soc. Quar.*, XXXIX(1960), 197-198. San Francisco *Chronicle*, February 7, 1872.

6. Wenzel, "Facts about the Stanfords," 254.

7. Sacramento *Union*, August 25, 1870.

8. Wenzel, "Facts about the Stanfords," 251.

9. San Francisco *Chronicle*, February 7, 1872.

10. Sacramento *Record-Union*, September 22, 1880.

11. Bancroft, *Stanford*, 194.

12. The complete membership list is given in a manuscript entitled "Records for 1857-1879," in the Sacramento Public Library.

13. Sacramento *Daily State Sentinel*, November 8, 1857, in Hugh S. Baker, "Rational Amusements in our Midst, Public Libraries in California, 1849-1859," *Calif. Hist. Soc. Quar.*, XXXVIII(1959), 311.

14. Stanford to Committee on Nevada University, February 21, 1872.

15. Robert C. Miller, "The California Academy of Sciences and the Early History of Science in the West," *Calif. Hist. Soc. Quar.*, XXI(1942), 369.

16. Edward B. Scott, *The Saga of Lake Tahoe* (Crystal Bay, Nevada, 1957), 27.

17. Marysville *Appeal*, July 7, 1868. Hittell, *Commerce*, 155.

18. Benjamin F. Gilbert, "Welcome to the Czar's Fleet, An Incident of Civil War Days in San Francisco," *Calif. Hist. Soc. Quar.*, XXVI (1947), 16. Admiral Popoff offered to defend San Francisco in the event of an attack by Confederate raiders. Peter F. Copeland and Marko Zlatich, "Imperial Russian Navy, 1863-1864," *Military Collector and Historian*, XVI (1964), 18-19.

19. San Francisco *Alta California*, January 1, 1867.

20. Berner, *Mrs. Stanford*, 15.

21. Wenzel, "Facts about the Stanfords," 253.

22. Mrs. Stanford to Mrs. W. H. Hobby, February 7, 1888, in Sacramento *Record-Union*, February 15, 1888.

23. Sacramento *Record-Union*, April 26, 1890.

24. *Ibid*.

25. Wenzel, "Facts about the Stanfords," 254.

26. *Ibid*.

27. Baird, "Architectural Legacy," 204. Sacramento *Bee*, April 18, 19, 1900.

28. Sacramento *Union*, February 27, 1938.

29. Wenzel, "Facts about the Stanfords," 245. Baird, "Architectural Legacy," 204. Sacramento *Bee*, March 13, 1860.

30. Baird, "Architectural Legacy," 204.

31. Sacramento *Bee*, September 9, 1937.

32. Palo Alto *Times*, June 13, 1940.

33. Fisher, "Stanford," 24-25.

34. San Francisco *Chronicle*, n.d., 1876, clipping in Stanford collection.

35. Berner, *Mrs. Stanford*, 17.

36. San Francisco *Chronicle*, n.d., 1876, clipping in Stanford collection.

37. Albert Shaw, *Review of Reviews*, August, 1893, p. 165.

38. The home, its furnishings, and all the rooms are described in considerable detail in Berner, *Mrs. Stanford*, 17-20; in unpublished "Notes from Miss Berner's talk about the Stanford Home," February 4, 1943; in Stanford collection; and in the San Francisco *Chronicle*, n.d., 1876, clipping in Stanford papers.

39. Berner, *Mrs. Stanford*, 16.

40. Shaw, *Review of Reviews*, August, 1893, p. 165.

41. Fisher, "Stanford," 25.

42. Archibald Treat, quoting Stanford, in unidentified newspaper clipping, SFS, X, 59.

43. Related by Governor George Stoneman as coming from Field, in Ayer, *Gold and Sunshine*, 281. Field was a Californian, and is sometimes regarded as a Stanford protege. Fred Rodell, *Nine Men* (New York, 1955), 157.

44. Ayer, *Gold and Sunshine,* 281-282.

45. San Francisco *Call,* October 17, 1882.

46. *Ibid.,* See Berner, *Mrs. Stanford,* 24-28, for a description of the car and how it was built, maintained, and handled by railroad workmen.

47. Henry Root, *Henry Root: Surveyor, Engineer, and Inventor,* (San Francisco, 1921), 25.

48. *Ibid.* 25, 52. The construction of the California Cable Railroad in 1877 was an epoch-making event in the use of concrete; it was the first time concrete was poured on wrought iron molded to a form.

49. *Ibid.,* 43.

50. *Ibid.*

51. *Carnival Record,* II (October 27, 1882), 4.

52. Evelyn Craig Pattiani, "Silk in Piedmont," *Calif. Hist. Soc. Quar.,* XXXI (1952), 337.

53. Bancroft, *Stanford,* 135.

54. Sacramento *Record-Union,* July 3, 1886.

55. Shaw, *Review of Reviews,* August, 1893, 165.

56. San Francisco *Examiner,* June 22, 1893.

57. Bancroft, *Stanford,* 135.

58. Berner, *Mrs. Stanford,* 24.

59. San Francisco *Examiner,* June 22, 1893.

60. Fisher, "Stanford," 28.

61. San Francisco *Examiner,* June 22, 1893.

62. Berner, *Mrs. Stanford,* 13-14.

63. Bancroft, *Stanford,* 63.

64. *Ibid.*

65. *Ibid.,* 64.

66. The itinerary of this trip can be reconstructed from letters and telegrams sent home by Mrs. Stanford and Leland and from Leland's "log book for 1881," now in Leland Junior collection. Some of the key guides to their locations and dates are Mrs. Stanford to Stanford, November 14, 1880, from Antwerp; *ibid.,* November 17, 1880, from Brussels; *ibid.,* March 16, 1881, from Naples; *ibid.,* March 28, 1881, from Rome. All in Jane Stanford collection.

67. Leland Junior to Stanford, November 8, December 19, 1880.

68. *Ibid.,* March 31, 1881.

69. Leland Junior to grandma, March 14, 1881.

70. Leland Junior to Stanford, March 19, 1881.

71. Berner, *Mrs. Stanford,* 29. Fisher, "Stanford," 29.

72. Berner, *Mrs. Stanford,* 24.

73. Sacramento *Record-Union,* n.d., 1881, dateline Paris, November 14, 1881.

74. *Ibid.*

75. Altrocchi, *Spectacular San Franciscans,* 243. Berner, *Mrs. Stanford,* 30.

76. Stanford to unidentified doctor, May 25, 1883.

77. Bancroft, *Stanford,* 72.

78. Leland Junior to Miss Hull, June 15, 1883, from London.

79. Leland Junior to Aunt Kate, July 2, 1883, from London. Leland Junior to Uncle Ariel, July 9, 1883, from London.

80. Leland Junior to Aunt Kate, August 2, 1883, from Paris.

81. Leland Junior wrote almost daily from Havre to his father during August; Aug. 9, 15, 16, 19, 21, 22, 25, 1883. Leland Junior to Miss Hull, September 2, 1883, from Paris. Leland Junior to Stanford, September 2, 1883, from Paris.

82. Fisher, "Stanford," 31. Bancroft, *Stanford,* 75.

83. Leland Junior to Uncle Ariel, October 17, 1883, from Paris.

84. *Ibid.*

85. Leland Junior to Uncle Ariel, December 25, 1883.

86. Leland Junior to Miss Hull, February 11, 1884, the last letter he wrote before his death.

87. *Ibid.*

88. *Ibid.*

89. Berner, *Mrs. Stanford,* 32.

90. This was narrated by Herbert C. Nash, in unidentified newspaper clipping in Stanford collection, and was reprinted in the Palo Alto *Daily,* September 4, 1893.

91. Lew Wallace, United States Minister to Turkey, to Stanford, January 16, 1884. Stanford to Jesse Grant, March 31, 1885.

92. Leland Junior to Miss Hull, February 11, 1884. Mrs. Stanford telegram to Timothy and May Hopkins, February 25, 1884.

93. Leland Junior to Miss Hull, February 11, 1884.

94. Stanford telegram to Ariel Lathrop, March 13, 1884, in San Francisco *Bulletin,* n.d., 1884, SFS, VIII, 12. In a similar telegram addressed to Mrs. Mark Hopkins, on the same date, Mrs. Stanford added: "Please pray for us." Jane Stanford collection.

CHAPTER XI

STANFORD UNIVERSITY

The crowning work of Leland Stanford's life was the creation of the university that bears his son's name; if he had never built a railroad, governed the state of California, or sat in the United States Senate, this achievement alone would have won him immortality. It was undoubtedly the most magnificent philanthropic gift that had ever been made at that date by a single American. At the time of its organization, the university was the most richly endowed school in the nation.

Following the unexpected and untimely death of their son, the grief-stricken Stanfords were both on the verge of nervous collapse. Life no longer seemed to hold any meaning for them, and it was well said that "the light of their lives went out with their boy."[1] On the first night Stanford sank into unconsciousness, a completely broken-hearted man, and his condition worsened to the point where his life, as well as his sanity, was despaired of.[2] Fearful that her husband might not survive the shock of Leland's death, Mrs. Stanford summoned all the courage she could to help lighten his burden. He gradually regained some of his strength only to have his wife overpowered by her silent grief and her anxiety for him, and for a time her life too hung in the balance.[3] Neither of them recovered completely, and their lives from that day on bore the imprint of this tragedy.

No one considered Stanford a deeply-religious man; he believed in God and in an after-life, and attended church occasionally, but religion never occupied a place as central to his life as it had his wife's. In Sacramento they sometimes attended a Baptist church, and when at home in Palo Alto they went to the Menlo Park Presbyterian Church.[4] When Stanford died, a Methodist Episcopal pastor in Washington considered the California Senator a member of his congregation.[5] All of which indicates that he was not indifferent to spiritual matters, but that he possessed no particular loyalty to any one doctrine or church. His religious position was aptly summarized by his wife, as follows:

If a firm belief in a beneficent Creator, a profound admiration for Jesus of Nazareth and his teaching, and the certainty of a personal life hereafter constitute religion then Leland Stanford was a religious man. The narrow walls of a creed could not confine him; therefore he was not a professed member of any church, for in each confession of faith he found something to which he could not subscribe. But for the principles of religion he had a profound veneration; in his heart were the true sentiments of Christianity, and he often said that in his opinion the Golden Rule was the corner stone of all true religion.[6]

The birth of Leland made such an impression upon Stanford that for the only time in her life Mrs. Stanford found him on his knees praying, thanking God for their baby and for her health.[7] From that moment on, there was more than an ordinary parental and filial affection between the father and son; each lived much of his life in the other, and it was hardly an exaggeration to say that, in the father's eyes, "the boy put the name 'sacred' upon everything which he touched in his gay, young life."[8]

A family friend said that the cruel blow of the son's death would have overwhelmed Mrs. Stanford had she not been supported "by a firm and confident reliance upon the Infinite Being."[9] She had a personal faith in Christ as her Savior. This faith and her belief in the immortality of the soul and that God never intended death as a punishment gave her the strength needed to bear her grief.

Several different accounts have survived of the first night following Leland's death. The exhausted father had a singular dream — some call it a vision — of his dead son; the phenomenon has been attributed to his "aching heart," "fevered brain," "fitful and disordered sleep;" in any case, he was lamenting in this dream his lack of reason for living, whereupon Leland appeared to him, as real as if in the flesh, and comforted him: "Father, be not cast down; all is well; you have much to live for; you can do much more and better for your fellow men than I."[10] The boy's charge assumed a different form with each retelling. In one he was much more specific: "Father, do not spend your life in a vain sorrow. Do something for humanity. Build a university for the education of poor young men."[11] Another has the son rebuking his distraught father: "Papa, do not say that. You have a great deal to live for; live for humanity."[12]

This "spiritual visitation" became a guiding force in the parents' lives, and on the following morning they decided to use their resources to found a university in memory of Leland; in this way they would take all the children of California to be their children. Ever since his wealth had begun to mount, with the completion of the transcontinental railroad, Stanford had been contemplating a substantial gift to some kind of public institution.[13] He had been undecided as to whether to give the money to a hospital or to a school, but was inclined toward the latter by the consideration that the safety of the country rested ultimately upon an educated people.[14] The death of Leland revived this interest. Later claims to the contrary notwithstanding, the idea for this memorial came to them at once, apart from any suggestion by others. Mrs. Stanford often attributed their inspiration to thoughts of the boy, and was quoted as saying that in dreams he helped her; every new thought and plan seemed to come from him.[15]

The Stanfords were unable to leave Paris until April 24, six weeks after the tragedy. During this interval, their idea for founding a university took definite shape, and Stanford began talking over his ideas with Dr. Augustus F. Beard, an American minister of religion who was in Paris. He confided to Beard:

> This bereavement has so entirely changed my thoughts and plans of life that I do not see the way before me. I have been successful in the accumulation of property, and all of my thoughts of the future were associated with my dear son. I was living for him and his future. This is what brought us abroad for his education. Now, I was thinking in the night, since Leland is gone what my wealth could do. I was thinking that since I could do no more for my boy I might do something for other people's boys in Leland's name.[16]

According to Beard, Stanford's experiences with poorly-trained railroad engineers had given him the idea of starting a school for training civil and mechanical engineers. Not content with merely reporting Stanford's views on the subject, Beard assumed credit for suggesting to him the idea of a school broader in scope, patterned after Cornell.[17] In point of fact, however, Beard had nothing to do with the idea of founding a university; it had already taken shape before he talked to Stanford. Beard was the first of a long line of people who claimed to have planted the idea in Stanford's mind or caused him to enlarge upon his own idea as a result of their suggestions.[18]

Before leaving Paris, the Stanfords drew up a new will, making provision for the projected university. They arrived safely in New York on May 4, but railroad business detained them until the fall. Stanford and his associates were then organizing the Southern Pacific of Kentucky holding company.

Shortly after the Stanfords returned from Europe, their plans to found a university were published in California by their friend Frank Pixley of the *Argonaut*. Pixley called upon them in their New York quarters to get the details of the plan, and then wrote home that they were intending to establish at Menlo Park a school for boys and girls which would prepare them for the scramble of life; it was going to focus upon practical learning rather than upon higher education.[19]

Meanwhile, Leland's body had been placed temporarily in a vault in Greenwood Cemetery in New York.[20] In November it was taken to Palo Alto, where a simple burial service was conducted with the employees of the farm acting as pallbearers.[21] The body was then placed in a small mausoleum on the farm, the same grounds on which the foundations had already been laid for his own home when he reached maturity.[22] Memorial services were held in a number of churches throughout the state, and scores of poems written in commemoration of the lad were sent to the mother in vain attempts to console her.[23]

II

Once back in California the Stanfords took immediate steps toward founding their school, but they ran into one difficulty: Stanford insisted upon retaining control over the university during his lifetime, whereas California law had no provisions for the incorporation of such an institution. His first move, therefore, was to have the legislature adopt a law that would allow this; he explained that had such a law not been passed, the school's trustees could have put him off the grounds. He explained further that he wanted his ideas carried out, so far as they were practical, and since he was going to place most of his fortune in this school, he would naturally like to humor his own whims.[24] He would not be satisfied making gifts to institutions over which he would have no influence or upon which he could not impress his own ideas. Stanford said that he had seen a number of large estates intended for public use devoured by attorneys and reduced to next to nothing by litigation following the death of the testators; seeing the possibility that this might happen to theirs, he and his wife had resolved to make the gift during their lifetimes and oversee its administration.[25]

An appropriate bill was quickly drawn up by Creed Haymond, one of Stanford's attorneys. The Senate passed it unanimously and the Assembly adopted it sixty-three to four; it was signed into law on May 9, 1885, Stanford's sixty-first birthday.[26] The enabling act provided for twenty-four trustees, each of whom was appointed by Stanford from among his business associates and personal friends.[27] The first meeting of the board was convened in the founders' San Francisco home on November 14, 1885; there, without pomp or ceremony, the trustees were received into the library and had the deed of grant read to them. In the presence of 100 people the Stanfords turned over to the trustees three large tracts of land as an initial endowment: the Vina ranch, the largest, had 53,000 acres; the Gridley farm, in Butte County, covered 18,000 acres, planted mostly in wheat; and the 6,000-acre Palo Alto farm.[28] The total value was estimated conservatively at $5,000,000, and was expected to increase to $20,000,000 by the end of the century.[29]

The founding grant defined the functions of the trustees and the purposes of the university. The twenty-four man board was empowered to appoint and remove presidents, fix the salaries of university employees, control the institution and its properties, and use the interest, but not the principal, of these properties.[30] The purposes of the university were to promote the "public welfare by exercising an influence in behalf of humanity and civilization," to teach the blessings of liberty, and to inculcate love and reverence for the principles of government. The grantors reserved to themselves "absolute dominion over the rents, issues and profits of the real property granted," as if the grant had not been made, and to guarantee a practical curriculum, not one purely theoretical or speculative, insisted that instruction be given in the arts, sciences, mechanics, and all branches of agriculture, in order to qualify students for "personal success and direct usefulness in life." Sectarian education alone was prohibited, but the trustees were to see that the immortality of the soul was taught, as well as the existence of an all-wise and beneficent Creator. The last requirement reflected the Stanfords' growing concern with religious matters.

Central to Stanford's plan was his insistence that the sciences be given their proper place, which was denied them by most other universities. Existing institutions allowed and indeed created a wide separation between the theoretical and the practical; this he would correct. Furthermore, his school was to be democratic: desire and willingness to work and learn were more important to him than were money, family, or social position. As a man who had worked hard himself and had succeeded, Stanford had great faith in the Horatio Alger path of success — success comes to those who work hard, save their money, invest wisely, and spend carefully.

The cardinal aim of the university was to cultivate individual potential in order to advance humanity. Stanford rejected the idea that there was only a fixed amount of wealth in the world and that only a few could be wealthy, that the rest were consigned to poverty: "I believe that the comforts and even the elegancies of life are the natural heritage of every provident, intelligent man. The earth is inexhaustible in supplies for the gratification of every reasonable want of man."[31] His university would develop the skills needed to help men help themselves; in other words, it would create Horatio Algers.[32] If some of his educational pronouncements had the ring of a farm-boy philosophy, they were sentiments that successful men all over the country could echo and applaud.[33]

Stanford University was to be coeducational so that girls could be taught how to be better mothers; those in whose hands rested the education of the young must themselves be properly educated. On this issue Stanford met with considerable opposition from his wife, who objected to a coeducational school. The topic was discussed at length, and he reportedly begged her to see it his way; but it was not until he reminded her that they had taken the children of California to be their children, and that girls as well as boys were children, that she finally gave in.[34]

Students at this school were to be inculcated in the necessity of living sober lives. Stanford estimated that twenty-five percent of the nation's productive capacity was lost in buying, selling, and consuming hard liquors.[35] In keeping with his belief that students were to be kept from the evils of alcohol, the founding deed prohibited forever any kind of "saloon" on campus. In 1888, when Stanford gave his approval for a railway station at Palo Alto, he did so with one reservation: whiskey must never be sold there near his school.[36]

Stanford always objected to conventional wisdom, rote learning, or traditional organization that stifled individual initiative, and he carried these dislikes with him in founding his school; freedom of individual development was to mark all curricular organization. Degree requirements and traditional sequences of courses were to take secondary place to practical, useful, individual development. Proper education necessitated absolute freedom of investigation on the part of teachers and students; thus Stanford endorsed *die Luft der Freiheit weht* as a proposed motto for the university.[37]

At Aix-les-Bains he had once met an acquaintance who believed that the Stanford fortune could be put to better use, since there was already an excess of education, in itself a prevalent cause of discontent.[38] Stanford contradicted him, insisting that there could no more be too much education than too much health or intelligence, and challenged him to produce one man who was too well educated. True, there was unwise or unfit education, but not too thorough or too much education.

III

There was an immediate, world-wide outpouring of praise for Stanford's plan; editors strained for adulatory adjectives with which to describe adequately his magnanimous bequest.[39] One called it the "most magnificent educational endowment of the world."[40] Another said that the entire plan was arranged from the "most unselfish and noblest inspiration."[41] Never was an act performed "with more singleness of purpose and with less ostentation."[42] This gift, "unique in the history of civilization," had no other end than the improvement of humanity.[43] One ecstatic writer called it an act of unparalleled magnificence; never in the whole history of civilization had there been a

EARLY CONSTRUCTION SCENE at Stanford University.

Stanford Library

gift "more princely than this."[44] The Stanford benefaction was unmatched by that of any private citizen in the "whole civilized world," so it was fitting that the giver as well as the gift was lauded: it was California's greatest citizen who created America's greatest university.[45] It was suggested that a monument to Stanford be erected in Santa Clara County to commemorate his creation of "the greatest and most richly endowed educational institution in the world."[46] And a preacher praised the projected university to the highest heaven, in a sermon in which he referred to it as the "epitome of the universe."[47]

The lopsided vote on Stanford's education bill and the response to his grant concealed the fact that there was considerable opposition. Some felt that there was no need in the area for another university, that the state school at Berkeley could handle all the students available and more. One New York editor remarked snidely that there was as much need for a new university in California as for "an asylum for decayed sea-captains in Switzerland."[48] Some argued that the grant was merely "restitution" for his having taken so much from the government and the public.[49] According to this line of reasoning, "Stanford" and "Central Pacific" had been synonymous during the heat of the antimonopoly agitation in California, and, having to bear the odium of much for which he was not personally responsible, being "a little less grasping" than his associates, he now wanted to do something to redeem his name. Granted that something of restitution did prompt his action, it still did not have to be done; taking all factors into account, it was an unselfish act of good will that evidenced a concern and a generosity that his detractors never appreciated. The question they did not face was this: was Stanford's grant evidence that he had always been different, or did his grant make him different? In short, was it an act of unadulterated magnanimity or an act of successful restitution? But regardless of the inner motives, the grant did work a profound change in the popular feeling toward him; from now on his former detractors would distinguish him even more clearly from his associates.

Others who opposed the school discovered or imagined even baser motives in Stanford's founding of this "unnecessary institution." According to one story, he founded the rival school out of spite for not having been confirmed a regent of the state university a few years earlier. On September 14, 1882, Republican Governor George C. Perkins had appointed him to the Board of Regents of the University of California. In January, 1883, when his name came before the Senate for confirmation, the opposition Democrats were then in control of the Senate, and Perkins had been succeeded by Democratic Governor George Stoneman. Stanford's nomination was referred to the State Judiciary Committee for reconsideration, which was tantamount to outright rejection. To avoid a partisan confrontation over a matter that should have transcended partisanship, Stanford withdrew his name.[50]

So far as he was concerned, this was the end of the matter; there is no evidence — nothing said or done by him — that he harbored any grudge over the incident, though for a time he was "deeply distressed," and very much resented the criticisms leveled at him because of his railroad associations.[51] But good relations between him and the University of California continued, and Martin Kellogg, its president, took part in the opening exercises of Stanford University a few years later.

Other critics said that Stanford's grant was prompted by partisan considerations, that he was merely using this "philanthropy" as a means of winning a seat in the United States Senate. During a lull in construction, when the Stanfords were touring abroad, Mrs. Stanford received newspaper clippings from the United States alleging that construction had been halted because Stanford had already won election to the Senate.[52] This charge was entirely baseless; if Stanford had wanted a Senate seat — and there is no evidence that he had given it any thought as early as 1884 — and if the position were for sale, he probably could have bought his way in for less than $20,000,000.

Stanford was convinced that a need existed for the kind of school he intended to build, and he wrote off the charge that he was duplicating the efforts of others by insisting that if his university were to be like others in the country, he would have given his money to one of them instead; but his school, he insisted, was to be "on a different plan."[53] Ironic as it now appears, one of the major differences between the "competing" universities was that Stanford's would be less expensive; its seven dollars per month for room and board was geared to help students who could not afford the twenty-five charged at Berkeley.[54]

IV

Stanford's "vision" after his son's death, as well as the boy's charge to him to do something for humanity, gave ammunition to people who maintained that Stanford University was established as a result of some kind of spiritualistic communication from the world beyond the grave. The Stanfords were not spiritualists, in the technical sense of the term, and he both denied and ridiculed allegations that his and his wife's so-called "monomania," their "devotion to spiritualism," had anything to do with their decision to dedicate their fortunes to beneficent purposes. Charges of spiritualistic influences persisted, however, despite all disavowals of faith in it. Perhaps the step from a faith in immortality to the belief that the departed soul can be contacted by the living is a short one: at any rate, in November, 1886, Stanford admitted to his attorney, Samuel M. Wilson, and Timothy Hopkins that just after Leland's death, when emotionally most unstable and most vulnerable because of their bereavement, he and Mrs. Stanford had attended seances in Paris in hopes of contacting their dead son. The boy was not dead, they thought, only spiritualized, and people in their psychological position were apt to be "beguiled by hope." But he explained further that they both gave up as futile all efforts to make such a contact.[55]

At times, however, Mrs. Stanford showed that she had a faint hope or belief that spiritualism was not all quackery. One woman requested and received from her a photo of Leland, from which she made a "physiognomical delineation" of his character.[56] Later, a Madame Diss de Bar said Stanford offered her a sizeable sum of money for a "spirit portrait," but he denied having any knowledge of her.[57]

In 1889 there appeared in a New York paper a six-column article on prominent men who believed in spiritualism. Stanford was listed among them, though the writer conceded that the California Senator denied any spiritualist connections and had no faith in mediums. The identification was based upon certain of Stanford's beliefs that smacked of spiritualism, though upon his flimsy evidence anyone believing in the supernatural could have been classed as a spiritualist.[58]

In the fall of 1891, rumors were again published in a number of newspapers that Stanford University had been founded through the agency and under the influences of spiritualism. Maud Lord Drake, a spiritualist medium, said she had been the link between the two worlds. Stanford saw her claim in a newspaper, and, wishing to put an end to all such speculation once and for all, asked David Starr Jordan to draw up a formal memorandum disavowing any faith in spiritualism and that spiritualistic influences had anything to do with his founding of Stanford University. Jordan wrote:

> Mr. Stanford made his will, looking to the endowment of the university, in Paris, April 24, 1884. Mrs. Stanford made her will also, and copies were sent to America. Mrs. Maud Lord Drake was unknown to them until they met her at a seance with the Grants in October, 1884. At about that time Mrs. Drake was detected in fraud. . . . No spiritualistic influence affected the decision [to found the university]. Mrs. Drake had no more to do with it than a babe unborn.[59]

The Stanfords' visits were prompted by curiosity as well as hope, but "they never received through mediums any evidence they regarded as convincing."[60]

Methodist minister John P. Newman, a friend of President Grant, who had preached in the church in Washington that the Grants attended, conducted the memorial services for Leland Junior in San Francisco. He wanted the presidency of Stanford University, but Stanford rejected all his hints about making the university a religious school, though Mrs. Stanford was interested.[61] Newman and his wife, apparently playing on Mrs. Stanford's interest in contacting her son, arranged a series of seances in their San Francisco home. Stanford was invited to join the cirle, but he refused. The Newmans eventually claimed a contact, but Mrs. Stanford was unconvinced; the voice she heard was not Leland's; yet she could not break away from the circle. Her husband reasoned with her, and advised her against further attendance, and she finally agreed to give them up. The unsuccessful Newmans then returned home to New York, but Mrs. Stanford's "preoccupation with the subject lasted for years."[62] Her secretary said that her whole subject of conversation was Leland; her grief was always in her mind, so much so that the San Francisco house itself seemed grief stricken.[63]

Patronizing spiritualistic mediums was not a socially acceptable practice then, as now, and the friends and relatives of the Stanfords, trying to protect their image, protested too much their interest in seances. Mrs. Stanford's interest simply could not be denied. Archibald Treat, for one, labeled the rumor that Mrs. Stanford was a spiritualist "alley gossip," and assured his readers that she was not a medium, as was sometimes alleged, nor did she hire them. To the undeniable report that she tried to commune with her dead son, all he could say was: "If that be true, then it is a beautiful thought."[64]

Following Mrs. Stanford's death, in 1905, the issue was revived. One journalist alleged that the Stanfords retired at eight o'clock each evening and extinguished all the lights in their San Francisco mansion or Palo Alto residence, wherever they happened to be, "so that the father and mother could commune with the spirit of the departed lad." "This nightly occurrence was an admitted fact," he added, but offered no evidence of any kind to substantiate his fantastic statement; nor did he identify the people by whom the fact was admitted.[65]

Mr. Simeon H. West, a Leroy (Illinois) spiritualist, later revived the story that the inspiration for the university came from the dead boy; that the Stanfords were faithful spiritualists, he said, had been known in California for a number of years. West identified a Mrs. J. J. Whitney of San Francisco as the Stanfords' private medium of sixteen years. He asserted that newspapers later attributed the founding of the university to a dream because it sounded "much milder to orthodox ears than to say spirits;" Stanford, like most men in high official positions, did not "proclaim his spiritualism from the housetops."[66] To have done so, West contended, would have forfeited his influence with the people with whom he dealt. Therefore, the Stanfords did not "mingle with the common herd of spiritualists," but employed their own private medium to hold family seances in their home. West's information came firsthand from the spirit world, he said, and was therefore as reliable as his report that Lincoln held private seances in the White House; Lincoln, a regular visitor at West's seances, had told him so.[67] With this kind of testimony, and irrefutable evidence, who could doubt West's explanations?

Stanford's brief dabbling in spiritualism followed him to his grave; it was reported after his death that his long illness had weakened him, and, turning to spiritualism for solace, he had become more of a "dreamer than actor." Following the death of his son, according to this fable, he developed a greater interest in spiritualism, "and inclined to a belief in the doctrines of the Spiritualists."[68]

Stanford's brother Thomas Welton, in Australia, was a confirmed spiritualist, and upon his death willed to his brother's university money for carrying on psychic research.[69] But in their letters there is not so much as an allusion to Leland Stanford's having any faith in spiritualism. After Stanford's death, his widow corresponded with his brother Thomas, and her interest in spiritualism was again quickened briefly by these letters; at the time of her death she was planning a trip to Australia where she hoped to see "an honest demonstration."[70]

V

The advice Stanford sought for establishing an educational institution came from much more concrete sources than fortunetellers. Immediately upon his return from Europe in the spring of 1884, he set about contacting a number of the nation's foremost college administrators. He knew the presidents of Harvard, Johns Hopkins, Cornell, and the Massachusetts Institute of Technology. One of the authorities consulted was Charles W. Eliot, president of Harvard, who later told of how the Stanfords had come to him and asked what his plant was worth. When given the figure of from five to six million dollars, Mrs. Stanford allegedly said, "Oh, Leland, we can do it." This conveys the intended impression that the Stanfords were so naïve that they did not appreciate that a university was more than buildings. Eliot said that this sum had a sobering effect on Stanford, but after an appreciable interval, he said, with a smile: "Well, Jane, we could manage that, couldn't we?"[71]

Eliot's version of their meeting, as improbable as it was, took on apocryphal lustre with each retelling, especially as embellished by his son, Samuel Eliot, who, a number of years afterward, had "a shabby little man and a shabby little woman" calling on his father for advice on building their projected university. The shabby little man asked: "How much would it cost to duplicate Harvard?" When told that Harvard had a history, a tradition, that could not be duplicated, the "shabby little man" replied: "I mean the plant, the *Plant* of Harvard, buildings, equipment and such." The story in all its grotesqueness suffers from paraphrase. In the words of young Eliot, the shabby multimillionaire bumbled out, "Oh, I see . . . well." The conversation continued:

My father decided to mention a hastily computed round sum and terminate the quite useless conversation: "Let's say twenty-five million dollars." Then the shabby little man turned to his shabby little wife in a sort of ecstacy [sic] and exclaimed: "Jane, we can do it! *Jane, we can do it!*"[72]

Eliot was wrong in everything: the amount of money was increased fivefold, the Stanfords were not little — Stanford himself weighed over 240 at the time, and his wife almost 170 — and they were far from shabby in their dress.[73] Mrs. Stanford was known as a tall, distinguished, and well-groomed lady of refinement — she was probably the only "shabby little old lady" in the world with a million dollars worth of jewelry and a reputation of being one of California's best-dressed matrons. Her husband's personal grooming was always impeccable, though at times a bit out of style. While in the Senate it was said of him that though neat, he was one of the most unassumingly-dressed men in the capital.[74] His wealth was not reflected in his clothes; he wore an old-fashioned (though not shabby) low cut vest, but his suits were of the best Irish linen.

One of the many college administrators from whom Stanford sought advice was General Francis A. Walker, president of the Massachusetts Institute of Technology. Walker spent a number of weeks at the Palo Alto farm, in the fall of 1886, advising on the building program.[75] He recommended construction of thirteen single story stone buildings. Walker's suggestions were accepted by the architects Shepley, Rutan, and Coolidge, successors to Henry H. Richardson, whose plans were eventually adopted. Charles A. Coolidge asked that his firm be considered for the job, and got it, probably through the influence of Walker, who was Coolidge's mother's cousin.[76]

With the adjournment of Congress, in March, 1887, Senator Stanford and his wife returned to California to begin actual construction on the university. He was anxious to get on with the building program so he could see the fruits of his labor.[77] On May 14, Leland's nineteenth birthday, the cornerstone of the university was laid, on a site chosen by Stanford and his houseguest, the famous architect Frederick Law Olmstead, with Senator Stanford performing the ceremony of mortaring it in place.[78] It was hoped that the school would open its doors one year from that date, but this proved impossible. Openings were subsequently announced for May 14, 1889, and the fall of 1890, but when this last date rolled around, the doors were still closed.

Building a university meant putting together a plant, finding the right man for the presidency, and assembling a faculty. The second of these tasks proved by far the most difficult. Stanford first offered the position to General Walker, at several times his MIT salary, but, fearful of the effects of a totally-new environment upon his family, and desirous of carrying his work where he was a bit further, the General declined.[79]

Unexpected setbacks such as this made Stanford realize the scope of the task before him. The talents he wanted were common enough, but getting them all in one man was another matter. "The scholars," he said, "are plentiful enough, but the executive ability is scarce."[80] He considered business ability more important than scholarship, and decided that if he could not combine the two qualifications he would get a businessman for the job, or possibly hold the presidency himself until he could get a suitable man.[81]

As opening day drew near, in the fall of 1891, and the university was still without a president, Stanford urged Andrew D. White, retired president of Cornell, to accept the position, but White declined. When asked whether there was anyone he would recommend for the position, White advised him to get David Starr Jordan, one of his former students, who was now president of Indiana University.[82] Soon afterwards, while Jordan was addressing a meeting at the University of Illinois, he was handed a telegram from White, with the cryptic message: "Decline no offer from California till you hear from me."[83] Upon his return to Bloomington, he found the Stanfords waiting to see him.

Jordan was immediately attracted to Stanford, the man — "he revealed an unusually attractive personality" — but, more important than this, the educational philosophies of the two men coincided very closely; both wanted students trained for "usefulness in life." After a short consultation with his wife, Jordan accepted the position, with some reservation, despite his $10,000 salary. First, California, with its "discordant elements," was still a very individualistic state; and, secondly, the university was to be "personally conducted," and that by a businessman active in political life. But the possibilities were so challenging that he could not decline.

The choice of Jordan and Stanford's consultation with President White had nothing to do with Cornell as any kind of pattern.[84] It is true that Cornell gave prominence to agriculture, engineering, mechanics, and science, but its curriculum differed little from any other land grant university.[85] As it turned out, Stanford University was organized, built, and then developed quite independently of any fixed model or pattern; its growth reflected the pragmatism and changing ideas of its founders as well as those of its first president.

VI

On October 1, 1891, opening exercises were held at Stanford University.[86] For three days trains brought visitors to Menlo Park, Mayfield, and Redwood City, and a special train of six cars was dispatched to carry those who overflowed the regular runs. When the dedicatory service opened, it was estimated that 5,000 people were crowded into the quadrangle, including many of the state's most distinguished citizens.[87] A stage decorated with palms, pampas grass, and grapevines, weighted down with fresh grapes, was erected at the north end of the quad, beneath a huge arch. The background was formed of American flags, and in the center was a full length oil portrait of Leland Stanford, Junior. Among the distinguished guests seated on the platform were faculty members from the University of California and the University of Santa Clara, two United States Senators, and a number of Stanford's intimate railroad associates. Collis P. Huntington was conspicuous by his absence.

Following the singing of "Glory Be to God on High," Stanford delivered the first address; it was brief, to the point, and, it must be said, inspirational, but contained nothing new in the way of ideas or charges to the faculty,

Wasp

DAVID STARR JORDAN, first president of Stanford University, 1891–1931.

trustees, and students. His comments hit time and time again upon the works of the Creator and his goodness and gifts to man. President Martin Kellogg of the University of California spoke briefly, and was followed by Stanford President David Starr Jordan. Trustee Dr. Horatio Stebbins offered a prayer, and Judge Lorenzo Sawyer, president of the Board of Trustees, delivered a brief, scholarly address, in which he praised the founders for their generosity and wisdom, and charged the trustees to carry out their intentions; if they developed the university according to the purposes of the founders, he predicted, its power for good would go on "from age to age, to the end of time."[88]

Ariel Lathrop, Stanford's brother-in-law and business manager, also managed the affairs of the university. This, as it proved, was unfortunate, since he did not approve of the university. Whether he thought Stanford could have done better with his money or whether he was concerned lest the Stanford heirs be left penniless is uncertain, but he was decidedly unfriendly toward the whole business. As in his other affairs, Stanford had not trusted the management of the university entirely to Lathrop, and when room and board were raised in Encina Hall at the end of the first year, Stanford wrote him ordering that the rate be cut to five dollars per week.[89] This, he said, was enough for poor students to pay, and it was these that he intended mainly to aid. Lathrop stood more and more in the way of smooth operation, and was unwilling to accept such rebukes; at about this time he resigned and returned to Albany.[90] But things got worse instead of better, because Mrs. Stanford's younger brother Charles replaced him, and Charles was harder to work with than Ariel. Complaints against him reportedly streamed into Stanford's office from workers at all levels, but Charles was kept on, undoubtedly because of the deep affection between him and his sister. The younger Lathrop, known for years as the university president's "hair shirt," saw the university completed and later became its treasurer and then business manager.[91]

The Romanesque style buildings were nearly completed in 1892, and, in the estimation of Andrew D. White, in their "simplicity, beauty, and fitness, far surpassed any other which had at that time been erected for university purposes in the United States."[92] White regarded the Palo Alto school and Jefferson's University of Virginia as the only exceptions to the general rule that American universities were a hodgepodge of incongruous styles.

Stanford continued active in the management of the university. He advised Jordan of the desirability of setting a good table for the students for less than three dollars per week.[93] He also made decisions in some fairly-trivial financial matters, as when he directed that students away from school for more than a week during holidays would be credited with the amount of their board during their absence.[94] He even assumed responsibility for naming the boys' and girls' dormitories.[95]

Stanford followed the completion of the initial building program with great care. He advised on the scope and cost and the kind of library needed, and when it came to building additional buildings, he traveled to California to advise Jordan about them.[96] He even advised on details such as the heating of the gymnasium.[97]

Even if he had wished, and there is no indication that he did, Stanford could not have retired entirely from the operation of the university. His name was too well known across the country, and he was considered much more accessible than a man like Jordan. Also, his philanthropic record would suggest that he might be a soft touch. There are hundreds of letters on file written to Stanford by parents hoping to get their children admitted to the university through his personal intervention.[98] Just as many wrote recommending others. In certain cases he intervened, as when he asked Jordan's special care for a potential student who had served for a number of years as his page in the Senate.[99]

For years prior to the opening of the university, Stanford had been inundated by requests for jobs.[100] Once President Jordan was hired, he nearly always referred this kind of correspondence to him.[101] The rule, however, was flexible, and on occasion he went beyond merely advising Jordan on faculty matters.[102] In one case that had perhaps more merit than others, Stanford responded directly: "I am leaving the selection of Professors to President Jordan, but when I see him I will confer with him in regard to your case."[103]

Stanford respected, sought, and accepted Jordan's advice. Once when a professor resigned whom Stanford wanted to keep, he offered to make him a vice-president, subject to Jordan's approval.[104] For the commencement speaker in the spring of 1893, Stanford chose George F. Edmunds of Vermont, then in Redlands, provided that Jordan had not already made other arrangements. He advised Jordan to contact Edmunds, if the position was still open.[105] At other times he was less solicitous, as when he telegraphed his president not to hire a certain professor, adding that he would explain later.[106] Occasionally Mrs. Stanford recommended someone to Jordan for a position on the staff, but this was rare.[107]

At times Jordan requested Stanford's permission to make certain appointments.[108] There is no record of such requests ever having been denied.[109] But, in cases where Stanford had no special concern or extraordinary knowledge about applicants, he refused to advise, telling Jordan to exercise his own judgment.[110] In one notable exception, Stanford made all the arrangements for a distinguished speaker to deliver a series of lectures at the university, and Jordan first read of the appointment in the newspapers.[111] Ex-President Harrison was invited to deliver a series of lectures on international law, in the fall of 1893, following his leaving the White House.[112]

Stanford also took part in making rules governing the extra-curricular activities of his faculty members. On one occasion he objected that Jordan let a professor travel to Pasadena at university expense to lecture there. Stanford suggested the need for a rule governing such matters, and then laid down the rule: "When our Professors lecture for other institutions it seems to me that

"THE DOORS THROWN OPEN"
"Senator Stanford — It is all for you, my boy, and for the coming
generations. My ambition is now satisfied. I have less desire to be
President than to be founder of an institution that will make Presidents!"

This Wasp caption was almost prophetic, considering the fact that
Herbert Hoover was a student in Stanford University's first graduating
class.

their expenses should be paid by the people for whom they lecture, especially if they have to go as far as Pasadena."[113]

Stanford and Jordan became close friends, though not intimates. On his European tours Stanford would write him about the university and discuss their educational philosophies. In one letter, for example, he expressed satisfaction with Jordan's belief that physics should be taught by experimentation rather than merely by lectures and recitation.[114] Such exchanges were common. These two men complemented one another very effectively; their personalities were different, but not abrasive. Stanford would write long, respectful letters to Jordan, expounding on educational, religious, and philosophic ideas, and on how best to put them into practice. He hoped that together they could make Stanford University an example in original methods of instruction.

As Stanford grew older and his health gradually worsened, he talked more and more often of God and immortality; even in his later letters to Jordan he evidenced a growing concern with religion. Musing on classical and contemporary world civilizations, he decided that the Greeks and Romans were highly educated, but lacked what he called "true human civilization." He was firmly convinced that a civilization could not long endure "without a belief in the immortality of the soul, and in the beneficence and justice of the laws of the Creator."[115]

All this had bearing on the university. The founder told his president that his aim was to "fit men to realize the possibilities of humanity." Their graduates, in a sense, were to be missionaries to spread correct ideas of civilization. The true foundation of humanitarianism was neither intellectual nor moral development alone, but the Golden Rule. This was to be the guide in the development of the "religious element in man."

As Stanford's plans matured and as the university began functioning as an institution of higher learning, plans for a comprehensive system from kindergarten through college were abandoned, and Leland Stanford, Junior, University began looking more and more like other American universities. Ultimately, its curriculum differed widely from what Stanford had in mind when he founded the school. Instead of an institution covering kindergarten to graduate school, and stressing the practical arts, it now has a traditional undergraduate system. And rather than being merely a trade school, one that is different from other colleges, it is now regarded by some Stanfordites as the Harvard of the West.

Stanford University's annual tuition, currently in excess of $2,000, over seven times as much as that at Berkeley, brings a smile to the lips of those who read that Stanford intended his institution as a place where poor boys could go to school. Its lands are still intact, including over 8,000 acres of the original grant, but portions have been taken under threat of condemnation by city, county, and state agencies; in 1955 federal authorities purchased eighty-seven acres for a veterans' hospital. Much of the land not used for university purposes is now leased for grazing, agriculture, and industry; the industrial park alone brings in over $500,000 per year in revenue.

Stanford's monument is complete: the university is his monument, but it is interesting to note that according to his own testimony, if he had known how his school was to turn out, he probably would not have founded it, but would have given his money to a school already in existence, such as, perhaps, the University of California.

1.   Clark, *Stanford*, 382.

2.   Berner, *Mrs. Stanford*, 33.

3.   *Ibid.*, 35.

4.   Oakland *Morning Times*, April 18, 1891. Berner, *Mrs. Stanford*, 49.

5.   Unidentified newspaper clipping, SFS, X, 70.

6.   San Francisco *Examiner*, June 24, 1893.

7.   Quoted in Clark, *Stanford*, 380.

8.   San Francisco *Examiner*, June 22, 1893.

9.   Frank Pixley, in the San Francisco *Argonaut*, June 2, 1884.

10. Bancroft, *Stanford*, 83.

11. Unidentified newspaper clipping, Box 6, folder 66, in Stanford papers.

12. Reported by newspaper correspondent George Alfred Townsend as told him by the Stanfords when he visited them at their Palo Alto home in 1887. Cincinnati *Enquirer*, October 21, 1887, and New York *Commercial Advertiser*, June 27, 1893. Both cited in Clark, 382. Still other forms appear elsewhere. J. H. Seals, "Leland Stanford's Dream," in Stanford papers.

13. Bancroft, *Stanford*, 89.

14. Address of George C. Vest, Senator from Missouri, in *Memorial Addresses on the Life and Character of Leland Stanford* (Washington, 1894), 65.

15. Maggie McClure to Boutwell Dunlap, April 30, 1923.

16. Cited in Clark, *Stanford*, 384.

17. David Starr Jordan agreed that Cornell was the model. *Leland Stanford's Views on Higher Education* (Stanford, 1901), 8. Tenth Annual Commencement Speech.

18. Berner, *Mrs. Stanford*, 34. Frederick L. Anderson claimed later that his father, an unknown Baptist preacher, spent much time in the Stanford home, and while there planted in his host's mind the "seed thought which later grew into Leland Stanford, Jr., University." F. L. Anderson, *Galusha Anderson, Preacher and Educator, 1832-1918* (no city given, 1933), 19-20.

19. San Francisco *Argonaut*, June 21, 1884.

20. Unidentified newspaper clipping, SFS, VIII, 7.

21. San Francisco *Call*, November 28, 1884.

22. Fisher, "Stanford," 33. *Memorial Addresses*, 88.

23. Berner, *Mrs. Stanford*, 37. SFS, VIII, 7.

24. Washington *Post*, December 19, 1886.

25. New York *Herald*, March 23, 1885.

26. This bill was given the awkward title, "An Act to Advance Learning, the Arts and Sciences, and to Promote the Public Welfare by Providing for the Conveyance, Holding, and Protection of Property, and the Creation of Trusts for the Founding, Endowment, Creation, and Maintenance within this state of Universities, Colleges, Schools, Seminaries of Learning, Mechanical Institutes, Museums, and Galeries of Art."

27. William Ashburner, Isaac S. Belcher, John Boggs, John Q. Brown, Charles F. Crocker, Horace Davis, Matthew P. Deady, Henry L. Dodge, Stephen J. Field, Charles Goodall, George E. Gray, Dr. H. W. Harkness, Timothy Hopkins, T. B. McFarland, John F. Miller, Lorenzo Sawyer, Irving M. Scott, James McM. Shafter, N. W. Spaulding, Francis E. Spencer, Josiah Stanford, William M. Stewart, Alfred L. Tubbs, and Henry Vrooman. George T. Clark, "The Romance that Founded Stanford," *Stanford Illustrated Review*, XXX (June, 1929), 462.

28. Horace Davis, *The Meaning of the University* (San Francisco, 1895), in Clark, *Stanford*, 389. Sacramento *Record-Union*, November 16,1885.

29. Sacramento *Record-Union*, November 16, 1885.

30. The Deed of Grant is reprinted in a number of places, including *ibid.*

31. Interview in Sacramento *Record-Union*, November 13, 1888.

32. Sacramento *Record-Union*, November 16, 1885.

33. Edith R. Mirrielees, *Stanford, the Story of a University* (New York, 1959), 23.

34. Berner, *Mrs. Stanford*, 45.

35. Unidentified newspaper clipping, Box 6, folder 63, Stanford papers.

36. Stanford to Timothy Hopkins, January 8, 1888.

37. "The winds of freedom are blowing," from an address of Ulrich von Hutten at the time of the trial of Martin Luther. "Wisset Ihr nicht," cried Hutten, "dass die Luft der Freiheit weht?" David Starr Jordan, "The Educational Ideas of Leland Stanford," *The Sequoia*, III (September 13, 1893), 20.

38. *Ibid.*

39. San Francisco *Commercial Record*, May 9, 1889.

40. Sacramento *Record-Union*, November 16,1885.

41. Vallejo *Chronicle*, quoted in *ibid.*, November 19, 1885.

42. Sacramento *Record-Union*, November 16, 1885.

43. *The Sequoia*, III (September 13, 1893), 19.

44. Chico *Chronicle*, and Marysville *Appeal*, quoted in Sacramento *Record-Union*, November 19, 1885.

45. West Oakland *Star*, October 26, 1889, in *ibid.*

46. San Jose *Mercury*, September 10, 11, 1889.

47. Horatio Stebbins, "The Great Gift," preached Sunday, November 22, 1885, in the First Unitarian Church of San Francisco. Reprinted in Sacramento *Record-Union*, November 28, 1885.

48. Unidentified editorial, quoted in Treat, "Golden Key," 60.

49. San Francisco *Examiner*, June 22, 1893.

50. Hittell, *History*, IV, 675. The antirailroad, anti-Stanford San Francisco *Bulletin*, on March 31, 1917, gave credence to this account in an absurd and erroneous front-page story. The writer had Stoneman withdrawing Stanford's name under pressure, and the humiliated Stanford vowing vengeance on the people of California for thus rejecting him.

51. San Francisco *Examiner*, June 21, 1893.

52. Treat, "Golden Key," 60. Lack of ready building funds caused no end of trouble, and building was very slow because of this. Whenever Stanford attempted to get some of his money out of the railroad, Huntington would tell him it was all loaned out and that there was no cash available. Most of the money he put into construction at this time came from income from the Pacific Improvement Company (Fisher, "Stanford," 41).

53. New York *Evangelist*, February 10, 1891.

54. Unidentified newspaper clipping, SFS, XXV, 15.

55. New York *Herald*, March 23, 1885.

56. Mary D. Stanton to Stanford, December 28, 1888.

57. San Francisco *Bulletin*, April 4, 1888.

58. New York *Press*, February 17, 1889.

59. Jordan, *Days of a Man*, I, 365-366. Jordan to H. C. Nash, July 27, 1901.

60. Jordan, *Days of a Man*, I, 366 note.

61. Berner, *Mrs. Stanford*, 42.

62. *Ibid.*, 43-44.

63. *Ibid.*, 39, 41.

64. Treat, "Golden Key," 93.

65. Chicago *Examiner*, March 2, 1905.

66. S. H. West to Bloomington [Illinois] *Pantograph*, June 19, 1906, printed in edition of June 22.

67. *Ibid.*, June 25, 1906.

68. San Francisco *Examiner*, June 21, 22, 1893.

69. See Thomas Welton Stanford papers. Stanford Library.

70. T. W. Stanford to Mrs. Leland Stanford, September 14, 1904. Berner, *Mrs. Stanford*, 43-44. Mrs. Stanford's interest in spiritualism reportedly carried her to the fringes of Swedenborgianism. Milwaukee *Journal*, May 23, 1895.

71. Eliot to David Starr Jordan, in Jordan, *Days of a Man*, I, 367.

72. Altrocchi, *Spectacular San Franciscans*, 243-244.

73. Unidentified newspaper clipping, SFS, XXV, 33.

74. Unidentified newspaper clipping, SFS, XVIII, 12.

75. San Jose *Mercury*, September 18, 1886. San Francisco *Call*, September 18, 1886.

76. Shepley, Rutan, and Coolidge Company letter to Jordan, January 29, 1913, in Clark, *Stanford*, 402-403.

77. San Francisco *Call*, April 16, 1887.

78. Berner, *Mrs. Stanford*, 48.

79. Sacramento *Record-Union*, November 13, 1888. James P. Munroe, *A Life of Francis Amasa Walker* (New York, 1923), 309.

80. San Francisco *Examiner*, April 17, 1889.

81. *Ibid.*

82. Andrew Dickson White, *Autobiography* (New York, 1922), II, 447.

83. Jordan, *Days of a Man*, I, 354.

84. Although Stanford had consulted a number of prominent administrators of the nation's top universities, none of their schools was the prototype for Stanford University. His close employee Henry Root, claiming firsthand knowledge in the matter, said that Girard College in Philadelphia was the model he had in mind (Root, *Root*, 30). Stanford later said that the Cooper Institute in New York was his prototype; it, like his projected institution, stressed the advancement of art, mechanics, and business (Ironically, Stanford University is at present one of the few remaining educational institutions in the country with no regular night school; except for a few seminars and classes held in the professional schools, the huge stone buildings stand empty the greater portion of the day). Stanford planned two prep schools, one for girls and one for boys, with a "central collegiate university" between them. Twelve-year-old children would be admitted to these schools for their preparatory work, and would be promoted to the university when they were advanced enough to begin studying for a particular vocation (San Francisco *Chronicle*, January 23, 1885).

85. Buffalo *Illustrated Express*, December 13, 1891.

86. *Exercises of the Opening Day*, October 1, 1891. Published by the university as Circular No. 5.

87. Sacramento *Record-Union*, October 2, 1891.

88. *Ibid.*

89. Stanford to Ariel Lathrop, May 30, 1892.

90. San Francisco *Examiner*, June 22, 1893.

91. Mirrielees, *Stanford University*, 28.

92. White, *Autobiography*, II, 448.

93. Stanford to Jordan, August 30, 1892.

94. H. C. Nash to unidentified correspondent, December 13, 1891.

95. Stanford telegram to Jordan, May 9, 16, 1891.

96. Stanford telegram to Jordan, May 26, 1891.

97. Stanford telegram to Jordan, February 18, 1892.

98. Box 1, Stanford papers.

99. Stanford to Jordan, May 29, 1891 [date is blurred, possibly 1892 or 1893].

100. See Mirielees, *Stanford University*, chapter 4, "Gathering the Faculty," for a detailed study of how the faculty was assembled.

101. Nash to M. St. Myrick, May 25, 1891. Nash to A. L. Ware, November 28, 1891.

102. Stanford telegram to Jordan, April 13, 1891.

103. Stanford to Professor Alexander Hogg, April 20, 1891.

104. Stanford to Jordan, April 3, 1893.

105. Stanford telegram to Jordan, March 10, 1893.

106. Stanford telegram to Jordan, May 30, 1891.

107. Mrs. Stanford to Jordan, October 15, 1891.

108. Stanford to Jordan, September 28, 1892.

109. Stanford to Jordan, August 24, 1892.

110. Stanford telegram to Jordan, February 17, 1892.

111. Stanford to Jordan, March 10, 1893.

112. *Ibid.* Harrison was to concentrate on certain aspects of international law, especially that relating to the solution of problems by arbitration. In the spring of 1894, a year after Stanford's death, he arrived at the university, and delivered one lecture per week on constitutional law, a modification of Stanford's original intention. San Francisco *Examiner*, March 7, 1894. All his lectures were reprinted in SFS, XXIII. See Box 2, Stanford papers, for considerable information on Stanford's part in the hiring of teachers.

113. Stanford to Jordan, February 17, 1892.

114. Stanford to Jordan, August 24, 1892.

115. *Ibid.*

CHAPTER XII

UNITED STATES SENATOR: PART I

Aaron A. Sargent, long a faithful supporter of the Central Pacific Railroad, was the leading contender in 1885 for Democrat James T. Farley's Senate seat, and he was justified in expecting Stanford's support. He had served the cause well, having helped engineer through Congress the railroad act of 1862, and had fought hard though unsuccessfully for the Goat Island grant. His service to the road had caused a number of people to oppose him as the railroad candidate when he had made an earlier bid for the Senate.[1] When the going got rough in early 1885, and it looked like he might lose the nomination, Sargent wrote Stanford asking him to return to California and use his influence with a number of influential Republicans in order to put a stop to their opposition.[2] Sargent was sure he had a safe majority at the time, but there was widespread concern within the party that his many political liabilities left him no chance of victory; besides, the San Francisco *Chronicle* was again opposing him as the railroad candidate. As requested, the Southern Pacific associates met and agreed to support Sargent.[3]

Stanford returned to Palo Alto and summoned Henry Vrooman, a close associate who was a confirmed enemy of Sargent, for a conference. He urged Vrooman to support Sargent despite their personal animosities, but Vrooman refused, and for two hours they argued the matter. A few days later the scene was repeated, whereupon Vrooman peremptorily refused to either vote for or assist in the election of his old enemy, and stated, furthermore, that he and his friends were determined to make Stanford Senator, in spite of all the latter could do for Sargent.[4] Though repeatedly urged to do so, Stanford refused to place himself in the running, and he called on Vrooman at least a dozen times, repeating his insistence that he and his associates relent and support Sargent.[5] Every man with whom Stanford discussed the senatorial race was so advised.

Frank Pixley complained on January 3 that Stanford was not a candidate and would not allow his friends to seek support for his potential candidacy. But Pixley was certain that if the Republican members of the legislature could not readily agree upon another man, and would tender Stanford "the unsolicited compliment" of a nomination, he would not feel at liberty to turn it down.[6] Was Stanford inviting a draft, or was this merely Pixley's wishful thinking? There is no way of answering this intriguing question. If Stanford was really seeking a call to the office, his tracks are too well covered to reconstruct what occurred behind the scenes; nothing has been found in the contemporary literature to suggest any other explanation than that Stanford did support Sargent and was not looking for the position himself.

Stanford's candidacy was not suddenly sprung upon the people of California. As early as December, 1884, a few California editors had endorsed him, and when rumors of a possible Stanford candidacy leaked to the press in early 1885, there was a widespread reaction that was almost universal in his favor.[7] It is possible that the antirailroad editors of the Stockton *Mail* and San Francisco *Chronicle* endorsed him because they saw the handwriting on the wall, that Sargent was going to win the nomination over their protests. Though they may have compromised on Stanford as less undesirable than Sargent, their support at the time appeared genuine.[8] Another journalist reported that since the "first gathering of the clans," a poetic allusion to the precaucus negotiations, Stanford's name had been mentioned prominently as a candidate.[9]

When rumors of an impending, or at least possible, switch in candidates reached Huntington, he found it incredible, and promptly dispatched to Stanford a telegram in code: "It is reported here that you are in the field against Sargent. I cannot believe it, please telegraph me at once."[10] Sargent himself begged Stanford to call off his friends, especially Creed Haymond, a Southern Pacific attorney and long-time associate, who was pulling Sargent votes from a number of legislators and pledging them to Stanford. The disgruntled Sargent said that the whole affair was inconsistent with a letter he had received from Stanford just a day earlier promising his support: "I appreciate the friendship these men have for you, & that their zeal for you is the cause of their acts. But they should not trifle with your honor, or force you into opposition to me, which they are now doing."[11]

The California legislature, elected in November, 1884, was composed of an evenly divided Senate, twenty Republicans and as many Democrats, and a heavily Republican Assembly, where the Democrats were outnumbered sixty to twenty. This made the election of a Republican Senator a foregone conclusion, unless one was nominated who was not acceptable to his fellow party members. A number of Republican hopefuls — Morris M. Estee, George C. Perkins, and Aaron A. Sargent — immediately entered the lists. Estee, the *Chronicle's* favorite, was expected to make the Republican party antimonopoly if he won; but his candidacy was largely a matter of seeking revenge for allegedly having been beaten earlier for governor by the railroad.[12] Perkins, thinking he had very little chance himself, joined in the scheme to elect Estee, but the whole cabal, according to Sargent's appraisal of the situation, favored Stanford's candidacy over his own for the reason that if Stanford won, it would be obvious that he had succeeded with railroad funds; this then would disgust the party with the railroad and make it anti-monopoly.[13]

The legislature was Republican, but it was also antirailroad, and apparently not just for public consumption. The railroad men in the legislature were almost solidly for Sargent, but the opposition to him was considerable and was growing. There was Vrooman's determined opposition, and he was now a state Senator from Alameda County; there was the genuine conviction among many who favored Sargent's candidacy that he could not win; and there was an equally-genuine popular movement for Stanford, once the subject had been broached. Californians who were against having the Central Pacific in politics had long made it a policy to distinguish between Stanford and the road which he headed, and his generosity in founding his university, the same month that the election of the legislature was held, made this distinction all the easier to accept. His friends rightly believed it an easy matter to persuade the people of California that he should be rewarded with a seat in the Senate.

The Republicans in the legislature caucused on Tuesday evening, January 20, 1885, to choose their candidate. Sargent was still confident of a majority of twenty, if Creed Haymond and Stephen T. Gage, another railroad man who was backing Stanford, would speak in his behalf, and a slight majority as it was if they remained neutral; in short, the only way he could be beaten was by Stanford supporters.[14] The eighty Republicans in the legislature showed themselves hopelessly divided on the first ballot: Sargent led the tally with twenty-six, followed by Perkins who got twenty-two, then came Estee with nineteen, and two minor candidates captured six votes. Stanford, the non-candidate candidate, received seven votes. On the second ballot, Vrooman, true to his promise — or threat, as the case may be — placed Stanford's name before the lawmakers. Perkins' vote immediately fell to one, and Sargent's and Estee's supporters plummeted to sixteen each; Stanford's name like magic drew forty-seven votes, more than enough for the nomination. Estee and Sargent supporters were understandably infuriated by this unexpected turn of events, and refused to make the vote unanimous. One disgruntled Assemblyman muttered, "This is the worst blow that has ever been struck at the Republican party in this State," and a Senator echoed these sentiments, "The Republican party has gone to hell."[15]

Stanford was still unwilling to allow the use of his name, but his friends finally persuaded him that he was the only hope for the party to field a winning candidate; furthermore, they impressed upon him that this was a popular call which he could not very well refuse.[16] Some of his friends believed that the Senate would be a kind of therapy for him; he needed to get away from the Palo Alto farm with its ubiquitous reminders of happier days. When the position was offered him, he reportedly left the decision entirely to his wife, suggesting to her that life in Washington might prove a welcome diversion.[17]

Stanford accepted the Republican nomination, but he did not seek it. This, of course, was the universal claim of all politicians, while they lobbied and manipulated economic and political strings behind a curtain of pious indifference. But Stanford did indeed seek to avoid it, and actively supported the candidacy of Sargent; but as much could not be said for his friends, and they were legion and powerful, as well as determined. Vrooman later said that Stanford's loyalty to Sargent and his own lack of political ambition were unique, that he was elected against his consent and over his protest.[18]

II

Jerome Hart, a contemporary, later attributed the whole Stanford boom to Frank Pixley, another of Sargent's confirmed foes. In 1859 Sargent had run for attorney general on Stanford's unsuccessful ticket, whereas Pixley had won the position in 1861 when Stanford was victorious. According to Hart, their enmity can be traced to the failure of the one and the success of the other. Pixley confided to Hart in early 1885 under pledge of secrecy that he was going to prevail upon Stanford to run for the Senate.[19] Hart doubted that Stanford would betray his "most loyal henchman," but events, he said, were to prove him wrong; the appeal to Stanford's vanity was irresistible, and he fell in with Pixley.[20] Hart said it was then left to Vrooman and William H. Mills, another railroad man, to persuade Stanford that Sargent would surely lose while he could easily win. Thus, the moving forces behind Stanford's election were Henry Vrooman, Stephen T. Gage, Creed Haymond, and William H. Mills. Gage, according to his brother, using the argument that the change in environment would be good for Mrs. Stanford, persuaded him to accept the nomination.[21]

This is possible, but how likely it is that this argument alone was that persuasive is another matter. If Stanford had wanted a more salubrious social climate he could have afforded it without the added burdens of Senate duties and the very insalubrious natural climate of the nation's capital city. And if there were something morally indefensible, or treacherous, or dishonest — depending upon one's point of view — in his supplanting Sargent, such an argument would not have mitigated the injustice and would not have persuaded him to do it. It seems obvious that Stanford was convinced — rightly or wrongly is another question — that the voice of his friends and the voice of the California legislature were indeed the voice of the people. Perhaps the tight first ballot convinced him that Sargent could not have beaten the Democratic candidate even if he had managed to win over the strong opposition in the Republican caucus.

Another contemporary referred to Stanford's nomination as a "daring, defiant, skillful, and expeditious piece of political work" that never had its equal in California.[22] A Sargent supporter himself, he did not recognize any opposition to Sargent except the railroad cabal, which foisted Stanford upon a reluctant legislature and equally reluctant state. The facts do not bear him out. If there was little likelihood that Sargent could have won, Stanford was entirely justified in replacing him; the purpose of political parties is victory in elections, and Stanford brought that.

Some question still persists. Stanford had heard that Sargent's railroad loyalties had become suspect and had asked his friend Marcus D. Boruck, editor of the *California Spirit of the Times*, to investigate the matter. Boruck did so, and wrote the Senator-elect on February 2, 1885, confirming a rumor that Sargent had been planning to doublecross the railroad. While supposedly a loyal railroad supporter, he was also posing as an antimonopoly candidate. It was reported that he was even denouncing the railroad in the privacy of his own room when there were no railroad men about.[23] This does not seem probable. It is more likely that this report was designed to make Stanford's own position more palatable to himself, to remove any doubts that he still might entertain as to the justice of what he had done. How better could this be done than to convince himself that he had supplanted a traitor?

Stanford's election was a foregone conclusion, and on January 28, seventy-nine of the state's 120 legislators — sixty-six percent — made his election final; his was the greatest vote received by a senatorial candidate in twenty years.[24] Democrat George Hearst ran second, drawing less than half Stanford's vote.[25]

Vrooman deserved most of the credit for this victory. One editor praised him as a maker of United States Senators, and predicted that Stanford's "spontaneous" nomination would restore faith in the material interests of the Pacific Coast — interests that had been demoralized by, of all things, communist ideas. If an honest man was the "noblest work of God," this enraptured journalist wrote, then California was going to be represented in the Senate by "one of the noblest works of the Creator." Stanford's victory was a defeat for the "corrupt and venal politicians" who wished to sell the Senate seat to the highest bidder.[26]

It was ironic that the man who could have outbid all others was able to win nomination singularly free from the corrupting influences of coin. Stanford's nomination was recognized as the result of a friendly conspiracy on the part of his friends, but was simultaneously accepted as an expression of public confidence in the man himself, further evidence that the people did not oppose railroad men, as such, but were able to discriminate between them. Stanford was praised as one of the few men who had no political ambitions; he would make an excellent Senator because he would transcend partisanship.[27]

III

With remarkably few dissenters, most of the newspaper editors of California and other sections of the country were happy with Stanford's nomination.[28] The unenthusiastic editor of the Los Angeles *Times* accepted it as the best possible, given the four candidates, saying that it was preferable that the head of the railroad be Senator without purchasing the position than to have one of its attorneys buy his way in with railroad money.[29] In this way the interests of the people would be protected by the "high character, known integrity, and distinguished ability" of Stanford. Most people, he said, trusted Stanford to do the right thing as Senator. He was a man who could not be bought with gold, of which he already had a surfeit; he was too wealthy to be corrupted. He mused that Stanford must have derived considerable satisfaction in being so popular with the same people who persistently and bitterly attacked the corporation at whose head he stood.

An inland editor predicted that the great "railroad king" would exercise a more beneficial influence in the Senate for the state of California than could any other candidate.[30] A northern editor rejoiced in the defeat of Sargent, who was "simply a politician of the narrowest and bitterest stripe," and saw the election of Stanford as a foreshadowing of the destruction of the Republican party, because he would not be partisan enough for his compatriots.[31] A Nevada County journalist traced the nomination of Stanford entirely to his popularity among the masses of people across the state; neither money nor manipulation was needed or used to elect the people's candidate. For a whole month, he said, there had been a "cyclone" of public opinion formulated in Stanford's favor, among Democrats as well as Republicans.[32] This agrees with Stanford's later claim that a great many Democrats had pressed the Republicans to run him.[33]

Bipartisan praise for Stanford's election was voiced in many big city papers. One editor who continued long a Stanford supporter was confident that his nomination met with the hearty approval of every honest man in the state. This "honest, patriotic, industrious, and unselfish gentleman" was not a seeker after office, and the senatorship was literally forced upon him.[34] Another said that the legislature had simply obeyed a public sentiment which was so emphatic and pronounced that no one dared resist or deny it, and predicted the dawn of a new and happier era in the state as a result of Stanford's election; it was proof that the "calm, reasoning intelligence" of the people would in the future guide the political affairs of the state.[35]

Boruck viewed the nomination as an honor, "unsought, unbought, unsolicited." The noted noncandidate, he wrote, was admired, respected, and esteemed for his "honorable impulses, ability and intelligence, for his clear intellect and magnificent brainpower." Certain that the Republican nominee was just a little lower than the angels, very little at that, he continued: "He is a man who, in all the great essentials which constitute manhood in its highest type, stands pre-eminent among men. His name is a glory to the state, and his life the brightest page in her history. Hail! All Hail! Leland Stanford, Senator!"[36]

If the practical unanimity with which the people of California accepted Stanford's nomination was any reflection on the wisdom of the move, the Republicans had made the best choice possible. As a popular candidate, rather than a machine politician, his selection seemed to some a return to the tradition of the founding fathers.[37] And since he was a railroad man, and the state's first ranking railroader at that, his selection and ready acceptance testified eloquently to the fact that people respected his personal integrity, and felt confident that the public good would hold first priority in his actions for the coming six years; his character alone was a sure guarantee that the trust reposed in him would be discharged impartially in the public interest.

Some were not easily reconciled to a railroad Senator; not that they had any personal animus toward Stanford the man, but they regarded his election as a "political outrage," an assertion that the people must not be allowed to rule.[38] Others, more cynical, could not believe that he had not purchased the Senate seat, as so many were doing in his day; one wit observed that Stanford's horseflesh was more creditable to him than his rank as a statesman, "though he paid as high for one as for the other."[39]

There seldom resides in one man the combination of qualities found in Stanford. He had political experience, far more than many of the Senators serving with him, and though not a brilliant man, his intellectual development was as great or greater than that of a number of his colleagues; and certainly no one would have denied that he was one of the foremost business managers in the upper house. In short, he had the material out of which statesmen are made: education, experience, political astuteness, a good business sense, integrity, and the respect of his constituents and colleagues.

Despite this, Stanford entered upon his new office with no little trepidation. Shortly after his election he reminded the California Republican League that this was his first experience with legislative office, and said that he felt much better suited for administrative position. Republican though he was, he was going to Washington with little partisan feeling; his main concern, he promised, was to advance the interests of California.[40]

IV

When Leland Stanford took the oath of office as a United States Senator on March 4, 1885, he was satisfied that he was answering a popular call; although he was the wealthiest man in the august body, and the seventh richest in the United States, he had neither bought nor bargained his way into office, and was therefore free of all political encumbrances.[41] He was where he was largely through the influence of his wealth, to be sure, through philanthropies and business connections and positions of respect, but not because he had used it illegally or immorally to purchase his position.

The first regular session of the Forty-ninth Congress did not convene until December 7, but Stanford's Senate career began on March 4, when a special Senate session was called. He quickly jumped into his official duties with a vengeance, and was soon known as the busiest man in the Senate.[42] At first the junior Senator from California found his duties irksome, for he missed the easygoing and efficient life he had lived before. After one month in office he began complaining that his constituents were working him to death, that they had made him an errand boy, a pack horse.[43] He had 100 letters a day to answer, and the writers all expected him to respond personally.[44] Accustomed as he was to direct action whenever he, the chief executive of the railroad, spoke, the deliberative processes of the Senate were especially annoying.[45] The only thing that kept him from resigning, said a number of Californians, was the probability that Governor Stoneman would appoint a Democrat to succeed him. They predicted that if California elected a Republican governor in 1886, thus eliminating this prospect, he would almost certainly resign.[46]

Stanford had spoken often during his business and political careers, and was known as a lover of speechmaking, but he was not an outstanding orator. He addressed the Senate during his eight years there fewer than two dozen times, but this was owing in part to his frequent and extended absences. He first spoke before the Senate on February 9, 1886, very early in his career, when he briefly stressed the necessity of a new post office in San Francisco.[47] Two months laters, on April 26, the neophyte legislator spoke at length against the Interstate Commerce bill, and argued the same point at greater length on January 10, 1887, adding nothing new to what he had said the first time. The ideas expressed in both these speeches were not new by any means; he had used them time and time again when resisting state regulation of railroads and when speaking outside the Senate against public control of private business. After all, he repeated, control was the essence of ownership; it destroyed the income-producing quality of private property.[48]

The California Senator recognized the bill for what it was, rather than what its title purported it to be: it was a bill to regulate railroads. Its authors had failed to define commerce, which included trading, bartering, and interchange of commodities; as it stood, Stanford suggested, it ought to be renamed "a bill to regulate carriers." He conceded that Congress had the right to regulate interstate commerce, but maintained stoutly that its selective meaning of commerce to cover railroads that crossed state lines would convert "nonphysical lines" into barriers, or "frontiers between the states." He appealed to his states' rights colleagues to oppose the bill on the ground that the rights of states were being infringed.

One argument used in the bill's defense, that a government has a right to regulate that which it creates, did not apply in this case, Stanford argued, since the states, not Congress, had incorporated the railroads. But by far his greatest objection was that this bill violated constitutional guarantees against having one's property confiscated without due process of law. Rate control was a form of confiscation, since it deprived railroads of anticipated profit, and anticipated profit was property. Stanford objected further that the proposed law destroyed competition. As it was, some railroads were making long hauls, often at a loss, at a lower rate than short hauls in order to get traffic from other roads. But if the federal government made them adhere to these long haul rates, and then cut the short rates to a proportion of the long rates, as it intended to do, the roads would go bankrupt.

In his second speech he pointed to cutthroat competition with water travel as evidence that the railroads did not have a monopoly, and he complained that the Interstate Commerce bill was a sure guarantee that water transport would be cheaper than rail, thereby making it impossible for railroads to compete. He omitted all reference to pools and gentlemen's agreements to avoid competition whenever possible, and failed to recognize that the waterways were either owned or controlled by railroad interests, that, in effect, competition had already been destroyed. He made this bill sound disastrous to all railroads, but in a later interview, after it was signed into law, he said that the recently enacted act would not hurt roads east of Chicago. These roads, in fact, would benefit from the law, because they already had pooling agreements that were more stringent than its terms; but West Coast railroads would be hurt by having their rates forced below water rates.[49]

Stanford attributed the antirailroad ICC law to the desire of politicians to draw votes. The "emergencies of politicians," he said, were an important factor in lawmaking, and the same demagogues responsible for this law would soon seek out new interests to assail, all with the intention of attracting votes. But he misjudged the mood of the nation. More was at issue than ambitious politicians seeking votes; there was going to be regulation of railroads, regardless of constitutional niceties, for state regulation had failed, as signaled by the reversal of the Granger cases. Regulation was wanted and it was needed, and since the Supreme Court had said in effect that the states could not regulate commerce that crossed state lines, the only agency left was the federal government.

The Interstate Commerce Act as signed into law on February 4, 1887, was weak and largely ineffective, but it was a beginning.[50] Once such a law was on the books and had withstood a court test, the old walls against regulation were doomed to collapse. It was much easier to strengthen such legislation to make it effective than to get it accepted in the first place.

V

As Stanford reflected upon his experiences as a young man in business and his observations of miners at work, he became more and more impressed

Stanford Library

LELAND STANFORD.

with the need for greater cooperation. This soon became a panacea for all social ills, especially the conflicts between capital and labor that were making the headlines with increasing regularity. He tried in various ways to encourage individuals who wished to form cooperative associations, and introduced a bill on December 20, 1886, that was designed to help them.[51] The bill was limited to the District of Columbia, but laws in the District allowed anyone to form corporations there, regardless of home state; besides, Stanford hoped some states would take this bill as an example for their own legislation.[52]

The following February 16, 1887, Stanford told the Senate that civilization itself rested ultimately upon principles of cooperation.[53] The cooperative associations he was espousing would allow workers to share the fruits of their industry. Not only would the material goals alone justify such legislation, but cooperation involved a moral dimension — it would create a more intelligent people.[54] The purpose of cooperation, as he saw it, was to allow those with little capital to unite in economic ventures which none of them could afford individually. The anticipated objection that this bill was merely asking for a right which was already guaranteed was true so far as it went, he conceded, but before a group could incorporate for any specific purpose under existing laws, it had to show financial solvency. His bill provided for the association of individuals with or without capital; it merely extended to people without capital provisions that had hitherto existed only for those with it. In this, it was far more democratic than existing laws.

A lengthy explanation of his ideas and his bill was published in the New York *Tribune*. There Stanford reiterated his earlier assertion that it would help people realize that there was no fundamental conflict between labor and capital, and then he went on to explain in greater detail how their interests were the same; each needed the other, and both were working for the same ends.[55] Capital was the product of labor, so there could no more be antagonism between them than between cause and effect. By bringing people to realize that capital was but labor organized, that corporations were but extended partnerships, and that all laborers with intelligence could organize cooperative societies and work for themselves, he hoped to show that all antagonisms were more apparent than real.

The employer was, temporarily at any rate, not only a necessity in the economic system, he was a benefactor; but as labor became more intelligent, and developed to the point where it could employ itself, the employer as a separate part of the system would no longer be necessary. Stanford justified the present profit system on the ground that the initiative of the employer had made profit possible and had put labor to work, and such initiative must be rewarded. Labor could organize and put itself to work, but was unwilling, or, from lack of intelligence, unable. But perfect cooperation, which was inevitable, would gradually eliminate the employer class. In other words, labor was indispensable; capital was merely useful.[56] Stanford believed, then, in the "Gospel of Wealth;" he agreed with the Carnegies and the Rockefellers that the wealthy were but trustees of their wealth, but he parted company with these men in holding that their usefulness as a class would someday end.

> What I believe is; the time has come when the laboring men can perform for themselves the office of becoming their own employers; that the employer class is less indispensable in the modern organization of industries because the laboring men themselves possess sufficient intelligence to organize into co-operative relation and enjoy the entire benefits of their own labor.[57]

All this was not intended as an endorsement of a primitive communism or share-the-wealth scheme. Any man who demanded of another a portion of his property was claiming a portion of his manhood, a share in his productive capacities. Stanford favored a distribution of wealth, but the only proper grounds for such a distribution was by the produce of labor. Distribution of wealth would come from a more equal distribution of the productive capacity of men, and this would result from cooperation. Stanford's plan would produce a distribution of wealth, but not a forced distribution that would destroy individual initiative and personal rewards for diligent work and self development. When he later wrote President Jordan that cooperation was one of the most important things that could be taught in the university, he gave as his reason that education tended to distribute wealth more generally.[58] Economic equality would introduce social equality, so that no industrious man would feel himself one whit the social inferior of any man alive.[59]

In this theorizing Stanford seemed at times to be a betrayer of his own class, but his ideas had no tinge of European radicalism, no socialism, no revolution; he merely insisted that all antagonism between labor and capital was foolish, that the two were mutually dependent. He recognized that overall prosperity depended upon an enlightened working class, a class that was involved personally in the products of its labors, a class that would possess the wherewithal to purchase and enjoy the products that it was paid to produce.

Stanford's bill passed the appropriate committee, but died on the Senate calendar without coming up again. He reintroduced it on December 22, 1891, and it came up for discussion on April 9, 1892, when he was absent from the Senate; thus his bill died once and for all.[60]

VI

Memories of the Civil War kept sectionalism alive in Congress, and occasioned much waving of the bloody shirt at election time or when bills of a sectional nature appeared or appointments were made. An event occurred in 1888 that proved Stanford disinclined to carry on this sectionalism and willing to bolt his party on an important vote when personal convictions directed him to do so.

President Grover Cleveland had nominated L.Q.C. Lamar, an outstanding Southern politician and former Confederate officer, to the United States Supreme Court. The Senate Judiciary Committee conceded that he was fully qualified for the office, but insisted that his former Confederate connections rendered him unfit for it. It was expected to be a close vote, and party whips worked overtime getting their members in line. Lamar was approved thirty-two to twenty-eight, with only two Republicans supporting him. Stanford was one of them.[61] The independent-thinking Republican was generally praised for this action. The editor of a San Francisco paper, for example, was sure that his stand "argued a great amount of moral force" for this man in whom there was "nothing of the politician."[62]

VII

Leland Stanford, President of the United States. This would have been the pinnacle of success for any United States Senator, and was the dream of many. Indeed, it was not beyond the pale of possibility for Stanford, at least to hear his friends and ardent supporters tell it. One of the most surprisingly-neglected aspects of Stanford's whole career consists of his presidential booms, not because there was any chance that he might have become president, but just because they happened, just because a number of people for over six years thought it a distinct likelihood or at least a remote possibility, because they catapulted him to a position in politics that was expected to bring him at the very least a cabinet position.

Even before his election to the Senate was confirmed, it was rumored that Stanford would capture the Republican nomination in 1888.[63] With the party conspicuously lacking in new talent, and with Grover Cleveland taking office in the spring of 1885, it was not surprising that rumor made every popular man a candidate. Stanford was interviewed on the subject, and took the trouble to deny emphatically that he was a candidate, but conceded what everyone already knew, that few men in the country would reject the nomination if it were offered.[64]

A number of California editors endorsed his candidacy, with one pointing to his "breadth of intellect of early American statesmen" and his thorough knowledge of business as prime qualifications for the office.[65] After all, political administrators needed to know business to run the government, and Stanford was a proven master in this area. By the spring of 1886 the Sacramento *Record-Union*, one of the most influential California newspapers, had also endorsed Stanford's candidacy. Several San Francisco journalists regarded Stanford as the strongest man in the Republican party in 1886, and endorsed him for the presidency, predicting that his nomination would please all classes and all parties in the state.[66] About the same time a Nevada politician asserted that Stanford probably had a better chance of winning in

1888 than any other hopeful, including Blaine, who was still hungering and thirsting after the first office. And if nominated, the California Senator could easily beat the unpopular Cleveland.[67]

Two years after his Senate career was launched, Stanford's boom was being heard more and more insistently in the East. An editor in the nation's capital predicted that his nomination would command the respect of all Americans, something that could not be said of very many Republican prospects.[68] As far away as the Midwest, Stanford was being groomed as the party's 1888 candidate.[69] And barely a year before the next presidential election, he was billed in California as the next president, on the ground that he alone could carry his home state, New York, where he was "universally admired."[70] What could be more natural than his "manifest destiny?"—Leland Stanford: railroad magnate, then governor of California, next United States Senator, and finally President of the United States.[71]

Stanford's most persistent booster was the editor of the San Francisco *Argus*. In his editorials, as well as with some of the cleverest political cartoons of the day, he promoted Stanford for the White House. The California Senator was a "fitting successor" to Lincoln; he was the strongest and most available man mentioned for the executive mansion; he had never been involved in party quarrels or dissensions, and therefore had no enemies to stab him in the back.[72] He was not only more likely to carry New York than any of the prominently mentioned candidates, he was also very strong in the South. If William T. Sherman, Roscoe Conkling, or Walter Gresham did not capture the nomination, Stanford would, and of these possibilities, only Stanford could carry any Southern states; and no one could possibly doubt his ability to carry the whole Pacific Coast.[73]

Early in 1888 this same editor was sure that all the leading journals wanted Stanford, especially since Blaine had by then withdrawn. One of his better cartoons showed Blaine leading Stanford to the presidential chair and bidding him sit there. Blaine's "withdrawal" was obviously taken too much at face value.[74] Other journalists wanted Stanford nominated, but did not see Blaine giving him the White House; rather, a political battle between the California Senator and the former Secretary of State was shaping up, and on its results depended the issue.[75] Another believed Stanford incapable of winning the machine support necessary to capture the nomination; he was "too much a man of the people for the party 'sachems' to accept."[76]

Stanford did not win the nomination in 1888, and did not try to get it. His name was not placed in nomination and he received no votes. That the people of California were "disappointed and chagrined" that the delegates at the Chicago convention passed him by, as was asserted by one of his friends, is not very likely. At any rate, General Benjamin Harrison, the Republican candidate, received all eight of the Golden State's electoral votes.[77]

Stanford was in Europe from the spring through the fall of 1888, and did not take part in the election. In October, just after returning home, he saw the tariff problem as the most important single issue in the presidential race; the free trade policy of the Democrats, to his way of thinking, would be ruinous to the industrialists as well as the workingmen. Cleveland's administration, he insisted, had been a failure ever since he struck at silver.[78] Protection was demanded, though at this point he made a distinction between a protective tariff, which he supported, and a revenue tariff, which he opposed, on the ground that the latter levied an inequitable tax upon the people. Riding the political currents of his day, and not allowing the country's anti-British prejudices to go unused, he summed up the whole campaign and defined all the issues in one terse sentence: "Every Englishman is for Cleveland."[79]

Stanford's friendship with Harrison, his faithfulness to the party and its candidate, and his unflagging popularity merited a cabinet position, and it was rumored that Harrison would reward him with one.[80] The expected appointment never materialized, and the matter was not pushed from either end, but Stanford did exercise a great deal of influence on the Harrison administration so far as West Coast patronage was concerned. He was characterized as the supreme arbiter in all matters relating to the distribution of patronage in California.[81]

VIII

From 1888 on, the Senator's health declined steadily. In May of that year another cure at Bad Kissingen was advised, and the Stanfords sailed on the *Alaska* that same month, in the middle of the long session of the Fiftieth Congress. The *Alaska* was built to carry half cargo and half passengers, but the entire passenger accommodations were reserved for the Stanford party.[82] The trip began just a few months after they laid the cornerstone for their university, and they followed the progress of its construction throughout the trip. This third European tour is the best documented of their five, owing to the copious correspondence sent and received about the building of the school, and because Miss Berner accompanied them and kept extensive records of their itinerary.

When they approached London, Captain Berryman, the European agent of the Southern Pacific and the Pacific Improvement Company, met the *Alaska* with a private tug and passed the Stanford entourage quickly through customs and into the private car of Baron Rothschild. While in London, Stanford took care of railroad business, attended to some shipments of wine from Vina, and went shopping for art treasures. He purchased an expensive Murillo painting and a number of items for the university, especially the museum.

The purpose of the trip had been the thermal cure, but his health had improved to the point that he did not go directly to Bad Kissingen; instead, the party made an extended tour of the continent. As it turned out, this trip was almost free of serious illness, and afforded the Stanfords some of the most tranquil and pleasant moments of their lives. They were honored everywhere they went. At Metz, on the border between France and Germany, two German officers invited him on a personally conducted tour of the fortifications. On the way out, they had a military escort. The officers had been told in advance of the Stanfords' impending visit, and were thus able to make arrangements to guarantee them a comfortable stay.

The party went from there to Frankfurt-am-Main, made a tour of the city, and then left, hoping to escape the depression of the martial atmosphere of the city, which at the time was virtually a military camp. Once domiciled at Kissingen, the California couple was invited to the home and garden of "Prince Bismarck." Following an extended stay of six weeks at the springs, Stanford was twenty pounds lighter — though still pressing 240 or thereabouts — but was weak, so doctors recommended the "aftercure" at St. Moritz. On the way to this Swiss resort, they visited Nuremberg for three days, and then spent a week in Munich. They reached St. Moritz on July 4th, after passing through a snowstorm on the way, and from there made their way to Italy, where Mrs. Stanford's sixtieth birthday was celebrated at Lake Como. Leaving the town of Bellagio, near the Lake, the peripatetic patients next went to Milan, and then passed ten days at Pallanza, on Lake Maggiore.

At each city they visited they went on buying trips, purchasing all sorts of antiques, woodcarvings, pictures, china, and furniture for their Palo Alto home, which was being renovated during their absence. In October, 1888, they returned from Europe to their remodeled home, now a three-storied building with a first floor library and a spacious dining room. They left for Washington on November 23, where they remained until April 5, 1889, following the close of the second session of the Fiftieth Congress.

Much of the summer and early fall of 1889 was spent either in Palo Alto, at the Del Monte lodge, or just touring the state. Everywhere the Stanfords went people turned out *en masse* to see them. At Red Bluff in early October they were given a brilliant reception at the Pavilion — where the whole depot was decorated with flags and bunting in their honor.[83] The next day the scene was repeated in Chico; there they were given a military escort to General Bidwell's ranch, where a large public reception was held.[84] Two brass bands whooped it up and 1,000 school children showered their carriage with flowers.

The Stanfords returned to Washington on November 28, 1889, just in time for the convening of the first session of the Fifty-first Congress, putting behind them one of the happiest periods of their lives, and entering — though they had no way of knowing it then — one of the most trying, with failing health and unprecedented railroad problems ahead.[85]

1. Stockton *Independent*, July 18, 1873.

2. Sargent to Stanford, November 11, 1884, January 11, 1885.

3. Skinner, *History of California*, IV, 454-455.

4. Henry Vrooman, "Honorable Leland Stanford," in H. H. Bancroft collection, Bancroft Library.

5. *Ibid.*

6. San Francisco *Argonaut*, January 3, 1885.

7. *California Spirit of the Times*, December 20, 1884.

8. Sacramento *Bee*, January 16, 1885.

9. San Francisco *Alta California*, January 13, 1885.

10. Huntington telegram to Stanford, January 12, 1885.

11. Sargent to Stanford, January 13, 1885.

12. Sargent to Stanford, January 11, 1885.

13. *Ibid.*

14. Sargent to Stanford, January 13, 1885.

15. Butte *Record*, January 24, 1885.

16. Bancroft, *History*, VII, 431-432.

17. Berner, *Mrs. Stanford*, 55.

18. Vrooman, "Stanford."

19. Jerome Hart, *In Our Second Century* (San Francisco, 1931), 127.

20. *Ibid.*

21. Norris L. Gage to Edgar E. Robinson, May 23, 1917, in Clark, *Stanford*, 431.

22. Frank A. Leach, *Recollections of a Newspaperman* (San Francisco, 1917), 264.

23. Marcus D. Boruck to Stanford, February 2, 1885.

24. Sacramento *Record-Union*, January 29, 1885.

25. California *Senate Journal*, 1885, 169-170.

26. Oakland *Tribune*, January 21, 1885.

27. *Ibid.*, January 22, 1885.

28. SFS XI and XII, 39-109, contain hundreds of clippings from scores of newspapers in California and the rest of the country almost all endorsing Stanford's candidacy and praising the legislature that elected him.

29. Los Angeles *Times*, January 21, 1885.

30. San Joaquin *Valley Argus*, January 24, 1885.

31. Butte *Record*, January 24, 1885.

32. Nevada *State Journal*, January 24, 1885.

33. Interview with correspondent of the Cincinnati *Enquirer*, reprinted in *California Spirit of the Times*, n.d., clipping in Stanford papers.

34. San Francisco *Argus*, January 24, 1885.

35. San Francisco *Newsletter*, January 24, 1885.

36. *California Spirit of the Times*, January 24, 1885.

37. *Ibid.*

38. Unidentified newspaper clipping, 1885, SFS, XII, 43.

39. Unidentified newspaper clipping, SFS, XXII, 1.

40. Speech before California Republican League, February 11, 1885, reprinted in unidentified newspaper clipping, SFS, XII, 23.

41. New York *World*, n.d., SFS, XXV, 55.

42. Unidentified newspaper clipping, SFS, X, 4.

43. Unidentified newspaper clipping, SFS, X, 1-2.

44. Unidentified newspaper clipping, SFS, X, 4.

45. Unidentified newspaper clipping, SFS, XXV.

46. Unidentified newspaper clippings, SFS, X, 1, 2, 4.

47. *Cong. Record*, 49 Cong., 1 Sess., 1,237.

48. *Ibid.*, 3,827, 4,316-4,318. *Ibid.*, 2 Sess., 490.

49. Cincinnati *Enquirer*, February 18, 1887.

50. *Cong. Record*, 49 Cong., 2 Sess., 1,435.

51. *Ibid.*, 272.

52. Cincinnati *Enquirer*, February 18, 1887.

53. *Cong. Record*, 49 Cong., 2 Sess., 1,804.

54. Stanford was neither espousing nor was he interested in the Rochdale-type distributive cooperative. See J. Murray Luck, "Cooperation — An Aspect of the Social Philosophy of Leland Stanford," *Co-op News*, April 13, 27, May 11, 1950.

55. New York *Tribune*, May 4, 1887.

56. San Francisco *Argonaut*, June 11, 1887.

57. New York *Tribune*, May 4, 1887.

58. Stanford to Jordan, his last letter, in San Francisco *Examiner*, June 22, 1893.

59. Leland Stanford, "The Future of Our State," in unidentified newspaper clipping, Stanford collection, Box 6, Folder 66.

60. *Cong. Record*, 52 Cong., 1 Sess., 92, 3,412.

61. George W. West eulogy, *Senate Memorial Addresses*, 66.

62. San Francisco *City Argus*, n. d., SFS, XVI, 3 and XIX, 4.

63. San Francisco *Newsletter*, January 24, 1885.

64. Unidentified newspaper clipping, n d., 1885, in SFS, X, 10. This scrapbook contains scores of clippings on his presidential prospects for 1888.

65. Yolo *Mail*, n. d., SFS, X, 10.

66. For example, San Francisco *Argonaut*, n. d., 1886, SFS, "C."

67. Sacramento *Record-Union*, March 31, 1886. Nevada man in unidentified newspaper clipping, January, 1886, SFS, X, 12.

68. Washington [DC] *National Republican*, June 22, 1887, in San Francisco *Argus*, n.d., SFS, XVI, 13.

69. Jerseyville [Illinois] *Republican-Examiner*, February 25, 1887.

70. San Francisco *Post*, November 11, 1887.

71. California *Farmer*, December, 1887, in Stanford collection.

72. San Francisco *Argus*, n. d., spring, 1888, SFS, XIX, 4.

73. *Ibid.*, n. d., SFS, XIX, 10.

74. *Ibid.*, n. d., SFS, XVI, 6, and September 4, 1886.

75. Marysville *Appeal*, n. d., SFS, X, 4.

76. Unidentified newspaper clipping, SFS, II, 151.

77. San Francisco *Argonaut*, August 13, 1888. Sacramento *Record-Union*, July 5, 1888.

78. Stanford interview, printed in San Francisco *Chronicle*, November 11, 1888, and Sacramento *Record-Union*, November 11, 1888.

79. Sacramento *Record-Union*, October 20, 1888.

80. New York *Herald*, October 27, 1888.

81. Unidentified newspaper clipping, SFS, XXV, 6.

82. Berner, *Mrs. Stanford*, 62-81.

83. Sacramento *Bee*, October 5, 1889.

84. *Ibid.*

85. Sacramento *Record-Union*, September 17, 1889.

CHAPTER XIII

SIDETRACKED

Late 1884 and early 1885 constituted a busy time for Stanford. In November of the earlier year, he founded his university, which he personally managed for a number of years; two months later he was elected to the United States Senate; and less than three weeks following this he was named president of the newly-formed Southern Pacific Company of Kentucky. Each of these was a full-time undertaking, and few men, regardless of drive, stamina, or good intentions, could have done justice to more than one, let alone all three.

Huntington, for one, was sure that the interests of their railroad empire were suffering from Stanford's neglect. Over the years, for this and other reasons, relations between him and Stanford had grown more and more strained, and finally Charles F. Crocker made a special trip to New York to mediate between them. He returned to San Francisco under the mistaken impression that matters had been smoothed out.[1] But they had not, and finally, when open war seemed imminent, these two old partners and the Crocker and Hopkins interests met in New York and negotiated and signed a veritable treaty of peace. An agreement was drawn up on February 28, 1890, providing that at the next annual meeting Huntington would replace Stanford as president of the Southern Pacific; for his part, Huntington was to destroy or hand over to Stanford for disposal all papers in his possession on the Sargent affair—this titillating point was not elaborated upon—and all parties having interest in the Pacific Improvement Company were to "refrain from hostile or injurious expression concerning each other." The signers also agreed "in good faith" that they would "cooperate for the election of Leland Stanford as senator to the next term."[2]

On his way back to California, in early April, 1890, just before the fateful annual meeting in San Francisco, Stanford told a reporter in Wadsworth, Nevada, that he had notified his associates to expect his resignation from the Southern Pacific presidency: "If I have my way I'll turn over the Presidency to another man at the directors' meeting next week."[3] He gave ill health as one of his reasons, but said nothing to suggest that this contemplated move was part of a prior agreement that had already been ratified, and that he no longer had any choice in the matter; he was obviously preparing the ground for the inevitable in order to soften the blow to his own morale and prestige. This was not a hasty move on his part, he assured the press; because he wanted to have more time to devote to the university and to his Senate duties, he had been considering it for four years.[4] When queried about a possible successor, he verified rumors that Huntington was to succeed him, admitting by doing so that all the details for the impending changes had been worked out in advance. Huntington was immediately contacted about Stanford's resignation, and with perfect composure lied to the press, saying he knew of no reason why Stanford should resign and that he had first heard of it himself in the newspapers.[5]

When the changeover in administration came, it was not as smooth and orderly and free from bitterness as the associates wished it to appear, but what went on just before the fateful meeting was not revealed until a number of years later, when Charles F. Crocker's account was leaked to the press. According to him, Stanford's resignation amounted to an ouster from the first position, and even though the change had been agreed to several weeks earlier, when it was actually made it came as a heavy blow. This agrees with Miss Berner's statement that Stanford returned from the meeting a sick man, looking as though he had aged several years in that one day.[6]

Just prior to the meeting of April 9, 1890, Huntington told Stanford that he hoped he would receive the office in as good shape as when it was turned over to him, a number of years earlier.[7] This was more than Stanford could stand. Without losing his temper, he launched into an attack on Huntington's long record of duplicity with his associates. He alone of the original four, Stanford said, had sought surreptitiously on a number of occasions to disrupt their friendship and business harmony. When Huntington had moved to New York to work for the interests of the whole group, he had become involved in other interests, and had used the Pacific railroad for his own selfish ends. The California group had even sent Crocker to New York on occasion as a spy to keep an eye on their wayward partner. Stanford warned Edward T. Searles that he was aligned with a man whom Mark Hopkins, Timothy Hopkins, and his own wife, the former Mrs. Mark Hopkins, had always distrusted, and then charged that his own work in the railroad had been made doubly hard because of the way Huntington had worked against him behind his back.

All this was said in the hearing of Huntington, who tried to laugh away the whole indictment, but a few moments later he had his revenge. Huntington was elected to the first office and was seated in the presidential chair by the outgoing chief. Other changes in the directorate reflected a general strengthening of the Huntington interests. Ariel Lathrop was dropped from the board, and Thomas E. Hubbard, one of Mrs. Searles' attorneys, was added. The Huntington-Searles interests on the new board outnumbered the Stanford-Crocker people two to one.[8] Huntington read his inaugural message from a prepared manuscript, thanking the officers for electing him president, as though it had been spontaneous, and pledging his continuing loyalty to the company. In a statement directed with studied malice at Stanford and the 1885 senatorial election, he said: "In no case will I use this great corporation to advance my personal ambition at the expense of its owners, or put my hands in its treasury to defeat the people's choice and thereby put myself in positions that should be filled by others."

Huntington's remarks created a sensation in the press. In an interview shortly thereafter with a San Francisco newspaper correspondent, he stated that the company had entered too far and too often into politics. Without embarrassment, he stated:

> This building [Fourth and Townsend headquarters] has been overrun with politics, and it is time to call a halt. . . . From this time on we are going to follow one business. We are railroad men and intend to conduct a legitimate railroad business. To do that successfully politics must be let alone. The two don't go well together.[9]

On top of this, he said he did not want to convey the impression that he and Stanford had fallen out; after all, he had nothing personal against the Senator, and intended in no way to offend him by any of his remarks.[10]

Huntington's statement that he, unlike Stanford, had kept the railroad out of politics was as far from the truth as it could possibly be; it was common knowledge that he had been up to his ears in politics throughout his whole railroad career. For years he had acted as a lobbyist in Washington, and afterward had employed salaried attorneys as his agents in Congress. He well appreciated the importance to their railroad empire of a few key, strategically-placed lobbyists.

In 1882, when George E. Whitney, a candidate for state Senator, learned that the railroad was against him, he confronted Stanford and Huntington in their offices. Stanford expressed his hope that Whitney would be elected, but Huntington said he was not interested in politics. Whitney, whose estimation of Huntington's political activities was widely accepted, retorted: "While you say you are not in politics, I think you are."[11] Stanford's friend Archibald Treat agreed; he charged that the "ruthless" Huntington was "steeped from his feet to his eyebrows in politics."[12]

A survey of the California press turns up only one editor who accepted at face value Huntington's statement that he was above politics.[13] Most California journalists recognized that it would be exceedingly difficult to persuade California that Stanford, not Huntington, was responsible for railroad politics, especially after Huntington's letters were aired at the Colton trial, letters that were "fragrant of a political fund."[14]

The editor of the San Francisco *Examiner* wrote a number of pro-Stanford articles in which he asserted that even the bitterest antirailroad critics would prefer Stanford to Huntington as the head of the Southern Pacific; he was more humane, more responsive to public opinion, and more interested in the prosperity of California.[15] Unlike Stanford, who was a Californian with California ideas, Huntington had become a New Yorker, and a bitterly anti-California, pro-Chinese New Yorker at that. This writer had earlier said that Huntington was not "loved greatly" or "respected overmuch" in California; but his stronger statement, that money was "Huntington's only god," seemed to fit better the low esteem in which the new Southern Pacific president was held by most Californians, as reflected by scores of letters that poured in to Stanford from total strangers supporting him in the controversy with Huntington.[16]

The editor of the *Chronicle* also championed the Stanford cause, identifying Huntington with Brutus and Stanford with Caesar, and attributed Huntington's attack to Stanford's scheme for lending government money at low interest; Huntington, Hubbard, and Thomas E. Stillman, another of Mrs. Hopkins-Searles' attorneys, were allegedly disgusted by his plan, believing it would injure their company.[17] In a similar vein, the editor of the Sacramento *Bee*, also one of Stanford's staunchest defenders, condemned what he called Huntington's "intentional public insult" to Stanford, and called the latter's retirement "a blow to the people," a "great public calamity."[18]

Creed Haymond, who subsequently resigned as head of the railroad's legal department, realizing there was no place in the company for him under the new regime, told the *Chronicle* that Huntington's statements about Stanford's election to the Senate were most unfortunate, and resulted from his not knowing the full details.[19] Circumstances that had nothing to do with railroad matters, and about which Huntington never dreamed, made Sargent's election impossible, but Huntington never tried to learn the full facts of the matter.[20] Haymond insisted again that Stanford had not wanted the senatorship, but that in accepting it he had wronged no one, especially Huntington. If Stanford had not taken Sargent's place, Haymond reiterated, someone else would have, but he added, cryptically: "The reason why Sargent was not elected Senator is known probably to only three men in all the world. Yes, one of them is Creed Haymond."[21]

From the inner circle of the railroad associates there came the story that Huntington and Stillman had gone after Stanford in an attempt to force him into retirement.[22] The basis for their discontent was Stanford's neglect of railroad affairs and his political ambition. But, this source confided, it was Stanford's scheme to lend government money at low interest that finally precipitated a declaration of war.

Stanford flatly denied that he had ever in his life used a cent of railroad money for his personal benefit, and reiterated that he had not been an active candidate for the United States Senate in 1885.[23] Struck to the quick by the insinuations that railroad money had bought his Senate seat, he immediately sent a letter to the Board of Directors demanding an investigation into the charges. In the event of an investigation, it was expected that Stanford would have been vindicated, but no matter who won, the railroad would be the loser.[24] It was believed at the time that the only thing that had prevented an open eruption before this was the knowledge that their securities would have "tumbled like a house of cards stricken by a tornado."[25]

Crocker leaped into action and left no stone unturned in an attempt to patch up the quarrel before it came before the directors for official consideration.[26] He, Stillman, and Hubbard, acting together, persuaded Stanford to withdraw the letter.[27] The argument that finally won him over was that he had no right to force the other railroad owners into the position of having to arbitrate or choose between him and Huntington over a personal quarrel.[28] But Stanford was said to have demanded of Huntington either a retraction of his charges or complete vindication by the board.[29] In a limited sense, he got the former.

Huntington was prevailed upon to sue for peace before the road was disrupted sufficiently to damage its position on the market. On April 15, 1890, he obligingly addressed a letter of apology to Stanford. He made it clear in his "Dear Governor" letter that their mutual friends had insisted upon his writing, and he then expressed his regrets that the words of his inaugural statement had been construed as an attack upon his partner:

> Allow me to say that I greatly regret this impression since I did not intend to make such attack or to charge that you had used the Company's money to advance your personal interests or in any improper manner, and I am satisfied that you have not done so. Allow me also to express the wish that our relations may continue as friendly hereafter as they have been heretofore.[30]

The two men remained in their offices at Fourth and Townsend all day long, with the press outside busily speculating about a rumored compromise.[31] Meanwhile, railroad officials continued to assure the public—and themselves —that the quarrel would have no adverse effects on the company's bonds or credit. On the sixteenth of the month, an *entente cordiale* was restored.[32] The two men greeted each other, amidst smiles and uncomfortable cordialities, and then the whole group went to lunch together. It was reportedly "not a hungry gathering," but it was sociable, and afterward they all returned to Stanford's office for the remainder of the afternoon; this was the longest Stanford and Huntington had been together for five years. Thus an armistice had been arranged, though not a peace, as evidenced by continuing jabs at Stanford by Huntington.[33]

When the shakeup in the Southern Pacific management failed to improve business relations, Stanford and Crocker insisted upon new ground rules for conducting business. They dispatched a letter to the Huntington-

Searles group demanding that harmonious relations prevail in the future; as long as there was one dissenting voice among the four, there were to be no new enterprises started. "Success without harmony is possible," they wrote, "but hardly probable."[34]

II

Much ink has been spilled over how Stanford's first Senate election had destroyed all remaining cordiality with his partner Huntington, who was sure that he and Sargent had been double-crossed by their politically ambitious associate. Stanford and Huntington had both promised to back their faithful legislator-politician-railroad attorney. Later events have shown that the importance of this incident has been greatly exaggerated, as evidenced by remarks made by Huntington himself. In 1886 he wrote Stephen Gage that he, Stanford, and Crocker had had a conference to decide on whom to support for the Senate in 1887, when the California legislature would be electing another Senator.[35] Huntington did not identify the man on whom they had agreed, but this letter contained some neglected remarks on Stanford's election a year earlier.

Huntington said that the election of Stanford was not expected when the two had met just before his election; in fact, Stanford's election had never entered his mind. This is not surprising, since it had not entered anybody's mind long before the event. But, Huntington went on, he could not say anything against Stanford's election, because, if it had been a subject of discussion, Stanford would have been his first choice. His colleague was a "clean," "pure," and "able" man; his only regret was that it placed him in an "equivocable" position with Sargent.

As for the 1887 election, Huntington once again endorsed Sargent, on the ground that he was the best man to look after the overall interests of the state. He would like to see Sargent elected, not only because he liked him personally, and thought he would represent the state ably, but to repay him for the loss of his promised seat in 1885: "I feel that in this way justice will be done to him as well as to myself and others who had promised him our support to the best of our ability."[36]

Stanford knew that Huntington had been less offended in 1885 than was generally believed, and he wrote Gage a short while afterward to collect a number of the adulatory letters written him by Huntington in 1886 and turn them over to Ariel Lathrop for safekeeping.[37] But something had obviously happened between 1886 and 1890 to destroy the cordial relations between Stanford and Huntington, and one does not have to seek far to find it.

Huntington's first "grumblings" about his associates were heard years earlier, when they began building their mansions on Nob Hill, but this had long since been forgotten.[38] Now he was rankled by Stanford's placing his fortune in a school. Many times when Californians called on Huntington in New York he would tell them that Stanford was a fool, throwing away his money on horses, and he would complain about the equally foolish project to build a school, which he termed "Stanford's circus."[39] Any money that Stanford had to throw around could best be plowed back into the railroad.

Huntington's major objection was that the Senator and university manager no longer paid sufficient interest to his railroad duties. Stanford himself realized this and had tried to resign from the presidency in 1889, but all his associates except Huntington prevailed upon him to stay on a while longer.[40] Meanwhile, he continued absenting himself from company business for long periods of time, as he had for two or three years. Huntington objected to this, and during the last year his complaints came with greater and greater frequency.[41]

Even before taking on all his added responsibilities in the Senate, wineries, horses, stables, travels, and railroad business had usurped much of Stanford's time. He had served for years as president of the Central Pacific, in fact as well as name; he was neither a figurehead nor a mere titular head (that road had always been known to its enemies as Stanford's road or Stanford and Company, never Huntington and Company).[42] But he was hardly more than titular head of the Southern Pacific, and Huntington reasoned that if Stanford was not going to use his favored position among Californians for the benefit of the railroad, he should be replaced by the man who was functioning as president, himself.

Some of Stanford's friends conceded that further widening of the breach between the old partners was caused by the lack of harmony between their wives.[43] Huntington's first wife had died and he had remarried. Mrs. Stanford had allegedly snubbed the new Mrs. Huntington, and refused to associate with her. When Huntington asked Stanford to have his wife call on Mrs. Huntington, he was told that Mrs. Stanford arranged her own social affairs.[44] It was later reported that the spite of Mrs. Huntington and her desire to humble Mrs. Stanford resulted in Huntington's attempt to purchase opposition to Stanford in his senatorial race, but a number of contemporaries attributed Huntington's attack on Stanford to his long-seething jealousy of his famous and respected colleague.[45] Stanford had been governor, Senator, and had his name on a thousand tongues for the presidency, while Huntington, in the opinion of one writer, remained basically a friendless, money-worshipping, glorified village trader, who remained unknown and unnoticed, regarded almost universally as "tricky, hypocritical, and insincere."[46]

Stanford's loss of the presidency of the Southern Pacific has too often been depicted as a total ouster from railroad affairs, but this was not the case. When he announced his intention of resigning, he made it clear that his interests in railroad affairs were as great as ever and that he was going to take an active part in these affairs.[47] When it was agreed that he would step down, an executive committee was created, consisting of himself, Huntington, C. F.

Crocker, and Thomas H. Hubbard. Stanford was made chairman of the committee. This position, many believed, relieved him of the details of the presidency while still allowing him to supervise many of the affairs of the corporation. Several people surmised, inaccurately as it proved, that as chairman of the newly-created executive committee he would still be at the head of the great railway system.[48] One editor was engaging in wishful thinking when he predicted, or hoped, that Stanford's voice would be as strong as ever in the company.[49]

Some of Stanford's friends asserted that his resignation was entirely his own decision, based upon his recognition that his poor health made it impossible to perform his Senate duties and kept him less active in university affairs than he liked. This appears little more than the work of an overanxious press that was trying in every way possible to protect him from the stigma of outright defeat.[50] In a similar vein, Stanford himself explained that his principal interest in railroads had been construction, and now that the Southern Pacific system was completed, he wished to leave its management to others.[51] If this were so, why did he remain president of the Central Pacific?

Though his position in the councils of the company was undoubtedly weakened, it was far from that of an absurd newspaper report that stated a few years later that he now had "as little to say about the exercise of the powers he had so long wielded as the boy which [sic] ran the elevator that took him downstairs after the meeting."[52] Stanford did not surrender his numerous positions with other railroads, and he continued as president of the Central Pacific until his death, with Huntington as first vice-president.[53] He also retained his position as president of the Amador, Berkeley, Sacramento and Placerville, San Pablo and Tulare, Stockton and Copperopolis, Vaca Valley and Clear Lake, and South Coast branch lines, all of which, of course, were part of the Southern Pacific system.[54]

With two personalities as different as Stanford's and Huntington's, perhaps conflict was inevitable. The remarkable thing is not that they fell apart, but that they had worked together so effectively for so long. Another remarkable thing was the way their railroad empire suffered so little from these internecine battles. This was due, no doubt, to their recognition of the consequences of all-out warfare and the willingness of both of them to swallow some of their pride and continue working together; the railroad battle in some respects, then, brought out the best in both their characters.

---

1.   San Francisco *Chronicle*, April 11, 1890.

2.   The Pacific Improvement Company now meant Stanford, Huntington, the Crocker family, and Mrs. Searles, the former Mrs. Mark Hopkins. A copy of this agreement, in Herbert Nash's handwriting, was later found among Mrs.

Stanford's papers. It is now in a bound volume of Stanford correspondence in the Stanford papers.

3. Sacramento *Bee*, April 5, 1890. San Francisco *Chronicle*, April 5, 1890.

4. San Francisco *Call*, April 8, 1890.

5. Los Angeles *Times*, April 7, 8, 1890.

6. *Ibid.*, July 24, 1897. Berner, *Mrs. Stanford*, 85.

7. Los Angeles *Times*, July 24, 1897.

8. San Francisco *Examiner*, April 10, 1890.

9. *Ibid.*

10. *Ibid.* San Francisco *Chronicle*, April 12, 1890.

11. Treat, "Golden Key," 43.

12. *Ibid.*, 44, 46.

13. Colusa *Morning Gazette*, May, 1890, in SFS, I, 106. Historian H. H. Bancroft agreed, but only after falling out with Stanford. According to him, Huntington had needed a California resident as head of the Southern Pacific, but now, to save the corporation from politics, he was exercising his option of placing himself at the head of the road. *Builders of the Commonwealth* (San Francisco, 1891), V, 98-101.

14. Eureka *Times*, April 19, 1890.

15. San Francisco *Examiner*, April 10, 1890.

16. *Ibid.*, January 7, 1889. San Francisco *Argonaut*, April 21, 1890. Box 2, Folder 11, in Stanford papers.

17. San Francisco *Chronicle*, April 10, 1890.

18. Sacramento *Bee*, April 10, 1890.

19. San Francisco *Chronicle*, April 11, 1890.

20. San Francisco *Examiner*, April 12, 1890.

21. San Francisco *Chronicle*, April 11, 1890.

22. *Ibid.*, April 10, 1890.

23. San Francisco *Examiner*, April 12, 1890.

24. *Ibid.*, April 13, 1890.

25. Stockton *Mail*, April 12, 1890.

26. San Francisco *Examiner*, April 12, 1890.

27. *Ibid.*, April 15, 1890.

28. *Ibid.* San Francisco *Chronicle*, April 15, 1890.

29. San Francisco *Chronicle*, April 16, 1890.

30. Huntington to Stanford, April 15, 1890. Stanford announced that he did not wish to be interviewed by the press on the contents of the letter, but he soon made it public, and allowed it to be printed in most of the San Francisco newspapers.

31. San Francisco *Examiner,* April 16, 1890.

32. *Ibid.,* April 17, 1890.

33. San Francisco *Argonaut,* May 19, June 2, August 4, 1890.

34. Stanford and C. F. Crocker to Huntington, Thomas E. Stillman, and Thomas H. Hubbard, April 22, 1892.

35. Huntington to Stephen T. Gage, May 8, 1886.

36. *Ibid.*

37. Stanford to Gage, April 29, 1890.

38. Huntington to Hopkins, March 23, 1877. San Francisco *Argonaut,* April 21, 1890.

39. Treat, "Golden Key," 45.

40. San Francisco *Examiner,* April 12, 1890.

41. *Ibid.*

42. San Francisco *Bulletin,* July 13, 1872.

43. Stockton *Mail,* April 12, 1890. San Francisco *Examiner,* June 21, 1893.

44. Berner, *Mrs. Stanford,* 86. San Francisco *Argonaut,* April 21, 1890. Chicago *Examiner,* March 2, 1905.

45. Stockton *Mail,* April 12, 1890.

46. San Francisco *Argonaut,* April 21, 1890.

47. San Francisco *Alta California,* April 8, 1890.

48. *Ibid.,* April 10, 1890. Bancroft, *History,* VII, 632.

49. Sacramento *Record-Union,* April 10, 1890.

50. San Francisco *Examiner,* April 7, 1890.

51. San Francisco *Alta California,* April 8, 1890.

52. Los Angeles *Times,* July 24, 1897.

53. San Francisco *Alta California,* April 10, 1890.

54. San Francisco *Examiner,* April 7, 1890.

CHAPTER XIV

UNITED STATES SENATOR: PART II

While he was engaged in his imbroglio with Huntington, Stanford tried his best to be present at most Senate roll calls, for a matter of special interest to him had come up with the introduction of the controversial Blair education bill. This bill frightened states' rights enthusiasts by providing for federal aid to schools where such aid was needed; an initial grant of $77,000,000 was to be apportioned among the states in proportion to their illiteracy rates.

Stanford spoke for the measure on February 25, 1890.[1] He rejected without consideration the argument that the bill was unconstitutional, maintaining that the important consideration was whether or not there existed a need for it. Believing that the national government could have no more important object than the improvement of the intelligence of the nation's citizens, and inasmuch as a number of states could not afford to meet the educational demands imposed upon them, he concluded that the bill was not only constitutional, but also necessary and essential. Reminiscent of his own school's founding grant, and reflective of his growing concern with religion, he argued that literacy and intelligence were needed to make possible the morality and religion which were in harmony with a "sublime, all-wise, always beneficent Creator." Education was his panacea for all problems, whether religious, political, or industrial, and this bill would certainly make humanity better, wiser, and happier. Earlier, Stanford had attributed the nation's poverty to the sale and use of liquor, lack of manual labor, and ignorance of how to save money. The Blair bill would help eliminate poverty by giving people the needed education, sense of values, and ability to work.[2]

At home, as expected, Pixley's *Argonaut* supported Stanford's position on the Blair bill, while the *Chronicle* came out against it, with such illogical, almost bizarre, reasoning that Stanford's stand seemed brilliant by contrast.[3] This editor rejected Stanford's assertion that education contributed to man's control of the various forces of nature and thereby helped him provide for his needs; chance and circumstance, not education, controlled these forces. He rejected as nonsense the Senator's statement that the wealth of one man in no way implied or necessitated the poverty of another. Wealth, after all, was fixed in amount. If the proponents of the Blair bill had had to contend with no more substantial arguments or opposition than this, their bill would not have been defeated, as it was.

Stanford's legislative interests were limited in number and scope, but he was greatly interested in national finances. He was sure that what was needed to solve the nation's economic problems was an increase in the amount of circulating currency. In this he agreed with the Populists and Alliance men, but their points of agreement ended there. The Senate's financial wizard surprised his fellow millionaires by reasoning himself to the conclusion that the nation's economic system should not only be more flexible, but ought to give every man the credit he needed, based alone upon his industry, character, and ability to repay.[4] And since it was the farmer who had the indestructible security that could best furnish the government with the means of supplying the needed money that would give the system flexibility, on March 10, 1890, Stanford submitted a resolution to the Senate requesting that the committee on finance inquire into the possibility of making loans directly to farmers, with their real estate as security.[5] When the committee sidetracked the resolution for two months without action, he pressed the matter on the floor of the Senate. On May 23 he introduced a bill which directed the Secretary of the Treasury to print $100,000,000 worth of paper money secured by land at no more than fifty percent of its value.[6] This, he said, was far safer than the present policy of lending ninety percent on government bonds, and would have the additional advantage of allowing those without liquid capital to "energize" their assets.

Stanford was asked to explain the difference between his bill and the subtreasury scheme advocated by the Farmers' Alliance. The alliance plan, he pointed out, called for temporary loans secured by the products of the farmers' lands, loans that had to be repaid as soon as a crop was harvested, whereas his scheme provided for long-term loans at two percent interest secured by the lands themselves.[7] Some critics could not see the difference.

II

While busy with official duties, as well as trying to resolve the railroad mess, the ailing California Senator again interrupted his routine, in April, 1890, long before the long session of Congress closed, to take the thermal cure again. He was suffering intensely, and some prominent New York physicians advised him to go to a number of German bathing resorts to arrest certain unidentified "incipient organic troubles."[8] He and his wife returned briefly to California before leaving for Europe. In Sacramento they were given one of the most "spontaneous and heartfelt manifestations of respect and esteem" ever tendered anyone in the state, as 10,000 people turned out to see them, including 1,000 school children.[9] Both were visibly touched by

Author's Collection

PRESIDENT BENJAMIN HARRISON, SENATOR STANFORD, and POSTMASTER GENERAL JOHN WANAMAKER, Palo Alto, 1891.

this public display of affection. They were back in Washington in May, when Stanford introduced his finance resolution, and they sailed for Europe later the same month.

As it turned out, this was one of their shortest trips abroad; by the middle of October they were back home in San Francisco, summoned to campaign for reelection to the Senate.[10] The campaign had not been progressing satisfactorily in his absence. The newspapers had blown his feud with Huntington into a balloon, and were telling the voters how even Huntington had conceded that Stanford's Senate seat had been purchased with railroad funds. Stephen M. White, the Democrats' favorite, realizing that if the Republicans captured the legislature no name other than Stanford's would be presented to the Republican caucus, used the occasion to barnstorm in favor of electing Senators by convention rather than caucus, thus approximating a popular vote.[11] As if these problems were not enough, a nationwide recession during Harrison's administration boded ill for Republicans everywhere. Stanford was also saddled with the liability of the unpopular McKinley tariff, which was credited with the high cost of living and which he had supported.

W. W. Stow, a San Francisco attorney who was managing Stanford's reelection campaign, fortunately recognized that things were out of hand for him, and called the Senator back from his European tour two weeks early.[12] The Stanfords were welcomed by tumultuous crowds everywhere they went, in Sacramento, Stockton, Auburn, and Colfax.[13] In the state capital a public reception with a torchlight procession from the train was given in his honor.[14] It was characterized as a spontaneous, nonpolitical affair, but the presence of several Republican organizations gave away its real purpose. On the following day, October 15, this scene was repeated at Stockton, where it was reported that multitudes of all political hues turned out to see this "great, good, and wise man," this "true servant of the people," this "benefactor of his race."[15] In honor of the Stanfords' generosity toward education, the public schools were closed at 11:30 to give the school children an opportunity to see them.[16]

Stanford delivered a nonpartisan address to the crowd assembled in the huge pavilion, and praised people of both parties for their patriotism and their consensus on most political principles; they differed on very few, most important of which was the tariff. He explained briefly that his protectionism was intended to induce people to engage in all classes of industry, but he soon passed on to less political topics. At the close of his talk the roof rang with three hearty cheers, and the Stanfords boarded their train for another city, eventually touring as far south as San Diego.[17]

Huntington, meanwhile, not only violated the February, 1890, agreement to support Stanford for reelection, but went out of his way to provide opposition. In August, for example, he spoke of the "rottenness of the politics of the state as conducted by Leland Stanford."[18] Much of the California press had by then written Huntington off as a hopeless, incorrigible hypocrite, but much more was to come.[19] In September he wrote that he was not going to make any organized effort to defeat Stanford, but he left no doubt where he stood: *"My preference is naturally for Republicans. But I would much rather have a good clean Democrat than a Dirty Republican."*[20] These remarks and the others like them prompted another flurry of rumors of an impending clash between the two railroad giants.[21]

It was an easy matter for Californians to choose between Stanford and his opposition, and when they spoke at the polls there was no doubt as to their choice. The immediate issue, of course, was control of the legislature. If the Republicans won this, Stanford was in. On election day the people not only voted in a Republican legislature, where the Democrats managed to capture only twenty percent of the seats, but, for the first time in nine years, chose a Republican governor. The heavy Republican victory was even more remarkable since the nation as a whole had gone the other way. When asked what made this lopsided victory possible, one California politician answered: "It was simply Stanford."[22]

He was right. Farmers of both parties had supported Stanford because of his land loan bill, and city workers and anti-Chinese labor groups supported him as well, because of his stand on immigration. The Chinese problem had caused Stanford considerable personal troubles, culminating in his getting rid of Chinese labor on a number of his farms in order to satisfy the public, and his ideas on this key issue had been solicited time and time again, especially after Huntington had come out against any kind of restriction whatsoever.[23] Stanford preferred his own race, as he made clear on a number of occasions, but he justified exclusion on other than racist grounds. Almost magnanimously, he conceded that even though the Chinese were a "disturbing element" in American society, it was only because the laws kept them from becoming citizens. On the ground that they were "sojourners," and not colonists, he felt that present restrictive legislation was sufficient.[24] He rejected the argument that their presence caused less demand for white labor; now that the mines, the principal attraction for Chinese labor, had almost given out, they presented even less a threat than ever.[25]

So far he had said little that would win the support of the racists in the state and much that would offend them. In fact, he said little else, but his support of restrictive legislation, his belief that the Chinese were racially inferior to Caucasians, and his opposition to all forms of amalgamation presented a position that was attractive or at least palatable to most voters. He also made it clear that the amalgamation of Negroes and Caucasians was just as much out of the question.[26]

On January 14, 1891, the California legislature demonstrated its satisfaction with Stanford as a Senator and its affection for him as a man by re-electing him by a vote of eighty-six to thirty, even though fragile health made it impossible for him to perform his duties with the drive needed.[27] His re-election was endorsed all over the country as a well-merited honor, as a trib-ute to the man who more than any other in the state deserved well at the hands of the people. Hardly anyone aside from hardcore antirailroad people even suggested that money had been used to win the support of the legisla-ture, but there can be no doubt that his continuing generosity toward the university and his other philanthropies had much to do with his reelection.[28]

III

In December, 1890, the Stanfords were back in Washington, ready to pick up their social and senatorial duties. Once there, Stanford took up his money bill again. On the preceding June 11, the Senate Committee on Fi-nance had postponed indefinitely his measure, so on December 19 he intro-duced another.[29] Since so many arguments had arisen in the interim about the nature of legal tender, this time he devoted more time to a discussion of it, and he concluded, simply: legal tender is created by the imprint of the United States government regardless of material used. But in February, 1891, the same committee killed his bill again.

When the Fifty-second Congress convened in December, 1891, the per-sistent California Senator prepared another finance bill, which he introduced on January 21, 1892. This time he fought for it more strongly inside as well as outside of Congress. He began by accusing the committee which had twice previously killed his bills with not having considered the economic principles underlying them. Rather, it had relied on some superficial comparisons of his system and those that had failed in some other countries; but those had failed, he insisted, because of insufficient security.

The major difference between Stanford and the members of the finance committee was that they believed that paper currency would inevitably de-preciate, whereas he was convinced that land security was just as substantial as specie.[30] But his scheme sounded too much like the Populists' "potato bank" plan for the orthodox to accept, a plan that in itself was designed to favor one particular class of people. Stanford emphatically denied this as one of his purposes, insisting that his only goal was to increase the nation's circu-lating medium, a goal accepted by a considerable portion of the Democratic party and perennial third parties, though it was very unpopular in his own. He recognized that farmers as a class would benefit from his measure, but not at the expense of other groups or the economy as a whole. If the farmers of his state alone could "energize" one-half the value of their lands at a nominal rate of interest, a volume of money would be placed in circulation that would develop the industries of the country as a whole.

Stanford was told that a legal tender dollar was not worth as much as a specie dollar, so on February 29, 1892, he introduced a bill to determine the value of legal tender currency. It was followed almost immediately by another calling for the coining of silver bullion. On March 30 he delivered his last Senate speech, in which he read that portion of his bill which directed that all legal tender, made so by the stamp of the government, be accepted at par for all debts public and private. To avoid the rush of speculators that followed the passage of the Sherman Silver Purchase Act, Stanford's bill did not provide that the government had to exchange one kind of currency for another; all would be accepted at par.

The California Senator unfortunately failed to recognize the strength of the widespread animus toward fiat currency, and he kept hitting at his old theme that legal money was entirely the creature of the law. To make matters worse, he actually preferred paper money to specie, since gold was hardly ever seen east of the Rockies and all the silver available, even if minted, would have been but a "drop in the bucket" of needed currency.[31] Paper money based upon unimpeachable security was what the country needed. When a "gold bug" Senator objected even to the use of silver, which he called a "debased" coin, Stanford met him on the practical level. Drawing from his pocket a silver dollar, he challenged his colleague: "You say that dollar piece is only worth eighty-five cents, do you? Well, sir, I will give you ninety-nine and a half cents each for a hundred thousand of them."[32] The gold enthusiast was silenced, and Stanford's challenge went unaccepted.

Another incident further confirmed him in his position: when he tried to pay for his lunch in the nation's capital with a gold coin, it was twice refused. Returning to the Senate, he told the story to some gold supporters and asked for an explanation. When told that the gold coin was not legal tender, he replied: "That's it exactly. It's the stamp that makes money and not the materials of which the money is composed."[33] This kind of argument silenced the opposition, but it converted no one to his cause. His financial measures never again came before the Senate.[34]

No aspect of Stanford's Senate career received more widespread publicity than his money bills; they were discussed from one end of the country to the other, with reactions ranging from the warmest praise and talk of electing him president to serious misgivings as to his sanity. His friend Pixley of the San Francisco *Argonaut* gave all the money bills his editorial endorsement, but a number of Midwestern editors saw it as nothing more than a crazy fiat scheme, and described its author as "a success as a railroad operator but a dreadful failure as a statesman."[35] The plan of this "most sagacious financier in the Senate" for increasing the currency struck upon the key note to a practical solution of the nation's financial problems, in the estimation of some, while to others it constituted an outright rejection of American capitalism, and showed that he was "fully impregnated with socialistic ideas."[36] Some felt that his plan demonstrated his "broad statemanship" and lack of self-interest, while others suspected that his own interests would profit more than they should, since railroads might qualify for low-interest, long-term loans secured by government land grants.[37]

The Lamar appointment of 1888 had showed Stanford's political independence, and this was demonstrated again in 1891 when the Elections bill,
sometimes called the Force bill or Lodge bill, after its author in the House of
Representatives, came before the Senate. Designed to provide federal protection for Negroes when they were voting, this proposal was one of the most
heated political issues of the time. Stanford opposed it, and in so doing
aligned himself against the overwhelming majority of his fellow Republicans.
He conceded that the present election system had a number of "evils" in it,
but the Force bill, in his estimation, was a greater evil than that which it
hoped to correct. By regulating the voting procedures of the states, it endan-
gered the principle of self-government. What was worse, by encouraging or
possibly requiring that local and national elections be held at the same time, it
would allow regulation of national elections as well as local.[38]

Senate Republicans were determined to pass this measure, and even tried
to press the cloture system into the service of their cause, but eight Western
Republicans joined the Democrats in sidetracking the bill. Stanford was one
of the eight, for though absent when the crucial vote was taken, he was paired
against it.[39]

If Stanford's bruited candidacy for the presidency in 1888 seems incredible, his second presidential boom, in 1892 as the Populist candidate, must
appear one of the all-time political absurdities. It is true that this movement
never got off the ground, but that it could even have been launched, or conceived, for that matter, is significant. For some Alliance men to give serious
consideration to the wealthiest man in the Senate as the candidate for a party
whose motto was "down with the money power" was indeed incredible, and
yet it happened. Stanford's money bill was too much for some of them to resist. It is clear that Stanford's financial plans alone prompted this interest, but
a similarity of views on this one point could not by any stretch of the imagination make him a supporter of the radical doctrines of the Populists. Some of
these he would have condemned as un-American or communistic: direct election of Senators, government ownership of railroads and utilities, a graduated
income tax, to name a few.[40] He went out of his way to state explicitly in the
summer of 1891 that he was not a candidate for the presidency.[41]

But some of his enthusiastic supporters would not take no for an answer,
even though they did not always make it clear for which party's nomination
they were endorsing him. The election of 1888 had hardly passed when his
boosters began touting him for the presidential candidate in the next quad-
rennial contest. His nomination in 1892 "would brand the American people
as being the greatest discriminators of human excellence on earth," one ecstatic fan proclaimed.[42] The Stockton *Mail* wanted him as the People's Party
candidate, and insisted that if one went over the country with a "moral garden
rake" he would not find a man better qualified for the position.[43] The editors
of the *Argonaut* and the San Francisco *Argus* also favored him as the Alliance candidate; with him running on the People's ticket, the party would

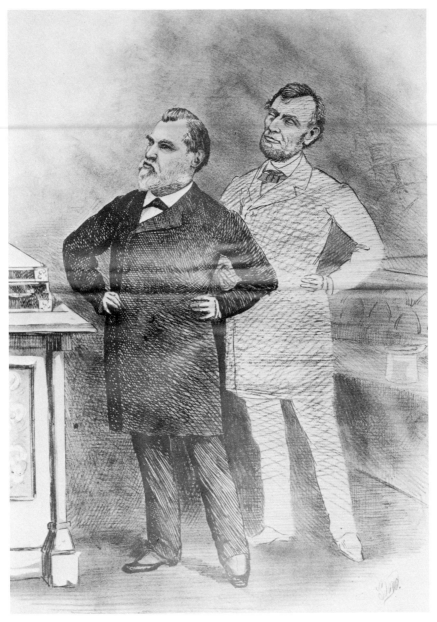

Stanford Library

A SAN FRANCISCO EDITOR SEES STANFORD as "A fitting successor to Lincoln."

sweep the country from Maine to Texas.[44] He was undoubtedly the "coming man," and one enthusiastic journalist listed thirteen prominent governors, Senators, other high-ranking public officials, and a number of outstanding businessmen who supported Stanford for the first office.[45]

An Alliance meeting in Florida was reported as discussing Stanford's candidacy. In spite of his own indifference, Stanford clubs began springing up all over the West; California people, it was said, were all behind him, as were many from the Mississippi Valley, silver people from the West, and farmers from the Pacific Northwest. All that remained was for the Alliance men to endorse him and they could elect him president.[46]

Unlike 1888, when Stanford's candidacy as a Republican could have been feasible, and few bothered to belittle it, in the 1891 boom there developed considerable opposition, as the ridiculousness of the whole affair was recognized by most people. The influential New York *Times* shrugged it off as a luxury that an active mind and a long purse could afford, but this was untrue; there is no evidence that Stanford himself had anything to do with it.[47] Most out-of-state people knew very little about Stanford other than that he was a millionaire, but this in itself somehow made him dishonest or crazed with ambition. One journalist suggested that if the Alliance men wanted a "bloated monopolist" they should go all the way and get Jay Gould.[48] Another judged Stanford entirely on his railroad connections and depicted him as the "embodiment of greed," having pockets that bulged with money that belonged to the government.[49] It was ironic that this kind of criticism should come after a number of his railroad connections had been weakened and after he had given the bulk of his fortune to Stanford University.

Another critic, claiming more knowledge of Stanford's political dealings than did his most astute and carping critics in his home state, said he was a hypocrite; he was merely pretending to befriend farmers, in order to get their votes.[50] But the criticism of the Stanford boom that made the most sense was heard the least often, that it was based upon too narrow a political affinity with the Alliance doctrines.[51]

IV

Stanford paid no attention to this talk of his candidacy. He at least recognized it for what it was: a form of tribute by his friends and admirers and the daydream of a handful of Alliance men who wanted a winning candidate at any cost. He and his wife, meanwhile, had turned to things within their reach, like lavish banquets and foreign travels. When they first arrived in Washington, in 1885, they had lived in an annex to the Arlington Hotel while searching for a home. They eventually leased a mansion at 1701 K Street, opposite Farragut Square. Stanford was by all odds the richest man in the Senate, and this big white stone house was one of the most beautiful and most fashionable in the capital. Nearby he kept a stable, though not all the twenty horses in his Washington stables were kept within the city.[52]

The Stanfords' first year in Washington was spent in mourning for their son; it was not until the second year that they entered Washington society, but when they did, it was with a bang.[53] When they drove by, people took notice, for it was said that they had the "handsomest equipage at the Capital."[54] Mrs. Stanford's lavish receptions and parties, not to mention her philanthropies, made her one of the most popular ladies in Washington.[55] Her dinners were regarded as the most fabulous the city had ever seen.[56] After reelection to the Senate, the Stanfords extended their dining room capacity far beyond the original eighteen which it seated; by then Mrs. Stanford's calling list in Washington included 1,000 names.

In 1888 they gave a huge reception for the widow of President Grant, a close friend of three years. But nothing compared to the gala party they held for President-elect and Mrs. Benjamin Harrison in January, 1891. Among the guests at this famous affair were a number of Senators and generals, Vice-president-elect Levi Morton, and Chief Justice Melville W. Fuller.[57] A few days afterwards, when the Stanfords were guests at a White House reception, Mrs. Stanford "literally blazed with diamonds," and one disgruntled editor snapped that one month's interest on her jewels would have carpeted the stone floor on which the ladies stood catching cold.[58] Her diamond collection alone was valued at $1,000,000, besides her emeralds, pearls, and rubies; her accessories surpassed the richest ever seen before in Washington, and a single diamond necklace was valued at $600,000.[59] Her jewels had long been a topic of conversation in social circles as well as a target for editors. Whole editorials were dedicated to her priceless collection, which included the jewels of the former Queen Isabella of Spain.[60] Mrs. Stanford was said to own more diamonds than any royal family in Europe, with the exception of the British and Russian.[61]

Hardly a day passed that some notable figure did not call at the Stanford home, and at their banquets they entertained not only Presidents, former Presidents, Senators, Representatives, and Supreme Court Justices, but scientists, artists, pageboys, and their own employees. On at least one occasion they played host to the whole Pacific Coast Congressional delegation.[62] Stanford's closest friends in the capital were Stephen J. Field of Marysville, California, a Democrat and Supreme Court Justice, who gave him some influence with the Cleveland administration; Congressman Joseph McKenna, who was later appointed to the high court; W. W. Morrow, who became a United States Circuit judge and who said later that he went often to the Stanford home because of the good company to be found there; John Carlisle, first Congressman, then Senator, then Cleveland's Secretary of the Treasury; Senator William P. Frye of Maine; Senator Justin S. Morrill of Vermont; and James G. Blaine.[63]

As the Stanfords took their place among the social elite of the nation's capital, their philanthropies increased. They received from twenty-five to forty "begging letters" per day; within one week requests came from Egypt,

Ireland, and India.[64] Wherever they were, needy causes received their assistance. At home in Menlo Park, Mrs. Stanford gave the Presbyterian Church a new organ, and she spent several small fortunes sponsoring five kindergartens in San Francisco, having given them a combined endowment of $100,000.[65] And in commemoration of the work of Father Junipero Serra, she erected a statue in his honor in Monterey. While attending a church in that small town she donated $200 for a badly needed carpet.[66] On a short trip to Portland, Oregon, she gave over $500 to an orphans' home.[67] Such philanthropies in the East were not as extensive as in the West, but they were considerable. Mrs. Stanford on one occasion gave $150,000 for an old woman's home in Albany, New York.[68] And the Senator gave $5,000 to Bates College in Maine.[69] These philanthropies are representative, but do not scratch the surface of the causes to which they contributed during their senatorial tenure.

Despite official duties and failing health, the California Senator and his wife continued to entertain often and regally. They once gave a feast for all of Washington's Western Union messenger boys.[70] And every Christmas the Senate pages were invited to a party and were given five dollars with which to buy a gift.[71] In one year alone the California millionaire spent over $100,000 entertaining.[72] With this kind of money to throw around, it is no wonder that Stanford could give his entire Senate salary of $7,000 to his private secretary, in addition to the regular salary of $2,500.[73]

The Stanfords and the first family shared more than political affinity; they soon became close friends. And in 1891, when the Harrisons made a trip to California and an extended tour of the Coast, rumor had it that Stanford footed the whole bill.[74] Harrison's presidential train reached Oakland on April 25, and the party spent that night at the Palace Hotel in San Francisco.[75] After a restful Sunday in San Francisco, Mrs. Harrison and other San Francisco ladies were entertained in the evening by Mrs. Stanford.[76] A few days later, when one of the city's most spectacular balls was given in honor of the President and his wife, hundreds turned out to meet them in the Nob Hill palace, which was reported ablaze with lights into the early hours of the morning.[77]

The Stanfords next took their guests to the Palo Alto farm, where they met California junior Senator Clark N. Felton and Governor and Mrs. Henry H. Markham.[78] Harrison enjoyed the farm immensely: he toured the university, then under construction, visited the world famous champion stables, had lunch at the Stanford home, and then pushed ahead to other parts of the state.[79]

Though many guests of note were entertained at the farm, it was generally known that the common as well as the great were welcome to call on the affable Senator.[80] On May 19, 1893, for example, a committee from the Palo Alto Improvement Club dropped by unannounced and uninvited to discuss some local problems with Stanford. Though a semi-invalid at the time, he welcomed them all. They talked about a number of problems with which Stanford promised to help them, and then the guests, realizing how fragile his health was, tried to excuse themselves. But he insisted that they stay, and they spent the rest of the afternoon discussing anything that happened to come up. The members of the committee were favorably impressed by their host's hospitality and homespun earnestness.[81]

V

On April 7, 1892, again in the middle of the session, the truant Senator returned briefly to California, only to be back in Washington at the end of the month, when he wrote his brother in Australia that he was suffering attacks of the "grippe," which affected his legs and his hearing, and said that he and his wife would soon leave again for Europe.[82] In June they sailed on their fifth and final trip together. Stanford was a sick man, worse than he had ever been before, and in a letter from Aix-les-Bains Mrs. Stanford lamented that his health had not improved after a dreary week on the continent, and she despaired of his life.[83] They took the advice of a physician who recommended a change of air, and made an excursion to Switzerland for the "reaction" part of the cure and then returned to Aix-les-Bains for the second cure. By July Mrs. Stanford wrote with considerable relief that he was feeling much better.[84] In the fall they spent some time in England, and on October 5 sailed for home on the *Majestic*. They were home in Palo Alto by the end of the month.[85]

PRESIDENT BENJAMIN HARRISON and party visit the Palo Alto Farm, 1891.

Stanford Library

The ailing Senator sat out the 1892 presidential campaign, unable to contribute much to Harrison's cause. He no longer believed that the tariff was the paramount issue, as in 1888. The nation was compelled to have a revenue tariff, so for all practical purposes the protective tariff men had things their own way.[86] Politically, he said, the only question was whether the Democrats or Republicans would control.

Ill health continued to plague Stanford, so much that he was unable to return to Washington until February 13, 1893, and he never attended the special session of the Senate, which lasted until April; his Senate career had thus ended a year earlier.

Stanford performed creditably as a Senator. He was neither an outstanding legislator nor a great orator, and he authored no great legislation, but he did serve faithfully on a number of committees, among them Civil Service, Education and Labor, Fisheries, Naval Affairs, and Public Buildings and Grounds. Until his health got to where he could no longer attend, he spent quite some time on the floor of the Senate. He was a Senator in fact as well as name.

During his Senate tenure, Stanford built, opened, and helped manage Stanford University; he continued his philanthropies; and he presented bills and voted on measures that on occasion won him the commendation of people of both parties in his state. He became a sort of political senior citizen; one hesitates to say senior statesman. Californians by and large were more than satisfied with his Senate career, and they, after all, were what really counted. Several of his votes showed that he was not an obsequious partisan, and his stand on occasion against railroad bills showed that he was unwilling to favor legislation that was not good for the nation as a whole, regardless of his own economic interests or those of his associates. When a railroad attorney reproached him for voting against a certain railroad bill, he replied, good-naturedly: "Oh, I forgot all about the fact that I was interested in railroads; I'll do better next time."[87] But he did not.

Perhaps no higher compliment could be paid Stanford as a public official than that of Senator William M. Stewart of Nevada: "Every suggestion he made, every speech he delivered, and every bill he introduced had for its object the good of all the people."[88] Little more could have been expected.

---

1. *Cong. Record,* 51 Cong., 1 Sess., 1,687-1,688.

2. Sacramento *Record-Union,* February 22, 1888.

3. San Francisco *Argonaut,* April 14, 1890. San Francisco *Chronicle,* March 31, 1890.

4. New York *Evangelist*, February 19, 1891. In Clark, *Stanford*, 459.

5. *Cong. Record*, 51 Cong., 1 Sess., 2,068.

6. *Ibid.*, 5,169-5,170.

7. Stanford interview with Cincinnati *Enquirer*, reprinted in pamphlet form, in Stanford papers.

8. San Francisco *Examiner*, April 5, 1890. The best documentation of their fourth European trip is found in the correspondence between Mrs. Stanford and Mrs. Timothy Hopkins. In Mrs. Jane Stanford papers.

9. Sacramento *Record-Union*, April 26, 1890.

10. Jane Stanford to May Hopkins, July 4, 1890.

11. San Francisco *Wave*, September 13, 1890. In Clark, *Stanford*, 444.

12. Washington *Post*, November 12, 1890. In *ibid.*, 446.

13. *Frank Leslie's Illustrated Magazine*, November 8, 1890.

14. Sacramento *Bee*, October 14, 15, 1890.

15. Stockton *Mail*, October 16, 1890.

16. *Ibid.*, October 15, 1890.

17. *Ibid.*

18. Huntington to editor of the Kern County *Californian*, August 8, 1890, in issue of August 23, reprinted in San Francisco *Examiner*, August 26, 1890.

19. San Francisco *Examiner*, August 28, 1890. Stockton *Mail*, September 13, 1890.

20. San Francisco *Examiner*, September 18, 1890.

21. *Ibid.* Stockton *Mail*, September 9, 10, 13, 1890.

22. Washington *Post*, November 12, 1890.

23. San Francisco *Examiner*, January 7, 1889.

24. *Ibid.*, January 6, 1889.

25. *Ibid.*, January 8, 1889. San Francisco *Call*, April 6, 1890.

26. San Francisco *Call*, April 6, 1890.

27. San Francisco *Alta California*, January 14, 1891.

28. Washington *Post*, January 1, 1891. Washington *National View*, February 7, 1891. Philadelphia *Record*, January 15, 1891. Unidentified newspaper clipping, SFS, II, 5.

29. *Cong. Record*, 51 Cong., 1 Sess., 5,919. *Ibid.*, 2 Sess., 667-668.

30. Stanford to Stockton *Mail*, February 18, 1892. In Clark, *Stanford*, 464.

31. Washington *Post*, April 27, 1893.

32. *St. Louis Journal of Agriculture*, quoted in unidentified newspaper clipping, SFS, X, 7.

33. Phoenix [Arizona] *Herald*, n.d., 1891, in SFS, II, 45.

34. To get his theories on money in print for distribution, an interview was arranged with Stanford at his Palo Alto home. It was published anonymously as a forty-two page pamphlet entitled *The Great Question, An Interview with Senator Stanford on Money.* In Stanford collection.

35. San Francisco *Argonaut,* March 23, 1891. Chicago *Tribune,* January 20, 1891.

36. Petaluma *Argus,* March 15, 1890. Unidentified newspaper clipping, SFS, I, 10.

37. Unidentified newspaper clipping, SFS, X, 3. SFS I contains scores of editorials on this issue. *Cong. Record,* 52 Cong., 1 Sess., 470.

38. New York *Evangelist,* February 19, 1891.

39. William M. Stewart, *Reminiscences of Senator William M. Stewart of Nevada* (New York, 1908), 305-307.

40. Washington *National View,* January 1891, SFS, II, 6.

41. Stanford to Col. Joseph K. Rickey, July 1, 1891, in San Francisco *Examiner,* July 22, 1891.

42. Twin Falls *Idaho Citizen,* October 25, 1889.

43. Stockton *Mail,* November 3, 1891.

44. San Francisco *Argonaut,* March 16, 1891. SFS II contains hundreds of newspaper clippings from all over the country endorsing Stanford as the alliance candidate.

45. San Francisco *City Argus,* various issues, 1891, in SFS, II, 89, 131; XVII, 76-77; XIX, 10.

46. Unidentified newspaper clipping, December, 1890, Box 6, Folder 66, Stanford papers.

47. New York *Times,* December 10, 1891.

48. Omaha *Bee,* January 25, 1891.

49. Atlanta *Journal,* January 23, 1891.

50. Omaha *Herald,* January 18, 1891. Albany *Evening Journal,* January 25, 1887.

51. The San Jose Grange opposed him as well as his financial schemes, as did a number of farmers from the Pacific Northwest. San Jose Grange meeting, May 17, 1890, reported in unidentified newspaper clipping, SFS, I, 38. *Northwest Pacific Farmer,* n.d., 1890, in SFS, I, 49.

52. A detailed description of the home and its furnishings is in an unidentified newspaper clipping, SFS, "C," 36. They also maintained a home on Fifth Avenue in New York.

53. Clark, *Stanford,* 450.

54. Washington *Critic,* n.d., in SFS "C."

55. Washington *News,* January 29, 1887.

56. Unidentified newspaper clipping, SFS, XVIII, 7-9.

57. Washington *Post,* January 16, 1891.

58. Fremont *News,* January 23, 1891.

59. Unidentified newspaper clipping, SFS, X, 1, 53.

60. San Francisco *Herald,* June 23, 1887. New York *Star,* January 18, 1891.

61. Unidentified newspaper clipping, SFS, XXV, 19, 22.

62. Fisher, "Stanford," 2-3.

63. *Ibid.,* 34. Morrow quoted in Clark, *Stanford,* 450.

64. Unidentified newspaper clipping, SFS, "C."

65. Unidentified newspaper clipping, SFS, XVIII, 1-4; XXV, 16. San Francisco *Bulletin,* May 14, 1886. Portland [Maine] *Argus,* July, 1891, in SFS, II, 111.

66. Monterey *Monitor,* July, 1891, in SFS, II, 110.

67. Portland [Oregon] *Sunday Mercury,* September 24, 1887.

68. Sacramento *Record-Union,* May 17, 1886.

69. William P. Frye to Stanford, January 17, 1889.

70. Berner, *Mrs. Stanford,* 82.

71. Testimony of Carl Loeffler, a Senate page during Stanford's tenure, at Stanford University Founders' Day celebration, in Washington, D. C., March 9, 1936, in Stanford collection.

72. Pittsburgh [Pennsylvania] *Times,* December 21, 1887.

73. *Ibid.*

74. A number of newspaper editorials repeated this rumor. SFS, II.

75. New York *Tribune,* April 27, 1891.

76. New York *Press,* April 27, 1891.

77. San Francisco *Examiner,* April 29, 1891.

78. New York *Herald,* April 29, 30, 1891.

79. San Francisco *Chronicle,* April 30, 1891.

80. Altrocchi, *Spectacular San Franciscans,* 213.

81. Reported in "A Tribute from Citizens of Palo Alto." In Stanford Collection.

82. Stanford to Thomas Welton, May 30, 1892.

83. Mrs. Stanford to Timothy and May Hopkins, June 22, 1892. Mrs. Stanford to Mrs. David Starr Jordan, June 16, 1892.

84. Mrs. Stanford to Dr. and Mrs. Jordan, July 13, 1892.

85. Stanford to Jordan, September 28, 1892. Mrs. Stanford to Timothy and May Hopkins, October 30, 1892.

86. Stanford to Thomas Welton, May 30, 1892.

87. Related by J. B. McCarthy, his Senate secretary, in Anonymous, *Military Order of the Loyal Legion of the United States,* Circular 38, November 29, 1904.

88. *Memorial Addresses,* 61.

CHAPTER XV

THE END OF THE LINE

Stanford lived in Palo Alto in a state of semiretirement from the summer of 1892. Though ill and confined to his home most of the time, he retained interest in public affairs, and occasionally had the whole California Congressional delegation in on business.[1] He made a brief trip to Washington in February, 1893, spent a short time in New York the following month, in greatly improved health, and in April stopped off in Chicago at the Columbian Exposition on his way home.[2] This was to be his last trip East, and it was rumored that he was planning to resign his senatorship soon.[3]

June 20, 1893, began no differently from the days preceding it, for Stanford's daily activities were fairly routine: he arose at 7:30, ate a leisurely breakfast, and rode down to the paddocks to watch the horses. After lunch, on this particular day, he went for a long ride in his low-wheeled cabriolet to see his friend Nick Smith in nearby San Carlos, eight miles away. In the evening, at home again, he had dinner and then did some reading on various economic problems facing the nation. Before retiring, Stanford was given his daily massage, to induce circulation; his poor health kept him from exercising on his own.[4] Just a week earlier he had been almost unable to move without assistance, and his hearing had been so impaired that it was difficult at times to carry on a conversation with him, though his mind was at all times alert. On this tragic night he had difficulty sleeping, and about midnight he was discovered dead.[5] His doctor attributed his death to overexertion of his weak heart from trying to get out of bed, adding that the eating of a too heavy dinner possibly aggravated his disorder.[6]

Stanford's body was kept in the second story room where he had died, pending funeral arrangements, and only a few intimate friends were admitted.[7] The funeral services were held in the open air in the Inner Quad at Stanford University, with an estimated 5,000 people in attendance, among them several high public officials and hundreds of railroad associates and employees, but not C. P. Huntington. The casket was carried to the place of funeral by eight locomotive engineers, according to Stanford's own directions, and was placed on a platform at one end of the quad.[8] The simple burial service was read by William Ford Nicholas, bishop of the Episcopal Diocese of California. Rector Robert C. Foute of the Grace Church in San Francisco read the Scriptures, and Horatio Stebbins, pastor of the First Unitarian Church of the same city, delivered the eulogy. Following the funeral, the casket was deposited in a granite mausoleum a half mile away.

Stanford's estate had long been the subject of much speculation, and had been estimated at between $50,000,000 and $100,000,000, but a court inventory set it at about $18,000,000.[9] Most of the estate was left to the widow to dispose of as she saw fit. She was the sole executrix of her husband's will, which left $2,500,000 to the university, $300,000 to his brother Thomas Welton, $100,000 to his brother Philip, $100,000 to each of his nieces and nephews on both sides of the family, and $15,000 to Herbert C. Nash.[10]

II

September 16, 1893, was set aside by the Senate for paying tribute to the deceased member from California. Statesmen from all parties and sections lauded their departed colleague: he was one of the most wonderful men the republic had ever produced; he was a great man, one of the truly unique figures in American life, the "best of the American type." The millionaire-Senator was never obtrusive or self-assertive, though his judgment in all things was unimpaired. He was a Christian in the highest and best sense of the term, and had showed himself a great man by throwing off the prejudices of education and section. Though his advantages were not superior to those of thousands of other boys, by his own ambition, moral character, good judgment, enterprise, energy, and industry, he had made a success of himself. He was as a father to his employees, a genial companion to all, a man simple in manners, generous in hospitality, and unostentatious in his dress and habits.

In the House of Representatives Stanford's career was called one of the most remarkable in history—romance in real life. He possessed all the positive attributes of kingship, and though he was admittedly not faultless, his virtues greatly outshone his shortcomings. No more impressive personality had ever walked the halls of Congress.

Californians in all walks of life vied with one another in offering Stanford their highest praises. Even his old associate C. P. Huntington offered a kind word, as, with trembling voice, he said that he had never known a more agreeable or more pleasant man.[11]

Stanford admirers were sure that he was California's greatest citizen. He was not only the most powerful, but the most popular man on the Pacific Coast. The story of Stanford was the story of California, and his death was a public calamity. This "greatest man that California ever produced" did more for his adopted state than any other ten men combined. In agriculture, no one

Stanford Library

A SAN FRANCISCO EDITOR DEPICTS STANFORD as California's best friend.

else had done a hundredth as much for the Golden State, and his business probity was unimpeachable.

When viewed from any number of perspectives, wrote one admirer, Stanford's character assumed a grandeur that challenged universal admiration. In the essentials of the highest degree of manhood, according to another, he stood preeminent among men, and his praises had to be sung rather than spoken: "His name is a glory to the State, and his life the brightest page in her history. Hail! All Hail! Leland Stanford."

Stanford's benefactions made him a philanthropist-philosopher. His eulogists further proclaimed that he was at the same time taciturn, deeply versed in the knowledge of "human nature," and respected for his "magnificent brain power." He was preeminently a thought-producing and not a thought-repeating man. Stanford became the "Sage of Palo Alto."

Praises were also sung to this spiritual giant because of the lofty aspirations of his inner life and his nobility of soul. His wealth, influence, and popularity all arose from the qualities of his character and his personal integrity. He was active when other men were idle, generous when others were greedy and grasping, lofty when others were base, and he was always actuated by the noblest and kindliest impulses. To top it all, no man ever lived with more character and goodness in his heart than Leland Stanford.

Following Stanford's death, those who attempted biographical sketches, editorials, or eulogies found superlatives constantly on their pens. He was brave, broadminded, courageous, courteous, democratic, earnest, effective, forceful, frank, generous, genial, gentlemanly, honest, humane, industrious, kind, liberal, lofty, patient, patriotic, pleasant, prudent, simple, suave, sympathetic, unselfish, and wise. Stanford was praised as a man of undoubted integrity, spotless private character, far-reaching benevolence, calm judgment, and masterly administrative abilities. He was one of the noblest works of the Creator.

III

Setting aside this tangled web of adulation, when all is said and done, Stanford was essentially a practical man, a builder, a doer. One of his secrets of success was getting as much out of his potentialities as possible. When something needed to be done, whether finding a way to construct railroads under snow slides or capturing a horse's stride on film, Stanford usually had a plan. His brain teemed with ideas, almost always of a practical nature.

This man was a gambler. He was willing to risk all he had to improve his position, as demonstrated when he went to Port Washington, and then, set back by a natural catastrophe, moved to California and began again. He gambled on railroads, mines, and a myriad of other business concerns and hobbies. At any time after his thirty-fifth year he could have retired with a comfortable fortune, yet he risked it all not merely for a greater fortune, but for greater challenges. Stanford was not merely a dollar chaser; achievement was the thing.

Most of all, Stanford was a many-sided man. We know a great deal about many of these sides, perhaps too much. He was simple and uncomplicated, and simplicity in Stanford's case was more baffling than subtlety or complexity. He possessed no secret or overpowering psychological drives that make for titillating biography, and he had no great, unrealized ambitions that sometimes explain peculiar character traits or personality quirks in other men.

No hidden vices or ideological or psychological drives have been uncovered in him. And, unfortunately for the biographer, he seems to have been guilty of no notable indiscretions. No scandals are attached to his name. Just one "the public be damned" would have won him greater fame. Even those who would denigrate him as a member of the "robber baron class" prejudge him on the basis of his business associates; but he was not in the same ethical league with the Fisks, Drews, and Huntingtons.

Was Stanford a great man, as many of his contemporaries believed? In his railroad projects, he ranks in the same bracket with James J. Hill and other great builders. His material accomplishments were among the most extensive in the nation. His wines, his farms, his homes, his political successes were all of the first order, and his philanthropies were prodigious. His career was indeed a conspicuous exemplification of a series of phenomenal successes in a great number of spheres. He worked hard and constantly, and grimly, leaving behind a record that shows very little sense of humor. His career was slow and plodding, but ever progressive.

There have been greater men in every one of the various fields that Stanford victoriously invaded. He spread himself thin over a number of different enterprises, and one could argue, perhaps, that greatness eluded him because of his lack of singularity of purpose. Each field he entered could have absorbed his full-time interest, and each would have brought him greater fame, and fame after all appears to be an ingredient of greatness.

Leland Stanford, unfortunately and unfairly, is largely a forgotten man. His life ended with the century that created such lives, or made it possible for such men to develop. It was partly—but only partly—due to the circumstances of his time that he was able to become what he was. His story was part of the great American legend of the farm boy who makes good through hard work and struggle—the embodiment of the Horatio Alger myth.

This is not to place Stanford on a pedestal; pedestals are made for statues, not men. A monument, perhaps, is more in order, and the university of his conception and founding is his greatest, self-made monument. However, some attempts at monument raising were made. By late 1889 a number of San Joseans were busy erecting a statue of him in Alum Rock Park, and in 1946 he was elected to the New York Hall of Fame.[12]

Stanford was a great railroad builder, a great horsebreeder, a great moneymaker, and a great philanthropist; still, something seems to be missing in his story, something elusive. Stanford possessed the qualities of a hero at the beginning of the age of antiheroes. In an earlier, less critical, less iconoclastic age, he would have been one. His life was the kind that could be held up as an example to youth, worthy of their emulation; yet he was not a paragon of moral perfection, for he had his human passions and frailties. In the debunking age of the antihero, created or heralded by muckrakers, progressives, and reformers, he became a robber baron, a selfish representative of the octopus-age of railroad growth. If a medium is struck between hero-worshipers and the belittlers of great men, Stanford would be found a good man, but not a saint. He was ambitious for power, money, and influence, but not greedy or without regard for others. The student of this man's life feels that he ought to have been great, that he hovered on the edge of greatness, but never quite made it. He was perhaps a near-great. To paraphrase Shakespeare, some people are born great, others achieve greatness, and still others have greatness pass them by. For one reason or another, some explicable and some elusive, Leland Stanford belongs in the last category.

1. *Memorial Address*, 82.

2. Mrs. Stanford to May Hopkins, March 31, 1893.

3. San Francisco *Chronicle,* June 21, 1893.

4. San Francisco *Examiner,* June 22, 1893.

5. Whether found by his wife, his valet, or both together is uncertain. San Francisco *Examiner,* June 21, 22, 1893.

6. San Francisco *Examiner,* June 22, 1893.

7. The best account of the funeral was published in *Memorial Addresses,* 19-26.

8. The engineers chosen were William Scott, Cornelius Collins, Barney Kelly, George Cornwall, Walter Lacy, Sam C. Clark, James E. Saulpaugh, and James G. Ressegine. Anonymous, *Eulogy of Leland Stanford,* published by Brotherhood of Locomotive Engineers, Leland Stanford Division, No. 238.

9. Stocks $12,000,000, bonds $4,000,000, notes $1,000,000. Cash on hand and household effects were incidental. All his stocks were identified and enumerated in San Francisco *Examiner,* October 3, 1893, and San Francisco *Chronicle,* January 18, 1894.

10. Will is in Stanford papers. Reprinted in San Francisco *Call,* July 1, 1893. Why Thomas Welton's gift was three times the size of his brother's was never explained, but Philip was as close to being a black sheep as any member the Stanford family ever had; this undoubtedly was the reason. He had a gift for wasting fortunes, and even though he received this handsome inheritance, he died in poverty in 1903, and his sister-in-law, Jane Stanford, was called upon to pay his burial expenses (Stanford, *Genealogy,* 55).

11. San Francisco *Examiner,* June 22, 1893.

12. Colusa *Daily Sun,* November 4, 1889. J. D. Hatch, Jr., ed. *Albany County Historical Association Record,* VII (April, 1948), 1.

BIBLIOGRAPHY

There are numerous obstacles to writing a biography of Leland Stanford, not least of which is that many essential documents have been either concealed or destroyed. Mrs. Stanford did posterity and history an unforgivable disservice by burning most of her personal letters from her husband, letters that would have filled many of the gaps in our understanding of him that must remain forever open. Largely because of her, not a single Stanford letter now survives regarding his first three years in California.

It is commonly believed that all the Central Pacific files were burned in the San Francisco conflagration of 1906, though this is not true. Many valuable records of the Pacific Improvement Company, for example, are now deposited in the Jackson Library at Stanford University. And some scholars suspect that the Southern Pacific Railroad has more records in its collections than most people realize. Some records undoubtedly have been lost, inadvertently or accidentally destroyed, or even suppressed. Others, besides Mrs. Stanford's, were purposely destroyed, including those of the Contract and Finance Company.

But the picture is not entirely bleak. Hundreds of Stanford's letters are preserved in his papers at the Stanford Library, in addition to those in the collections of his wife and son. Besides these, there are available scores of letters to Stanford from C. P. Huntington, Mark Hopkins, and Charles Crocker. The Stanford collection also houses a valuable collection of letters between Hopkins and Stanford.

George T. Clark's life of Stanford, published in 1931, is incomplete as a biography. The author knew nothing of men like Henry Root; he hardly touched upon the various railroad-owned construction companies; and he barely recognized Stanford's position in the Occidental and Oriental Steamship Company — but he did give us a useful source book. He quotes in their entirety a number of letters that Stanford wrote during his school days, letters never again seen after Clark used them. Most of these letters have been used in this book.

An almost untapped source of information is a series of over thirty bound volumes of family scrapbooks filled with newspaper clippings on a number of subjects from papers all over the country. The collectors were selective; most of the clippings treat their subject favorably. But one can retrace many of Stanford's steps from them, and can reconstruct a number of controversies surrounding his political career by reading scores of editorials on them.

The only Stanford diatribe the author has found was published in 1876 by the editor of the San Francisco News Bureau, at the height of antirailroad feeling in California. This was a fifteen-page pamphlet entitled *The California King: His Conquests, Crimes, Confederates, Counsellors, Courtiers, and*

Vassals. Stanford's Post-Prandial New-Year's Day Soliloquy in *Southern Pacific Railroad Pamphlets,* Stanford Library).

As in the life of any prominent public man, the act of judging evidence in order to separate fact from fiction is a challenging undertaking, and is perhaps never completely successful. The historian's role as detective is taxed to the limit by H. H. Bancroft's puzzling "History of the Life of Leland Stanford: A Character Study," left by him in manuscript form in the Bancroft Library and published in 1952. This was an impressionistic and adulatory sketch of his subject's career, but two decades later, in his *Retrospection, Political and Personal* (New York, 1912), 238-239, Bancroft evened the score over a grievance against Stanford, presumably over the latter's cancellation of his subscription to Bancroft's *Chronicles of the Builders of the Commonwealth.* Bancroft decided in his later work that the California Senator was pure "pose and piety." His "Asiatic eyes" were placed too close together and they "rolled heavenward in hypocritical ecstasy whenever he wished to be impressive." In his earlier work, Bancroft felt that Stanford's founding of his university was enough in itself to make his life worth recording, but in the latter piece he said that in default of an heir, Stanford gave his money to found a university which was to make high crime respectable. Most eulogists inclined toward Bancroft's earlier view of Stanford; but, unlike him, they had no loss of revenue to prompt a later reevaluation.

Bancroft's "Life of Stanford" included among its contributors a half dozen of Stanford's closest associates, as well as Stanford himself. This manuscript mixes fact, adulation, and sheer nonsense in a way that leaves the historian-detective never completely sure of its reliability, but a judicious use of the data contained in it does provide some insight into the life of Stanford.

1. MANUSCRIPTS

Hubert Howe Bancroft Papers, Bancroft Library.
Charles Crocker Papers, Bancroft Library.
George Davidson Papers, Bancroft Library.
Henry H. Ellis Papers, Bancroft Library.
Collis P. Huntington-Mark Hopkins Correspondence, Hopkins Transportation Collection, Stanford Library.
Frederick F. Low Papers, Bancroft Library.
Herbert C. Nash Papers, Bancroft Library.
Jane Stanford Papers, Stanford Library.
Leland Stanford Papers, Stanford Library.
Leland Stanford, Junior, Papers, Stanford Library.
Thomas Welton Stanford Papers, Stanford Library.

2. UNITED STATES GOVERNMENT DOCUMENTS

Congressional Globe, 34 Congress, 1 Session.
_____ , 37 Congress, 2 Session.

_____, 42 Congress, 2 Session.

Congressional Record, 44 Congress, 2 Session.

_____, 49 Congress, 1 Session.

_____, 49 Congress, 2 Session.

_____, 51 Congress, 1 Session.

_____, 51 Congress, 2 Session.

_____, 52 Congress, 1 Session.

House Executive Document 7, 48 Congress, 2 Session.

House Executive Document 60, 49 Congress, 1 Session.

House Executive Document 238, 55 Congress, 3 Session.

Senate Executive Document 51, 50 Congress, 1 Session.

United States *Statutes*, 1856, 1862, 1863-1865, 1865-1867, 1869-1871.

Population of the United States in 1860: Compiled from the Original Returns of the Eighth Census. Washington, 1864.

3.   CALIFORNIA STATE GOVERNMENT DOCUMENTS

Senate Journal, 1855, 1860, 1862, 1863-1864, 1885.

Appendix, Senate Journal, 1863, 1874.

Assembly Journal, 1860, 1862, 1863-1864.

Appendix, Assembly Journal, 1863, 1874.

Statutes, 1853, 1855, 1857, 1862, 1863-1864, 1867-1868, 1875-1876.

Supreme Court Reports, 1856, 1862, 1864-1865.

Ellen M. Colton versus *Leland Stanford*, et al., in the Superior Court of the State of California in and for the County of Sonoma, 1883.

Colton Case Depositions. 2 vols.

Report on the Fifth Viticultural Convention. San Francisco, 1887.

Report of the Sixth Annual Viticultural Convention, Sacramento, 1888.

Bundschu, Charles. *The Vineyards in Alameda County, The Report of Charles Bundschu, Commissioner for the San Francisco District, to the Board of State Viticultural Commissioners of California*. Sacramento, 1893.

4   TEHAMA COUNTY DOCUMENTS

Tehama County Records, Book Q.

Tehama County Book of Deeds, Book R.

Tehama County Index to Deeds, Grantor and Grantee, 1880-1889.

5.   NEWSPAPERS

A.   California

Alameda *Telegram*

Auburn *Placer Herald*

Butte *Record*

Chico *Chronicle*

Chico *Enterprise-Record*

Chico *Record*

Colusa *Morning Gazette*
Colusa *Sun*
Eureka *Times*
Fremont *News*
Fremont *News-Register*
Hollister *Free Lance*
Los Angeles *Times*
Marysville *Appeal*
Monterey *Monitor*
Nevada City *State Journal*
Nevada City *Transcript*
Oakland *Inquirer*
Oakland *Morning Times*
Oakland *Tribune*
Petaluma *Argus*
Petaluma *Daily Sentinel*
Placerville *News*
Red Bluff *News*
Red Bluff *Sentinel*
Sacramento *Bee*
Sacramento *California Times*
Sacramento *Record*
Sacramento *Record-Union*
Sacramento *State Journal*
Sacramento *Union*
San Diego *Seaport News*
San Francisco *Alta California*
San Francisco *Argonaut*
San Francisco *Bulletin*
San Francisco *Call*
San Francisco *Chronicle*
San Francisco *City Argus*
San Francisco *Commercial Record*
San Francisco *Daily Times*
San Francisco *Examiner*
San Francisco *Herald*
San Francisco *Newsletter*
San Francisco *Post*
San Francisco *Wave*
San Joaquin *Valley Argus*
San Jose *Daily*
San Jose *Mercury*
San Jose *Times*
Santa Barbara *News-Press*
Santa Cruz *Sentinel*
Sausalito *Herald*
Stanford University *Stanford Daily*
Stockton *Independent*

Vallejo *Chronicle*
West Oakland *Star*
Woodland *Mail*
Yolo *Mail*

B.   Other States

Phoenix *Herald*
Atlanta *Journal*
Twin Falls *Idaho Citizen*
Bloomington [Illinois] *Pantograph*
Chicago *Examiner*
Chicago *Post*
Chicago *Tribune*
Jerseyville [Illinois] *Republican-Examiner*
Louisville *Post*
New Orleans *Times-Democrat*
Boston *Courier*
Boston *Transcript*
Portland [Maine] *Argus*
Minneapolis *Minnesota Tribune*
Omaha *Bee*
Omaha *Herald*
Albany *Journal*
Albany *Press*
Albany *Times-Union*
Buffalo *Illustrated Express*
New York *Commercial Advertiser*
New York *Evangelist*
New York *Herald*
New York *Press*
New York *Recorder*
New York *Star*
New York *World*
Cincinnati *Enquirer*
Portland [Oregon] *Mercury*
Philadelphia *Record*
Philadelphia *Times*
Pittsburgh *Times*
Washington [D.C.] *Critic*
Washington *National Republican*
Washington *National View*
Washington *News*
Washington *Post*
Washington *Sun*
Cedarburg [Wisconsin] *News*
Milwaukee *Journal*

Milwaukee *Sentinel*
Port Washington *Democrat*
Port Washington *Pilot*
Sheboygan *Press*

6. MISCELLANEOUS PERIODICALS

American Wine Merchant, VI (1947).
California Farmer, December, 1887.
Carnival Record, II.
Frank Leslie's Illustrated Magazine, November 8, 1890.
Golden Argosy, VI (June 23, 1888).
New York *Spirit of the Times*.
New York Sportsman.
Pacific Wine and Spirit Review, XXVII (November 5, 1891).
––––––––––, XXX (July 6, 1893).
Resources of California, 1886.
Review of Reviews, August, 1893.
St. Louis Journal of Agriculture.
San Francisco *California Spirit of the Times and Underwriters' Journal*.
Scientific American, XXXIX (October 19, 1878).
––––––––––, XLII (June 5, 1880), 353.
Scientific American Supplement, VIII (August 9, 1879).
, XIII (January 28, 1882).
Yearbook of Agriculture, 1898.

7. JOURNAL ARTICLES

Anonymous, "Atlantic and Pacific Railroad," *California Mail Bag*, II (May, 1872), 30-32.

––––––––––, "Leland Stanford," *ibid.*, I (August, 1871), 1-4.

––––––––––, "Leland Stanford," *ibid.*, V (August, 1874), i-xxiv.

Arrington, Leonard J., "The Transcontinental Railroad and the Development of the West," *Utah Historical Quarterly*, XXXVII (1969), 3-15.

Athearn, Robert G., "Contracting for the Union Pacific," *ibid.*, 16-40.

Baird, Joseph A., Jr., "Architectural Legacy of Sacramento," *California Historical Society Quarterly*, XXXIX (1960), 193-207.

Baker, Hugh S., "Rational Amusement in Our Midst, Public Libraries in California, 1849-1859," *ibid.*, XXXVIII (1959), 295-320.

Best, Gerald M., "Rendezvous at Promontory: The 'Jupiter' and No. 119," *Utah Historical Quarterly*, XXXVII (1969), 69-75.

Betts, John R., "The Technological Revolution and the Rise of Sports, 1850-1900," *Mississippi Valley Historical Review*, XL (1953-1954), 231-256.

Boerner, Arthur R., ed., "Early Letters of Dr. Theodore E. F. Hartwig, Cedarburg's Physician and Surgeon," *Wisconsin Magazine of History*, XXIX (1946), 347-356.

Bowman, J. N. "Driving the Last Spike at Promontory, 1869," *California Historical Society Quarterly*, XXXVI (1957), 97-106, 263-274.

Brayer, Herbert O., "Preliminary Guide to Indexed Newspapers in the United States, 1850-1900," *Mississippi Valley Historical Review*, XXXIII (1946-1947), 237-258.

Bridgman, Louis W., "Leland Stanford of Port Washington," *Wisconsin Freemason*, XII (1955), 5-6.

Brown, James L., "More Fictional Memorials to Mussel Slough," *Pacific Historical Review*, XXVI (1957), 373-377.

Carman, Harry J. and Charles H. Mueller, "The Contract and Finance Company and the Central Pacific Railroad," *Mississippi Valley Historical Review*, XIV (1927), 326-341.

Carranco, Lynwood and Mrs. Eugene Fountain, "California's First Railroad: The Union Plank Walk, Rail Track, and Wharf Company Railroad," *Journal of the West*, III (1964), 243-256.

Clark, George T., "Leland Stanford and H. H. Bancroft's 'History,' A Bibliographical Curiosity," *The Papers of the Bibliographical Society of America*, XXVII (1933), 12-23.

_____, "The Romance that Founded Stanford," *Stanford Illustrated Review*, XXX (1929), 461-467.

Clendenen, Clarence C., "A Confederate Spy in California: A Curious Incident of the Civil War," *Southern California Quarterly*, XLV (1963), 219-233.

Coman, Edwin T., Jr., "Sidelights on the Investment Policies of Stanford, Huntington, Hopkins, and Crocker," *Bulletin of the Business Historical Society*, XVI (1942), 85-89.

Copeland, Peter F. and Marko Zlatich, "Imperial Russian Navy, 1863-1864," *Military Collector and Historian*, XVI (1964), 18-19.

Cotterill, R. S., "Early Agitation for a Pacific Railroad, 1845-1850," *Mississippi Valley Historical Review*, V (1918-1919), 396-414.

Crothers, George E., "Historical Outline of the Founding of Stanford," *Stanford Illustrated Review*, XXXIII (1931), 14-15, 26-28, 33-34, 36, 38, 40.

Drury, Clifford M., "John White Geary and his Brother Edward," *California Historical Society Quarterly*, XX (1941), 12-25.

Dunlap, Boutwell, "Some Facts Concerning Leland Stanford and His Contemporaries in Placer County," *ibid.*, II (1923), 203-210.

Fanning, Peter, "Early History of California," *Douglas 20, Police Journal*, IV (1926), 17, 42-43.

Ford, de Miriam A., "Palo Alto's Mysterious Frenchman," *California Historical Society Quarterly*, XXXIII (1954), 169-174.

Gilbert, Benjamin F., "California and the Civil War: A Bibliographical Essay," *ibid.*, XL (1961), 289-307.

——————, "The Confederate Minority in California," *ibid.*, XX (1941), 154-170.

——————, "Welcome to the Czar's Fleet, An Incident of Civil War Days in San Francisco," *ibid.*, XXVI (1947), 13-19.

Goldman, Henry H., "Southern Sympathy in Southern California, 1860-1865," *Journal of the West*, IV (1965), 577-586.

Gregg, Elizabeth, "The History of the Famous Stanford Ranch at Vina, California," *Overland Monthly*, LII (1908), 334-338.

Hammond, George P., "Manuscript Collections in the Bancroft Library," *American Archivist*, XIII (1950), 15-26.

Hatch, J. D., Jr. [Stanford's election to New York Hall of Fame], *Albany County Historical Association Record*, VII (1948), 1-4.

Hichborn, Franklin, "The Party, the Machine, and the Vote: The Story of Cross-filing in California Politics," *California Historical Society Quarterly*, XXXVIII (1959), 349-357.

Hood, Mary V. Jessup and Robert Bartlett Haas, "Eadweard Muybridge's Yosemite Valley Photographs," *ibid.*, XLII (1963), 5-26.

Hopkins, Caspar T., "California Recollections of Caspar T. Hopkins," *ibid.*, XXVI (1947), 175-183.

——————, "California Recollections of Caspar T. Hopkins," *ibid.*, XXVII (1948), 165-174, 264-274, 339-351.

Hurt, Peyton, "The Rise and Fall of the 'Know Nothings' in California," *ibid.*, IX (1930), 99-128.

Jordan, David Starr, "The Educational Ideas of Leland Stanford," *The Sequoia*, III (1893), 19-22.

Kemble, John H., "The Big Four at Sea, History of the Occidental and Oriental Steamship Company," *Huntington Library Quarterly*, XXX (1940), 339-357.

Ketterson, F. A., Jr., "Golden Spike National Historic Site: Development of an Historical Reconstruction," *Utah Historical Quarterly*, XXXVII (1969), 58-68.

Kibby, Leo P., "California, the Civil War, and the Indian Problem: An Account of California's Participation in the Great Conflict," *Journal of the West*, IV (1965), 183-209, 377-410.

——————, "Union Loyalty of California's Civil War Governors," *California Historical Society Quarterly*, XLIV (1965), 311-321.

Kraus, George, "Chinese Laborers and the Construction of the Central Pacific," *Utah Historical Quarterly*, XXXVII (1969), 41-57.

Lesley, Lewis B., "The Entrance of the Santa Fe Railroad into California," *Pacific Historical Review*, VIII (1939), 89-96.

_____, "A Southern Transcontinental Railroad into California: Texas and Pacific versus Southern Pacific, 1865-1885," *ibid.*, V (1936), 52-60.

Luck, J. Murray, "Cooperation — An Aspect of the Social Philosophy of Leland Stanford," *Co-Op News*, April 13, 27, May 11, 1950.

Mann, David H., "The Undriving of the Golden Spike," *Utah Historical Quarterly*, XXXVII (1969), 124-134.

May, Ernest R., "Benjamin Parke Avery," *California Historical Society Quarterly*, XXX (1951), 125-149.

McDonald, P. A., "Ships and Record Pacific Passages, Part I," *Nautical Research Journal*, XIV (1967), 17-22.

McKee, Irving, "Historic Alameda County Wine Growers," *California Magazine of the Pacific*, XLII (1953), 20-23.

_____, "Notable Memorials to Mussel Slough," *Pacific Historical Review*, XVII (1948), 19-27.

_____, "Three Wine-Growing Senators," *California Magazine of the Pacific*, XXXVII (1947), 15, 28-29.

Mighels, Ella Sterling, "A Memory of the Governor," *Grizzly Bear*, X (1912), 5.

Miller, Robert C., "The California Academy of Sciences and the Early History of Science in the West," *California Historical Society Quarterly*, XXI (1942), 363-371.

Morrow, William W., "The Founders of the University," *Leland Stanford Junior University Publications*, Trustees' Series, XXV (1914), 11-31.

Mosher, Francis W., "The Stanford Vina Ranch," *Stanford Illustrated Review*, XXXIV (1933), 182.

Netz, Joseph, "The Great Los Angeles Real Estate Boom of 1887," *Historical Society of Southern California, Annual Publications*, X (1915), 54-68.

O'Meara, James, "The Union or the Dominion?" *Overland Monthly*, XIV (1889), 414-428.

Pattiani, Evelyn Craig, "Silk in Piedmont," *California Historical Society Quarterly*, XXXI (1952), 335-342.

Peterson, H. C., "The Birthplace of the Motion Picture," *Sunset Magazine*, XXXV (1915), 909-915.

Pomeroy, Earl, "California, 1846-1860: Politics of a Representative Frontier State," *California Historical Society Quarterly*, XXXII (1953), 291-302.

Rodecape, Lois, "Celestial Drama in the Golden Hills," *ibid.*, XXIII (1944), 97-116.

Shutes, Milton H., "Republican Nominating Convention of 1860," *ibid.*, XXVII (1948), 97-103.

Smith, Grant H., "Bodie; The Last of the Old-Time Mining Camps," *ibid.*, IV (1925), 64-80.

Stoll, H. F., "The Wineries of Northern California," *Wines and Vines*, XVIII (1937), 3-5.

Tegeder, Vincent G., "Lincoln and the Territorial Patronage: The Ascendancy of the Radicals in the West," *Mississippi Valley Historical Review,* XXXV (1948-1949), 77-90.

Traxler, Ralph N., "Collis P. Huntington and the Texas and Pacific Railroad Land Grants," *New Mexico Historical Review,* XXXIV (1959), 117-133.

Tutorow, Norman E., "Leland Stanford, Midwife of the Movies," *Pacific Historian,* XIV (1970), 85-96.

_____ , "Leland Stanford, the Successful Failure," *Wines and Vines,* LI (1970), 61-62.

_____ , "Leland Stanford's Wisconsin Years," *Wisconsin Then and Now,* XV (1969), 1-4.

_____ , "Stanford's Response to Competition: Rhetoric versus Reality," *Southern California Quarterly,* LII (1970), 231-247.

Wagner, Henry R., "Edward Bosqui, Printer and Man of Affairs," *California Historical Society Quarterly,* XXI (1941), 321-332.

Wenzel, Caroline, "Finding Facts about the Stanfords in the California State Library," *ibid.,* XIX (1940), 245-255.

Wheat, Carl I., "The Journals of Charles E. De Long, 1854-1863," *ibid.,* X (1931), 355-395.

_____ , "A Sketch of the Life of Theodore D. Judah," *ibid.,* IV (1925), 219-271.

White, Chester Lee, "Surmounting the Sierras: The Campaign for a Wagon Road," *ibid.,* VII (1928), 3-19.

8. COLLECTED DOCUMENTS, LETTERS, AND WORKS

Anonymous, *Memorial Addresses on the Life and Character of Leland Stanford.* Washington, 1894.

_____ , *State Register and Year Book of Facts.* San Francisco, 1859.

Clark, George T., ed., "Letters of Leland Stanford to Mark Hopkins," *California Historical Society Quarterly,* V (1926), 178-183.

Evans, Elliot, ed., "Some Letters of William S. Jewett," *ibid.,* XXIII (1944), 227-246.

War of the Rebellion: A Compilation of the Official Records of the Union and Confederation Armies. Washington, 1897-1902.

9. DIARIES, AUTOBIOGRAPHIES, AND REMINISCENCES

Bancroft, Hubert Howe, *Retrospection, Political and Personal.* New York, 1912.

Bell, Horace, *Reminiscences of a Ranger.* Los Angeles, 1881.

Cole, Cornelius, *Memoirs.* New York, 1908.

Fremont, John Charles, *Memoirs of My Life.* Chicago, 1887.

Harpending, Asbury, *Great Diamond Hoax and other Stirring Incidents in the Life of Asbury Harpending*. San Francisco, 1913.

Jordan, David Starr, *The Days of a Man*. 2 vols. New York, 1922.

Leach, Frank A., *Recollections of a Newspaperman, A Record of Life and Events in California*. San Francisco, 1917.

Root, Henry, *Henry Root: Surveyor, Engineer, and Inventor*. San Francisco, 1921.

Stewart, William M., *Reminiscences of Senator William M. Stewart of Nevada*. New York, 1908.

White, Andrew Dickson, *Autobiography of Andrew Dickson White*. 2 vols. New York, 1922.

10. BIOGRAPHIES

Anderson, F. L., *Galusha Anderson: Preacher and Educator, 1832-1918*. n.p.,1933.

Bancroft, Hubert Howe, *Chronicles of the Builders of the Commonwealth*. 7 vols. San Francisco, 1891.

—————, *History of the Life of Leland Stanford: A Character Study*. Oakland, 1952.

Berner, Bertha, *Incidents in the Life of Mrs. Leland Stanford*. Stanford, 1934.

Clark, George T., *Leland Stanford, War Governor of California, Railroad Builder, and Founder of Stanford University*. Stanford, 1931.

Curtis, Edward, *Two California Sketches: William Watt and Leland Stanford*. San Francisco, 1880.

Evans, Cerinda W., *Collis Potter Huntington*. 2 vols. Newport News, 1954.

Grant, Joseph Donohoe, *The Stanfords*. Palo Alto, 1938.

Hunt, Rockwell D., *California's Stately Hall of Fame*. Stockton, 1950.

James, George Wharton, *Heroes of California: The Story of the Founders of the Golden State as Narrated by Themselves or Gleaned from other Sources*. Boston, 1910.

Lavender, David, *The Great Persuader*. Garden City, 1970.

Loughead, Flora H., ed., *Life, Diary, and Letters of Oscar Lovell Shafter*. San Francisco, 1915.

Munroe, James P., *A Life of Francis Amasa Walker*. New York, 1923.

Parton, James, *et al. Sketches of Men of Progress*. Cincinnati, 1870-1871.

Phelps, Alonzo. *Contemporary Biography of California's Representative Men, 1881-1882*.

Shuck, Oscar T., ed., *Representative and Leading Men of the Pacific*. San Francisco, 1870.

Stanford, Arthur Willis, *Stanford Genealogy, Comprising the Descendants of Abner Stanford, the Revolutionary Soldier*. Yokohama, 1906.

Tutorow, Norman E., *The Early Years of Leland Stanford: New Yorker Who Built the Central Pacific Railroad.* Pamphlet, Ithaca, New York, 1969.

11. GENERAL WORKS

Altrocchi, Julia Cooley, *The Spectacular San Franciscans.* New York, 1949.

Anonymous, *Annual Report of the Southern Pacific Railroad Company,* year ending December 31, 1869. In California State Archives, Sacramento.

_____ , *Appeal to the California Delegation in Congress Upon the Goat Island Grant to the Central Pacific Railroad Company.* San Francisco, 1872.

_____ , *Catalogue of the Officers and Students of Clinton Liberal Institute.* Utica, 1844.

_____ , *The Great Dutch Flat Swindle: The City of San Francisco Demands Justice.* San Francisco, 1864.

_____ , *Memorial and Biographical History of the Counties of Fresno, Tulare, and Kern, California.* Chicago, 1892.

_____ , *Military Order of the Loyal Legion of the United States.* San Francisco, 1904.

_____ , *The Pacific Railroad: A Defense Against its Enemies.* San Francisco, 1864.

_____ , *Palo Alto Stock Farm Eleventh Annual Catalogue.* San Francisco, 1894.

_____ , *Railroad Lands in California, Nevada, and Utah.* San Francisco, 1875.

_____ , *Speech of Honorable Leland Stanford in the Constitutional Convention of Nevada, July 13, 1864.* San Francisco, 1865.

_____ , *Statement Made* [by Leland Stanford] *to the Senate Committee of the Nevada Legislature.* Sacramento, 1865.

_____ , *The Struggle of the Mussel Slough Settlers for their Homes.* Visalia, 1880.

Ayers, James J., *Gold and Sunshine: Reminiscences of Early California.* Boston, 1922.

Bancroft, Hubert Howe. *History of California.* 7 vols. San Francisco, 1886-1890.

Barber, John W. and Henry Howe, *Historical Collections of the State of New York.* New York, 1842.

Bean, Walton, *California: An Interpretive History.* New York, 1968.

Beebe, Lucius, *The Central Pacific and the Southern Pacific Railroads.* Berkeley, 1963.

Blumann, Ethel and Mable W. Thomas, ed., *California Local History, A Centennial Bibliography.* Stanford, 1950.

Brotherhood of Locomotive Engineers, Leland Stanford Division, *Eulogy of Leland Stanford.* 1893.

Brown, James Lorin, *The Mussel Slough Tragedy.* Fresno, 1958.

Butterfield, C. W., *History of Washington and Ozaukee Counties*. Chicago, 1881.

Colburn, Frona, *Wines and Vines of California*. San Francisco, 1889.

Coy, Owen C., *Guide to the County Archives of California*. Sacramento, 1919.

Daggett, Stuart, *Chapters on the History of the Southern Pacific*. New York, 1922.

Davis, Horace, *The Meaning of the University*. San Francisco, 1895.

Davis, John Francis, *An Index to the Laws of the State*. Sacramento, 1911.

Davis, John P., *The Union Pacific*. Chicago, 1894.

Davis, Winfield J., *History of Political Conventions in California, 1849-1892*. Sacramento, 1893.

Delano, Alonzo (pseudonym "Old Block"), *The Central Pacific Railroad*, or *Forty-nine and Sixty-nine*. San Francisco, 1868.

Dumke, Glenn, *The Boom of the Eighties in Southern California*. San Marino, 1944.

Eldredge, Zoeth Skinner, ed., *History of California*. 5 vols. New York, 1915.

Elliott, Orrin Leslie, *Stanford University, the First Twenty-five Years*. Stanford, 1937.

Fitzgerald, Oscar Penn, *California Sketches, New and Old*. Nashville, 1897.

Goodwin, Charles C., *As I Remember Them*. Salt Lake City, 1913.

Greeley, Horace, *Overland Journey from New York to San Francisco*. New York, 1860.

―――――, and John F. Cleveland, comp., *A Political Text-Book for 1860: Comprising a Brief View of Presidential Nominations and Elections, etc*. New York, 1860.

Griswold, Wesley S., *A Work of Giants*. New York, 1962.

Grodinsky, Julius, *Transcontinental Railway Strategy, 1869-1893*. Philadelphia, 1962.

Hall, Carroll D. and Hero E. Rensch, ed., *Old Sacramento*. Sacramento, 1958.

Halley, William, *Centennial Yearbook of Alameda County*. Oakland, 1876.

Halstead, Murat, *Caucuses of 1860: A History of the National Political Conventions*. Columbus, 1860.

Haney, Lewis H., *Congressional History of Railways, 1850 to 1887*. Madison, 1908-1910.

Hart, Jerome, *In Our Second Century*. San Francisco, 1931.

Hendricks, Gordon, *The Edison Motion Picture Myth*. Berkeley, 1961.

Historical Records Survey. *Guide to Depositories of Manuscript Collections in the United States: California*. Los Angeles, 1941.

Hittell, John S., *The Commerce and Industries of the Pacific Coast*. San Francisco, 1882.

Hittell, Theodore H., *History of California*. 4 vols. San Francisco, 1885-1897.

Holbrook, Stewart H., *The Story of American Railroads*. New York, 1947.

Howell, George R. and Jonathan Tenney, ed., *History of the County of Albany, New York, from 1609 to 1886*. New York, 1886.

Howell, George R. and John H. Munsell, ed., *History of the County of Schenectady, New York, from 1662 to 1886*. New York, 1886.

Jackson, W. Turrentine, *Wagon Roads West: A Study of Federal Land Surveys and Construction in the Trans-Mississippi West, 1846-1869*. Berkeley, 1952.

Jones, Idwall, *Vines in the Sun*. New York, 1959.

Jordan, David Starr, *Leland Stanford's Views on Higher Education*. Stanford, 1901.

Judah, Theodore D., *Central Pacific Railroad Company of California*. San Francisco, 1860.

_____ , *A Practical Plan for Building the Pacific Railroad*. San Francisco, 1857.

_____ , *Report of the Chief Engineer on the Preliminary Surveys and Future Business of the Sacramento Valley Railroad*. May 30, 1854.

_____ ; *Report to the Executive Committee of the Pacific Railroad Convention of 1859*. Sacramento, 1860.

Kennedy, Elijah R., *The Contest for California: How Colonel E. D. Baker Saved the Pacific States to the Union*. Boston, 1916.

Lawson, Will, *Pacific Steamers*. Glasgow, 1927.

Marvin, Charles, *Training the Trotting Horse*. New York, 1891.

Melendy, Brett and Benjamin F. Gilbert, *Governors of California*. Georgetown, California, 1965.

Mirrielees, Edith R., *Stanford, The Story of a University*. New York, 1959.

Muybridge, Eadweard, *Animal Locomotion*. Philadelphia, 1887.

_____ , *The Human Figure in Motion*. London, 1901.

Myers, Gustavus, *History of the Great American Fortunes*. New York, 1936 edition.

Nevins, Allan, *Grover Cleveland*. New York, 1934.

Occidental and Oriental Steamship Company Record. Minutes of the Board of Directors, 1874 to 1908.

Orton, Richard H., *Records of California Men in the War of the Rebellion, 1861-1867*. Sacramento, 1890.

Paul, Rodman W., *California Gold: The Beginning of Mining in the Far West*. Cambridge, Massachusetts, 1947.

Ramsaye, Terry, *A Million and One Nights*. New York, 1926.

Riegel, Robert, *The Story of the Western Railroads*. New York, 1926.

Royce, Josiah, *California from the Conquest in 1846 to the Second Vigilance Committee in San Francisco*. Boston, 1886. R. G. Cleland edition, 1948.

_____ , *The Feud of Oldfield Creek: A Novel of California Life*. Boston, 1887.

Rudd, Helen N., *A Century of Schools in Clinton*. Clinton, New York, 1964.

Ramsaye, Terry, *A Million and One Nights*. New York, 1926.

Riegel, Robert, *The Story of the Western Railroads*. New York, 1926.

Royce, Josiah, *California from the Conquest in 1846 to the Second Vigilance Committee in San Francisco*. Boston, 1886. R. G. Cleland edition, 1948.

_____, *The Feud of Oldfield Creek: A Novel of California Life*. Boston, 1887.

Rudd, Helen N., *A Century of Schools in Clinton*. Clinton, New York, 1964.

Sabin, Edward L., *Building the Pacific Railway*. Philadelphia, 1919.

San Francisco News Company Editor. *The California King*. San Francisco, 1876.

Scherer, James A. B., *The Lion of the Vigilantes: William T. Coleman and the Life of Old San Francisco*. Indianapolis, 1939.

Scott, Edward B., *The Saga of Lake Tahoe*. Crystal Bay, Nevada, 1957.

Silliman, Benjamin, *Remarks Made on a Short Tour Between Hartford and Quebec in the Autumn of 1819*. New Haven, 1820, second edition, 1824.

Smith, Eugene W., *Passenger Ships of the World, Past and Present*. Boston, 1963.

Smith, Wallace, *Garden of the Sun: A History of the San Joaquin Valley, 1772-1939*. Fresno, n.d.

Smyth, W. S., *First Fifty Years of Cazenovia Seminary, 1825-1875*. Cazenovia, 1877.

Southern Pacific Railroad Company, *Historical Outline of the Southern Pacific Company*. San Francisco, 1933.

Stanwood, Edward, *A History of the Presidency*. 2 vols. Boston, 1916.

Stille, Charles H., *History of the United States Sanitary Commission*. Philadelphia, 1866.

Stillman, J. D. B., *The Horse in Motion*. Boston, 1882.

Taggart, Frederick J., *Catalogue of the Hopkins Railway Library*. Palo Alto, 1895.

Taylor, Deems, *A Pictorial History of the Movies*. New York, 1943.

Underwood, Tom R., ed., *Thoroughbred Racing and Breeding*. New York, 1945.

Van Zile, Edward S., *That Marvel - the Movie*. New York, 1923.

Wallace, J. H., ed., *Wallace's Year-Book of Trotting and Racing*. 17 vols. New York, 1886-1902.

Wetmore, Charles A., *Treatise on Wine Production and Special Reports on Wine Examinations, Appendix B, The Report of the Board of State Viticultural Commissioners for 1893-1894*. Sacramento, 1894.

Whicher, John, *Masonic Beginnings in California and Hawaii*. n. p., 1931.

White, Gerald T., *Formative Years in the Far West, A History of the Standard Oil Company of California and its Predecessors through 1919*. New York, 1962.

Wilson, Neill C. and Frank J. Taylor, *Southern Pacific*. New York, 1952.

Winther, Oscar O., *Express and Stagecoach Days in California, from the Gold Rush to the Civil War*. Stanford, 1936.

————, *The Transportation Frontier: Trans-Mississippi West, 1865-1890*. New York, 1964.

Wood, Dallas E., *History of Palo Alto*. Palo Alto, 1939.

Wood, Leslie, *The Miracle of the Movies*. London, 1947.

12. UNPUBLISHED MATERIALS

Fisher, Helen Dwight, "Leland Stanford, 1824-1893." Unpublished manuscript, Stanford papers.

Gundelfinger, Edward R., "The Pacific Mail Steamship Company, 1847-1917: Its Relations with the Railroads." Unpublished B. A. thesis (University of California, Berkeley, 1917).

McAfee, Ward M., "Local Interests and Railroad Regulation in Nineteenth Century California." Unpublished Ph. D. dissertation (Stanford, 1965).

McConnell, John A., "The Stanford Vina Ranch." Unpublished M. A. thesis (Stanford, 1961).

McKinney, William Clyde, "The Mussel Slough Episode, A Chapter in the Settlement of the San Joaquin Valley, 1865-1880."Unpublished M. A. thesis (University of California, Berkeley, 1948).

Mudgett, Margaret Holt, "The Political Career of Leland Stanford." Unpublished M. A. thesis (University of Southern California, 1933).

Treat, Archibald, "The Stanfords and their Golden Key." Unpublished manuscript (San Francisco, 1937), Stanford papers.

Vrooman, Henry, "Honorable Leland Stanford." Unpublished manuscript. In H. H. Bancroft papers, Bancroft Library.

13. INTERVIEWS

Author with Fred Weibel, Jr., July 1, 1969.

Author with Edgar E. Robinson, August 2, 1969.